The Barnes & Noble
Guide to
Children's
Books

BARNES & NOBLE

NEW YORK

Barnes & Noble
NEW YORK

ISBN 978-1-4351-4528-3

Packaged for Sterling Publishing by
p.s. ink publishing solutions, Fairfield, CT

Selected and reviewed by Kaylee N. Davis

Designed by Sequel Creative, Fairfield, CT

Distributed in Canada by Sterling Publishing c/o Canadian Manda Group,
165 Dufferin Street, Toronto, Ontario, Canada M6K 3H6

Distributed in the United Kingdom by GMC Distribution Services
Castle Place, 166 High Street, Lewes, East Sussex, England BN7 1XU

Distributed in Australia by Capricorn Link (Australia) Pty. Ltd.
P.O. Box 704, Windsor, NSW 2756, Australia

For information about custom editions, special sales, and premium and corporate purchases,
please contact Sterling Special Sales at 800-805-5489 or specialsales@sterlingpublishing.com

Manufactured in China

2 4 5 8 10 9 7 5 3 1

Table of Contents

"The more that you read, the more things you will know. The more that you learn, the more places you'll go."

—Dr. Seuss, *I Can Read with My Eyes Shut*

The joy of snuggling up with a child on your lap and reading together is one that all parents and caregivers know. That precious lap time and story-before-bed time is the simplest way to raise a reader and instill in children a lifelong love of books and

reading. But how do you choose the right book for your child when there are so many choices, formats, and new technologies? This book has been created to assist you with the selection process and to advise and guide you through the world of children's literature. Organized by age, subject, and reading level—and alphabetically by author—this guide will help you choose the best books for your family library—and you can be sure that we have carefully vetted every single book we recommend.

Today's children are constantly exposed to all forms of media: movies, television, computers, the Internet, and even apps on phones; there is no question that this generation of children is more tech savvy than any previous generation. But when it comes to engaging their imaginations and exposing them to magic, whimsy, laughter and tears, silliness and play, heart-stopping suspense, and a love of language, and teaching them to read, there is nothing better than a book shared together!

Walking into a children's book department can be an intimidating experience for many parents and caregivers, and shopping online can be a challenge if you don't already know exactly what you are looking for. This book will guide you in making the right choices for your children by offering a carefully curated shopping experience. Each title in this guide is reviewed with an eye toward assisting you in selecting the right books at the right time in your child's development. There are more than 1,000 titles reviewed and categorized; start with your child's age and interests, and keep it by your side when you shop online or in the bookstore. Soon you'll be able to open the entire world of books to your children with confidence. And with new classics written every day, this guide will help you choose titles that incorporate similar themes and formats as they are published.

It all starts with board books, full of vibrant images that teach simple concepts, designed for the littlest hands and built to withstand a fair amount of chewing and tossing. Children then grow into picture books that present new, story-focused experiences with wonderful art, charming stories, laughs, and language awareness. When a child begins to identify letters and sounds and is ready to learn to read, beginning readers will help turn those squiggles on the page into "sight words," and genuine reading begins. Then it's on to reading independently, first with short chapter books that may or may not include illustrations, soon followed by full-length novels. There are other alternatives along the way, such as nonfiction books about favorite topics and innovative formats that pop up, pull, and dazzle, and the next thing you know, you have helped to raise a reader!

And now a word about new technologies: there is no reason to fear the digital revolution. Nothing will ever replace the bonding moments of lap-time or bedtime stories or the joy

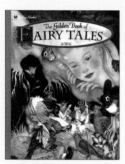

of reading a physical book with your child and turning pages to see what comes next. But any technology or format that keeps them reading and encourages their love of the written word is to be embraced. Every day more and more children's books are becoming available as ebooks, enhanced ebooks, and apps. Go ahead and experiment to see what works for your family. Each time you go online to barnesandnoble.com, look through the new digital choices available for every age.

Throughout this book you will also see short essays from some of your favorite children's book authors and illustrators, sharing what inspires them and why they chose to write or illustrate books for children. Each and every author or illustrator featured in this book started out just like your child—being read to and learning to read but, more important, being encouraged to keep reading, drawing, and creating by someone who cared and understood the importance of books in the development of children. You can be that person, too. When you give children the gift of books and reading, you give them access to the world around them—and all you have to do is **remember to read with your children every day!**

Kaylee N. Davis

Author & Editor
The Barnes & Noble Guide to Children's Books

Newborn to 2 Years

A baby's first books are the stepping-stones to a lifetime of reading. Reading to infants and toddlers is all about story time, and that starts with your voice. As the infant learns to focus, attention shifts to the image on the page and eventually to the words. Reading with babies and toddlers is essential to their developing senses: the sound of your voice, the feel of the book in their hands, differentiating the visual elements on the page, and yes, even the smell and taste of books as they chew on them, which of course they will do! But these books are created to stand up to all the wear and tear that babies and toddlers can subject them to and still be read again and again.

In this section you'll find books that originated in the board-book format. Many of today's most popular board books are actually shorter versions of the most loved picture books, such as *Goodnight Moon* or *The Very Hungry Caterpillar*. You'll find the original, complete versions of those titles in the Picture Book section of this guide. Many favorite entertainment-based licensed characters are also readily available in this format, and your child may enjoy them; however, licensed or brand-driven characters tend to be trend driven and can wax and wane in popularity over time. Therefore we chose to concentrate on more timeless selections that offer more variety for babies and toddlers.

Here are some guidelines to keep in mind when choosing books for newborns to two-year-olds:

- Let children experience the physical book. These books are designed to be sturdy enough to take a beating and be wiped clean after a good chewing or being thrown onto the floor.

- Select sturdy books with rounded edges that are the right size for little hands.

- Choose concepts that are simple, with clear text and bright graphics or photographs.

- Look for photographs that represent everyday objects in baby's world and are easy to identify.

- Select books with simple, repetitive, or rhyming text and basic word/object identification.

- Look for subjects or stories that connect to a baby's world.

- Find books that focus on basic skill building, such as shapes, colors, sizes, opposites, numbers, or letters.

- Don't forget cloth, vinyl/bath, touch-and-feel, and lift-the-flap books! You'll find a few of them here, but many more are listed in the chapter on Innovative Formats (page 199).

Eileen Christelow

Five Little Monkeys Jumping on the Bed

This favorite children's rhyme is presented here, charmingly illustrated, with those cheeky monkeys kissing mom good night and then bouncing on the bed until one by one they fall off and the doctor is called, resulting in the familiar refrain, "The mama called the doctor. The doctor said, 'No more monkeys jumping on the bed!'" Eventually, of course, they all end up a bit bandaged but finally and happily sound asleep.

1989 Clarion Books

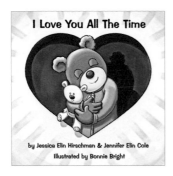

Jessica Elin Hirschman and Jennifer Elin Cole
Illustrated by Bonnie Bright

I Love You All The Time

This book is a gentle reminder to children that no matter how busy their parents or extended family, and no matter how far away they live from one another, they are always loved. In this day and age, when both parents often work and grandparents, aunts, and uncles may be in different cities or even countries, this reassuring book for toddlers reminds them that they are loved all the time.

2000 Cookie Bear Press

Michelle Sinclair Colman

Illustrated by Nathalie Dion

What do you buy for those ultra-hip parents who have the latest of everything? How about an ultra-hip book or set of books to match their oh-so-fabulous lifestyle? With tongue firmly in cheek, these books address the lifestyles of the uber-fabulous baby, from their snappy black togs, trips to the farmer's market, and the wonders of "country life," to flying on jets, proper rocker attire, and warm winter wear. It's all here, charmingly illustrated with a large dollop of humor for those city-slicker parents and their sophisticated (though drooling) offspring.

Artsy Babies Wear Paint *(2011)*

Beach Babies Wear Shades *(2007)*

Country Babies Wear Plaid *(2006)*

Eco Babies Wear Green *(2008)*

Foodie Babies Wear Bibs *(2008)*

Jet-Set Babies Wear Wings *(2009)*

Rocker Babies Wear Jeans *(2009)*

Sporty Babies Wear Sweats *(2010)*

Urban Babies Wear Black *(2005)*

Winter Babies Wear Layers *(2007)*

Tricycle Press

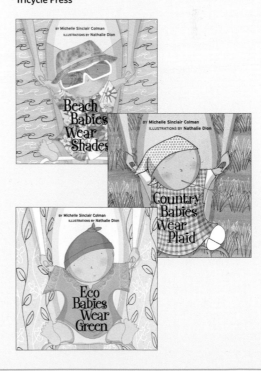

Sandra Boynton

If anyone can be said to "own" the board book category, it would have to be Sandra Boynton. Her books continue to be among the bestselling board books, and most families have at least one of her titles—some hilarious, some sweet, and often a mix of both. Sandra started out designing greeting cards, many featuring the lovable animals that also populate her books for children. Perhaps it was that training that made her a master of being able to tell an entire story in six pages or less. Her understanding of rhythm and rhyme, her inherent ability to distill a story to its most basic level, her whimsical animal illustrations, and her willingness to embrace the ridiculous have made her books favorites with babies, toddlers, and their parents. Many are available in Spanish as well.

Belly Button Book!

Featuring a slew of hippos with bare tummies, this ode to baby's tummy will take the "where's your belly button?" game to a whole new and very silly level.

2005 Workman Publishing

Barnyard Dance!

Tied with *Moo, Baa, La La La!* for the bestselling Boynton board book, this lively book offers a sing-song romp through the barnyard as the animals square dance together. The book teaches both animal identification and animal sounds.

1993 Workman Publishing

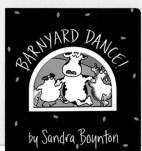

Blue Hat, Green Hat

Teach your child about basic colors and animals with this seriously silly bunch of animals—an elephant, a goofy turkey, and more—wearing hats in some very unusual ways.

1984 Little Simon

Pajama Time!

This rollicking bop through silly animals getting ready for bed will have kids doing the "Pajama-Dee-Bop" and snuggled in for the night in no time.

2000 Workman Publishing

But Not the Hippopotamus

A classic among board books, this riotous rhyming book features pairs of animals engaging in all sorts of activities with the common refrain, *"But not the hippopotamus."* Children will scream it out each time—until the end, when the hippo is triumphant.

1982 Little Simon

The Going to Bed Book

This upbeat tribute to bedtime features all sorts of animals on an ark preparing to settle in for the night. They find their pj's, brush their teeth, do their exercises, and engage in serious silliness, ending with a calming bedtime.

1982 Little Simon

Snuggle Puppy!

A sweet bedtime rhyme between a mother dog and her "Snuggle Puppy" will send your children to sleep with a smile and a good-night kiss—literally and in book form.

2003 Workman Publishing

Moo, Baa, La La La!

If you only buy one Boynton book for your baby, let it be this bestseller! Your baby will learn the sounds each animal makes and laugh along the way with Boynton's silly animals.

1982 Little Simon

Photographic images in books for infants are very effective for teaching basic concepts. The images in the *DK Baby Touch and Feel* and *Peekaboo!* series are clean, clear, and relatable, and the text is simple, with names and sounds like *kitten* and *meow*. When you add in padded covers and a variety of touch-and-feel novelties, you have a board book that not only teaches, but also engages a baby's senses of sight, touch, and sometimes smell. These books feature large images and wonderful textures, which have the added benefit of being appropriate for children with visual impairments or developmental delays that require a more tactile approach to learning.

Baby Touch and Feel: Animals *(2008)*

Baby Touch and Feel: Bedtime *(2008)*

Baby Touch and Feel: Colors and Shapes *(2009)*

Baby Touch and Feel: Playtime *(2001)*

Baby Touch and Feel: Things That Go *(2009)*

Baby Says Peekaboo! *(2006)*

Bathtime Peekaboo! *(2005)*

DK Publishing

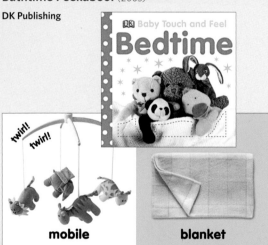

twirl! twirl!

mobile   blanket

Baby says peekaboo!

touch-and-feel and lift-the-flap

DK Baby Touch and Feel
Playtime

DK Wheelies

These books feature all the appeal and wonderful photographic style of the DK line, with the added play value of actual turning wheels, taking a simple concept board book to a level suitable for a more active toddler. There are many other vehicles in this series, but parents should be counseled to supervise play with these books as they do have small moving parts and are not recommended for very young infants.

Fire Truck *(2003)*

Bus *(1999)*

DK Publishing

DK My First Board Books

These simple, single-concept books feature clean, crisp images of letters and colors on clean white backgrounds with three to four accompanying photographic images of objects that reinforce the concept presented and teach colors, letters, and object identification. For example, the uppercase and lowercase *A* are shown with photos of an apple, apron, acorn and airplane. Strawberries and cherries show the color red. There are many more books in this series, such as numbers, shapes, and more.

My First ABC Board Book

My First Colors Board Book

2004 DK Publishing

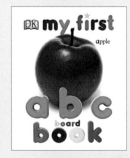

DK my first
apple
a b c
board
book

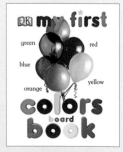

DK my first
green   red
blue
orange   yellow
colors
board
book

Newborn to 2 Years

Lois Ehlert

Color Zoo

This concept book by award-winning author Lois Ehlert is brilliant at using shapes and colors to create various animals. The concept features nine animals, nine shapes, and sixteen colors. By removing a shape with each page turn, a new animal is created on the following page. As the book progresses, each shape removed is named and children learn about shapes, juxtaposition, animals, and colors.

Caldecott Honor

1989 HarperCollins

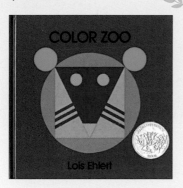

Fish Eyes:
A Book You Can Count On

Caldecott Award-winner Lois Ehlert takes on numbers, counting, and simple addition in this bright and colorful undersea adventure with a school of fish. The child is asked if he or she "could put on a suit of scales, add some fins and one of these tails" and join the fish as they increase in number. Children will learn to count as well as exercise their imaginations as they turn each page of this colorful counting book that uses vivid, easy-to-count images and rhyming text.

1990 Harcourt Children's Books

Sarah Gillingham

Illustrated by Lorena Siminovich
Board Books with Finger Puppets

These interactive board books include die-cut pages and an attached, high-quality felt finger puppet in each book, which allows the parent or child to wiggle and move the main character on each and every spread of the book. The sweet and simple text and added play value will make these books family favorites from the very first reading.

In My Den

In My Flower

In My Nest

In My Pond

In My Meadow

In My Tree

2009 Chronicle Books

Sandra Boynton on her eclectic early influences…

I've always loved to draw—especially cartoonish things—and I've always loved to write. I absolutely adore little kids, I adore books, and I remember vividly and happily being a child. (Whereas I only have the dimmest recollection of being an adult.) So creating children's books makes great sense for me. It's a comfortable fit.

I'm so lucky that I get to write and illustrate these books, AND to pretend it counts as a real job.

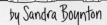

It's hard to really say with any certainty what my influences are, because of course we are all influenced by whatever—and whomever—we admire. I guess the first answer is my parents. My father was a literary scholar and a superb English teacher; my mother, an artist—a Fine artist, not a cartoonist. And then my teachers: I went to Germantown Friends School in Philadelphia from Kindergarten through 12th Grade, and the dynamic education that a good Quaker school offers is nothing short of incredible.

Beyond this, naming influences is a fraught enterprise, as it can so quickly become pretentious and even vaguely delusional. Wait. What a good idea! Delusional pretention actually sounds like fun! Here goes: In much of my work, the echoes of Rachmaninov, Edward Hopper, and early Soupy Sales are unmistakable.

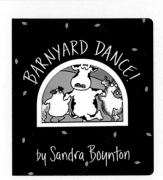

I have loved as well:

George Eliot, Charles Schulz, Jessie Wilcox Smith, Glenn Miller, Ronald Searle, Sempé, Ella Fitzgerald, William Steig, Jimmy Stewart, Dave Barry, William Butler Yeats, Jane Austen, James Marshall, George Booth, Fred Astaire, Jack Benny, Arthur Rubinstein, The Beatles, Bill Watterson, Dylan Thomas, Alan Rickman, Johannes Brahms. And Buddy Holly.

See individual listings for books by Sandra Boynton on pages 10 and 11.

Tana Hoban

Studies have shown that young infants respond best to simple images in black and white, making Tana Hoban's *Black & White* perfect for babies whose vision is still developing. Each wordless spread includes a simple silhouetted image of a recognizable object—a button, a leaf, keys—in an accordion fold-out format that allows babies to identify objects with the words their parents speak as they interact their way through the book. In *Who Are They?* Hoban again uses simple black silhouettes of animals: each left-hand page features a full-grown animal, and the facing page depicts a baby version of the same animal—a duck and a duckling, a sheep and a lamb, a cat and a kitten, and more—for parents and babies to identify. *Red, Blue, Yellow Shoe*, originally published in 1986, was one of the first board books to display color photography on a white background. In this book about colors, each page features a recognizable image—a red alarm clock, a purple flower, a yellow shoe, and more. These simple images are a wonderful way to introduce babies to the basic colors in their world.

Black & White (2007)

Red, Blue, Yellow Shoe (1986)

Who Are They? (1994)

Greenwillow Books

Karen Katz

Featuring multicultural babies and parents, and some with lift-the-flap peek-a-boo features, these sweet and charming board books offer families many hours of interactive play, along with lots of hugs and kisses. There are many more books in this series than are featured here, but these offer a variety of family play, including teaching numbers by counting down the kisses from ten to one, lifting the flaps to find baby's belly button, and identifying all the different kinds of hugs from Daddy, from scared-of-the-dark hugs to kiss-it-all-better hugs, and everything in between. The multicultural aspect of these books, and also that they give Daddy equal time, make them a must-have for your family library.

Counting Kisses (2003)

Daddy Hugs (2007)

Where Is Baby's Belly Button? (2000)

Where Is Baby's Puppy? (2011)

Little Simon

Newborn to 2 Years

Sandra Magsamen

Snuggle-Me Stories

Acclaimed artist and author Sandra Magsamen started out designing everything from wall art to coffee mugs with her recognizable art and life-affirming text. This series of cloth and novelty books for infants and toddlers brings her signature style to the youngest members of your family. Her line of books is extensive, and only a few examples are noted here, but those that are feature plush finger puppets, soft and cuddly cloth, plush or glittery images, and embedded sound chips to sing along with, effectively combining reading and play for infants and toddlers.

Bedtime Bunny *(2009)*

Butterfly Kisses *(2007)*

Love Bug *(2007)*

Twinkle, Twinkle, You're My Star *(2010)*

LB Kids

Illustrated by Jenn Ski

Soft Shapes Books

The Soft Shapes series of books for babies and toddlers (there are many more titles than listed here) pack a whole lot of learning into each title. They teach simple concepts, they are made of foam, and they have pop-out puzzle pieces on each page. Perfect for playtime, bath time, or anytime, these brightly colored, versatile, huggable, touchable, squeezable books teach basic concepts like shapes or colors and offer simple puzzle play for very young children. In addition, these books are excellent for use with children with visual impairments or developmental delays that require a more tactile approach to learning.

Soft Shapes: Animals

Soft Shapes: Counting

Soft Shapes: Trucks

Soft Shapes: Shapes

2010 innovativeKids

My First Taggies

The Taggies books were created by a mom who realized that her child was more fascinated by the textures and feel of the edging of her blanket and the tags attached to plush toys than she was by the toys themselves. Many Taggies books are made of soft, plush fabric, and each features different looped, textured ribbons and multiple textures on each page. The stories are simple, but the point is to offer your child a tactile and visually stimulating book, perfect for touching and cuddling. These books are excellent for use with children with visual impairments or developmental delays that require a more tactile approach to learning.

Will Grace
Illustrated by Jill McDonald
Hey, Diddle, Diddle
2006 Cartwheel Books/Scholastic Inc.

The Itsy-Bitsy Spider
2007 Cartwheel Books/Scholastic Inc.

If You're Happy and You Know It
2006 Cartwheel Books/Scholastic Inc.

Will Grace
Who Do You See?
2009 Cartwheel Books/Scholastic Inc.

Kaori Wantanabe
I Love You
2004 Cartwheel Books/Scholastic Inc.

Kaori Wantanabe
Sweet Dreams
2003 Cartwheel Books/Scholastic Inc.

Dorothy Kunhardt
Pat the Bunny

Published in 1940, this book started the concept of touch-and-feel books, and it's still one of our favorites. Four generations of toddlers have played with this book, and now your child can as well! It is still in the original spiral-bound format, and features the same wonderful interactivity: who can forget the peek-a-boo mirror, trying on Mommy's ring, or Daddy's scratchy beard? We should warn you: this book will be well-loved and well-used, and it's not unusual to have to buy another copy after a few months of serious loving and playing by your children.

1940 Golden Books

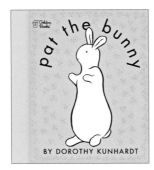

Bill Martin Jr and John Archambault
Illustrated by Lois Ehlert
Chicka Chicka ABC

An abridged board format of the well-loved classic picture book *Chicka Chicka Boom Boom* (featured in the Picture Book section of this guide), this rollicking, romping rhyme tells the tale of the letters climbing to the top of the coconut tree with text that simply begs to be sung and danced to along with Ehlert's brilliant, brightly colored illustrations. This marriage of text and art created a classic that your children will be able to recite by heart in no time at all.

1990 Little Simon

Helen Oxenbury

Multicultural

These big board-books, with their oversize format and bright graphics, deal with simple, relatable concepts for babies—but what makes them unique is how they do it. In these books, originally published in 1987, British author and illustrator Helen Oxenbury takes care to show multicultural images of babies doing all the things babies do together: clapping, tickling, playing games, and going to sleep under the loving supervision of their (also multiracial) parents. These roly-poly little citizens of the world will win your hearts and provide hours of fun as you and your children play along.

All Fall Down

Clap Hands

Say Goodnight

Tickle, Tickle

1987 Little Simon

Leslie Patricelli

These adorable little books are all about opposites, explained with a wonderful sense of humor and quirky art style, using examples that every toddler and parent can relate to. Whether it's what makes baby happy compared to what makes baby sad or the concept of big and little or quiet and loud, the omnipresent words *no* and *yes*, and everyone's favorite, *yummy* and *yucky*, these books use the juxtaposition of opposites on facing pages to explain the concept to the littlest learners, who will be laughing all along the way.

Baby Happy Baby Sad *(2008)*

Big Little *(2003)*

No No Yes Yes *(2008)*

Quiet Loud *(2003)*

Yummy Yucky *(2003)*

Candlewick Press

Kaaren Pixton
Indestructibles

They're not kidding. These thin, six-inch-square, twelve-page wordless books are printed on the same sort of material used for those impossible-to-open mailing envelopes. They are drool-proof, rip-proof, chew-proof, unbreakable, and best of all 100 percent washable! Don't let the thin, lightweight material fool you; this material allows for some amazingly bright and deep color graphics that will never fade. Kaaren Pixton's brilliant art style is reminiscent of Eric Carle's, featuring things that creep, crawl, fly, swim, and wiggle. These books are creatively rendered to teach early concepts, and you and your child will be talking through these wordless stories for hours at a time, for years to come.

Creep! Crawl! *(2009)*

Flutter! Fly! *(2009)*

Jungle Rumble! *(2010)*

Mama and Baby! *(2010)*

Plip-Plop Pond! *(2010)*

Wiggle! March! *(2009)*

Workman Publishing

Amy Wilson Sanger

"World Snacks" Board Books

No matter what their ethnic background, today's toddlers know that there is a world of food out there beyond the "happy meal." Each of these books deals with a specific ethnic food group—African American, Indian, Japanese, Mexican, Jewish, Italian, and Chinese—and all feature simple rhymes and accurate food names, and are illustrated with really fun cut-paper collage art. With rhymes like "Corn tortillas make my tacos, my tostada, and my chips. Tomato salsa, por favor, and guacamole dip!" each of these books is both appetizing and irresistible, and makes a perfect book to tuck into the diaper bag for tonight's dinner at your favorite ethnic restaurant!

A Little Bit of Soul Food *(2004)*

Chaat and Sweets *(2008)*

First Book of Sushi *(2001)*

¡Hola! Jalepeño *(2002)*

Let's Nosh! *(2002)*

Mangia! Mangia! *(2005)*

Yum Yum Dim Sum *(2003)*

Tricycle Press

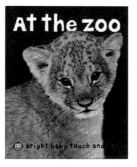

Roger Priddy

With over two hundred of his books in print, Roger Priddy has made it his business to use big, bright, photographic images to teach babies and toddlers first words and concepts. Each book features not only easy-to-identify objects, numbers, colors, and letters, but also simple learning activities to reinforce the concepts. The "Bright Baby Touch and Feel" books are subject specific and feature some of the best texture interactivity available. The topics addressed are toddler-friendly, whether it's animals, counting, or first words, and will help your child to quickly develop proficiency in sight words, object identification, and basic skills. These sturdy books are large in format and built to last.

Bright Baby: Colors, ABC, Numbers *(2008)*

Bright Baby: First 100 Animals *(2006)*

Bright Baby: Touch and Feel Slipcase: On the Farm, Baby Animals, At the Zoo, Perfect Pets *(2006)*

My Little Counting Book *(2005)*

My Little Word Book *(2004)*

Priddy Books

Nick Bruel on being provocative…

Maurice Sendak once told me not to be afraid to be provocative. That was one of the many happy and unforeseen consequences of working in a children's bookstore as I did for over seven years: sometimes an otherwise unremarkable day can change dramatically when one of the genre's greatest luminaries calls you with an insignificant question that turns into a half-hour conversation.

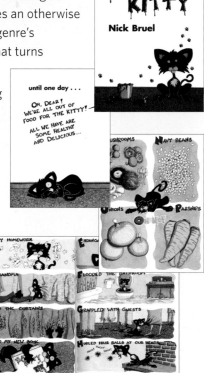

During the conversation, I discussed with Maurice something I once heard him say during an interview, about how adults and children will read a book differently. Adults will open a book, begin reading it, and then more often than not feel compelled to slog their way through it to the end regardless of how dull or unenlightening it might become. But for a child…a child will open a book, begin reading it, and throw it across the room the moment it loses his or her interest.

Writing a book is easy. Illustrating it is easy. Maintaining a child's interest…that's the challenge.

As Maurice and I spoke, we struggled to find the right word to describe the solution to the challenge. We concluded that one should not be afraid to be *controversial*. No, that wasn't quite right. The point isn't to anger or disturb the reader. *Provocative*. That was the word we agreed upon. Each page needs to tell the reader that he or she NEEDS to turn the page, that there is a promise of something unexpected or unique on the next spread. Fail to live up to that promise, and that's when the book hits the wall.

My own books did not exist yet. The idea of making a book that travels through the alphabet five times while telling the story of a cat with a bad attitude or a book about how the same little boy is perceived differently by all the family and friends and monsters in his life or a book about giving that same ornery cat a bath over the course of 140 pages—these ideas were at best mere flickers somewhere in the back of my subconscious.

The conversation I had with Maurice did not propel my not-yet-existent career, but it certainly did influence it once my books began to take shape. "Am I being provocative?" is the question I ask myself each and every time I start a book or even a page. "Am I convincing my reader to turn that page?" I don't know. It's the right question to ask. But it's not for me to answer.

See individual listings for books by Nick Bruel on pages 30 and 117.

Count My Blessings 1 Through 10

This simple twist on a traditional "thank you" prayer offers toddlers a way to express their thanks—anytime—for the simple things in their life, while also learning to count to ten, beginning with one house, two parents, three friends, and so on, all the way up to Grandfather painting ten toy cars, and the final blessing, "I count my blessings, one through ten. Keep us safe, I pray. Amen." With no mention of a specific deity, this book is ecumenical in nature and would make a good addition to any family library regardless of specific religious belief.

2008 Putnam

Peek-A-Love

This charming love-themed version of peek-a-boo incorporates both heart-shaped die-cuts on every page as well as lift-the-flaps that allow maximum toddler interaction with the book and the text. Children will enjoy looking through the sparkling heart die-cut to find the next animal, perhaps a playful buzzing bee, and then lifting the flap to find what the bee loves—a blooming bright yellow flower.

2010 Little Simon

Five Rubber Duckies

Not every child looks forward to bath time, but this bright board book, featuring silver holographic foil bubbles and a stunning, yet simple, almost three-dimensional art style, might be just the thing to get those crusty toddlers into a nice, warm bath before bedtime. And while they're at it, they will learn to count to five with the familiar rubber duckies and can continue that lesson once they are in the actual tub with their own rubber ducky or other bath toys.

2008 Price Stern Sloan

Old MacDonald Had a Farm

There are plenty of board-book versions of this classic nursery song to choose from, but this version stands out for its charming art as well as its value-added format. There are five fuzzy, flocked tabs incorporated into this book for each of the animals—the duck, lamb, horse, pig, and cow—which add a charming touch-and-feel aspect to this traditional song for toddlers.

2008 Price Stern Sloan

Barney Saltzberg
Peekaboo Kisses

This fully interactive, touch-and-feel book has many fun features for children: lift-and-look flaps, fabric and fur textures, a mirror, and even a squeaker built right in! Barney Saltzberg has written and illustrated a number of titles in this "kisses" series, all featuring cute, boldly colored and simply drawn familiar animals that even the littlest babies can easily relate to. And, of course, there are kisses galore, which makes it a fun book to read and act out with your child.

2002 HMH Books (Franchise)

Newborn to 2 Years

Picture Books Ages 2–6

"Read it again!" When you hear these three little words, you know that you have selected the right picture book for your child. When your child loves a story, you WILL be reading it over and over again, so it's important to find books that both of you will enjoy. Welcome to the amazing world of picture books, filled with wonderful stories, life lessons, beautiful art, laughs and silliness, and favorite characters who will become your child's first friends. These are books that you may remember from your own childhood, and now they can be cherished by the next generation of your family.

There is an abundance of wonderful picture books to choose from, and all have something unique to offer your family. We think you'll agree that this section contains the best of the best.

The interests of a toddler differ greatly from those of a first-grader, but what they do have in common is a love of story, a fascination with illustration, favorite characters, and the ability to learn life lessons from a tale well told. As you read the reviews in this section, you will be able to select books that are appropriate for your child at every stage of his or her development, as well as find books that address everyday issues like sibling rivalry, going to school, fitting in, sharing, and more.

In this category, animals often stand in for children and while it's true most bunnies don't wear jackets and ties, most frogs don't speak, and most mice aren't friendly to adults, don't be confused by this—your child won't be. For children, it's a perfectly normal way to relate to a story or character, and it's all about fun, using one's imagination, and developing a sense of humor.

Here are some guidelines to keep in mind when choosing picture books:

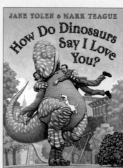

- Find stories that will interest your child as well as elicit questions and discussion.

- Funny stories will develop your child's sense of humor.

- "Relatable" stories can help children deal with issues and concepts they are experiencing in ways they can understand.

- Pay attention to art styles and photographs of images that your child responds to.

- Be sure to include books and favorite characters that you loved as a child to share with your own children.

- Award-winning authors and illustrators are usually a sure bet; we've included a list of award winners in the back of this guide.

- Use picture books as an opportunity to introduce your children to other cultures.

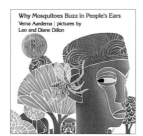

Verna Aardema
Illustrated by Leo and Diane Dillon

Why Mosquitoes Buzz in People's Ears

Aardema's retelling of this African folktale, magically illustrated by the Dillons, who won a Caldecott Award for this book, illustrates the consequences of one little lie. As the cumulative effects of a little fib told by Mosquito to Iguana (and passed "telephone style" from animal to animal) mount, serious consequences result. In the end all is resolved—but legend has it that the reason mosquitoes buzz in people's ears is that they will always be checking to see if we are still upset with them.

1975 Dial

Harry G. Allard
Illustrated by James Marshall

Miss Nelson is the nicest teacher in the school—but her students still misbehave. Miss Nelson has an idea: she "goes missing," and is replaced by a substitute teacher, the evil Viola Swamp, who lays on the homework and is not very nice. Miss Nelson returns to a very grateful class and a much better behaved one as well. Parents will quickly figure out what's going on, but children will be wondering what happened to Miss Swamp when Miss Nelson returns. In the second volume, Miss Nelson goes on vacation—but instead of the scary Miss Swamp, who students fear will return, they are subjected to the very boring and aptly named principal, Mr. Blandsworth.

Miss Nelson is Missing! *(1977)*

Miss Nelson is Back *(1982)*

Houghton Mifflin Books for Children

Giles Andreae
Illustrated by Guy Parker-Rees

Giraffes Can't Dance

As all the animals in the jungle prance and dance at the Jungle Dance, poor giraffe is teased because he can't dance very well at all. His legs are skinny and his neck too long, and he is jeered off the dance floor. He meets a wise cricket, however, who gives him good advice that builds up his self-esteem, and when he returns to the dance he is confident and graceful. This is a great story about self-esteem with quirky and fun illustrations.

2001 Orchard Books/Scholastic Inc.

Molly Bang

Ten, Nine, Eight

Though this charming, award-winning picture book features an African American father and daughter, its cozy bedtime rhyme, wonderful illustrations, and expressions of the love between a father and his "little big girl" are appropriate for all families. As they count down from ten to one, beginning with "Ten small toes all washed and warm," quiet playtime turns into a loving bedtime ritual.

1983 Greenwillow Books

Ludwig Bemelmans

Judi Barrett

Illustrated by Ron Barrett

Cloudy With a Chance of Meatballs

This tasty tale of a town called Chewandswallow is told by a grandfather to his grandchildren. Imagine a town where the weather provides your meals, and they come like clockwork three times a day—just carry your plate and fork with you and wait for lunch! Then one day, inexplicably, the food becomes huge and dangerous— a tomato tornado, a pea-soup fog. In this hilarious tale, filled with illustrations loaded with food-related gags, the people of Chewandswallow use their really big food to construct boats to sail away to another town—where they actually have to buy and cook their food.

1978 Atheneum

Karen Beaumont

Illustrated by David Catrow

I Like Myself!

This ode to self-esteem is fun, and features Catrow's signature quirky art style, but holds a serious message for all little girls, especially African American girls. With laugh-out-loud images and wonderful rhyming language—"Inside, outside, upside down, from head to toe and all around, I like it all! It all is me! And me is all I want to be."—this exuberant little girl celebrates all she is and does. Whether she has polka-dotted lips, beaver breath, or stinky toes, she is still exactly who she wants to be, and that is her own unique self.

2004 Harcourt Children's Books

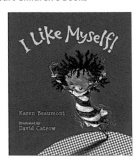

Madeline Books

"In an old house in Paris that was covered with vines lived twelve little girls in two straight lines." So begins one of the best-loved (by both girls and boys) and most delightful tales in children's literature, the story of Madeline and her exciting adventures. Beginning with the story of Madeline's appendectomy (complete with scar!) in *Madeline*, we follow our plucky heroine through three more books of escapades, each featuring Bemelmans' brilliant rhyming text and charming illustrations. Since *Madeline* first appeared in print in 1939, these books have been a must for any family library.

Madeline *(1939)*

Madeline's Rescue *(1953)*

Madeline and the Bad Hat *(1957)*

Madeline in London *(1961)*

Viking

Barbara Helen Berger
Grandfather Twilight

Each night, Grandfather Twilight gets out of his comfy chair, opens his wooden chest, takes a single pearl from an apparently endless strand, and begins his walk through the forest to the sea. As he walks, a magical mist of twilight follows him, and the pearl in his hand grows bigger. When he reaches the sea, he tosses the now-large pearl into the sky, where it becomes the moon, and then he returns to his own bed for the night. This extraordinary bedtime book is notable not just for its amazing illustrations, but also for its spare text and calming effect on children as they prepare for bed.

1984 Philomel

Claire Huchet Bishop
Illustrated by Kurt Wiese
The Five Chinese Brothers

This Chinese folktale is not without its controversy. The basic story line is a tale of five identical brothers who use their special powers to save the life of the brother who is unjustly accused of murder. One brother (the accused) can hold unlimited amounts of water, one has an iron neck that can't be broken, one can hold his breath forever, one cannot be burned, and one can stretch his legs to any length. Each of the brothers uses his special skill to save the first brother from execution. Some parents may find the illustrations in this book, written in 1938, disturbing in today's more politically correct climate, but most children are more interested in the characters' superpowers. Parents should pre-read this book and decide for themselves if their child will enjoy this well-loved, classic story.

1938 Putnam

Serge Bloch
Butterflies in My Stomach and Other School Hazards

This book is about two things—school, and literal interpretation of common idioms—both represented here in Bloch's witty pen-and-ink drawings and some photographic collage as well. For example, Bloch shows a boy laughing "with ants in his pants" while his teacher tells him to "zip his lip." Kids will enjoy the visual interpretations of idioms such as "the big cheese," "happy as a dog with two tails," a "long face," and so many more. And all of the visual mayhem is built around the first day of school, which can make that transition an easier one for your child.

2008 Sterling

Jan Brett
The Mitten

In this lushly illustrated Ukrainian folktale, a boy asks his Baba (grandmother) to knit him some snow-white mittens. She warns him they will be hard to find if he loses one in the snow—which he promptly does. Animals climb into the mitten for warmth: first a mole, then a rabbit, a hedgehog, an owl, a badger, a fox, and even a bear—and then a little mouse climbs in, and his whiskers cause the bear to sneeze. Brett's realistic and detailed art will keep children poring over each illustration.

1989 Putnam

Caldecott Honor

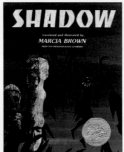

Caldecott Award

(Translated from the French of Blaise Cendrars)

Shadow

What is a shadow? This book addresses this question by setting the story as an African folktale, though it is actually based on a French poem by Blaise Cendrars. The illustrations in this book are as mystical as the poem itself, representing the shadows and characters in black silhouette, block-printed over amazing watercolors. Children will be entranced by both the legend of the shadow and the artwork that so compellingly supports the story, and parents can use this book to explain their children's own shadows to them as well.

1982 Atheneum

Multicultural

Caldecott Honor

Dick Whittington and His Cat

Notable for its award-winning, linoleum-cut, two-color artwork, this English folktale is based on a true character: Lord Mayor Richard Whittington, who was born in London in the 1300s. This is the story of how, from his humble beginnings as a orphaned waif living on the streets of London, he eventually became the city's Lord Mayor—with the help of his very clever cat. Dick keeps a cat to keep the rats away and, needing money, must sadly sell the cat to a Moorish ruler whose island is overrun by rats. The cat is such an expert ratter that the ruler rewards Dick, who becomes a successful merchant and eventually Lord Mayor of London.

1950 Atheneum

Stone Soup

This favorite French tale has been retold, set in different cultures, and re-illustrated countless times—but this version of the story remains the classic. As soldiers approach a village, the townspeople hide all their food because they know those soldiers are always hungry. The soldiers, however, outwit the townspeople with their recipe for "stone soup." All they need is a carrot or two, and maybe an onion, a bit of meat, and a few more things to make it complete. The townspeople can at least provide that, right? This classic children's story allows the reader to be in on the joke, and children quickly learn the inherent lesson of sharing as well.

1947 Atheneum

Norman Bridwell
Clifford the Big Red Dog

You've seen the TV show, the merchandise, the clothing —but it all started with the book. This easy-to-read classic tells the story of Emily Elizabeth and her well-loved pet Clifford. Normal dog behaviors change drastically when your pet is a giant red dog, and this book and all the books that follow in the Clifford series (available in multiple formats) reinforce not only early reading with simple sentences, but also visual humor and the obvious love of a child for her pet. Start with this book—then there are many more in the series for you and your family to enjoy.

1963 Cartwheel Books

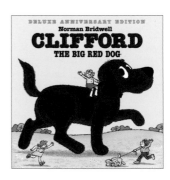

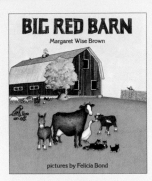

Illustrated by Felicia Bond
Big Red Barn

"By the big red barn/In the great green field..." Fans of the classic *Goodnight Moon* will recognize the language style of this book immediately. This book takes little ones on a tour of the animals large and small that live in and around the barn. Brown's wonderful rhythmic language and Bond's clean, clear art style will keep kids interested as they learn to identify farm animals and their offspring.

1989 HarperFestival

Illustrated by Leonard Weisgard
The Important Book

Teaching your children about the world around them is important—but what is important about all the things in the world? This book uses rhythmic language and beautiful art to teach them what really is important about rain, sunshine, daisies, bears, and so on. Written by the author of *Goodnight Moon* and stunningly illustrated by Leonard Weisgard, the book begins a learning pattern that goes on even after you are done reading, as children continue to discern the importance of every part of their world.

1949 HarperCollins

Illustrated by Clement Hurd
Goodnight Moon

This classic book is the gold standard to which all other bedtime books are compared. The first generation who grew up listening to it each night are now reading it to their grandchildren. The little bunny in his blue-and-white pajamas says goodnight to everything he sees in his room. Babies and toddlers love to find the little mouse on every page and watch the moon as it rises in the window. The rhythmic language and subtly darkening illustrations will lull children to sleep, that is, until they say the inevitable words: "read it again."

1947 HarperFestival

Illustrated by Clement Hurd
The Runaway Bunny

This reassuring tale of motherly love by the author of *Goodnight Moon* was actually written first, and, in fact, a copy of this book can be found on the nightstand in that classic tale. When a little bunny decides to go off on his own, he discovers that no matter where he might wander or what he might do, the reassuring love of his mother will always be there waiting for him. A comforting tale of motherly love, this classic will be read time and time again and be just as soothing each and every time.

1942 HarperFestival

Picture Books 2–6

Picture Books 2–6

Virginia Lee Burton

Jeff Brown

Illustrated by Macky Pamintuan

Flat Stanley: His Original Adventure!

At some point in your child's school reading, you will meet Flat Stanley. Stanley Lambchop was flattened by a bulletin board—he is now about four feet tall, a foot and a half wide, and one inch thick. This allows him to be mailed all over the world, and his friends and family send him on all sorts of adventures, photograph him, and send back the pictures. Many schools have kids create their own "Flat Stanley" and do the same—and it's entirely possible that somewhere in the world Flat Stanley is being photographed every day. This book has been reissued and re-illustrated many times, so if the original edition is not available, pick up the most recent one—the story remains the same.

1964 HarperCollins

Nick Bruel

Bad Kitty

With the words "She wasn't always a bad kitty," a new children's classic was born, and the alphabet will never be the same. When Kitty's family runs out of her favorite foods, mayhem ensues, alphabetically of course, and as the situation is rectified and Kitty makes amends, we are treated to three more hilarious romps through the alphabet. Kids will giggle as the narrator reports Kitty "hurled hair balls at our heads" and later "hugged the little mouse." This book takes children on a rollicking romp through the alphabet five times, but you'll be reading it many more times than that!

2005 Roaring Brook Press

Mike Mulligan and His Steam Shovel

This classic story about Mike Mulligan and his trusty steam shovel, Mary Anne, addresses the issue of how technology and progress affect the way we get things done but in a way children can understand. When new machines come along that may be able to do the construction jobs Mike and Mary Anne have been doing all along, they need to figure out a way to show that they are still useful and important. Children love the wonderful illustrations, done with the same sort of crayons they color with today, and the book's message, which reinforces the important concepts of loyalty and perseverence.

1939 Houghton Mifflin Books for Children

The Little House

Caldecott Award

One of the best things about children's books is that it is perfectly normal for inanimate objects to have a "life," along with thoughts and feelings. This is the award-winning story of a little house in the country, who was happy watching the passing seasons and the family who grew up within her walls. She always wondered what city life was like, but when the city eventually grew and enveloped her, she was left alone and neglected. Rescued by the descendents of the people who built her, she is moved back to the country and restored to her former glory. The charming watercolor illustrations will keep children turning the pages, and the story of simple country living vs. urban sprawl will enchant them no matter where they live.

1942 Houghton Mifflin Books for Children

Ashley Bryan
Let it Shine

Coretta Scott King Award

This joyously illustrated book celebrates three traditional spirituals that all children will likely hear or sing throughout their lives: "This Little Light of Mine," "Oh When The Saints Go Marching In," and "He's Got the Whole World in His Hands." Illustrated with astounding cut-paper collages of multicultural children and families in both urban and rural settings, this book comes complete with musical notations in the back for those who may be able to play along on the piano or other instrument. This is a wonderful, visual way to introduce children to traditional American music.

2007 Atheneum

Janell Cannon
Stellaluna

Janell Cannon has made a career of writing lovable stories about traditionally not-so-lovable creatures. When a baby bat is knocked from her nest by an owl and lands in a bird's nest, she quickly has to learn to fit in by acting like a bird, not a bat. The illustrations are both beautiful and accurate in their renderings as to what the animals look like in nature, and the story about feelings and finding your place are issues that all children can relate to.

1993 Harcourt Children's Books

The Very Busy Spider

A very busy spider is spinning her web, and none of the other animals' questions can distract her from the task at hand. The way that Carle manages to portray animals, such as dogs, goats, and spiders, with nothing more than brightly colored paper collages and watercolor paint is remarkable— and in this book the web itself is tactile, embossed on every page. This story of industriousness and not giving up until the job is done provides valuable reinforcement for children who may lack focus and patience.

1984 Philomel

The Very Hungry Caterpillar

This book is one of the "must-haves" for your family library. Featuring Eric Carle's vibrantly colored tissue-paper-and-paint collage art on a white background, it follows the growth of one VERY hungry caterpillar from egg to caterpillar to butterfly. As children turn the pages with holes punched in them, the holes and the pages grow bigger and bigger, and they joyously repeat the refrain, "But he was still hungry." as the caterpillar munches his way through all sorts of food. It is a counting book, but also a story of metamorphosis and simple science, and the bold art style will inspire many future art projects as well.

1969 Philomel

Chief Seattle
Illustrated by Susan Jeffers
Brother Eagle, Sister Sky

The text of this picture book is adapted from a speech purportedly delivered by Chief Seattle at treaty negotiations in the 1850s. Beginning with the words "How can you buy the sky?" this vivid interpretation of Chief Seattle's respect and love for Earth and all its creatures is as relevant today as it was more than two hundred years ago. Jeffers' art is an inspiration; done in pen and vibrant color, the detailed, mystical drawings portray concern for the environment as eloquently as Chief Seattle's words.

1991 Dial

Babette Cole
Princess Smartypants

One look at the cover of this book will tell your children that not every princess wants to wear a crown and a gown, or, for that matter, marry a prince. Princess Smartypants is perfectly happy living with her pets, and when her parents tell her it's time to get married, she devises another plan to retain her single status. She sets up a series of "tasks" for her suitors, and as they fail at them one by one, she enjoys every minute of it—until Prince Swashbuckle appears on the scene. This book reinforces independence in little girls who dream of becoming a princess, or something more, one day.

1991 Putnam

Barbara Cooney
Miss Rumphius

This glorious picture book is as well-loved by parents as it is by children because of its simple message: "You must do something to make the world more beautiful." Little Alice hears those words from her grandfather as a little girl. After she grows up to travel the world and becomes Miss Rumphius, she returns to his home by the sea and fulfills his wish for her by scattering lupine seeds wherever she goes. This sweet story will certainly spark discussions in your home about how you and your children can make the world more beautiful as well.

1982 Viking

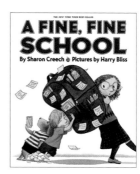

Sharon Creech
Illustrated by Harry Bliss
A Fine, Fine School

In this book the author explores the concept of "too much of a good thing." Tillie loves school but she also loves her free time, because that's when she can teach her younger brother to skip and climb trees. When her aptly named (and very gung-ho) principal, Mr. Keene, decides his students and teachers are so fine that they should have school every day, even on weekends and holidays, Tillie knows that something must be done—and that she is just the one to do it.

2001 HarperCollins

Caldecott Honor

Freight Train

This colorful book by award-winning author and artist Donald Crews uses simple text and vibrant art to do two things very well: teach colors and motion. By blurring the colors on the train cars to indicate movement, and utilizing simple descriptive text, it helps children understand the concept of motion as well as learn the six basic colors, a rather impressive achievement for a white static page.

1978 Greenwillow Books

School Bus

As children get ready to attend school, even preschool, the biggest fascination (and sometimes fear) is the school bus. Using a few words per page and his signature artwork, Donald Crews demystifies the school-bus experience for both nervous and excited preschoolers. Children will learn about kind bus drivers and meeting their classmates, as the big yellow bus picks up the children, brings them to school, and brings them back home again in this simply told tale about an important transition in their lives.

1984 Greenwillow Books

Truck

This nearly wordless book follows a big red truck throughout its busy day, from the loading dock to the highway, to roadside diners, and into the city. Though there is no narrative text, there are plenty of words built into the art—on the truck, on road signs, and on other objects along the way. These are "sight words" that will be easy for those just beginning to read to identify; for those too young to read there are plenty of visual clues for children to narrate as the truck makes its daily rounds.

1980 Greenwillow Books

Caldecott Honor

Maryann K. Cusimano
Illustrated by Satomi Ichikawa

You Are My I Love You

This sweet and simple book is all about the love between a calm and gentle parent and an exuberant child, represented by a teddy-bear parent and child. There is no gender mentioned, so the parent can be either Mom or Dad, depending on who is doing the reading. The similes used in each rhyming couplet are simple enough for babies and toddlers to understand, such as "I am your parent; you are my child. I am your quiet place; you are my wild," as the story follows the parent and child through their day from morning to bedtime.

2001 Philomel

Picture Books 2–6

Little Golden Books

In September 1942, a new children's book classic was born when the first twelve Little Golden Books were published, and today there are now more than two billion Little Golden Books in print. For many children, the classic Golden Book characters were their first literary friends: *The Poky Little Puppy* (still the bestselling Little Golden Book of all time), *The Little Red Caboose*, *Scuffy*, *Tootle*, and so many more. Many of the best-known children's book authors and illustrators are part of the Golden Books family: Richard Scarry, Hilary Knight, Margaret Wise Brown, Eloise Wilkin, Gustaf Tenggren, Tibor Gergely, Alice Provensen, Frank Oz, and many others. Over the years, Little Golden Books have featured the hottest licensed characters from Disney, Sesame Street, and other major brands, but never stopped printing and selling the classic, character-driven books that built the brand. This guide includes a representative sampling of the books available. Many others can be found online or in your local bookstore, and, yes, still in grocery stores as well! The format remains the same today, and though the price has increased from the original twenty-five cents each, they remain some of the most affordable books available.

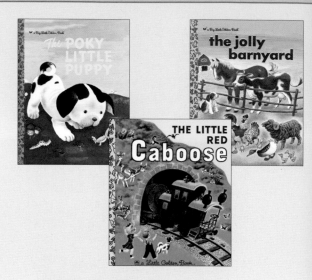

Marian Potter
Illustrated by Tibor Gergely

The Little Red Caboose

The little red caboose wants to be as popular and as useful as the steam engine at the front of the train, but alas, he is stuck at the back. Until one day it's the little red caboose's turn to be the hero, when he saves the train from rolling down the mountain and earns the respect he has always wanted.

1953 Golden Books

Annie North Bedford
Illustrated by Tibor Gergely

The Jolly Barnyard

It's a big day on the farm. Today is farmer Brown's birthday, so he gives all the animals their favorite foods to eat. But what will the animals decide to give Farmer Brown? As you might expect, the cow will give milk, the chickens will give eggs, the sheep will give their warm wool, and so on, until all the animals have given their loving farmer their very best gifts.

1950 Golden Books

Janette Sebring Lowrey
Illustrated by Gustaf Tenggren

The Poky Little Puppy

This is the bestselling Little Golden Book of all time, with over fifteen million copies sold since 1942. Generations of children have loved the little puppy who is always dawdling and poking around to explore and investigate things, and who comes home so late that he has to go to bed without his strawberry shortcake.

1942 Golden Books

Kathryn and Byron Jackson
Illustrated by Gustaf Tenggren

The Saggy Baggy Elephant

Little Sooki is a very happy fellow who dances through the forest, until he encounters a mean-spirited parrot who tells him that his skin is too loose and his ears and nose are too big, and he should be called "saggy baggy" instead of Sooki. The little elephant tries everything to fix his appearance, until he meets a herd of dancing elephants just like him.

1947 Golden Books

Gertrude Crampton
Illustrated by Tibor Gergely

Scuffy the Tugboat

Scuffy the Tugboat is sure that he is meant for "bigger things," and so he leaves the toy store owned by the man with the polka-dot tie, and takes off to explore the world. He sees many amazing things on his journey but, in the end, realizes that he is meant to be back home, safe in his bathtub in the toy store.

1946 Golden Books

Cathleen Schurr
Illustrated by Gustaf Tenggren

The Shy Little Kitten

Up in the hayloft there are five frisky, roly-poly kittens and one shy little striped kitten. One day, the shy little kitten ventures out of the hayloft to explore the world. As she meets all sorts of strange and wonderful animals and other types of creatures along the way, she also learns to not be shy about making new friends.

1946 Golden Books

Gertrude Crampton
Illustrated by Tibor Gergely

Tootle

This family favorite is the story of a little train that is going to school to learn how to stay on the tracks and become a big locomotive. Tootle is easily distracted by the flowers and meadows that the tracks run through, and he goes off the rails to investigate. Of course in the end he understands that he needs to stay on track to reach his goals.

1945 Golden Books

Kathryn Jackson
Illustrated by Gustaf Tenggren

Tawny Scrawny Lion

There once was a tawny scrawny lion that just couldn't get enough to eat. He chased monkeys on Monday, kangaroos on Tuesday, zebras on Wednesday, and so on. Until one day he met a family of ten chubby rabbits who taught him to eat carrot stew—instead of them.

1952 Golden Books

Jon Stone
Illustrated by Michael Smollin

The Monster at the End of this Book

Grover is nervous. He knows there is a monster at the end of this book, and he warns readers not to turn the pages. Children will scream and laugh along with Grover as they disobey him and turn the pages all the way to the end to discover the only monster there is Grover himself, who is a bit embarrassed but laughing as well.

1971 Random House Children's Books

Jon Stone
Illustrated by Michael Smollin

Another Monster at the End of this Book

Grover is still worried that this time there *really* is a monster at the end of this book and tries to do everything he can to stop curious Elmo from turning the pages and getting to the end. What monster lurks at the book's end? It's just Elmo, of course!

1996 Random House Children's Books

Illustrated by Betsy Lewin

Click, Clack, MOO Cows That Type

Caldecott
Honor

The most improbable things can happen in children's literature, and a bunch of cows that start typing notes to Farmer Brown about their living conditions may be unlikely, but the laughter this story brings is not. The cows are cold, and they want electric blankets. When the farmer refuses, they go on strike. A compromise is finally reached, thanks to a negotiation by the duck. Lewin's wacky illustrations convey the emotions of the cows and the other farm animals with broad humor, and the message of peaceful protest and compromise is one children can readily understand.

2000 Atheneum

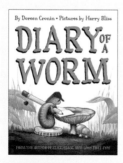

Illustrated by Harry Bliss

Diary of a Worm

The droll humor in this book and the wonderful illustrations will have both parents and children laughing in no time. Worm lives a life not too different from the child reading the book—except, of course, he's a worm. He has friends, goes to school, goes to dances—all very normal activities; now imagine doing all of that without arms and legs! It makes doing the "Hokey Pokey" a bit of a challenge. There are valuable lessons here about ecology and the worm's place in the circle of life, but there are also laughs galore for the whole family.

2003 HarperCollins

Alexandra Day
Good Dog, Carl

This nearly wordless book—it has only twelve words in forty pages—tells a story the way only a gifted writer and illustrator can, through vivid narrative art. Parents need to set aside their own issues to embrace a rottweiler who babysits for a toddler, but children will not have any such issues. They will laugh as the clever Carl cares for the baby he obviously loves, even bathes her and cleans up the house, all before mother returns from shopping. This is a great book to encourage children to tell you the story by "reading" the art.

1985 Simon & Schuster Books for Young Readers

Jean de Brunhoff
The Story of Babar

This classic tale of a little elephant that comes into the big city to find his fortune after the death of his mother has been loved around the world since its introduction in France in 1931. Once he enters the city, Babar becomes the toast of the town, is crowned King, and takes a Queen when he marries his cousin Celeste. The adventures of Babar, Celeste, and their children carry on through many more books, some written by de Brunhoff's son Laurent after his father's death. While there is much to love about these books, parents are advised to pre-read them to assure that they are appropriate for their child. The death of Babar's mother is skillfully handled, but there are other problematic depictions regarding race and violence in later books due to the time and place in which they were written.

1931 Random House Children's Books

Beatrice de Regniers
Illustrated by Beni Montresor

Caldecott Award

May I Bring a Friend?

When a little boy is asked to tea by the King and Queen, he asks politely, "May I bring a friend?," and the King answers, "Any friend of our friend is welcome." So he brings a series of friends to a series of teas and other meals, but his friends turn out to be a giraffe, a lion, a monkey, and other animals that are not quite as well behaved as he is. This award-winning book's pen-and-ink art style and humorous theme, along with a fun twist at the end, will make it a family favorite in no time.

1964 Atheneum

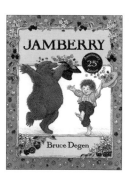

Bruce Degen
Jamberry

A boy and a bear go off together to pick berries in this rollicking poetic celebration of the simple joys of summer. Its language is almost musical in nature; you may find yourself making up songs and dances as you read aloud. The frolicking joy is evident in the artwork that beautifully accompanies this rhyme. Berry picking is a common theme in children's literature—but there is nothing common about this book. Don't be surprised to find yourself craving a few berries or at least some toast with jam by the end.

1983 HarperCollins

Tomie dePaola
Strega Nona

Caldecott Honor

The Italian folktale of the local Strega Nona, or "Grandma Witch," quickly reveals that Strega Nona is a very good witch and not at all scary. She uses the magic in her always-full pasta pot to cure the ills and troubles of the townsfolk in her medieval village. With her big nose and big chin, this adorable grandma will entertain children with her good heart and good deeds, as well as with a whole lot of magic. There are other books in this series as well, but this award-winning title is the one that made Strega Nona a classic children's character.

1975 Simon & Schuster Books for Young Readers

Julia Donaldson
Illustrated by Axel Scheffler
The Gruffalo

When a little mouse walks through the forest, he is threatened by some natural predators: a fox, an owl, a snake, and others. In each case, he tells them a story he has made up about the terrible "gruffalo," who is searching for them for dinner. Each runs off in terror, as the mouse wanders on, laughing about his feat, saying, "Doesn't he know? There's no such thing as a gruffalo!" Until, of course, he runs into you-know-who, and has to convince the gruffalo that all the animals of the forest fear him! Lots of laughs and fun art make this not-too-scary thriller one that your children will ask for again and again.

1999 Dial

Picture Books 2–6

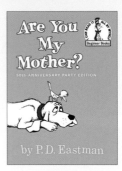

Are You My Mother?

This favorite in the "Beginner Books" series was written in 1960 and is often one of the books today's parents loved best from their own childhoods. The illustrations offer wonderful visual clues to the text, as a small bird hatches from his egg while his mother is out shopping and proceeds to try and figure out who his mother is. Children will laugh and shout "NO!" as the silly little bird asks everything from a bulldozer to a dog, a cat, and a boat, "Are you my mother?" All ends well, of course, in this reassuring and very funny tale that may well get you and your children asking the same question of your household appliances and pets.

1960 Random House Children's Books

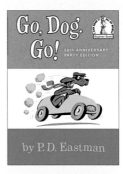

Go, Dog. Go!

This favorite beginning-reader book features simple sight words and also introduces children to simple prepositions, opposites, and colors, as dogs of every shape, size, and color—even some with polka dots—speed through the pages on many forms of transport, from cars and scooters to ferris wheels. There are only seventy-five words in this book, and the visual clues will help young readers work them out as they see them on the page. That, and a budding romance between a big yellow dog and a poodle with a hat, will keep the laughs and the learning moving along as quickly as the dogs in the book.

1961 Random House Children's Books

The first book in this series, *Llama Llama Red Pajama*, deals effectively with children's night terrors. It tells the tale of a little llama who gets scared after being left alone in his bed, and his Mama who doesn't immediately respond to his cries as she is on the telephone. The second title, *Llama Llama Mad at Mama*, deals with the issue of controlling emotions, when our adorable little llama, who doesn't want to go shopping with Mama, gets bored and throws a tantrum in the store. And the third title in the series, *Llama Llama Misses Mama*, is about the new experience of going to preschool, and what will happen when Mama leaves. There are more books in this series, and the wonderful thing about all of them is the way the author uses simple rhyme and very expressive art to render common childhood anxieties in a manner that both children and parents can appreciate. These universal themes are dealt with by using humor and reassurance to calm the transitions that are difficult for toddlers.

Llama Llama Red Pajama (2005)

Llama Llama Mad at Mama (2007)

Llama Llama Misses Mama (2009)

Viking

Ian Falconer

Olivia

For every parent who has a precocious and rambunctious child, Olivia is just the pig for you. Falconer's black-and-white art with bright red highlights and spare text propels this tale of a bundle of energy who is supremely confident, very sophisticated, and "good at lots of things." Olivia is exhausting to her patient parents, and when her mom tucks her in at night and says, "You know, you really wear me out. But I love you anyway," what else can Olivia say but, "I love you anyway too." There are many other books in this series, and each of them is tons of fun and filled with ATTITUDE, something Olivia possesses in abundance.

2000 Atheneum

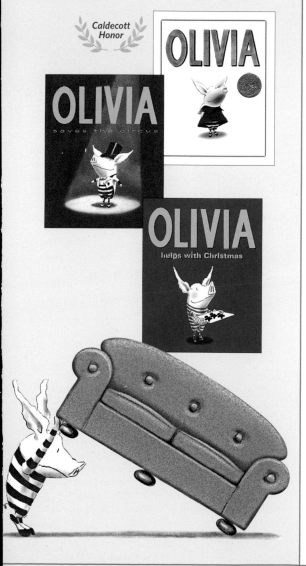

Jules Feiffer

Bark, George

Noted cartoonist Jules Feiffer scores big time with this simple, visual tale of a dog who cannot bark. When his mother asks him to bark, he meows. Then moos. Then quacks. They go off to the vet, who reaches down into George and pulls out a cat, a cow, a duck, and, well, you get the idea. Of course it can't end that simply; when George is asked to bark at the end of the book, he opens his mouth and out comes..."Hello." Kids will enjoy the simply drawn yet very funny visuals and love making all the animal sounds and guessing what will come out of George next.

1999 HarperCollins

Marjorie Flack
Illustrated by Kurt Wiese

The Story About Ping

This classic tale is about a little duck named Ping, who lives with his outrageously large extended family on a boat on the Yangtze River in China. When Ping is accidentally separated from his family while looking for food, he embarks on a series of adventures, along with a few close calls, before being reunited with them in the end. This story of family love is reassuring to young children, and the artwork beautifully evokes rural life along the Yangtze in China. It is a true classic for every family library.

1933 Viking

Picture Books 2–6

39

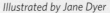

Picture Books 2–6

Illustrated by Jane Dyer
Time for Bed

When it's time for bed, parents look for a comforting and calming story, and this one perfectly fits the bill. Short rhyming couplets featuring a variety of baby animals and their parents—and a final illustration of a child with his mother—will help to lull children to sleep. The soft and beautiful art that accompanies the text, whether depicting a lamb or a baby mouse, is charming and soothing, making this just the right sort of book to send your child off to dreamland.

1993 Harcourt Children's Books

Illustrated by Steve Jenkins
Hello Baby!

The short, simple text of this book about baby animals of all sorts is perfect for babies and toddlers, but the real star of this book is award-winning artist Jenkins' beautiful collage art that appears almost three-dimensional against flat white backgrounds. Monkeys, warthogs, hippos, lions, and more, including a human baby at the end, nearly leap off the pages of this stunning picture book, which is perfect for the very young.

2009 Beach Lane Books

Illustrated by Judy Horacek
Where Is the Green Sheep?

This hardworking title is actually a great beginning reader with simple, bold, black, repetitive text. It also teaches simple colors and comparisons, all while telling a truly entertaining tale. With text like "Here is the blue sheep. And here is the red sheep. Here is the bath sheep. And here is the bed sheep. But where is the green sheep?" and rowdy illustrations of sheep frolicking on the playground or playing music, this book inspires children to chant the refrain "But where is the green sheep?" Until, of course, he is found on the final spread, asleep under a bush.

2004 Harcourt Children's Books

Wanda Gag
Millions of Cats

Considered by many to be one of the first modern picture books, this classic tale of vanity versus humility was written in 1929 and remains a popular classic. When an old man goes out to find his wife the most beautiful cat in the world, he can't decide on one cat, and brings home every cat he can find. It is up to the cats to determine who is the most beautiful and who can stay with the old couple. The cat that remains after all the fuss is a scrawny little kitten—who, of course, becomes the most beautiful cat. This is a wonderful tale of love, which teaches that you must look beneath the surface for true beauty.

1928 Putnam

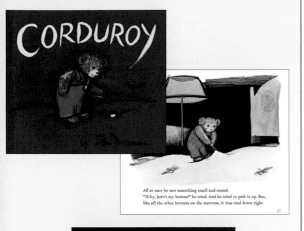

All at once he saw something small and round.
"Why, here's my button!" he cried. And he tried to pick it up. But,
like all the other buttons on the mattress, it was tied down tight.

17

Corduroy

A little brown bear wearing corduroy overalls with a button missing on one strap sits on a shelf in the store, just waiting for someone to take him home. When Lisa tells her mother she wants the bear, her mother only sees the missing button, and says no. During the night, Corduroy explores the store to find a new button, but is restored to his shelf by the night watchman. The next morning, Lisa comes in to buy him with her own money, and a classic story is born. Featuring Hispanic and African American main characters, this book is a classic story of the love of a little girl for her favorite bear.

1968 Viking

A Pocket for Corduroy

In this charming sequel, Corduroy is at the laundromat with Lisa, and notices her checking all the pockets before washing her clothes. He notices that his overalls don't have any pockets and sets off to look for something to make one. In the confusion of his adventure, he is left behind in someone else's laundry. Corduroy is rescued by the laundromat owner, and Lisa returns the next day to find him. She promptly sews a pocket on his overalls and puts in a card with his name, so he'll never be lost again.

1978 Viking

Nikki Giovanni
Illustrated by Bryan Collier

Rosa

This award-winning picture book retelling of a seminal moment in the civil rights movement—the story of Rosa Parks, an African American woman who refused to give up her seat on the bus to a white person—brings history to life for young children. Illustrated with Collier's brilliant collage-and-watercolor art, this book is a sensitively told tale of how one person and one simple act can change the world. Children will learn more about Parks in school, but this book makes a perfect non-preachy introduction to the civil rights movement and an unlikely hero.

2005 Henry Holt

Paul Goble

The Girl Who Loved Wild Horses

This award-winning story of a Native American girl will entrance any young readers who love horses. The girl in the story has an unusual ability to communicate with wild horses, and when a storm drives her and the horses far from her tribe, she learns to live with and as one of them. Eventually she is rescued—but her tribe understands her unique relationship with the animals. She is allowed to return to them and is transformed by the experience. The art is stunning, and the story of finding your own special gifts and following your dreams is very well done.

1978 Atheneum/Richard Jackson Books

Picture Books 2–6

Picture Books 2–6

Hardie Gramatky
Little Toot

In children's books there are two things you can count on: stories about tugboats and stories about a character who is frightened or teased but who eventually summons enough courage to save the day. This book has both. Little Toot is afraid of the rough waters of the ocean, so he stays mostly in the harbor, and the other tugboats call him a sissy. One day his very special skills are needed out in the ocean, and of course, he rises to the occasion and succeeds beyond his own dreams. This classic title remains a favorite for its charming art and wonderful story about conquering your fears.

1939 Putnam

Virginia Hamilton
Illustrated by Leo and Diane Dillon
The People Could Fly: The Picture Book

This African American folktale, brought to life by its award-winning author and illustrators, is a story of hope and freedom. In ancient days some Africans could fly, and when they became slaves, some of them still remembered how to do so. This tale is the story of how that magical skill was used to rescue some African Americans from slavery. With its lyrical storytelling and astounding art, this magical book is a must have for any family library, no matter your ethnic background.

2005 Alfred A. Knopf

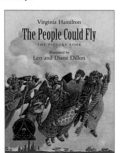

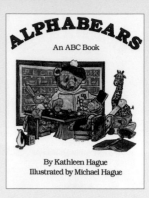

Illustrated by Michael Hague
Alphabears: An ABC Book

In this unique alphabet book, children will learn the alphabet by way of twenty-six soft and cuddly teddy bears, each with an alphabetically inspired name and rhyme, such as: "B is for Byron, who snuggles in bed. Mom tucks him in with a kiss on the head." Hague's art for this book reflects the coziness and comfort of teddy bears, and the ones featured look like they are ready for a quick snuggle and squeeze.

1984 Henry Holt

Illustrated by Michael Hague
Good Night, Fairies

This bedtime book offers fairy lore that is perfect for toddlers, with quiet, calming text and lovely, detailed artwork. Children will pore over the artwork on every spread, wondering at the magical fairies who hang the stars in the sky and teach flowers to bloom and unicorns to fly. Little ones will love locating the little red-capped fairy that appears on each page, and counting the 321 winged fairies shown in the book.

2006 Chronicle Books

David A. Carter on the perfect combination of drawing, coloring, and building...

Like many people from my generation, my early favorites were the books of Dr. Seuss. The first book that I read by myself was *Green Eggs and Ham*, and the wild creatures in *If I Ran the Circus* and *If I Ran the Zoo* fascinated me. Even before I began reading Dr. Seuss, I would become lost in a Golden Book called *Cowboys and Indians*, illustrated by Gustaf Tenggren. Every night I would ask my mom to read *The Biggest Bear*. The Lynd Ward illustrations of Johnny and the bear still hold a very special place in my heart.

I have been an artist for as long as I can remember; maybe I was influenced by Tenggren and Seuss. As a child not only did I spend hours drawing and coloring, but I also built sculptures with wood and nails from my dad's workshop. In high school, when a car accident kept me in bed for many months, I spent my time filling sketchbooks with drawings. When I finally got back to high school, my art teacher, Roger Cushing, introduced me to the world of illustration and helped me get a scholarship to attend college. In the early 1980s, after studying illustration in college, I moved to Los Angeles, where I went to work for Intervisual Books, the company that started the renaissance in pop-up books. It was there that I was inspired by two pop-up books, Jan Pienkowski's *Robot* and Robert Crowther's *The Most Amazing Hide-and-Seek Alphabet Book*. I knew from that moment that I wanted to pursue the art of the pop-up book. For me, it was the perfect combination of drawing, coloring and building. I see my art as entertainment for the mind. From pop-up bugs to red dots and everything in between, I hope my art tickles your mind.

See individual listings for books by David A. Carter on page 202.

Author/Illustrator David A. Carter

Stoo Hample
The Silly Book

Sometimes a perfectly silly book is what is called for—and this one is so silly that it is absolutely perfect in every way. With wild and silly illustrations, silly songs, silly poems, and silly jokes, this book is meant to deliver the laughs, and it does so with every reading. The humor is simple and child-friendly and is the perfect distraction for kids at a restaurant or in the car or for just sitting in the living room for a good long chuckle together. There's no plot and no deep message—the book is purely and simply chock-full of fun—and really, deeply silly!

2004 Candlewick Press

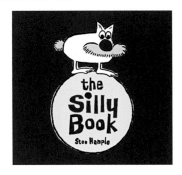

Martin Handford
Where's Waldo?

Trying to find the intrepid Waldo (and his friends Woof, Wenda, Wizard, Whitebeard, Odlaw, and others) in his signature red-and-white striped hat and shirt in these densely illustrated spreads provides hours of fun for families and children alike. We know he's there on every spread, but discovering just where he is takes some keen observation. Every page of this book is a visual smorgasbord of images, and everyone in the family will love the search. It's perfect for long car trips or for antsy children who need a fun distraction.

1987 Candlewick Press

Eric Hill
Where's Spot?

Eric Hill may not have invented the concept of lift-the-flap books, but there is no question that he is a master of the form. There are many Spot books available, in every conceivable format, but this book, the original title, has taught countless toddlers how to seek and find the lovable pup as he hides throughout the book. Each book in the series teaches simple concepts, such as colors, shapes, and sizes, and encourages children to interact by lifting and looking for answers to the questions.

1980 Putnam

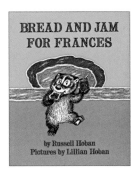

Russell Hoban
Illustrated by Lillian Hoban
Bread and Jam for Frances

There are several books available that feature Frances the badger, including *Bedtime for Frances*, *Best Friends for Frances*, *Happy Birthday Frances*, *A Baby Sister for Frances*, and *A Bargain for Frances*, and each one deals with a specific aspect of typical toddler behavior. Frances is a typical toddler, sweet and earnest, sometimes stubborn and sometimes naughty, and in this book she decides that she will only eat bread and jam—because that's what she loves best. You can imagine where this goes after a few days of the same thing for every meal. All of these books are timeless and deal with issues that all children can relate to.

1964 HarperCollins

Caldecott
Award

Kitten's First Full Moon

This award-winning title is masterfully executed in black, white, and gray, and perfectly evokes the nighttime and the big round moon that the little kitten thinks is a bowl of milk. As the thirsty and determined little kitten tries to get to the bowl of milk, she ends up falling down the stairs, getting a bug on her tongue, and making a veritable feast of errors easily understandable visually, even to toddlers. In the end, there is a bowl of milk for her on the porch, and the moon remains in the sky. This sweet story of determination rewarded also features great visuals of round items throughout for children to identify and name.

2004 Greenwillow Books

Chrysanthemum

When it comes to dealing with the emotions of pre-schoolers and primary-grade children, nobody is better than Kevin Henkes. This book focuses on teasing and bullies, and how one mouse family deals with it. Chrysanthemum thinks her name is perfect, but when she gets to school, the children taunt and tease her about it—after all, with thirteen letters, it does take up half the alphabet. Fortunately she does talk to her parents about her feelings, and it all comes out all right in the end. This is an important topic, and many families need a way to open the discussion. This book will help to do so in a very positive way, even with very young children.

1991 Greenwillow Books

Julius: The Baby of the World

Sibling rivalry has never been so much fun or so easy for kids to relate to. Lilly is thrilled with her new brother at first, but it doesn't last long when he starts getting all the attention. Her truly creative taunts ("if you were a food, you'd be a raisin") and slights of her brother stop abruptly when a visiting cousin starts to insult baby Julius. Suddenly we see the other side of sibling rivalry—an abiding love and loyalty. This issue is common in most families when the second child arrives, but dealing with it can be stressful. This book helps explain those feelings to young children and may even preempt some of that jealousy.

1993 Greenwillow Books

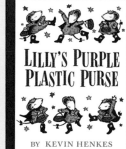

Lilly's Purple Plastic Purse

She's *baaack*—and the irrepressible Lilly is up to her usual shenanigans in this hilarious romp of a book about feeling angry, making mistakes, and learning to apologize. Lilly loves her teacher, but when he takes away her new and exciting purse because she is playing with it in class, she turns on him and draws a nasty picture of him. When he returns the purse to her at the end of the day—with a nice note inside—Lilly realizes that she went too far and makes amends. This is a simple lesson in humility but told with great humor and heart.

1996 Greenwillow Books

Picture Books 2–6

Picture Books 2–6

Mary Hoffman
Illustrated by Caroline Binch
Amazing Grace

Every once a while, a book comes along that changes how we think; this is one of them. Grace is a lover of stories, and like many primary graders, she loves to act them out. When her school selects *Peter Pan* as the school play, she knows the title role is right for her. When her classmates tell her she can't play Peter because she isn't a boy and she's black, she is shattered. But her grandmother reminds her that she can do and be anything, and Grace's courage and belief in herself win the day. The book is about self-esteem, but it also deals with how we are different and how we are also all the same.

1991 Dial

Katharine Holabird
Illustrated by Helen Craig
Angelina Ballerina

For every little girl who ever wanted to be a ballerina or graceful ice skater, there's Angelina, an energetic and determined little mouse who is both. Little girls will love the tutus and plenty of pink, as Angelina spins her way into their hearts. This is the first in a series of books about Angelina, a mouse that wants nothing more than to dance, dance, dance, and will let nothing stand in her way. This is a wonderfully illustrated tale that expresses both the grace and joy of dance with compelling visuals and a well-told story about letting nothing get in the way of your dreams.

1983 Viking

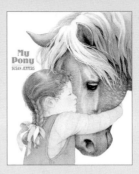

My Pony

In this book, Susan Jeffers manages to capture the longing that so many girls have for a horse of their own. A young girl understands that horses are expensive and require a lot of room, but that doesn't change her desire for a pony of her own. She begins to draw, and what she draws is a magical pony named Silver who comes to life in her dreams. The pony takes her on galloping dream adventures and brings her back to her bedroom each night. Even the artwork in this book is transparent and dreamlike and utterly beautiful.

2003 Hyperion

The Nutcracker

Rather than base this book on the E.T.A. Hoffman fairy tale, Susan Jeffers tells her version in a manner that might be more familiar to fans of the annual holiday extravaganza—she bases her retelling on the *Nutcracker* ballet. Using spare text and lovely paintings that capture all the magic of a live performance and the Christmas season, this is a *Nutcracker* that will be adored by every little girl or boy who ever strapped on their own ballet shoes or hopes to do so in the future.

2007 HarperCollins

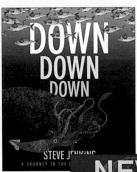

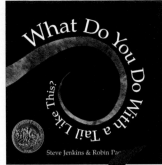

Actual Size

Children understand the basic concepts of *big* and *little*, but *huge* and *tiny* can be a bit of a challenge. This book by Steve Jenkins uses his mastery of collage and watercolor to teach children not only about wild animals both familiar and not, but also about size and perspective, by comparing them, and illustrating the animals—or at least parts of them—in actual size. Kids can compare their hands, eyes, ears, and tongues to all sorts of animals in this fascinating book.

2004 Houghton Mifflin Books for Children

Down, Down, Down: A Journey to the Bottom of the Sea

In this book, children will learn about all the amazing, scary, weird, and strange creatures that live deep in the sea, such as squid, neon jellyfish, and whales, as well as all the other creatures that live in, around, and above our oceans. These thrilling and rarely seen creatures are presented in their dramatic undersea world via Jenkins' clever use of collage and paint in a way that can sometimes appear almost three dimensional. Your children will be so entranced by the art and text that they will have no idea how much science they are learning—but you will.

2009 Houghton Mifflin Books for Children

Never Smile at a Monkey

We teach our children what to not do when approaching an animal or strange pet—but what if you find yourself face-to-face with a monkey, a hippo, a platypus, or a jellyfish? Using alliterative language ("Never jostle a jellyfish" or "harass a hippopotamus") and his brilliant art style, Jenkins provides a humorous and fact-based explanation of the not-so-obvious reactions that the wrong approach to a wild animal might prompt. The science behind the information is solid and presented with humor, and the lesson of caution when dealing with wild animals is important as well.

2009 Houghton Mifflin Books for Children

Steve Jenkins and Robin Page
What Do You Do With a Tail Like This?

Written in the format of a guessing game, each page of this book asks a question and features art depicting a specific part of an animal—its tail, nose, ear, etc.— and then the following spread shows more of the animal and answers the question. The repetitive concept engages young children, and Jenkins' signature collage and watercolor art will astound them with its brilliance and accuracy in representing the animals. Both educational (facts are built into the text) and entertaining, this book and its sequel, *What Do You Do When Something Wants to Eat You?* will keep children entranced the entire time.

2003 Houghton Mifflin Books for Children

Crockett Johnson
Harold and the Purple Crayon

One of the most beloved characters in children's literature is bald-headed Harold, who, with his purple crayon, goes out and creates his own world. As he walks, he draws his own landscape to enter, always careful to keep the moon and a few other landmarks in sight. When he approaches the sea, he draws a boat; when he gets hungry, he draws some pies; and when he is tired, he draws the window to his room. This lesson in creativity and fantasy will resonate with children, as do the simple purple lines that create Harold's world. Caution to parents: you might want to pick up the crayons after reading this book with your children!

1955 HarperCollins

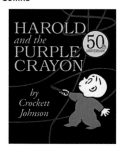

Alan Katz
Illustrated by David Catrow
Are You Quite Polite?

Children love to sing silly songs, and, in addition to being silly in the extreme, these songs will go a long way toward teaching good manners. The team of songwriter Katz and illustrator Catrow has turned the concept of sing-a-long verses set to familiar music into an art form, using unconventional concepts and wild and wacky illustrations. And this book takes manners way past "please" and "thank you." With songs like "Jimmy Picks Boogers," sung to the tune of "Blue Tail Fly," or "Don't Talk with Beans in Your Mouth," sung to "Michael Row the Boat Ashore," this book will make children laugh and sing but also learn what is and isn't appropriate behavior and why.

2006 Margaret K. McElderry

Pictures by Maurice Sendak

These two charming and hilarious books tackle the very conventional issue of manners and etiquette in a most unconventional way. Children are only too familiar with hearing the words "What do you say?" when they have forgotten to insert a "please" or "thank you" in conversation, and this book reinforces that message by taking those teachable moments to the most extreme. Joslin's sublime-to-ridiculous social situations, such as "You are downtown and there is a gentleman giving baby elephants to people. You want to take one home because you have always wanted a baby elephant, but first the gentleman introduces you to each other. What do you say, dear?" combined with Sendak's classic, humorous illustrations make teaching children proper manners a breeze. The basics are all here—"please," "thank you," "excuse me"—but the situations in which they are used will keep your children laughing the whole time they are learning proper etiquette. And should they ever actually be walking backward down the street and bump into an alligator, they will know exactly what to say and do!

What Do You Say, Dear? *(1958)*
What Do You Do, Dear? *(1961)*
HarperCollins

Picture Books 2–6

The Snowy Day

Caldecott Award

A little boy wakes up to discover that the world outside has been transformed by an overnight snowfall. Out he goes to experience the snow by making footprints and snow angels, shaking snow from tree branches, and doing all the things a little boy might do on a snowy day. The quiet magic of a fresh snowfall comes alive through cut paper, watercolors, and collage. Prior to Ezra Jack Keats (a white, Jewish man from Brooklyn) there weren't any books featuring African American characters for toddlers and preschoolers outside of folktales. The beauty of the way he wrote and illustrated his books is that his characters are just kids doing things kids do and, as such, are perfect for all children but very special for African American children who may not have seen images that look like themselves in books.

1962 Viking

Hi, Cat!

This is the simple story of a little boy named Archie who greets a stray cat and what happens when that cat follows him through his day. The cat's antics cause mayhem, but in the end, when the cat follows him home, Archie realizes he has made a friend for life. As in Keats' other books, the fact that Archie is African American is incidental to the story but important in many other ways. All children relate to the story and to the character and rarely even notice Archie's race—a testament to a timeless story well told and beautifully illustrated.

1999 Viking

Peter's Chair

In this story about sibling rivalry, Peter's parents have a new baby girl, and suddenly everything is changing. First they paint Peter's old cradle pink, then his old crib too. When Peter realizes his favorite chair is next, he decides enough is enough and plans to run away with his dog, Willie. Eventually, of course, all is well and Peter learns that the new baby is small, and he is big; his parents still love him, while he kind of loves his baby sister, too. Peter and Willie are characters who reappears in other Keats books (*Whistle for Willie* and *The Snowy Day*), and children feel comfortable with him and can relate to the way that Peter feels about the new addition to the family.

1998 Viking

Whistle for Willie

Peter wants to learn to whistle more than anything. He wants to be able to whistle for his dog, Willie, like other kids whistle for their dogs. But as hard as he tries, no sound comes out, and his cheeks are starting to hurt, too. Children will relate to Peter's frustration in this sweet tale of perseverance, but they will also learn that determination can bring results as long as you don't give up. The character of Peter runs through many of Keats' books, and readers who loved him in *The Snowy Day* will be rooting for him all the way through to this book's successful ending.

1964 Viking

Pinkalicious

If your little girl loves everything pink, this is the book for you. On a rainy day, Pinkalicious and her mom make cupcakes—all pink of course. But when she eats too many, she finds that she has turned pink herself, and exclaims, "I'm Pinkerbelle!" Mom whisks her off to the doctor, who prescribes some green food; Pinkalicious resists, eats more pink, and suddenly turns bright red. At that point, she relents and eats enough of the green stuff to return to normal—but there is a clever twist at the end involving her brother. This book is a sly way to teach children about eating a balanced diet with lots of vegetables. There are many offshoots of this book involving various colors if pink is not your child's particular obsession.

Elizabeth and Victoria Kann
Illustrated by Victoria Kann

Pinkalicious *(2006)*

Purplicious *(2007)*

Victoria Kann

Goldilicious *(2009)*

Silverlicious *(2011)*

HarperCollins

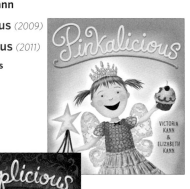

Laurie Keller
The Scrambled States of America

Learning geography can be challenging, but this clever book makes learning the fifty states a cinch and provides laughs along the way. At the annual "states party," Virginia and Idaho decide to switch places so they can see new things. Soon all the states want to do the same; the landlocked states want to see the ocean, and those northern states could use a sunny break from the cold winters. Filled with crazy asides and states with definite personalities, this book delivers learning and laughing hand-in-hand. And ultimately the states learn their lessons and find ingenious ways to get back to their original locations on the map.

1998 Henry Holt

David Kirk
Miss Spider's Tea Party

The vividly colored paintings that accompany the story in this book are as much of a draw as the story itself. The colors virtually jump off the page in this tale of a lonely spider who can't understand why none of the other bugs will come to her web for a tea party. Kids are in on the joke—they know how spiders kill their prey—but this spider has to prove she is harmless by nursing a wounded moth back to health, and eventually the other bugs see that she "ate just flowers, and drank just tea." The rhyming language and subtle counting exercises as the bugs finally join her for tea teach basic numbers, and the theme of the book makes it perfect for tea party readings.

1994 Scholastic Press/Scholastic Inc.

William Kotzwinkle and Glenn Murray
Illustrated by Audrey Colman

Walter the Farting Dog

Say what you want about the title and topic of this book—children find it hilarious. When dealing with reluctant readers, children (especially boys) who don't like to read or don't want to be read to, go for the humor—and the more scatological the better. There is a message here as well! Walter is rescued from the pound but turns out to have one really bad habit—farting. The family is disgusted, but when Walter's horrid habit helps foil a crime, he repays the family's kindness to him, and they accept him, farts and all. Besides all that, it really is pretty funny, and the illustrations are pretty great, too.

2001 Frog Books

Karla Kuskin
Illustrated by Marc Simont

The Philharmonic Gets Dressed

This brilliant book was published to immediate acclaim. The simplicity of the story of all the different ways the members of the philharmonic get up, get dressed, and get to work, complemented by Simont's simple, cartoon-style art, make this one for every family library. Kids will laugh at the orchestra members bathing, showering, trimming their mustaches or putting on powder, and especially at all the varieties of underwear that can be worn by 105 different people. Then the musicians get into their black-and-white clothes and off they go, in trains, taxis, or limos, to reach the performance hall. The subtext here is that although everyone gets ready for the same event, they all do it in their own way, that we are more similar than different, but everyone is special.

1982 HarperCollins

Munro Leaf
Illustrated by Robert Lawson

The Story of Ferdinand

One of the bestselling children's books of all time, this charming story about a serene bull who would rather smell the flowers than participate in the bullfights of his native Spain has taught children about peace and tranquility since 1936. Ferdinand is big and strong, and not a coward at all, he's just very mellow and happy. Until one day when he accidentally sits on a bee, which promptly stings him. His wild reaction is witnessed by the men who have come to find the "biggest, fastest, roughest" bull for the bullfights in Madrid, and so our peaceful bull finds himself in the ring. Fear not, Ferdinand sticks to his principles. Lawson's black-and-white illustrations effectively portray both the drama of the bullfight and Ferdinand's very happy ending.

1936 Viking

Phillippe Lechermeier
Illustrated by Rébecca Dautremer

The Secret Lives of Princesses

Oversized and nearly one hundred pages long, this "field guide" to princesses is perfect for girls who have curiosity, a sense of humor, and a willingness to accept all things magical. It is vividly illustrated and filled with unusual charts, graphs, and diagrams; there are stories, entire pages showing royal residences, coats of arms, lists of jewels, educational requirements, and bios of some very magical princesses, who often bear strong resemblances to fairy queens children may already be familiar with.
Note: this book is also appropriate for older readers.

2010 Sterling

Eoin Colfer on being the hero in his own stories…

I wanted to write books for children because growing up, kids' writers were my heroes and the worlds they created were in many ways my playgrounds. I was rubbish at football and worse at schoolyard games, but I could write a little story or draw a caricature, so most of my leisure hours were spent off in a corner somewhere making my own comic books. The first time I remember breaking through the membrane between reality and imagination was with Mark Twain's *Huckleberry Finn*. That cheeky first-person narrative sucked me into Huck's world, and I realized that a person did not have to be a perfect superhero to be the hero of a book. Huck was a pipe-smoking, cussing truant, and yet here was a story all about him. Anyone could be a hero. I could be a hero, at least in stories. And so from then on, I imagined myself in all the lead roles, especially the flawed ones, which were the only ones I was really interested in. In fact, whenever I read a book, I searched for the flaw that would help me to identify with the main character, and if he didn't have one, I invented some dark secret from his past.

Many years later, when I became a teacher, I read *Huckleberry Finn* to the kids in my class and I watched their faces light up with the same magical glow that I imagine mine did all those years ago, and I wondered what it must be like to be Mark Twain, the person who had brought so much joy, so I decided to find out and spent the next ten years or so trying to get a book published. When it finally happened I was too nervous to read it to my own class, but my colleague did and he assures me that the kids thought it did not stink too much. Which is not bad for a first effort.

See individual listings for books by Eoin Colfer on page 135.

Author Eoin Colfer

Suzy Lee
Wave

This book is completely wordless, but the black, gray, and blue illustrations of a little girl enjoying her day at the beach tell the story so completely that no words are needed. Her facial expressions and body language convey her excitement upon arriving at the beach, her joy in confronting and teasing the waves, and her interactions with some very expressive seagulls. This book is a story that young children can tell to themselves with or without a parent "reading" to them, and it will reinforce visual communication and self-expression for children of all ages.

2008 Chronicle Books

Kevin Lewis

Illustrated by Daniel Kirk
Chugga-Chugga Choo-Choo

A child's playroom comes to life in this vibrantly illustrated tale of a train loaded with toys that makes his way around the tracks laid out in a child's bedroom. With wonderful rhythmic language and art that almost seems three dimensional, this story and its classic "toys come to life" theme will entrance even the littlest readers.

1999 Hyperion

Illustrated by Daniel Kirk
My Truck is Stuck!

This lively, rhyming tale features a simple plot, but is filled with humor and brought to life by Kirk's brilliantly colored illustrations. Two burly dogs who are hauling a load of yummy bones get their truck stuck in a prairie dog hole. As the dogs try in vain to get their truck unstuck, the prairie dogs have been sneaking off with the bones. This is a perfect book for the very young who are fascinated with all things vehicle-related.

2002 Hyperion

Illustrated by Daniel Kirk
Tugga-Tugga Tugboat

This bath-time favorite by the team of Lewis and Kirk features a tugboat who is clearly the master of the harbor, pulling the big boats, putting out fires—but little readers will soon figure out that the harbor looks pretty familiar, and those boats look a lot like bars of soap... and the action is really all taking place in the bathtub. As in their previous books, Lewis and Kirk once again utilize rhythm and rhyme and vibrant art to their full advantage, making this a book that makes children look forward to bath time.

2006 Hyperion

A Color of His Own

This story of finding your own true self and the value of friendship is told in words and beautiful images that even very young children can readily understand. The chameleon realizes that everything has a color—elephants are gray, pigs are pink—except him. He can be any color, depending on where he is sitting. He decides to become just one color, and off he goes to find the greenest leaf to sit upon. Which is fine until autumn comes, and he turns red, then yellow, and then brown. He meets another chameleon who suggests they travel together; once he makes a friend, he realizes that they will always be alike and always be friends, whatever their color.

1975 Random House Children's Books

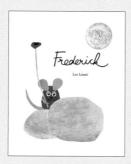

Frederick

In one of Lionni's most stunning picture books, a little mouse named Frederick is sitting alone on a rock while all the other mice are running around gathering up nuts and grains for the upcoming winter. On one day Frederick says he is gathering sun rays for the cold dark winter days, and on another day he is gathering words and colors. When the other mice run out of food in the middle of winter, it is Fredrick who uses his warm body and store of words and colors to feed their spirits until spring. This beautifully illustrated picture book teaches that there is more to life than work—there is also creativity and an appreciation of the beauty of words and the world around us.

1967 Alfred A. Knopf

Little Blue and Little Yellow

Lionni's skills as a graphic designer are in full display in this deceptively simple book about primary colors. Only in children's books can two blobs of color, in this case torn paper, come to life as characters. Little Blue and Little Yellow are best friends. One day they can't find each other, and when they are reunited they are so overjoyed that they hug and hug until they blend and become Green. But what happened to Little Blue and Little Yellow? This story of friendship and acceptance also teaches colors and how two colors can make one new color. It's simple and brilliant.

1959 Alfred A. Knopf

Swimmy

The use of subtle watercolor washes plus the addition of graphic images of little red fish and our hero Swimmy, the little black fish, make this story a treat for the eyes as well as the ears as it is read aloud. Swimmy has many brothers and sisters, and they are all red. He is the only black fish, and he is also faster, braver, and smarter than his siblings. Swimmy realizes that the other fish are hiding behind the rocks because they are scared of being eaten, and he convinces them that teamwork and camouflage will help them to live more freely. Children will learn the importance of thinking things through and working together in this beautiful book.

1973 Alfred A. Knopf

Caldecott Honor

Picture Books 2–6

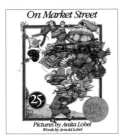

Arnold Lobel
Illustrated by Anita Lobel

On Market Street

There is no shortage of ABC books available, but this book by the multiple award-winning team of Arnold and Anita Lobel is in a class by itself. The concept is simple enough: a young boy heads to Market Street to shop for one item for each letter of the alphabet. In this case it's the execution of the art that sets the book apart, as each shopkeeper and vendor on Market Street is composed entirely of the item he or she is selling, be it apples, books, or oranges. Since its publication in 1981, this book has taught children the ABC's and given them tons of fun identifying each item alphabetically and laughing and wondering over the pictures of the shopkeepers.

1981 Greenwillow Books

Melinda Long
Illustrated by David Shannon

How I Became a Pirate

Who doesn't want to be a pirate? You don't have to mind your manners or brush your teeth, and think of all that pirate lingo and adventure! When little Jeremy Jacob is whisked off the beach with some pirates, he's thrilled—until he realizes that there is nobody to tuck him in, read him a story, and when a storm hits at sea, no one to comfort and reassure him. Shannon's illustrations are swashbuckling fun, the pirates are not too scary (though their rotten teeth are), and kids will learn tons of fun pirate talk. *Avast! Aaarrgh! Ahoy, mateys!* With a sweet message reinforcing that there really is no place like home, this book is fun for all.

2003 Harcourt Children's Books

James Marshall
George and Martha

This classic title from a beloved author/illustrator is all about best friends, who in this case happen to be two adorable hippos named George and Martha. The simple text is perfect for those just beginning to read, and the lively art holds many visual clues to the text. There are two separate stories about the friends in this book. In one, about how friends can work out differences, George is really tired of Martha's pea soup; and in the other, about making good decisions and staying safe, George tries to fly off in a balloon. There are many other George and Martha books in the series, but this book is where it all began.

1972 Houghton Mifflin Books for Children

Bill Martin Jr and John Archambault
Illustrated by Lois Ehlert

Chicka Chicka Boom Boom

This exuberant verse about the alphabet became a classic as soon as it was published. In the brightly colored, cut-paper illustrations by award-winning illustrator Lois Ehlert, the letters race to the top of the coconut tree. Then, with rhythmic language and clever renderings, the slightly bruised letters fall to the ground with a resounding "Chicka Chicka... BOOM! BOOM!" As each letter begins its assent, children will happily recite the sing-song verse "Chicka chicka boom boom! Will there be enough room?" This book's verse begs to be sung and danced to and is a welcome replacement for the standard ABC song. You and your children will be rockin' and rollin' from start to finish.

1989 Beach Lane Books

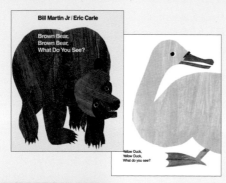

Illustrated by Eric Carle

There are many books in this series by two of the stars of children's books, Bill Martin Jr and Eric Carle, and they all follow the same pattern. One animal sees or hears another, which then appears on the following page, for example, "Blue horse, blue horse, what do you see? I see a green frog looking at me." Toddlers love the repetition and will easily learn to predict the next animal after a few readings. The most striking part of all the books is the combination of a simple text pattern with Carle's signature collage and watercolor art. Though the basic format and pattern of the books is the same, each book offers a different educational premise. *Brown Bear, Brown Bear* is about learning colors, *Polar Bear, Polar Bear* is about the sounds made by animals found in the zoo, and *Panda Bear, Panda Bear* is about more rare or endangered animals. No family library should be without at least one of these books, and two or three would be even better!

Panda Bear, Panda Bear, What Do You See? *(1966)*

Brown Bear, Brown Bear, What Do You See? *(1967)*

Polar Bear, Polar Bear, What Do You Hear? *(1991)*

Henry Holt

A Boy, a Dog, and a Frog

Whenever you select a "wordless" book for your children, you are creating an opportunity for them to use their visual observations to tell you a story. In this charming book, which is the first in a series of six books, children will easily learn to read the visual clues in the beautifully rendered art that tells the very simple story of a young boy out for a walk with his dog and the frog they try to catch. The fun twist is that, although the frog eludes capture, he rather misses the boy and the dog, follows them home, and joins them in the bathtub. This book encourages observation, storytelling, and creativity, and it also allows children to "read" the story to themselves or to their parents.

1967 Dial

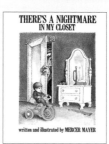

There's a Nightmare in My Closet

One of the most common issues that parents seek help with is what to do with a child who is afraid of the dark or suffers from night terrors. There have been many children's books that address the "scary monster" fears, but this book does it remarkably well, with a great deal of humor, charming pen-and-ink illustrations, and a clever twist. The tone is set from the first line, "There used to be a nightmare in my closet." A little boy goes on to tell the story of how he conquered that nightmare, which turned out to be fairly goofy looking, when he found out that the nightmare was scared of him! The solution? They climbed into bed together, snuggled up, and went to sleep. This book offers a not-so-scary and empowering way for toddlers to overcome their fears at bedtime.

1968 Dial

Anne Mazer
Illustrated by Steve Johnson and Lou Fancher
The Salamander Room

For every little boy or girl who has caught a frog, a butterfly, or in this case, a salamander, and wanted to keep it, there is always a mother who calmly asks, "But where will he sleep?" This book addresses that question as a little boy fantasizes how he can change his room for his new "pet." The art is realistic and very detailed as the fantasy spins deeper, until the boy's room actually becomes the forest. There are many bugs and wild creatures to be found in the art, which will entertain for hours. The lesson of being responsible about nature is implicit but never interferes with the child's own vibrant fantasy.

1991 Alfred A. Knopf

Sam McBratney
Illustrated by Anita Jeram
Guess How Much I Love You

This book is about the love between Little Nut Brown Hare and his father. The little hare tries to find ways to express how much he loves his father. The story ends with him saying "I love you right up to the moon" as he drifts off, and his daddy responding quietly, "I love you right up to the moon—and back." These expressions of love are common between parents and toddlers, but that doesn't make them less poignant. The soft and comic illustrations coupled with the two hares' reassuring declarations of love make this the perfect bedtime story—whether parents can get through it without crying is an entirely different matter.

1995 Candlewick Press

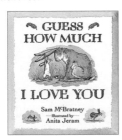

Gerald McDermott
Anansi the Spider

Anansi the Spider is an old "trickster" tale from Ghana, West Africa, in the Ashanti tradition. What sets this book apart from other versions of this traditional tale is the interweaving of traditional African motifs, along with the bold cut-paper and collage style art that so effectively evokes the tribes and culture of Ghana. Anansi is setting out on a long and difficult journey, and along the way is threatened by some natural foes, the fish and the falcon. When his six sons cleverly save his life, he must decide which son to reward and how. This folktale will entrance young adventurers, and teach them valuable lessons about doing the right thing regardless of any rewards for their actions.

1972 Henry Holt

David McKee
Elmer

This ode to individuality and humor is a favorite among young children, and this book about fun-loving Elmer the patchwork elephant has spawned many other titles. In this story we meet Elmer, whose brightly colored patchwork hide doesn't look anything like any of the other elephants. Elmer is a happy elephant, but he slowly grows concerned about being different. When he finds an elephant bush, he rolls around in the gray berry mash until he is as gray as everyone else. Of course he realizes that things are rather boring when he's not his usual patchwork, practical-joking self, and his "true colors" once again emerge. This is a great story for children about fitting in and accepting who you are.

1968 HarperCollins

Blueberries for Sal

Caldecott Honor

Sal and her mother decide to go out and pick some blueberries, and in a parallel story, a mother bear and her little cub are doing the same. Sal is eating the blueberries as she picks them, and her mother is planning on making jam with hers. As they continue to pick the berries, mother and daughter wander away from each other—Sal ends up picking and eating berries next to the mother bear, and her mother ends up picking berries with the cub. This classic story, simply written and beautifully illustrated, remains as popular today as it was when it was published in 1948.

1948 Viking

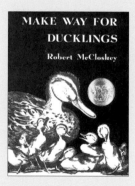

Make Way for Ducklings

Caldecott Award

Mr. and Mrs. Mallard decide to nest on an island in the Boston Public Gardens to raise their family, safely away from the foxes and other predators. The real action begins when Mrs. Duck decides to move her ducklings to the pond through busy downtown Boston, and is aided by the citizens and a very nice policeman. Children will rejoice in this story and its wonderful sepia-colored art and root for the ducks all the way through. Residents and visitors to Boston can still see the statue of Mrs. Mallard and her eight adorable ducklings in the Boston Common today.

1941 Viking

One Morning in Maine

The first real sign of growing up is your first loose tooth. In this story, we once again meet Sal (the character in *Blueberries for Sal*), who is a little older now and very excited about her first wobbly tooth. As she goes about her day in Maine, she tells every person and creature she meets about her loose tooth. While she is digging for clams, the most terrible thing happens—her tooth pops out and is lost in the muck. She is sure that some crab is going to get her wish for a chocolate ice cream cone from the tooth fairy and is desolate. This sweet story about growing up has a happy ending, of course, and the sweeping illustrations of the Maine coast and relatable story are perfect for children approaching this first major milestone in their lives.

1952 Viking

Caldecott Honor

Time of Wonder

For anyone who has ever gone on a vacation by the sea, this book set on the coast of Maine evokes all that is wonderful about vacations and coastal living. The family in this book is packing up to leave their vacation and head back home, and as they do so they recall all that was wonderful about their coastal holiday, from foggy mornings to sailing, from quiet evenings to hurricanes. This book powerfully evokes the bittersweet pleasures of a summer holiday and will help children learn to express their emotions and understand what it means to create good memories to take back home with you.

1957 Viking

Caldecott Award

Picture Books 2–6

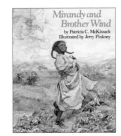

Multicultural

Patricia McKissack
Illustrated by Jerry Pinkney
Mirandy and Brother Wind

In this charming story, told in southern dialect, Mirandy wants to win her town's upcoming Cake Walk Jubilee, and believes that if she "captures the wind" he will do her bidding; it's just that she doesn't know how to do so. Through Pinkney's award-winning paintings, we follow Mirandy as she tries to and eventually believes she has captured the wind. But what children learn, as Mirandy does her cakewalk with the clumsy Edzel, is that the joy of living and being kind and generous to others is what causes her grandmother to comment about Mirandy and Edzel, "Them chullin' is dancing with the Wind!"

1988 Alfred A. Knopf

David McLimans
Gone Wild:
An Endangered Animal Alphabet

By using twenty-six endangered animals to teach the alphabet, McLimans accomplishes two things at once: introducing youngsters to some truly rare, endangered species, and creating an amazingly stunning graphic black-and-white pictographic way of teaching the alphabet. Has your child ever heard of the naked characin, the St. Helena earwig, or the crested ibis? Better yet, have you ever seen them illustrated as letters in the species' name? This award-winning book is a marvel of information, which is presented in black-and-red boxes on every letter-specific page and is sure to be pored over long after the alphabet is learned. The message here is conservation, but it is presented in a totally fresh, new way.

2006 Walker Books for Young Readers

Susan Meddaugh
Martha Speaks

Ever wonder what your dog is thinking? Maybe you should try feeding her some alphabet soup. That's what happens in this riotous tale of a dog named Martha, who learns to talk, and talk, and talk after eating some alphabet soup. Martha just won't stop talking, and her amazing social gaffes and nonstop patter are charmingly rendered in the text, speech balloons, and many hilarious asides. Eventually the family wishes Martha would "just stop talking," until, of course, her special skills save the family from a robbery. Children will learn about manners and social graces here, but mostly they will learn to laugh at Martha's antics.

1992 HMH Books (Franchise)

Arlene Mosel
Illustrated by Blair Lent
Tikki Tikki Tembo

This retelling of an ancient Chinese folktale will have your children trying to memorize the full name of the title character and chanting it along with you as you read. This book illustrates the legend of why the Chinese give their children such short names. Since an honorable name must always be pronounced in full, problems arise when Tikki tikki tembo-no sa rembo-chari bari ruchi-pip peri pembo falls into a well, and it takes his brother so long to say his name in full that he is out of breath and no one understands him when he tries to explain what happened. Tikki is rescued, of course, and this book will provide tons of fun with every reading.

1968 Henry Holt

Multicultural

Picture Books 2–6

What is it about Winnie-the-Pooh that has made him one of the most popular and well-loved characters in all of children's literature? That question may be answered differently depending on who you ask, but one thing that is certain is that children relate to this fuzzy bear and his friends because they understand him. He acts like them, talks like them, and thinks like them. He gets excited about the same things they do, and he gets scared of the same things, too. Parents also see the simple wisdom in the things that Pooh and friends do and say. What parent doesn't understand lines like, "When you are a Bear of Very Little Brain, and you Think of Things, you find sometimes that a Thing which seemed very Thingish inside you is quite different when it gets out into the open and has other people looking at it." There is wisdom in these books and love and joy and mystery and wonder galore. But mostly there are friends here, characters that may be your child's very first friends, characters they will remember and continue to learn from at every stage of their lives.

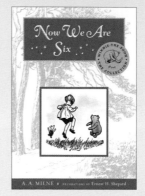

Illustrated by Ernest H. Shepard
Winnie-the-Pooh

Meet Christopher Robin and his toy friends: Pooh Bear, Piglet, Eeyore, Owl, Rabbit, Kanga, and Roo. Each of these characters embodies some aspect of childhood: Pooh is lovable and not too bright, Piglet is young and often frightened, Eeyore is insecure, Owl is wise, Rabbit is friendly and outgoing, and so on. Each chapter encapsulates a complete adventure and can be read a chapter a night at bedtime or all together when children are old enough.

1926 Dutton

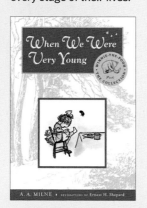
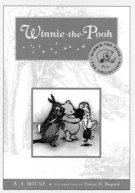

Illustrated by Ernest H. Shepard
When We Were Very Young

It is in this volume of poems that we first come to meet Christopher Robin, Milne's son, who will eventually be immortalized in *Winnie-the-Pooh* and Milne's subsequent stories about the "bear of very little brain." Many children first learned here about the changing of the guard at Buckingham Palace and also met John and his rain boots, but they mostly enjoyed the simple beauty of words and poetry, with lovely illustrations, in a volume created just for children.

1924 Dutton

Illustrated by Earnest H. Shepard
Now We Are Six

This is the sequel to *When We Were Very Young*; in the introduction the author mentions that Pooh "...walked through it one day, looking for his friend Piglet, and sat down on some of the pages by mistake." These sweet poems are just right for little children: short in length, whimsical in theme, and completely charming. Add Shepard's classic illustrations, and you and your child will be reciting poems to each other in no time at all.

1927 Dutton

Illustrated by Ernest H. Shepard
The House at Pooh Corner

Christopher Robin, Winnie, and the gang are back in the Hundred Acre Wood—but in this book we also meet bouncy, irrepressible Tigger, who so perfectly embodies the energy of your average toddler. Here, the friends have many new adventures together and learn more about the world and each other. But the take-away lesson here is really the eternity of youth and the love and support of close friends.

1928 Dutton

Illustrated by Sheila McGraw

Love You Forever

This book is really geared more toward parents than children and is a common gift at baby showers. Parents have definite feelings about it—they either love it or hate it—but it's difficult to argue with sales that top twenty million copies and still growing. This book deals with the love of a mother for her son, from his birth to his adulthood, and all that falls in between, to her death and the birth of his own son. Many parents are moved to tears by this book's expression of motherly devotion, but parents should be cautioned about reading this book to children who are easily upset or not yet ready for a book in which a grandparent dies.

1986 Firefly Books Ltd.

Illustrated by Michael Martchenko

The Paper Bag Princess

This hilarious "fractured" fairy tale with its humorous illustrations turns the tables on the traditional fairy tale narrative. In this case, our heroine, Princess Elizabeth, sets out to rescue her Prince Ronald. Ronald has been abducted by a dragon that burned down Elizabeth's castle, leaving her wearing a dirty paper bag. But after she cleverly outsmarts the dragon, using her wits and without violence, she realizes that Ronald is, in her words, "a jerk." Children and parents alike will laugh when Ronald shows his true colors and cheer when the Prince and Princess do not live happily ever after. Elizabeth happily dances off into her future alone, providing a great lesson in independence and using your head to solve problems.

1980 Annick Press

Mazeways: A to Z

Roxie Munro proves that interactivity can be combined with just about anything—and this time she's managed to create twenty-six dazzling mazes, one for each letter of the alphabet. *A* is for *Airport*, *K* is for *Kitchen*, *Z* is for *Zookeeper*, and so on, and each one is a separate and distinct maze. Along the way there are also more than 700 items for children to search for, count, and name, with answers at the back of the book. It's a book, it's an alphabet, it's mazes, and it's a game, too. Perfect for long car rides and family vacations, this book is a challenge and a pleasure for young readers.

2007 Sterling

Ecomazes: 12 Earth Adventures

Just when you thought it wasn't possible to pack this much activity into a picture book, along comes Roxie Munro's oversized tribute to the world's various ecosystems, in maze form. Children can visit the tropical rain forest, the penguin-filled ice-floes of Antarctica, and ten other biomes—but it's not just the mazes that need solving. There are also over 350 hidden animals scattered throughout the mazes, which allows for hours of maze-solving search-and-find adventures and a lot of eco-learning along the way.

2010 Sterling

Note: these books are also appropriate for older readers and puzzle enthusiasts.

The Three Questions

This book is based on a Tolstoy story that poses three questions: "When is the best time to do things? "Who is the most important one?" and "What is the right thing to do?" Pretty big questions for a children's book, but the way that the story and art portray the answers, in simple terms that children can understand and relate to, makes this story worth reading. The answers? "There is only one important time, and that time is now. The most important one is always the one you are with. And the most important thing is to do good for the one who is standing at your side." Ultimately, the moral of this story is about doing the right thing at the right time, and though it might be too obscure for the very young, it will be easily understood by those of preschool age and older.

2002 Scholastic Press Scholastic Inc.

Zen Ghosts

It's Halloween, and Michael, Addy, and Carl are looking forward to trick-or-treating. They are especially looking forward to a special treat from their friend Stillwater the panda, who has promised to dress as a ghost this year and introduce them to a storyteller. The ghost story that is told by someone (who may or may not be Stillwater) about a woman who appears to be in two places at once, is all about the concept of duality. Of all Muth's books, this one may be the most challenging for young children; however, the lyrical art and story with its mysterious ending is appropriate for Halloween. Parents should be prepared for discussion at the end of this book, as younger children may not fully understand the story.

2010 Scholastic Press/Scholastic Inc.

Caldecott Honor

Zen Shorts

A children's book that explains simple Zen parables to children seems an unlikely idea. But when you and your child meet Stillwater the panda, listen to his amazing tales, and lose yourself in Muth's soft and evocative art, you will realize that the moral concepts do not differ that much from the Aesop's fables you grew up with. The three children in this story—Addy, Michael, and Carl—each learn something different from Stillwater: forgiveness, good versus bad, and the real worth of material possessions. These are valuable lessons for children to learn, and in this case they are told gently, lovingly, and in terms that can be easily understood.

2005 Scholastic Press Scholastic Inc.

Multicultural

Zen Ties

Stillwater the panda is back in a story about a lesson in which even the title is a play on words; *Zentai* is Japanese for the "whole" or "the entire," as in all of us together. In this story, Michael is worried about an upcoming spelling bee, and Stillwater has an unexpected solution. He introduces Michael, Addy, and Carl to Miss Whitaker, the mean neighbor they are all rather frightened by but who Stillwater can see is really just very lonely. She turns out to be a great spelling coach! Michael wins the spelling bee—but actually so does everyone in the class, and they all receive red ties as rewards. This book also introduces children to Haiku poetry and, not incidentally, to Stillwater's nephew Koo—which results in the play-on-words greeting "Hi Koo!"

2008 Scholastic Press

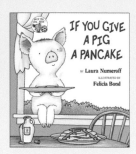

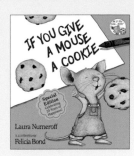

The first story in this series became an immediate bestseller upon publication and then spawned more volumes. The concept is simple enough— the relationship of things to each other, as well as cause-and-effect—but the perfect execution of the language and the playfulness of the art has created a classic. It all starts simply: if you give a mouse a cookie, he's going to ask for a glass of milk. But things escalate from there to requests for a straw for the milk, a napkin for his face, a mirror to check for a milk mustache, scissors for a quick mustache trim, a broom to clean up...and on and on, until the last page, which leads us back to the mouse wanting yet another cookie. Children will quickly memorize and be able to predict the next thing the mouse will want.

If You Give a Mouse a Cookie *(1985)*

If You Give a Moose a Muffin *(1991)*

If You Give a Pig a Pancake *(1998)*

If You Take a Mouse to The Movies *(2000)*

If You Give a Pig a Party *(2005)*

If You Give a Cat a Cupcake *(2008)*

If You Give a Dog a Donut *(2011)*

HarperCollins

Margaret Musgrove
Illustrated by Leo and Diane Dillon

Caldecott Honor

Ashanti to Zulu: African Traditions

There are many alphabet books and even a few specifically aimed at the African American reader, but this award-winning book is magnificently illustrated by the Dillons in fascinating detail and also offers many interesting facts. Each of the twenty-six letters of the alphabet represents a different African tribe; its customs, language, traditional apparel, history, and more are carefully explained. This book is filled with information that will be of interest to all families, not only those of African descent—but for those who are, it is a must-have addition to the family library.

1976 Dial

George O'Connor

Kapow!

This book is for every youngster who ever threw a towel or blanket around his or her shoulders and was instantly transformed into a superhero. The art and theme pay homage to the superhero comic books we are all familiar with, yet is decidedly aimed at toddlers and preschoolers with vivid imaginations. It is loaded with text in word bubbles and sound effects galore, and children will love playing along as the action builds. Our hero is transformed by his cape into "American Eagle," his sister into "Bug Lady," and their little brother into the nemesis, "Rubber Bandit," as they begin their crime-fighting missions. This book reinforces creative play and imagination—just add the towel/cape.

2004 Simon & Schuster Books for Young Readers

Picture Books 2–6

Illustrated by Robin Preiss Glasser
Fancy Nancy

Meet Fancy Nancy, a tiara-and-feather-boa-wearing little girl who likes everything fancy, much to the bemusement of her loving but non-fancy family. This premise could get annoying quickly if it weren't for two things: the adorable art, which includes lots of fancy details but clearly establishes the "dress-up" aspects of Fancy Nancy's style without going over the top, and the text itself, which offers a vocabulary word on every page, for example, "I like to write my name with a pen that has a plume. That's a fancy way of saying feather." Nancy offers her family "fancy" lessons, which they gamely sit through, and convinces them to dress up "fancy" and go out. When Nancy commits an inadvertent "faux pas"—that's fancy for accident (everything sounds fancier in French) she realizes that her family's love and support is more important than how they dress or act. The popularity of this book has already spawned many sequels that deal with typical family subjects like getting a dog (fancy=papillion, plain=mutt), Christmas (you must have a very fancy tree), and other very fancy topics. Warning to parents: be prepared to buy a feather boa or a tiara or both.

2005 HarperCollins

Bill Peet
The Caboose Who Got Loose

For all the young train buffs out there, this book about a caboose who longs for a different life is just the ticket. Katy Caboose is tired of trailing along behind the train and longs for a simpler life in the country that she passes through daily. One day, she talks to the switchman's shack at a station, and while she envies his stationary life, he envies her extensive travels. Katy reconsiders that her life might not be so bad, yet when a coupling breaks and she spends some time in one place surrounded by nature, she is finally happy. Bill Peet's colorful, energetic illustrations give life and personality to normally inanimate objects, allowing kids to relate to them.

1971 Houghton Mifflin Books for Children

Audrey Penn
Illustrated by Ruth E. Harper and Nancy M. Leak
The Kissing Hand

Chester Raccoon is nervous about starting school. Like most preschoolers, he doesn't know what to expect and would rather stay with his mother. Chester's mother kisses the palm of his hand, and assures him that whenever he gets lonely he should hold his hand to his cheek and the warm thoughts will rush to his heart and comfort him—and that it won't wash off when he washes his paws for lunch. Chester responds by kissing her hand so that she, too, will be comforted while he is at school. This sweet story will be very reassuring for toddlers and preschoolers (and their nervous parents) who are apprehensive about starting school.

1993 Tanglewood Press

Beatrix Potter

The World of Beatrix Potter

Perhaps there is no better-loved set of books for children the world over than the Tales of Beatrix Potter. While some of the characters from her garden of little animal stories are better known than others, they remain, when taken as a group, the most charming of children's stories. Though her books have been published in every conceivable size and shape over the more than one-hundred years since their original publication, these books were originally drawn and created in a small format (which is still available today) because the author wanted to create little books for little hands. Undoubtedly the best known of the twenty-three books is the first title in the series, the classic *Tale of Peter Rabbit*. Potter created her characters from the world that surrounded her home and garden, and they have all the characteristics that they would have in nature—with the additions of some human clothing and emotional attributes. Beyond Peter Rabbit, families have grown to love Flopsy, Mopsy, and Cottontail; Squirrel Nutkin; Jemima Puddle-Duck; Tabitha Twitchit; and Mrs. Tiggy-Winkle. All of Potter's characters—cats, frogs, pigs, squirrels, rabbits, and mice—are animals that children are deeply familiar with. Children have named their pets and parents their children after the lovable characters of these stories, stories that were read to them as children, and the same stories they now read to their own children and grandchildren. There are perils and dangers in these books as in the natural world—farmers with rakes and guns, as well as mean and fierce animals —but also simple lessons and nothing that can't be resolved by a sip or two of chamomile tea and some calming words at the end of the day.

The Tale of Peter Rabbit (1902)

The Tale of Squirrel Nutkin (1903)

The Tailor of Gloucester (1903)

The Tale of Benjamin Bunny (1904)

The Tale of Two Bad Mice (1904)

The Tale of Mrs. Tiggy-Winkle (1905)

The Tale of the Pie and the Patty-Pan (1905)

The Tale of Mr. Jeremy Fisher (1906)

The Story of A Fierce Bad Rabbit (1906)

The Story of Miss Moppet (1906)

The Tale of Tom Kitten (1907)

The Tale of Jemima Puddle-Duck (1908)

The Tale of Samuel Whiskers or The Roly-Poly Pudding (1908)

The Tale of the Flopsy Bunnies (1909)

The Tale of Ginger and Pickles (1909)

The Tale of Mrs. Tittlemouse (1910)

The Tale of Timmy Tiptoes (1911)

The Tale of Mr. Tod (1912)

The Tale of Pigling Bland (1913)

Appley Dapply's Nursery Rhymes (1917)

The Tale of Johnny Town-Mouse (1918)

Cecily Parsley's Nursery Rhymes (1922)

The Tale of Little Pig Robinson (1930)

Neil Gaiman on remembering what it was like to be a child and a reader...

When I was a boy, I read as an escape and to learn about the world. I read to meet people who were nicer or braver and wiser than I was. I read because the world inside my head was more interesting than the world outside and books helped me build that world. I read because I was scared of many things, and books calmed my fears, and people in stories went through much worse than I did. I read because books I loved became familiar places that would always be waiting for me and would welcome me home.

I loved the Narnia books, which first fed my love of myth and legend and the idea that there were worlds only a paper's thickness away; the Mary Poppins books, which taught me that there is a joy in not understanding everything; Kipling's *Stalky & Co.*, which told me that people had survived school experiences worse than mine, and his Jungle Book stories, which set me free in my mind to walk the jungle as a wild animal.

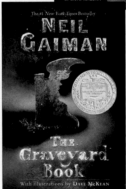

(One more writer made me a children's writer, though I was probably seventeen when I found my first book by her. The book was *Charmed Life* by Diana Wynne Jones. That a writer so good and so imaginative and so wise was writing for children meant that the golden age was not over.)

I wanted to write children's books initially perhaps because when I first wanted to be a writer I was still a child, and those were the books I was reading. But there was another reason. The other kind of books I read: patronizing and foolish books that convinced me the author had forgotten what it was to be a child. When I grow up, I would tell myself, *I shall not forget.*

See individual listings for books by Neil Gaiman on page 151.

Marcus Pfister
The Rainbow Fish

One of the very first books to use special effects, in this case holographic foil, *The Rainbow Fish* is a story about a very beautiful yet vain and selfish fish who learns a valuable lesson. The rainbow fish is proud of his sparkling scales, but his constant bragging to the plain fish has left him without many friends. Eventually, the lonely rainbow fish seeks advice from the wise old octopus, who encourages him to change his ways, give away some of his beauty, and "discover how to be happy." As he gives his scales to the other fish, a wonderful feeling overcomes him, and he learns to not be greedy and vain, but to share and be generous. This underwater fable teaches children the virtues of sharing and how to be a good friend to others.

1992 NorthSouth Books

Caldecott Award

Jerry Pinkney
The Lion & The Mouse

This wordless retelling of the Aesop fable is set in the African Serengeti, and Pinkney's detailed paintings propel the story forward so well that no words are needed. The tale of a lion that spares a mouse and in return is assisted by the mouse in his time of need is clearly illustrated by the art. All the animals portrayed clearly show emotions of fear, pain, gratitude, and compassion by their expressions. One of the great advantages of wordless books is that they allow children to use the visual clues in the art to tell the story or to "read" it on their own.

Caldecott Award

2009 Little, Brown and Company

Robin Pulver

Illustrated by Lynn Rowe Reed
Nouns and Verbs Have a Field Day

When Mr. Wright's class has a field day, the Nouns and Verbs decide they need one too. The problem is that they tend to stick to their own, verbs with verbs and nouns with nouns, which isn't really much fun. The rollicking art and the funny asides, plus the mayhem that the nouns and verbs have left for the students to sort out, will change the way children relate to learning proper grammar forever. These nouns and verbs come to life; they whine and exaggerate and become very self-important. Sometimes a whole lot of laughter is all it takes to make sense of basic sentence structure—that and a very funny (adjective) concept (noun) for a book.

2006 Holiday House

Illustrated by Lynn Rowe Reed
Punctuation Takes a Vacation

Poor punctuation marks. Day after day, they show up for class and are treated so badly. Erased, moved, used wrong or not at all. One day the teacher, Mr. Wright, declares "Let's give punctuation a vacation"— and off they go. But the children are left confused. They can't seem to write anything that makes sense, and they can't even punctuate a decent letter to get them to come back. Meanwhile the punctuation marks are writing lots of postcards to the class. This hysterical book demonstrates the importance of proper punctuation with a heavy dose of humor and a lot of personality.

2003 Holiday House

Picture Books 2–6

Watty Piper
Illustrated by George and Doris Gauman

The Little Engine That Could

There have been many versions of this story created over the years, but this original, with its classic and immediately recognizable art, remains the most loved version. In this clear message of positive thinking, a little blue engine takes on the task of pulling a train loaded with Christmas toys over a mountain that the bigger and more powerful engines will not attempt. The refrain of "I think I can...I think I can" soon turns to "I thought I could...I thought I could," as the determined little engine gets the job done. Written in 1930, this tribute to the power of positive thinking will stay with children throughout their lives, as they learn to try harder, never give up, and believe in themselves no matter what obstacles arise.

1930 Grosset & Dunlap

Patricia Polacco

The Keeping Quilt

Based on the true story of a quilt that was passed down through the author's family, *The Keeping Quilt* is a testament to memory and heritage and a celebration of family. In order to remember their previous life, a family pieces together a quilt from bits of the family's clothing worn prior to their emigration from Russia. The quilt becomes a family talisman of sorts, used to cover the Sabbath table, as a wedding canopy at marriage, on picnics, and to wrap each new baby when he or she is just born. This celebration of family and traditions is not just for a Jewish audience but for any family who cherishes its heritage.

1988 Simon & Schuster Books for Young Readers

Faith Ringgold

Tar Beach

Children born and raised in the heart of the city will understand the concept of "Tar Beach"—using the flat, black roof of an apartment building as a place to play and picnic. And for those not familiar with the cityscape, this beautiful story, told via a combination of fabric "story quilts" and paintings, will enchant. Cassie uses her imagination to fly far beyond her own tar beach and to express her hopes and dreams for her future and that of her family. This magical tale of a young girl's fantasy flight into the future she hopes for is one that all children can relate to and understand.

1991 Crown

Coretta Scott King Award

Caldecott Honor

Michael Rosen
Illustrated by Helen Oxenbury

We're Going on a Bear Hunt

This classic rhyme about a fantasy adventure is a favorite among preschoolers. A family of four sets out for an adventure near the sea to catch a bear. In addition to the rhyming text, there are also many fun sound effects that children will love, including *swishy* grass and mud that goes *squelch*—as well as the repeated refrain "We're not scared"—as they continue on their quest to find the bear. Oxenbury's richly colored paintings alternate with black-and-white drawings as the family finally meets the bear, find that they are in fact scared, and beat a hasty retreat home to snuggle as a family under the comforter on the parents' bed.

1989 Margaret K. McElderry

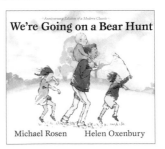

Officer Buckle and Gloria

Sometimes good intentions can go terribly wrong. This ode to friendship teaches children what it means to be a friend and more than a few safety tips as well. Officer Buckle's job is to teach school children about safety, but the truth is that the children of the aptly named town of Napville find his lessons so boring, they tend to fall asleep. Until one day when Officer Buckle brings Gloria the police dog with him to class. Unbeknownst to him, Gloria helps her friend by enacting his safety tips behind his back as he presents them. Now Officer Buckle is in great demand, but he has no idea that it's really Gloria who is captivating the attention of the audience. Children will understand the concept of hurt feelings, and also learn how two friends can work out their differences.

1995 Putnam

The Day the Babies Crawled Away

Illustrated entirely in black silhouettes on the colorful background of a sky that changes as day progresses to night, this book is a favorite with young children who can easily relate to both the story and the bits of humor in the art itself. As the parents in this story enjoy a pie-eating contest at the fair, five little babies crawl off to the woods unobserved by all, except for a little boy in a fireman's hat who shouts, "HEY! You babies, Stay!" He follows them and makes sure that those adventurous babies are safe and eventually returned to their parents. There are lots of laughs built into the art, and the rhyming text is fun to read as well.

2003 Putnam

Good Night, Gorilla

Sometimes it's fun to change up the bedtime story ritual with a tale that offers fun and giggles instead of calm and quiet. As the tired zookeeper bids good night to each of his charges, he is unaware that the gorilla has lifted his keys and is unlocking the animals' cages. Children are in on the joke from the first page and will be laughing as the oblivious zookeeper trudges home with a line of animals behind him. The fun continues as they all climb in bed with the now-exhausted zookeeper, until the bold gorilla snuggles up to the zookeeper's wife, and they are discovered. With very few words, this picture story easily communicates the action and the laughter, even for very young children.

1994 Putnam

H. A. Rey
Curious George

"This is George. He lived in Africa. He was a good little monkey and always very curious." These familiar lines begin the many adventures of two of the best-loved characters in children's literature, Curious George and the Man with the Yellow Hat. As millions of readers know, George's curiosity gets him into all sorts of humorous predicaments. The ultimate message of the book is threefold: think before you act, learn from your mistakes, and understand and forgive youthful errors. Some parents find the situations that George gets into disturbing, but our experience is that children do not. They can relate to George's antics and are not judgmental about them in the least. However, for cautious parents it might be appropriate to pre-read this volume to assure that you feel comfortable discussing George's mischievous behavior.

1941 HMH Books (Franchise)

Picture Books 2–6

Dog Heaven

When a young child loses a cherished pet, in this case a dog, parents have some explaining to do. This book and its sequel, *Cat Heaven*, can go a long way toward reassuring children about death and the hereafter. In this book we learn that in heaven all dogs are good dogs; they have comfy beds of inside-out clouds, treats from a jolly biscuit-making deity, and lots of angel children to play with. The simple, childlike, acrylic paintings are bright and appealing, perfect for young children and toddlers. Parents should pre-read this book to assure that the concept is presented in a way in which you are comfortable.

1995 Blue Sky Press

Illustrated by Stephen Gammell

Caldecott Honor

The Relatives Came

This vibrant celebration of a summertime visit by family members from around the country is full of what summer visits should be: lots of hugs and kisses, berry-picking, music, and playtime for the kids and cousins of every age, shape, and size. The whimsical art keeps the action moving along, as the visit moves from joy at their arrival to sadness when they leave to return home. The ending is upbeat, however, with the knowledge that the relatives will, of course, return for another visit. This story is an especially poignant one for today's families, with cousins who no longer all live in the same city, state, or even country and reminds us to make the most of the visits and times when we are together.

1985 Atheneum/Richard Jackson Books

Carl R. Sams II and Jean Stoick

Stranger in the Woods

This self-published book of wildlife photographs became an instant success when it was published. The authors, who are both wildlife photographers, started with a simple premise: how would animals in nature respond to a snowman suddenly appearing in their natural habitat? Add in some simple text and stunning photographs of deer, owls, muskrats, and other animals interacting with the snowman, and you have a magical story that children will request again and again, as they spend hours examining the amazing full-color photography of the animals in winter. This book has also spawned many sequels in multiple formats for children who want to learn more about animals in their native environment.

2000 Carl R. Sams II Photography

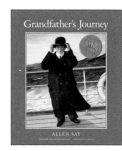

Caldecott Award

Allen Say

Grandfather's Journey

The theme of this remarkable book is the concept of home. This biographical story of the author's grandfather's journey to America from Japan and the discoveries he makes by boat, by train, and on foot, is a dual one, as it also reflects the author's own journey. In a tale told through paintings that mimic a family album, we learn that grandfather loved the new land, returned to Japan to marry, and then came back to California to start his family. While Grandfather and his family eventually returned to Japan, he always missed America.

1993 Houghton Mifflin Books for Children

Cars and Trucks and Things That Go

All children are fascinated by "things that go," and this book is the gold standard for portraying all forms of transportation, from those children will recognize to some purely imaginary. The real point of this book is object identification and vocabulary; children will pore over each jam-packed, action-filled page to find their favorite characters and vehicles (as well as little Goldbug, who appears on every spread of the book) far past their toddler years. Many parents and grandparents will remember this book from their own childhood, and enjoy sharing their favorite pages with their children and grandchildren. This book remains a true classic that will continue to be a must-have for the family library for generations to come.

1974 Golden Books

What Do People Do All Day?

Welcome to Busytown, where Richard Scarry's familiar anthropomorphic animals (that somehow manage to look human) live and work all day long. Children are curious about the world of "work," and this book will go a long way toward explaining the variety of jobs that people do every day. Children will identify workers both familiar and new, while losing themselves in Scarry's detail-filled art—including searching for favorite character Lowly Worm on each spread. As with all of Scarry's books, this well-loved classic teaches vocabulary and object identification along the way. There are many other Scarry titles about Busytown, including *Richard Scarry's Best Word Book Ever* and *Richard Scarry's Best Storybook Ever.*

1968 Random House Children's Books

Judy Schachner
Skippyjon Jones

Skippyjon Jones may be a Siamese cat, but he knows deep inside that he is actually a crime-fighting Chihuahua superhero named Skipito Friskito. This hilarious tale of one kittyboy's imaginary adventures during a time-out, and the mayhem that follows, is wonderfully portrayed with playful illustrations that will keep children laughing along with Skipito's crazy antics. Filled with short Spanish phrases and Spanish-sounding slang, this ode to creative and imaginary play will also teach some Spanish words and allow the reader to work on developing a convincing Spanish accent along the way. There are several other Skippyjon Jones titles in the series, so fans and devotees of El Skipito will have many solid follow-up choices for future reading.

2003 Dutton

Roslyn Schwartz
The Complete Adventures of the Mole Sisters

The ten stories in this collection about two sweet, tiny, and loving moles can be read individually or as a group, depending on the time available—but be forewarned that once you read one, your children will be clamoring for more. These calming stories are perfect for bedtime reading but are also appropriate when there might be a need to slow things down and relax into a story. The Mole sisters have many simple adventures, and each one teaches a loving lesson: helping each other, optimism, making the best of a bad situation, how to cool off on a hot day, what to do on a rainy one, and more. As the Mole Sisters would say, "How lovely!"

2004 Annick Press

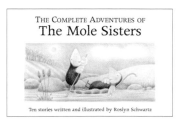

Jon Scieszka

David Shannon

Illustrated by Lane Smith

The Stinky Cheese Man and Other Fairly Stupid Tales

The team of Scieszka and Smith takes the concept of "fractured" fairy tales to an entirely "stupid" place in this award-winning collection. In this zany gathering of brief retellings of classic tales, it is possible that kissing a frog will leave a princess with a face full of frog slime and no prince or that an ugly duckling will grow up to be a really ugly duck. The characters interact with the art and the text, and the typefaces are used effectively to communicate pace and emotions and serve to move the stories along to their witty, revisionist endings. Reading this book is not recommended for bedtime—unless you find breathless laughter to be exhausting.

1992 Viking

Caldecott Honor

Illustrated by Lane Smith

The True Story of the 3 Little Pigs!

This "fractured" fairy tale retells "The Three Little Pigs" from the perspective of Alexander T. Wolf, who claims it was all a big misunderstanding. He was really just baking a cake for his dear granny's birthday and went to the pig's house to borrow some sugar. He had a really bad cold, and when he sneezed, the house collapsed. Since the "rude little porker" was already dead and the wolf was hungry, he ate him. And so it goes, and little listeners will have to decide who to believe. Smith's quirky and humorous illustrations will keep kids laughing along with the hilarious text from Scieszka, who was named as the first U.S.A. Ambassador for Young People's Literature in 2008.

1989 Viking

A Bad Case of Stripes

Children learn at a very early age that it is important to fit in; the tricky part is learning to fit in without giving up who you are. This book addresses that rather complicated issue in a very literal sense, as Camilla Cream actually "changes her stripes" at the least suggestion. Camilla has what she thinks is a terrible secret: she loves the one thing that children are supposed to universally hate—lima beans. Until she learns to be true to herself and be who she is, she is prone to breaking out in stripes, stars, feathers, and even, at one point, a long furry tail. The message is presented with Shannon's very visual sense of humor, and the allegorical nature of the art is often laugh-out-loud funny, but the underlying message is one that all children need to learn.

1997 Blue Sky Press/Scholastic Inc.

Caldecott Honor

No, David!

Being a toddler isn't easy. Not for the toddler, and certainly not for the parents. With independence and curiosity come the potential for trouble, and this book is a perfect child's-eye view of the mayhem one reckless toddler can render in a single day. The text is simple enough, but the childlike pictures tell the real story, as David does everything he shouldn't, page after page. Using crayons on the walls, making noise, jumping on the bed, running outside without clothes on—these transgressions get the predictable parental responses of "No, David!," "Be quiet!," and "Come back here!," but mostly lots of "No!" until the last spread, when naughty David finally gets the "yes" he's been waiting for, when his mother tells him, "Yes, David, I love you."

1998 Blue Sky Press/Scholastic Inc.

Rob Scotton
Splat the Cat

The first day of school can be a scary proposition for anyone, and Splat the Cat is nervous. Will he have friends? What if he gets lonely? Splat does everything he can to avoid going to school, but go he must; and just to be sure he isn't lonely, he brings his pet mouse Seymour with him. But this is cat school, and Splat is shocked to learn that cats chase mice. He doesn't chase mice. He likes mice, and he has one with him. The chaos that ensues when his fellow students find out about Seymour, and the story of how Seymour saves the day round out this story of first-day-of-school jitters. There are also many other books about Splat's adventures available for interested readers.

2008 HarperCollins

Maurice Sendak

Caldecott Award

Where the Wild Things Are

When Max puts on his wolf suit and misbehaves, his mother calls him a "wild thing" and sends him to his room without his supper. So begins one of the best-loved stories in all of children's literature. Through its spare text and glorious full-bleed illustrations, children who are familiar with a "time out" will relate to Max's imaginary adventures in the land of the wild things. With the famous line, "Let the wild rumpus start!" Max imagines himself as king of the not-too-scary beasts, and romps and plays with them until he gets lonely and hungry. So he returns to reality and finds comfort in his home, his room, and a hot meal waiting for him. This loving tribute to imagination and wonder is required reading for all families and a tale that every imaginative child can relate to.

1963 HarperCollins

Caldecott Honor

In the Night Kitchen

Little Mickey goes to bed...and we next see him literally "falling" asleep and into his dream of drifting down below, into the night kitchen, where the chefs are busily preparing a cake. This slightly surreal story is very like a dream; the things that happen are full of magic and imagination. Mickey falls into the dough and then kneads it into an airplane, which he uses to fly off to get the milk needed for the recipe. And in the end, there is cake for breakfast—yum! Sendak's art is bright and loose, allowing readers to imagine that they, too, are in the dream right along with Mickey.

1970 HarperCollins

Nutshell Library

This little boxed set of four small, hardcover books is perfectly sized for little hands and includes the following classic Sendak titles: *Alligators All Around*, an alphabet book; *Chicken Soup with Rice*, a calendar rhyme about the months of the year; *One Was Johnny*, a counting book; and *Pierre*, a cautionary tale about a boy who always says "I don't care!" Each book is charmingly told and beautifully illustrated on its own; grouped together in this format, they become a cherished collectible for your family library. The books can also be purchased in larger paperback editions for those who find the small size and small text difficult.

1962 HarperCollins

Theodore Seuss Geisel—Dr. Seuss—was asked to write a book using only 225 "new reader" vocabulary words; the result was *The Cat in the Hat*. Its whimsical illustration style and rhythmic story line about a crazy cat in a tall red-and-white hat who appears, creates mayhem, and then disappears, changed children's literature forever—and yes, he did it using only those 225 words.

Dr. Seuss books fall into two general categories: the "Bright and Early" books focus on reading, vocabulary, and early concepts, and the storybooks that often have a serious message buried in the rollicking rhyme and mayhem. And sometimes the books do both at once, as in the unforgettable language in *Green Eggs and Ham*, which encourages children to try new things. *Fox in Socks* is one long tongue-twister of a book that helps children sound out sight words, and *One Fish, Two Fish, Red Fish, Blue Fish* is chock-full of early concepts, including sizes, opposites, colors, and counting—and it all rhymes. *The Lorax* is about preserving the environment, *Horton Hatches the Egg* is about being faithful and fulfilling a promise, *Horton Hears a Who* is a story of humanity and equality, and *Oh, the Places You'll Go!* is a long meditation on achievement and following your dreams. There are many more books available, and though we may not have mentioned your favorites, the books presented here should be considered only the beginning of your Dr. Seuss collection.

These books are not easy to read; there are words that are pure nonsense, tongue-twisters galore, and frequent repetition, and each book has its own specific rhythm patterns. All of those things are what have made generations of children *love* these books. The illustrations are amazing, but it's really all about the language, the rhythm, the words themselves. When you read a Dr. Seuss book to your child, you are teaching him or her that there is magic and beauty in words, that language can be made to do tricks, to teach, to entertain, and to amaze, and, most importantly, that reading is *fun*. So practice reading these books alone if you find them difficult, but read them you must, because as the good doctor says, "And will you succeed? Yes indeed, yes indeed! Ninety-eight and three-quarters percent guaranteed!"

Horton Hatches the Egg (1940)

Horton Hears a Who! (1954)

The Cat in the Hat (1957)

Green Eggs and Ham (1960)

One Fish, Two Fish, Red Fish, Blue Fish (1960)

Hop on Pop (1963)

Fox in Socks (1965)

The Lorax (1971)

Oh, the Places You'll Go! (1990)

Random House Children's Books

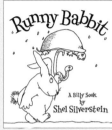

Lafcadio: The Lion Who Shot Back

This modern fable features a very docile lion who offers to give himself up to the hunter rather than be shot. He offers to lay quietly like a rug in front of the fireplace and eat the marshmallows the hunter toasts. The hunter refuses his offer, so Lafcadio does what the hunter expects—he eats him up and takes his gun. Lafcadio practices with the gun and becomes a famous sharpshooter, wearing smart clothes and traveling the world. But in the end—is he really still a lion at all? This moral tale for young children is all about being true to yourself and being exactly who you were meant to be. Children understand the lesson immediately, and the humor inherent in Silverstein's prose and witty line drawings will make this a family favorite.

1963 HarperCollins

The Giving Tree

Shel Silverstein often tackled subversive subjects in unconventional ways in his children's books, and this book's message may not be appropriate for every family. This is the story of a tree who loves a boy and gives him all that she has—her apples, her branches, and so on—until she is left as only a stump for the now-grown man to sit on. Parents generally feel one of two ways about this book: they either find it a story of the limitless love a parent has for his or her child, or they find it sad or disturbing. With sales of millions of copies, this book is seen by many as a message of giving without limits. Young children generally find the story to be a comforting one; parents may feel differently.

1964 HarperCollins

The Missing Piece

Using his signature illustration style to graphically depict a circle with a missing wedge-shaped piece, Silverstein tackles a much larger concept with the simplest of visual imagery. The circle is actually pretty happy, but wonders if he might be happier if he found his "missing piece." He goes on a quest in hopes of finding completion, fulfillment, and true happiness. What he actually finds along they way is that true happiness comes from within and not from finding something or someone who completes you. This is powerful stuff for adults to learn, and yet this simple book sends a clear message that Silverstein has repeated in some of his other books: that being the best person you can be, no matter who or what you are, is good enough.

1976 HarperCollins

The Missing Piece Meets the Big O

In Silverstein's *The Missing Piece,* a circle seeks fulfillment by trying to find his missing piece. In this sequel we meet the Missing Piece, who is seeking his circle in order to find independence. The Missing Piece is a simply drawn wedge, who is just sitting alone waiting for someone to take him somewhere. He searches for his missing circle, his "perfect fit," but nothing feels just right. Eventually he meets the Big O, who lovingly teaches him that he is not helpless, and how to "roll all by yourself." This empowering message of independence is made more powerful by the simple graphic style, which is used to communicate the frustration of helplessness and the joy of independence and how little really stands between the two.

1981 HarperCollins

Runny Babbit

The concept of this book is deceptively simple: reverse a few letters and then write a poem. Except that only a master like Silverstein could pull it off so well and then use his signature black-line drawings to give visual clues to the reader. The narrative is filled with clever inversions, like Sea Poup (pea soup), and a poetic visit to Rount Mushmore (Mount Rushmore), as Runny Babbit (Bunny Rabbit) has all sorts of letter-flipping adventures that parents and children will laugh at, while trying to decipher the real words. This clever book could be overwhelming if it weren't for the brilliance of the actual poems, which have just enough "real" words to hint at the inversions and drawings that give kids more clues to decipher the text.

2005 HarperCollins

Meet Madlenka, a little girl with a loose tooth who lives "in the universe, on a planet, on a continent, in a country, in a city, on a block, in a house, in a window, in the rain..." So begins Madlenka's story of telling her neighbors all about her loose tooth. In meeting her neighbors, we also take a trip around the world, for Madlenka lives in New York City, where everyone is from somewhere else. Through Sís' cut-out pages and detailed illustrations, we view Madlenka's world and all of her friends: the French baker, the Indian news vendor, the Italian ice cream man, the German lady who tells her stories, the Latin American grocer, the Asian shopkeeper, and her African American playmate Cleopatra, creating a trip around the world all on one block. Madlenka's neighbors help her celebrate her loose tooth, a sure sign of growing up, and in the process we learn all about the places, the food, and the traditions of all the homelands of her loving neighbors as well. In the sequel, *Madlenka Soccer Star*, Madlenka gets a shiny new soccer ball and takes it outside to play. She challenges everything she meets on the street to a game, including the mailbox, the parking meters, and finally a team of cats, all of whom come to life long enough for a quick kick or two. The final message that "The whole world wants to play soccer!" and the endnotes about the global history of the game and everywhere it is played will be a hit with young, aspiring soccer players right here in the United States.

Madlenka *(2000)*
Madlenka Soccer Star *(2010)*
Farrar, Straus & Giroux

The Wall

This autobiographical book tells the author's story of growing up in Cold War-era Prague. Sís does this by illustrating the history of the events during his youth, using graphic-novel-style panels with a parallel personal narrative below. Sís loved music and loved to draw; he wanted to listen to the Beatles and wear blue jeans, but none of that was allowed. This visual, biographical history lesson takes Sís from life under a totalitarian regime, with its many restrictions and fears, to his eventual defection to the United States. This astounding picture book is bursting with history and personal reminiscences and is suitable for primary-grade readers up to adults but may not be understood by or appropriate for the very young.

2007 Farrar, Straus & Giroux

Caldecott Honor

Multicultural

Esphyr Slobodkina
Caps for Sale

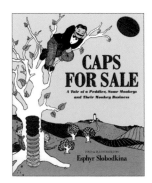

Written in 1938 and translated into more than a dozen languages, with over two million copies sold, this tale of a peddler and some very mischievous monkeys remains a classic. A peddler walks from village to village selling his caps—all of which he wears stacked on his head. When he decides to take a nap under a tree, he awakens to discover that a bunch of monkeys have taken his hats while he slept. Children have delighted for years in the antics of the monkeys as they taunt the peddler by imitating everything he does to get his hats back. The illustrations and naughty monkeys will keep children laughing, and the ending teaches how to use your wits to solve problems.

1938 HarperCollins

Lane Smith

It's a Book

In this ode to the printed word, a monkey is reading a book across from a jackass on a computer. The jackass begins peppering the monkey with questions, "Do you blog with it?" "How do you scroll down?" "Does it need a password?" "Can you make the characters fight?" to which the monkey continually responds with growing exasperation, "No, it's a book." Eventually the jackass grabs the book and starts to read, and the art vividly communicates his growing interest in the story of *Treasure Island*, while he assures the monkey he'll "charge it up" for him when he's done. The droll yet somewhat naughty response, "You don't have to...It's a book, Jackass." may not be every parent's cup of tea, but it is sure to get a laugh.

2010 Roaring Brook Press

John, Paul, George & Ben

In this hilarious revisionist history of America's founding fathers, Smith "rewrites" the personal histories of the participants. The truth is John Hancock always wrote his name big enough "to read it from space!", Paul Revere had an embarrassing habit of yelling everything, George Washington actually chopped down an entire orchard of trees, Ben Franklin annoyed everyone with his constant spewing of platitudes, and Thomas Jefferson was always writing lists, even presenting his teachers with a list of grievances. Smith's art is filled with humorous clues to the future roles these men will have in signing the Declaration of Independence, and a "Taking Liberties" quiz at the back sets the historical record straight.

2006 Hyperion

Madam President

We may not have a female president yet, but this book's lead character has the prerequisites, and she is available for the job—even if it's only in her own home and school life. This pony-tailed girl gives executive orders (to her cat), leads by example (by cleaning her room), vetoes as needed (no tuna casserole), and delegates to her Secretary of Agriculture (aka Mr. Potato Head) and the Cabinet Secretaries (inside a cabinet, of course), including a piggy bank in charge of the treasury. This clever book teaches children about the responsibilities of the president, by way of Smith's smart humor and graphics and his hilarious takes on getting the job done.

2008 Hyperion

Picture Books 2–6

David Soman and Jacky Davis
Illustrated by David Soman

Ladybug Girl

For every younger sister told by her older siblings that she is too little to play, enter *Ladybug Girl*—a tribute to creativity and enthusiastic independent play. Lulu's brother says she's too little to play with him, so she creates her own fun. She dons her red tutu and boots, her ladybug wings and antennae and, along with her faithful dog Bingo, goes off to seek adventure as Ladybug Girl. She rescues ants from a big rock that is in their way, imagines overcoming sharks lurking in puddles, and learns along the way that she can have fun all by herself. This empowering book for young girls is the first in a series of *Ladybug Girl* books.

2008 Dial

Peter Spier
People

This detailed picture book is a visual treat for young children, who will be fascinated by the art and the topic. The concept, that the world is filled with an enormous variety of people, and that they have both commonalities and differences, is presented here in a way children understand. Through illustrations that tell the story, we learn there are many races in the world—they live differently, write differently, speak different languages, eat different foods, live in unique homes, excel in a variety of activities, dress differently, celebrate different holidays, and worship differently—and it's all demonstrated without being preachy or pedantic.

1980 Doubleday

Judith St. George
Illustrated by David Small

So You Want to Be President?

This irreverent look at our nation's presidents doesn't stint on facts, but presents them along with some lesser-known anecdotes in a way that will offer as much laughter as learning. Small's art is reminiscent of political cartoons, and there are all sorts of funny asides scattered throughout the book. In addition to our presidents' accomplishments, children will learn which president was most handsome, tallest, shortest, oldest, and youngest, what jobs they had before they were presidents, and much more. There is also a listing in the back with the facts and a short biography of each president. This book brings history to life in a manner that reinforces the idea that anyone, even the children reading the book, can become president.

2000 Philomel

Caldecott Award

David Ezra Stein
Interrupting Chicken

Caldecott Honor

In this clever twist on the bedtime-story ritual, little red chicken is snuggled in for her bedtime story, and her father reminds her not to interrupt him as he reads. Through humorous art and cleverly-inserted text bubbles, we see that little chicken just can't stop herself—she jumps in and warns Hansel and Gretel not to enter the witch's house, she tries to calm Chicken Little by telling her it was just an acorn and not the sky falling, and of course, she warns Little Red about the lurking wolf. Her father then suggests that she should tell the story—which she happily does—and guess who falls asleep? For any parent who has read the same story over and over again, this book will be a welcome and very funny relief.

2010 Candlewick Press

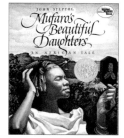

Coretta Scott King Award

Caldecott Honor

John Steptoe
Mufaro's Beautiful Daughters

A traditional tale from Zimbabwe, this Cinderella-like story is about two beautiful sisters: the good and virtuous Nayasha and the selfish and proud Manyara. The story may be familiar, but in the breathtaking paintings, Africa becomes as much a character as the sisters. When the king sends word that he is seeking a wife, he asks that "the most Worthy and Beautiful Daughters in the land" appear before him. Manyara rushes off to get to the king first and secure the crown, but Nayasha takes her time along the way to offer help and kindness to the poor and the elderly. You can guess who wins the king's favor and even extends generosity to her spoiled sister.

1987 HarperCollins

Michael Hague on the fascination and joy of drawing…

From an early age I wanted to be an artist. My family didn't go to museums. I didn't know that artists did paintings for galleries. I hadn't a clue that they designed everything from clothing and cars to my bubble-gum wrappers. In my little world, if you were an artist, you did paintings for books. I saw that a few lucky souls got to work for Walt Disney and created those contours and forms that I so loved. Fewer still got to draw the comics that appeared in the Sunday morning papers. But, it was books that got me excited and wanting to be an artist. I loved my Little Golden Books and spent hours making copies of my favorites. Eventually I graduated to studying my mother's set of colored fairy-tale books illustrated by H. J. Ford. I cherish the joy I had copying the details in his drawings. Soon there was my fascination with the Ernest Shepard drawings I discovered in my mother's edition of *The Wind in the Willows*. I wonder how many times I drew Mr. Toad. Years later, *The Wind in the Willows* would be one of the first books I illustrated as a professional. "Keep it cozy," was my mother's advice. My earliest and favorite memories are of sitting alone in my room on a rainy day making cozy little drawings. How strange it is that these many years later, that simple act of drawing is still my favorite thing to do.

See individual listings for books illustrated by Michael Hague on pages 42, 152, and 215.

Illustrator Michael Hague

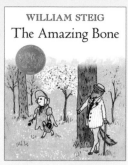

Picture Books 2–6

The Amazing Bone

This cautionary tale may not be just right for every child, but it's perfect for those who like a little bit of slightly scary adventure in their stories. If your children are easily frightened, you should pre-read this book prior to sharing it with them. Pearl the pig is out for a stroll and is enjoying the beautiful forest when she hears a voice among the flowers and discovers a talking bone. The bone had fallen from a witch's basket but would much rather play and frolic with someone like Pearl. The bone's ability to talk and imitate any sound soon saves Pearl from some scary robbers, and later a wily fox who wants to eat her. While this story can be too much for very young children, there is a solid message here about going off alone and avoiding "stranger danger." And as it is a book for children, all will be resolved happily at the end.

1976 Farrar, Straus & Giroux

Doctor De Soto

In this classic title from one of the preeminent children's book author/illustrators, we meet Doctor De Soto, a mouse who is also a wonderful dentist. He painlessly treats animals of all sizes and varieties, except (as the sign outside warns) "cats & other dangerous animals"—dangerous to mice that is. One day, a fox shows up in a great deal of pain, and the kindly doctor and his wife and assistant just cannot turn him away. However, when the fox returns the next day to pick up his new gold tooth, his feelings for the mice have changed from grateful to menacing. The De Sotos are ready for this, and their sly antics outwit their potential adversary. The theme of this book will be familiar to anyone who has ever read Aesop's fables: good deeds must sometimes be coupled with quick wits. This also provides a great and comforting story for children who may be anxious about visiting the dentist.

1982 Farrar, Straus & Giroux

Pete's a Pizza

In this book, award-winning author and illustrator William Steig delivers a delicious and loving recipe for rainy-day fun that parents and children will soon be playing as well. Pete is bored, and flops on the couch because he can't go outside to play ball with his friends. His father decides that it might be fun to make Pete a pizza in the literal sense, and scoops him up, brings him into the kitchen and begins to add ingredients like flour (talcum powder), oil (water), and tomatoes (checkers), and to knead him, prompting this exchange: "Pizzas are not supposed to laugh!" to which Pete responds, "Pizza-makers are not supposed to tickle their pizzas!" Pete is then returned to the couch to "bake." This fun game is presented as an actual recipe, and it certainly is a foolproof recipe for family fun.

1998 HarperCollins

Sylvester and the Magic Pebble

In this story Sylvester, a young donkey, finds a small red pebble that allows him to make wishes that come true. As he runs home to show his parents, he encounters a fierce lion; without thinking he wishes he was a rock so the lion could not eat him, and his wish is granted. Sadly, he is trapped as a rock; his worried parents miss him terribly and cannot imagine what has happened to him. Some time later, his lonely parents go on a picnic and unknowingly sit on the rock that was Sylvester. They pick up an unusual red pebble and wish that their son was with them. Their wish is granted, and the family is happily reunited.

1969 Simon & Schuster Books for Young Readers

Susan Marie Swanson
Illustrated by Beth Krommes

The House in the Night

This award-winning bedtime story is both calming and quiet in its language and art. Done entirely in black-and-white scratch-board images with pops of gold representing light, the art itself is calm and serene, and the cumulative rhythmic text, "Here is the key to the house. In the house burns a light. In that light rests a bed. On that bed waits a book...." leads the reader on a magical nighttime journey into the skies and then back home to bed. Rarely has a bedtime book been so simply illustrated and matched with such elegant language. This serene story will surely become a treasured part of your family bedtime ritual.

2008 Houghton Mifflin Books for Children

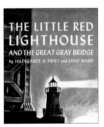

Hildegarde H. Swift
Illustrated by Lynd Ward

The Little Red Lighthouse and the Great Gray Bridge

The Little Red Lighthouse fears that it has outlived its usefulness when the massive George Washington Bridge is built above it, spanning the Hudson River with its bright, flashing lights. The Great Gray Bridge, however, knows better, and offers reassurance to the Little Red Lighthouse: "I call to the airplanes...I flash to the ships of the air. But you are still master of the river. Quick! Let your light shine again. Each to his own place, little brother!" The lesson that all things have their place resonates with children, who often feel too small and too young for many things. And for residents or visitors to New York City, both the bridge and the lighthouse still proudly stand together today.

1942 Harcourt Children's Books

Sam Swope
Illustrated by Barry Root

The Araboolies of Liberty Street

Every once in a while a children's book comes along that takes a political stand regarding tolerance, diversity, and conformity versus individuality—and manages to convey all of those difficult concepts in one stunningly illustrated and joyful story. The people of Liberty Street are controlled by mean General Pinch; all the houses and people look alike. Then the Araboolies, a crazy band of colorful types, who paint zig-zags on their house and watch TV in their front yard, arrive. The General is not happy and calls in the army to remove the house that is different. Fortunately, the children of Liberty Street take action by crazily painting all the houses except the General's—which the army dutifully removes.

1989 Farrar, Straus & Giroux

Kay Thompson
Illustrated by Hilary Knight

Eloise

One of children's literature's most memorable characters is Eloise, the six-year-old girl who lives in New York City's fabled Plaza Hotel. This exuberant little girl runs riot through the hotel, and her exploits are bound to leave both the reader and the listener breathless. The listener, because of Eloise's boundless energy and hilarious take on the world, and the reader, because there is no punctuation in this book (take a breath now and again), and because Eloise likes to repeat things three times for emphasis. Children love Knight's brilliant pink, yellow, and black artwork, the pages that open up and out, the ways Eloise amuses herself, and all the mischief a six-year-old can create in a stuffy hotel.

1955 Simon & Schuster Books for Young Readers

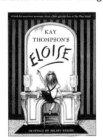

There Was an Old Lady Who Swallowed a Fly

Nancy Tilman

Caldecott Honor

Everyone is familiar with this outrageous and gruesome nursery song, but rarely has it been so effectively and riotously told as in this rowdy narrative. Using die-cuts in the pages to show the gory details of what's going on in the old lady's ever-growing stomach, along with humorous asides and commentary, this book will give children a hard time singing because they are laughing at the same time. A quick warning to parents: between the singing and the laughing, eating is not recommended as it would definitely lead to a choking hazard—as we all know, "she died, of course."

1997 Viking

Joseph Had a Little Overcoat

With wry visual humor and die-cut pages that hint at the action to come, Taback tackles a Yiddish folk song (reproduced in the back of the book) about a man and his well-loved coat, which, often-patched, is continually transformed into something else. Children will love guessing at the clues offered by the colorful folk art and die-cut pages as to the coat's next transformation, as the coat becomes a jacket, the jacket a vest, the vest a scarf, and so on, until all that is left is a button—which is then lost. The reader is then shown that Joseph is making a book about the coat, which proves the moral of the story: you can make something out of nothing! The simplicity of the concept, along with the beautifully executed art and die-cuts, will make reading this story a very interactive experience for small children.

1999 Viking

Multicultural

Caldecott Award

On the Night You Were Born

This celebration of the birth of a new baby will entrance little ones with its wondrous paintings of the natural world, from polar bears and giraffes to the moon itself rejoicing in the birth of a baby. With each painting, set against a deep-blue night sky, children will clearly see the joy that accompanies the birth of a very special baby: themselves—"Because there had never been anyone like you...ever in the world." The language is loving without being cloying, and the message is reassuring to toddlers that they are unique, important, and very much loved.

2006 Feiwel & Friends

Janice May Udry
Illustrated by Marc Simont

A Tree is Nice

Caldecott Award

This ode to trees is simply written and beautifully illustrated, half in color and half in black and white. The language is, at first glance, deceptively simple, but it is exactly the spare nature of the language that makes the book and the art so eloquent, with phrases such as "Trees are beautiful. They fill up the sky," and "A tree is good to have around. A tree is nice." Paired with this expressive text are Simont's award-winning illustrations of all the fun and funny things you can do with trees. With instructions at the end of the book on how to plant a tree and enjoy watching it grow, this book is one that your child will request again and again, and maybe they will want to plant a tree of their own. Because, as the author says, "Even if you have just one tree, it is nice too."

1957 HarperCollins

Deborah Underwood
Illustrated by Renata Liwska

The Quiet Book

Of all the words toddlers hear each day, *quiet* may be the most frequent. There are many kinds of quiet in a child's day, from the time they wake until they go to sleep at night. *Quiet* can be happy, lonely, cozy, tired, even impatient, and the softly drawn animals in this book demonstrate what *quiet* means, especially at bedtime. This book should help even the most rambunctious toddler settle in for naptime or bedtime.

2010 Houghton Mifflin Books for Children

Chris Van Allsburg

Jumanji

Caldecott Award

This astounding book is a wonder on many levels. The pencil drawings are detailed and realistic, but they portray events that are so fantastical it is difficult to believe what you are seeing. This haunting story explores the fine line between fantasy and reality, when two children find a game called Jumanji under a tree. The game bears the warning, "Free game, fun for some, but not for all. P.S. Read instructions carefully." Parents should take this warning to heart; this book is not for children who are easily frightened. But for adventurous children with active imaginations, the mayhem that ensues when the children begin to play the game will be compelling reading.

1981 Houghton Mifflin Books for Children

The Garden of Abdul Gasazi

Caldecott Honor

When a young boy named Allan is asked by Miss Hester to watch her rambunctious bull terrier, Fritz (who makes cameo appearances in all of Van Allsburg's books), while she visits a friend, he agrees, unaware of the adventure that awaits him. Van Allsburg's incredibly detailed gray-toned art sets the eerie mood for what happens next. When Fritz escapes his leash and runs into the garden of the magician Abdul Gasazi, nothing is what it appears to be. Has the towering magician turned Fritz into a duck or has it all been some sort of dream? The lines between reality and dream have been intentionally blurred here, and children will puzzle over the quixotic ending with every reading.

1979 Houghton Mifflin Books for Children

The Polar Express

Caldecott Award

Late one Christmas Eve, a young boy who is skeptical about Christmas magic reluctantly boards a mysterious train filled with other children in their pajamas, bound for the North Pole. At the North Pole, Santa Claus offers him any gift he desires, but he modestly asks only for a bell from Santa's sleigh. On the train ride home, the bell is lost. Was it a dream or did it really happen? On Christmas morning, the boy finds the bell under the tree with a note signed "S.C." His mother shakes the bell, and thinks it's broken. But the boy and his sister can hear it loud and clear, as it always will be audible to those who believe in magic.

1985 Houghton Mifflin Books for Children

Bernard Waber

Lyle Books

Only in children's books is it possible that a large green crocodile named Lyle could live with the Primm family on the Upper East Side of Manhattan, and it would seem perfectly logical. Lyle spends a fair amount of time in the bathtub, of course, but he also helps Joshua with his homework, jumps rope with the neighborhood kids, and helps Mrs. Primm with the shopping. *The House on East 88th Street* is the first book in the series, and tells the story of how the Primms came to find Lyle in their bathtub. *Lyle, Lyle, Crocodile* is probably the most popular book in the series and tells the story of a mix-up in a department store managed by a mean neighbor, Mr. Grumps, that lands Lyle in the Central Park Zoo, until the Primms come to his rescue. In *Funny, Funny Lyle,* the lovable croc faces two challenges: preparing for the Primms' new baby and introducing his mother to New York City and the family he loves. In *Lovable Lyle,* Lyle has to try extra hard to be lovable when he finds out that he has an enemy. These books all have simple storylines that children can relate to, and, most important of all, a very kind and lovable hero in Lyle himself.

The House on East 88th Street *(1962)*

Lyle, Lyle, Crocodile *(1965)*

Lovable Lyle *(1969)*

Funny, Funny Lyle *(1987)*

Houghton Mifflin Books for Children

Judith Viorst
Illustrated by Ray Cruz

Alexander and the Terrible, Horrible, No Good, Very Bad Day

Everybody, including children, has bad days when absolutely nothing goes right. This book goes a long way toward explaining that we all have to learn to handle our feelings of frustration or anger or sadness— just hopefully not all on the same day like Alexander. His day starts badly and gets worse: he went to bed with gum in his mouth, and now it's in his hair; he dropped his sweater into the sink while the water was running; Mom forgot to put dessert in his lunch; the dentist found a cavity; and it goes on from there. All the while, Cruz's illustrations portray exactly how awful Alexander's day is, while the repeated refrain throughout the book will have children chanting along, "I am having a terrible, horrible, no good, very bad day."

1972 Atheneum

Ellen Stoll Walsh

Walsh's brightly colored paper-collage art makes these three early-concept books standouts. Each book not only teaches a basic concept—counting, colors, and shapes—but also is enhanced by the simple story lines that are incorporated into each. In *Mouse Paint*, three white mice find some jars of paint and dip themselves in to demonstrate colors and color blends; in *Mouse Count*, our three little mouse friends are captured by a slithery snake and use their wits and ingenuity to count themselves out of trouble; and in *Mouse Shapes*, the mice use a cluster of brightly colored shapes to build a house in which to hide from a predatory cat.

Mouse Count *(1991)*

Mouse Paint *(1989)*

Mouse Shapes *(2007)*

Harcourt Children's Books

David Wiesner

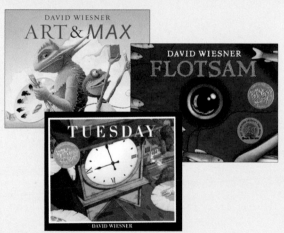

Art & Max

This book about the nature of art successfully explores several issues at once: creativity, friendship, that there is never just one way to look at art, and that we must keep learning in order to keep growing. It seems like heavy stuff for a children's book, but Wiesner pulls it off in a perfectly child-friendly way. Lizards Art and Max are friends. Art is a painter of traditional portraits; Max is younger and wants to learn to paint, too. Through a series of funny accidents, children will be introduced to realism, pointillism, and a bit of abstract expressionism, as Max learns to paint and Art learns to be open to new ideas. This book encourages children to think creatively.

2010 Clarion Books

Caldecott Award

Flotsam

The first thing you must do when reading this wordless book is let go of any preconceived notions of reality, and literally go with the flow of this miraculous seaside tale. There may not be any words here, but the pictures alone tell a magical story. A little boy is at the seaside when he is knocked over by a big wave and finds an old underwater camera deposited next to him. He rushes the camera to a photo store to develop the film within, and it's the last picture that gets his attention—a shot of a boy holding a picture of a boy holding a picture of a girl holding a picture...going back in time for decades.

2006 Clarion Books

Caldecott Award

Tuesday

One Tuesday evening around eight o'clock something magical happens: the frogs in the local pond mount their lily pads and begin to fly. Children will rejoice at the harmless disruption these fun-loving frogs create as they enter a suburban town. They mess with the laundry hanging on the line, switch TV channels on a sleeping granny, and scare the heck out of a dog—and that's just some of what they do in this surreal fantasy. When they return to their pond at the end of the evening, all that's left of their eerie presence in town are a few lily pads and a hint about the next flying visitors, who may be pink and porcine in nature.

1991 Clarion Books

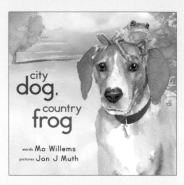

Illustrated by Jon J Muth

City Dog, Country Frog

When two award-winning author/illustrators get together to create a book, the results are bound to amaze, and this book does not disappoint. The text sings with Willems' familiar wit, as we meet a city dog who comes to the country in the spring and strikes up an unlikely friendship with a frog. Muth's paintings are filled with light and color, as we follow the friends through subsequent meetings in the summer and fall. They play together joyously until one day, when the frog is tired and wants to play "remembering," so together they relive the joys of their friendship. This foreshadows what happens in the winter, when dog returns and cannot find his friend the frog. In the spring friendship comes alive again, but in a new way. This story is ultimately about both friendship and loss but also renewal, as told through the metaphor of the seasons.

2010 Hyperion

Leonardo the Terrible Monster

Leonardo is terrible at being a monster. He can't seem to scare anyone. Leonardo decides to study hard and become a really scary monster, so he can finally "scare the tuna salad" out of someone. When he sees small, bespectacled Sam, he gives it his best shot, and Sam bursts into tears. Initially Leonardo is proud, until he realizes that Sam isn't scared—he's just having a bad day, and Leonardo decides that he'd rather be a friend than a scary monster. This tale offers parents an opportunity to teach children to face their fears, to not back down when they want to achieve something, and the value of friendship—a perfect trifecta of a book.

2005 Hyperion

We all know that it isn't reasonable for a pigeon to drive a bus, but this pigeon really, really wants to and is willing to do whatever it takes to get us to let him—whether it involves begging, cajoling, bribing, or throwing a fit. All of which is accomplished in a frame-by-frame narrative of the simply drawn bird, whose physicality and clever speech bubbles move the story forward, as the clever pigeon negotiates directly with the reader. In the next book, he wants a hot dog, and he wants it bad, and in the third book the pigeon is determined to convince us to get him a puppy. Children relate to the pigeon both because to them his requests are not totally unreasonable, just kind of silly, and, more importantly, they *are* him. This pigeon easily communicates the desires and frustrations of young children who sometimes want what they want just because they want it—except that this pigeon is way funnier than your average three-year-old throwing a tantrum.

Don't Let the Pigeon Drive the Bus! *(2003)*
Don't Let the Pigeon Stay Up Late! *(2006)*
The Pigeon Wants a Puppy! *(2008)*
Hyperion

Knuffle Bunny Books

The illustrations in this series are not only unique, but also serve the story perfectly. The main characters, the father and his daughter Trixie, are drawn as animation-style cartoon figures against a background of sepia-toned photographs of their neighborhood. In the first book, Dad and toddler Trixie are doing errands together, but when Trixie leaves her beloved Knuffle Bunny at the laundromat, the problem starts. Pre-verbal Trixie tries everything she can think of to let Dad know the problem, and nothing is working. Parents will relate as Trixie "goes boneless" in despair, but of course, Knuffle Bunny is eventually retrieved. In *Knuffle Bunny Too,* Trixie brings Knuffle Bunny to school for show and tell—and discovers a classmate has the same bunny! Mayhem ensues—there is a bunny mix-up, but a midnight exchange between dads brings Knuffle Bunny safely home, and a new friend is made. In the third book, the family and Knuffle Bunny head off to Holland to visit the grandparents, and Knuffle Bunny is left on the plane. Trixie must deal with the loss of her beloved toy and the pangs of growing up. These books teach children valuable lessons about love, security, friendship, and growing up.

Knuffle Bunny: A Cautionary Tale (2004)
Hyperion

Knuffle Bunny Too: A Case of Mistaken Identity (2007)
Hyperion

Knuffle Bunny Free
2010 Balzar + Bray

Margery Williams
Illustrated by William Nicholson

The Velveteen Rabbit

A boy is given a velveteen rabbit for Christmas, which joins the other toys in the nursery, just waiting for the boy to play with him. Because children naturally believe that their toys have real lives, they intuitively understand the message the wise Skin Horse offers to the young Velveteen Rabbit: "'Real isn't how you are made,' said the Skin Horse. 'It's a thing that happens to you. When a child loves you for a long, long time, not just to play with, but REALLY loves you, then you become Real.'" There have been entire books written about the "message" of this story, but it's really very simple— we are all deserving of love, and love makes you real.

1922 HarperCollins

Jeanne Willis
Illustrated by Tony Ross

Misery Moo

This story about a morose cow that refuses to be cheered up has a clear but humorous message about how depression and bad behavior can affect others. The little lamb tries everything she can to cheer up her friend the cow, and nothing works. Eventually the lamb gives up and goes away. Suddenly the cow realizes he is lonely, and goes looking for the lamb, only to find her depressed because she could not help her friend. The cow realizes that his mood is the problem, smiles for the lamb, and all is resolved. The story is deceptively simple, but the humor is built into the sly watercolor artwork, and children will understand the message of the book immediately.

2005 Henry Holt

Multicultural

A Chair for My Mother

Caldecott Honor

Three generations of an African American family—a grandmother, mother, and child—have survived a fire that destroyed all their possessions. They have a place to live and donated furniture, but they long for a big, cozy chair that they can all curl up in together. They also have a big jar that is slowly filling up with coins, saved from their mother's tips earned as a waitress and what Grandmother saves by shopping for bargains. Lovingly narrated by the young girl and illustrated with beautiful, brightly colored paintings accompanying the text, this story of family love, hope, and survival will help children understand that it is possible to achieve your dreams if you are patient and determined.

1982 Greenwillow Books

Multicultural

"More More More," Said the Baby

Caldecott Honor

This beautiful picture book by multiple award-winner Vera B. Williams is all about families and affection. The three adorable, multicultural tots in this simple concept book are feeling the love of their parents and grandparents, who kiss their tummies, their toes, and their sleepy eyes as they joyously request "more, more, more!" The stunning art and simple concept will have families reading and kissing along with the book in no time.

1990 Greenwillow Books

Illustrated by Laura Rader

Dinos in the Snow!

This winter frolic is perfect for all those toddlers who are fascinated with all things dinosaur-related. This book is a joyous celebration of all forms of winter sports, from skiing and snowboarding to sledding and skating. The colorful illustrations of a variety of dinosaurs bundled up in their winter gear, enjoying everything winter has to offer and the rhyming descriptive text make this a perfect read on a cold winter's day.

2005 Little, Brown and Company

Illustrated by Laura Rader

Dinos on the Go!

Combining two of toddlers' favorite things—dinosaurs and transportation—this rhyming story of dinosaurs from around the world racing to attend a dinosaur reunion is sure to please. There are dinos on bikes, in cars, and on trains, planes, trucks, and ships, and the exuberant illustrations of these prehistoric creatures zooming off to a party and the vibrant rhythmic text are just perfect for the youngest dinosaur fans.

2004 Little, Brown and Company

Illustrated by Don Wood

King Bidgood's in the Bathtub

Caldecott Honor

What do you do when the king is having so much fun playing in the bath that he won't get out of the bathtub and do his kingly duties? The members of his royal court, in full Elizabethan garb, try everything. But they all seem to end up in the tub with the king, enacting battles with toy ships, eating outrageous meals, pretending to fish, and even dancing. Children will love poring over the colorful and detailed oil paintings that illustrate this book and laughing at the jolly king's antics. This book makes the perfect pre- or post-bath bedtime story, especially for those children who are reluctant to take their daily bath.

1985 Harcourt Children's Books

Illustrated by Don Wood

The Napping House

This lovely naptime or bedtime classic begins with a simple premise: "There is a house, a napping house, where everyone is sleeping." But the hilarious paintings that accompany the story are anything but simple, as every creature in the house joins the snoring granny in bed for the night. Children will laugh as Granny is joined by a child, a cat, a dog, a mouse, and, eventually, a very wide-awake flea. What happens when the flea bites the mouse sets in motion a hilarious chain reaction that will have children laughing as the napping house becomes the house where "nobody is sleeping!"

1984 Harcourt Children's Books

Douglas Wood
Illustrated by Jon J Muth

Old Turtle and the Broken Truth

This moral tale is difficult for youngsters, but children in the primary grades will understand its message of love and equality between people and animals. A "truth" falls from the sky, breaking into pieces. The animals ignore it because they sense something is missing. A human finds a piece of the "truth" and takes the message "you are loved" back to share with his people, who become proud and ignore the wonders of the world around them. Eventually a young girl consults Old Turtle about her people's ways, and he shows her the missing part of the "truth," which says "and so are they." In this way, humans come to understand that there is more than one universal truth.

2003 Scholastic Press/Scholastic Inc.

Arthur Yorinks
Illustrated by Richard Egielski

Hey, Al

Caldecott Award

This classic book cleverly illustrates the adage that "home is where the heart is" in a way that children can easily grasp. Al is a janitor who lives with his dog Eddie in a one-room apartment on the Upper West Side of Manhattan. They love each other and do everything together, but their closeness turns to bickering when they feel the pressure of all that togetherness. One day, a mysterious bird offers them a life in paradise, with no worries or cares, and, after a bit of discussion, off they go. Happy at first, they soon begin to miss home, and how they manage to return brings the story to a close.

1986 Farrar, Straus & Giroux

Picture Books 2–6

Kevin Henkes on doing the work he loves…

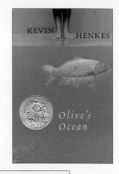

For as long as I can remember, I've wanted to be an artist. It wasn't until I was a junior in high school that I began to think of writing as a career. Because I was attracted to both writing and drawing, creating children's picture books seemed to be the perfect job for me.

That choice seems even more fitting because I was one of those kids who loved books dearly. Although I didn't own many books when I was a boy, my family went to our local public library regularly, so I had all the books I needed.

My love of books, my need to make art, and my desire to write stories led me down a path I'm still on today.

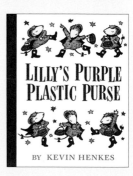

Growing up, I particularly admired the work of Crockett Johnson, Maurice Sendak, and Garth Williams. I was captivated by the worlds they brought to life, and I returned to their books again and again.

I'm drawn to small, domestic stories. They are what I know best and feel most comfortable creating. I suppose no story is truly new—what makes each one fresh are the telling details in both the art and the words; dialogue that sparkles and moves the narrative; the rhythm of the words; the specific, unexpected touches that elevate a story and allow it to sing.

Some of my favorite books are: *Bedtime for Frances*, by Russell Hoban, illustrated by Garth Williams; *Harry the Dirty Dog*, by Gene Zion, illustrated by Margaret Bloy Graham; and *Little Bear*, by Else Holmelund Minarik, illustrated by Maurice Sendak.

I'm lucky that I can spend my days doing the work I love. I wouldn't trade it for anything.

See individual listings for books by Kevin Henkes on pages 45 and 156.

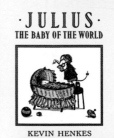

Essay by Kevin Henkes. Copyright 2011 by Kevin Henkes. Used with permission. All rights reserved.

Author/Illustrator Kevin Henkes

Dan Yaccarino

Every Friday

A charming salute to a family ritual of father and son bonding, this book may just start a new tradition in your family. Every Friday, a father and son go off to breakfast together before the boy goes to school and the father to work. They enjoy the routine and sameness of their Friday mornings together, from the waitress at the diner who knows just what they'll order, to the shop windows they linger in front of every week. Yaccarino's nostalgic art recalls a bygone era but also the fact that some things never change, especially the bond between father and son. A perfect Father's Day gift for Dad, and a loving story for sons, this book will quickly become a family favorite, and not just on Fridays.

2007 Henry Holt

Unlovable

Alfred is a pug dog who thinks he's unlovable. All the other dogs tease him about his short legs and funny pushed-in face; even the goldfish joins in. One day a new dog named Rex moves into the neighborhood, and he is the mirror image of Alfred. But Alfred makes a mistake—he is so desperate to be loved that he tells a little fib, and now he is afraid that Rex will not like him either. This sweet story of self-confidence and the meaning of friendship is enhanced by Yaccarino's charming, graphic illustrations, which cleverly express emotions and beautifully support the theme of the book.

2002 Henry Holt

Peter Yarrow

Illustrated by Melissa Sweet

Day Is Done

This picture book version with musical CD of Yarrow's well-loved song, made famous by Peter, Paul & Mary, has been lovingly transformed into a comforting bedtime story. Not every song can be converted successfully into a children's book, but this one succeeds both because of its strong, reassuring message to children that no matter what, "I am here," and Sweet's charming illustrations of young animals being tucked into bed by their parents, culminating with a human father tucking his son into bed. Whether you choose to read the book, sing the song, or listen to the accompanying CD, this book will soon become a comforting part of your family's bedtime ritual.

2009 Sterling

Peter Yarrow and Lenny Lipton
Illustrated by Eric Puybaret

Puff, the Magic Dragon

With over a million copies in print, this magical picture book retelling of a song most of us learned around the campfire has quickly become a book cherished simultaneously by three generations of readers. Though you may remember this song as a sad ode to growing up, Puybaret's illustrations are filled with all the wonder and magic of childhood and allow a new, happier ending to the song by virtue of a visual trick at the end, although the lyrics remains the same as you remember. This favorite family sing-along has now become a book that can stand on its own and is made all the better with the included CD, which also offers two bonus songs.

2007 Sterling

Illustrated by Mark Teague

The books in this series are popular for toddlers and preschoolers for a few reasons: they are about dinosaurs, they explore familiar childhood issues, and they are brilliantly and sometimes hilariously illustrated. Each features a page that identifies the various species of dinosaurs in the book, and while the subjects may be familiar to young readers, the images of these gigantic creatures trying to fit themselves into human-sized beds, tubs, tables, and desks are sure to cause many a giggle.

How Do Dinosaur's Eat Their Food? *(2005)*

How Do Dinosaurs Go to School? *(2007)*

How Do Dinosaurs Say Good Night? *(2000)*

How Do Dinosaurs Say I Love You? *(2009)*

How Do Dinosaurs Play All Day? *(2011)*

Blue Sky Press/Scholastic Inc.

Illustrated by John Schoenherr

Owl Moon

On a cold winter's night, brightly lit by a full moon, a young girl and her father bundle up and go "owling" to see if they can find the Great Horned Owl. As they make their way through the forest, they are watched by other forest animals, including a fox, a raccoon, and a deer. Father calls to the owl, and eventually the owl calls back. This appreciation of nature is enhanced by the atmospheric paintings that illustrate the book, which bring the winter's night in New England so vividly to life. Filled with nighttime mystery, this tale has become a well-loved, family favorite read-aloud.

1987 Philomel

Caldecott Award

Gene Zion

Illustrated by Margaret Bloy Graham

In *Harry the Dirty Dog,* we meet lovable Harry, a white dog with black spots who really hates to take a bath. So he takes the scrub brush, buries it in the backyard, and runs away before his family get him in the tub. During Harry's adventures, he manages to get really dirty, so when he finally comes home, he is a black dog with white spots, and nobody recognizes him. Harry quickly digs up the scrub brush and begs for a bath—which of course reveals that he is in fact their beloved dog. The other books in the series are equally charming. There is another case of mistaken identity when Harry is taken for a sea monster after a large wave covers him in seaweed in *Harry by the Sea.* In *No Roses for Harry*, Harry must deal with an embarrassing rose-covered sweater given to him by Grandmother, and in *Harry and the Lady Next Door,* Harry tries to handle a tricky situation with a loudly singing neighbor.

Harry the Dirty Dog *(1956)*

No Roses for Harry *(1958)*

Harry and the Lady Next Door *(1960)*

Harry by the Sea *(1965)*

HarperCollins

Beginning Readers
Ages 4–7

Every parent looks forward to that moment when their child begins to read. Pictures prompt the desire to read, scribbles on a page become letters, letters become sounds, and then sounds become words. If only it were that simple. There are sight words, long and short vowels, consonants, blends, compound words, paragraphs, chapters—it can all be so overwhelming! And if you are overwhelmed, you can bet your child will be, too.

Eventually it all clicks and your child hits that "ah-ha!" moment when sounds form words, *S* plus *A* plus *T* becomes *sat*, then *hat*, then *mat*, then *cat*...and your child is now ready for beginning readers.

Each publisher's beginning reader program works on the same basic "level" principle that increases in complexity from one level to the next. Some series use numbered levels, others use grade levels or letters, and some a combination of all three. It's important to remember that there is no set age or grade when a child is ready to learn to read or gains reading proficiency. The best approach for you is to let your child set the pace and to continue to read with your child every day.

This section has been organized by numbered levels, from Pre-Level 1 to Level 4. Here are some definitions and guidelines that summarize each level to help you select books for your child:

PRE-LEVEL 1 Ready to Read/My First Readers
(Generally for Preschool–Kindergarten)
Large type, easy words, and word repetition make for a shared reading experience with children who are just learning or already know the alphabet.

LEVEL 1 Reading with Help *(Generally for Preschool–Grade 1)*
Short and simple sentences, for children who recognize familiar words or can sound them out, in simple stories and concepts, often with picture clues.

LEVEL 2 Reading with Limited Help or On Your Own *(Generally for Grades 1–3)*
Engaging stories and characters that bring high-interest and/or easy-to-follow plots to life through basic vocabulary, longer sentences, and language play.

LEVEL 3 Reading Independently *(Generally for Grades 2–3)*
Complex plots and more challenging vocabulary for children reading on their own.

LEVEL 4 Reading with Confidence *(Generally for Grades 2–4)*
Longer paragraphs broken out into chapters, featuring exciting, high-interest themes that are perfect for children getting ready to read chapter books.

Here are some guidelines to keep in mind when choosing books for beginning readers:

- Find books that focus on concepts and topics of interest to your child.

- In the very young levels, look for books with pictures that are cued to the text.

- If you can find your child's favorite picture book characters in beginning readers, they are great bridges to a first reading experience.

- Find books that you enjoy, and don't be afraid that your child isn't ready; beginning readers, especially at the younger levels, also make great read-aloud stories.

- For an older reader, find high-interest subjects, especially nonfiction such as dinosaurs, dramatic weather, or historic events.

Reading Programs

Bobby Lynn Maslen
Illustrated by John R. Maslen
BOB Books

The BOB Books are sold in boxed sets of ten books and are designed to slowly build confidence in beginning readers by introducing four letters or sounds per book, working their way up to short vowels and simple sentences by the last book in the box. There are more than a dozen sets of BOB Books from which to choose, from simple alphabet books in the first set through all stages of reading competency.

1976 Cartwheel Books/Scholastic Inc.

Nora Gaydos
Now I'm Reading!

Each set in this leveled program contains ten books, as well as forty stickers and a parent's guide. In the set shown here, *Animal Antics* (Level One), the phonics books feature short vowel sounds. For each vowel sound there are two books with fun illustrations that use repetition to reinforce learning, as well as other enhanced activities—and the addition of stickers is always a plus for youngsters. There are twelve sets of books in the program that move a child from reading readiness to independent reading.

2001 innovativeKids

Beginning Readers 4–7

Alyssa Satin Capucilli
Illustrated by Pat Schories
Biscuit Books

All of the many books in the Biscuit series fall under the category of "shared reading"—reading with an adult or older sibling. Each book features a simple story, effectively told via short, one-syllable words with one or two sentences per page over thirty-two pages. The charming watercolor art helps new readers with the text by offering clear visual clues to the action. The books featured here all offer relatable stories for little learners; in *Biscuit Goes to School,* Biscuit tries to go to school with his owner, and a bit of mayhem follows; in *Biscuit Finds a Friend,* the little golden dog finds a lost duckling and helps him back to his pond; and in *Biscuit and the Little Pup,* he meets a very shy puppy and tries to get the pup to come out and play. All the Biscuit books are available in hardcover and paperback as well as bound storybook collections.

Biscuit *(1996)*

Biscuit Finds a Friend *(1997)*

Biscuit Goes to School *(2002)*

Biscuit and the Little Pup *(2008)*

Biscuit's First Trip *(2010)*

HarperCollins

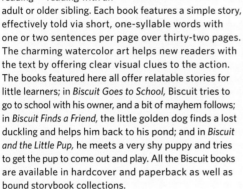

Caron Lee Cohen
Illustrated by S. D. Schindler
How Many Fish?

Featuring three to four words per page, this book uses repetition and rhyme to tell the story of six little fish swimming close to shore, who meet the six feet of three children who come to play at the beach. The story is simple, and though one fish is temporarily caught under a bucket, no real peril is faced by anyone. The illustrations are vivid, and the tale is told from a fish-eye view, which is a fun change of pace for new readers.

1998 HarperCollins

Mercer Mayer
Going to the Firehouse

By the time children are ready to read, there is a good chance they have already met Mayer's classic character, Little Critter, and his family and friends. This tale of a school visit to the firehouse offers the comfort of a familiar character taking a trip to one of the most fascinating places for children: the firehouse. With the book's simple text and bright, colorful art, children will not only learn to read, but also about fire trucks and some fire-safety tips, including how to stop, drop, and roll.

2008 HarperCollins

Joan L. Nodset
Illustrated by Paul Meisel

Go Away, Dog

A little boy is playing outside when he is approached by a big, black-and-white dog. He doesn't really like dogs, but he can't seem to make this one go away. The dog does tricks, runs, and plays with the little boy, until he finally wins him over and the boy takes him home. The clear and simple text is enhanced by the visual clues and expressive illustrations with recognizable facial expressions and body language.

1963 HarperCollins

Meet the Dinosaurs

Dorling Kindersley is known for the clear, photographic images that children love; however, when dealing with the subject of dinosaurs, this poses a problem. That problem is cleverly solved by using photos of lifelike models as well as realistic illustrations and picture strips to support the simple text. The text on this subject, which is fascinating to all young children, utilizes the concept of high-frequency words and picture labels to reinforce reading, as well.

2006 DK Publishing

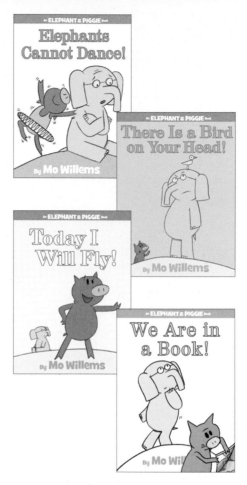

Elephant & Piggie Books

Award-winning author and illustrator Mo Willems turns his focus to early readers with this hilarious series of books about two friends: an elephant named Gerald and a pink pig named Piggie. These books feature simple text and easy sight words, and the plots and illustrations are fun from start to finish. Filled will incredibly expressive line drawings, speech bubbles, and visual gags, these books will have children laughing all the way through and reading in no time. There are more than a dozen books in the series, and we hope there are many more to come.

There Is a Bird on Your Head! *(2007)*

Today I Will Fly! *(2007)*

Elephants Cannot Dance! *(2009)*

We Are in a Book! *(2010)*

Hyperion

Beginning Readers 4–7

Esther Averill
The Fire Cat

In three very short chapters, we meet Pickles, a stray cat who is yellow with black spots and who lives in a barrel. Pickles has big paws and big plans but isn't sure how to achieve them until she is lovingly adopted by the crew at the firehouse. Pickles soon learns how to fit in and even assists with a rescue. The cartoon-style art is simple yet expressive, the text is large and easy to read, and the story of one stray cat who learns how to be the best possible cat she can be is a great lesson in striving for your goals and not giving up.

1960 HarperCollins

Linda Hayward
A Day in the Life of a Firefighter

There are many books in the DK Reader series, but this look at a firefighter's day is one that will fascinate all children. Rob is an African American fireman, who says good-bye to his family and heads off to work. Children have an opportunity to learn to read but also to understand what a firefighter does each day via the DK signature format of simple text and visual picture-dictionary squares that identify objects and the words that represent them.

2001 DK Publishing

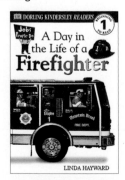

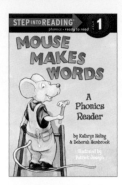

Kathryn Heling and Deborah Hembrook
Illustrated by Patrick Joseph
Mouse Makes Words

This phonics-based reader has a simple concept: a carpenter mouse on a ladder who makes words change by changing one letter at a time. His handiwork is perfect for emergent readers who are just learning phonics as he changes *cup* into *pup* and *hog* into *log*. With large text and simple words, this book's premise cleverly teaches reading, sight words, and phonics while helping children become successful readers.

2002 Random House Children's Books

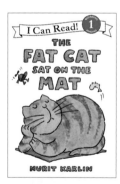

Nurit Karlin
The Fat Cat Sat on the Mat

The rhyming text in this book teaches phonics via a loose storyline about a witch's fat cat who is lying on a rodent's mat. The rodent tries everything to move the cat, including a hat and a bat (the flying kind), but nothing works until the witch comes home. The storyline isn't really as important as the visual prompts in the art, and the quick and fun repetition of short, rhyming words is perfect for emerging readers.

1996 HarperCollins

Jean Marzollo
Photographs by Walter Wick
I Spy: I Love You

The "I Spy" series is known for its detailed photographs filled with objects for children to find within the crowded pictures. This early reader takes that concept to the next step by using object-and-word association to help children read the words as they search for the objects in the pictures. A combination of reading and playing a visual game is perfect for readers who need more immediate gratification to encourage reading.

2009 Cartwheel Books

Karen Wallace
Rockets and Spaceships

Using vivid photographs of children in actual spacecraft, with simple text and visual picture-dictionary squares, this book makes a perfect introduction to space travel and satellites for beginning readers. The book features simple sentences, limited vocabulary, and word repetition to reinforce early reading skills and clear images to reinforce word identification.

2001 DK Publishing

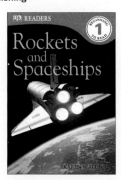

Else Holmelund Minarik
Pictures by Maurice Sendak
Little Bear Books

Little Bear was actually the first book ever written specifically for the now beloved "I Can Read" series, and the pairing of Else Homelund Minarik and multiple award-winning illustrator Maurice Sendak created a now-classic series of five books for beginning readers, as well as an entirely new category of children's books. Using simple text in large type, these books feature stories about a gentle little bear and his mother and friends. Sendak's illustrations are detailed pen-and-ink drawings, featuring one or two colors and lovely borders that not only enhance the text, but also keep young readers entranced. These books are an excellent introduction to reading simple text and short chapters, but the sweet stories and lovely illustrations also make these books excellent read-aloud choices before children are ready to read them independently. *Little Bear*, the first book in the series, contains four individual stories; "What Will Little Bear Wear?," "Birthday Soup," "Little Bear Goes to the Moon," and "Little Bear's Wish." *Little Bear's Friend* includes "Little Bear and Emily," "Duck, Baby Sitter," "The Party at Owl's House," and "Your Friend, Little Bear." *A Kiss for Little Bear* is a longer story of how a loving kiss is passed from one person to another.

A Kiss for Little Bear *(1968)*

Little Bear *(1957)*

Little Bear's Friend *(1960)*

HarperCollins

Captain Cat

Captain Cat is an orange-striped cat who snuck into the barracks when no one was looking and joined the army. Always the first to jump out of bed when the morning bugle blows, he has more stripes than all the other members of the troop (obviously) and is the perfect soldier. But this early reader is really a story of the power of friendship, one that uses simple text and many visual clues in its cartoon-style art to teach young children to read.

1993 HarperCollins

Chester

Chester is tired of living out west and being a wild horse. He wants to be tamed, to be loved, and to have someone take care of him—so he heads off to the big city to find a loving home. He tries being a carousel horse, a rocking horse, and even a statue, but none of those really work for him. Children will love learning to read as they follow along with Chester's quest to find a home where he will truly be loved and cared for.

1961 HarperCollins

Danny and the Dinosaur

This beginning reader is probably the most popular of Syd Hoff's many wonderful books for children. Of course the text is simple, the words large and easy to read, and the art is picture perfect—but it's really all about the story here. A young boy goes to a museum, sees a dinosaur, and thinks it would be fun to play with him. The dinosaur agrees, and they leave the museum together for a day of adventure and play. There are four books in this particular series, and each one is full of fun and clever adventures.

1958 HarperCollins

Danny and the Dinosaur Go to Camp

Danny and his dinosaur friend need a vacation, so it's off to camp they go. It turns out that it's pretty helpful to have a dinosaur at camp; if you get tired on a hike, you can all climb on his back and ride home. You can even use him as a boat, and remember he only has to take one step to win a race. The use of perspective in the illustrations, showing how much bigger the dinosaur is than the campers, adds plenty of visual humor as children learn to read.

1996 HarperCollins

Grizzwold

Grizzwold is big bear who is having trouble finding a place to live. The problem is that this gentle giant is pretty big, so big that the river only comes up to his knees, and three rabbits can sit in his footprint. Children will learn to read with the large, simple text as they follow this lovable bear on his quest to find the perfect place to live.

1963 HarperCollins

The Horse in Harry's Room

Harry has a horse in his room and nobody knows—well, not a real horse, an imaginary horse. They have fun and play all the time, but when Harry goes to the country and sees how real horses live, he starts to wonder if his horse would rather be free, too. This early reader not only teaches reading, but also cleverly addresses imaginary playmates and growing up. The art clearly depicts Harry's horse as imaginary with see-through line drawings, and kids will easily relate to and understand this story.

1970 HarperCollins

Mrs. Brice's Mice

Mrs. Brice has twenty-five pet mice. Twenty-four of them do everything together. The twenty-fifth mouse is always doing his own thing. When the other mice are exercising, this mouse sleeps; when the other mice go out for a walk in uniform lines, he prefers to ride on Mrs. Brice's hat. But one day, when a cat threatens the mice on their daily walk, the independent little mouse saves the day. This tale of a nonconformist mouse is sure to entertain youngsters just learning to read.

1988 HarperCollins

Oliver

Oliver is an elephant who wants to dance with the circus, but what will he do when he finds out that the circus already has enough elephants? Syd Hoff hits the mark again in this early reader with a sweet story of a gentle giant, which encourages early reading skills. As always, the illustrations are bright and offer visual support to the text, but Syd Hoff's books could stand alone as great picture books even if they didn't teach children to read.

1960 HarperCollins

Sammy the Seal

This fish-out-of-water tale is a perfect fit for Syd Hoff's funny and charming illustrations, as Sammy the seal leaves the zoo to join a group of school children for a day of fun and play. Sammy goes to school with the children, and, like the young readers of this book, he even learns to read! This beginning reader is a story about learning to read, a delightful twist that children just learning to read themselves will enjoy.

1959 HarperCollins

Stanley

Stanley isn't like the other cavemen. First of all, he doesn't like living in a cave at all, and he loves planting seeds and drawing pictures. He's so different that the other cavemen chase him away, but that doesn't bother Stanley. He's okay with being different, and when he invents the first house to live in and shows others a better way to live, he becomes a hero. This ode to being different is perfect for young children just learning what it means to fit in and still be true to themselves.

1962 HarperCollins

Who Will Be My Friends?

Moving to a new house in a new neighborhood can be scary for young children. Freddy likes his new house and his new room, and the new mailman and neighborhood policeman are also really nice. But what Freddy really wants is to make new friends, and he won't stop until he finds them in this charmingly illustrated early reader. This sweet story of how Freddy doesn't give up until he finds his friends can help young children with the difficult transition to a new home or school.

1960 HarperCollins

Illustrated by Arnold Lobel

Dinosaur Time

This book is perfect for curious children who want to learn everything there is to know about dinosaurs, including how to pronounce those really long and complicated names of the various species. The book focuses on eleven specific species of dinosaurs, and the simple text is easy to read, except for those long dinosaur names, which children will no doubt be happy to practice until they master them. The art is detailed enough to portray these fierce creatures but not to the degree that it is frightening.

1974 HarperCollins

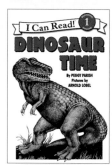

Illustrated by Marc Simont

No More Monsters for Me!

You know you are in for some fun when the main character's name is Minneapolis Simpkin, and the good news is that those are two of the longest words in this funny story. Minneapolis really wants a pet, but Mom says no to everything she suggests. She huffs out of the house, and when she hears a funny noise, she discovers a baby monster who clearly needs a home. So she takes it home and hides it in the basement. But the monster cries, and gets the hiccups, and is getting bigger by the hour. This silly romp of a book is perfect for early readers—especially if they have been wanting a pet of their own.

1981 HarperCollins

B. Wiseman

Morris Goes to School

Morris the moose can't read, and if you can't read you might end up going to the fish store when you really want candy. So Morris decides to go to school with the children in the neighborhood so he can learn to read and count, and sing and paint, too. Now Morris can go to the candy store and read the labels on the candy, and even count the gumdrops! This early reader is a lot of fun and also addresses why children need to go to school and learn to read.

1970 HarperCollins

Bonnie Worth

Illustrated by Christopher Moroney

Cooking with the Cat

This bright and colorful reader features everyone's favorite feline, the Cat in the Hat, as he whips up some treats that only he could dream of, like purple cupcakes. You can be pretty sure that cooking with this particular character will be seriously crazy and tons of fun. Simple rhyming word combinations and heavy-handed humor paired with art that is filled with visual clues make this a recipe for reading success.

2003 Random House Children's Books

Harriet Ziefert

Illustrated by Norman Gorbaty

Sleepy Dog

This early reader is perfect for reading before bedtime, as it follows a sleepy dog and cat as they prepare for bed, exchange hugs and kisses, and dream playful dreams until they wake up in the morning. The book features large type with very few words on each page, so beginning readers can feel a sense of accomplishment when they are able to read the entire book by themselves before bedtime—or anytime.

1984 Random House Children's Books

Level 2

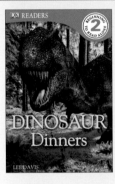

Lee Davis

Dinosaur Dinners

Using the Dorling Kindersley winning combination of photographs of models and realistic illustrations to explain the facts about dinosaurs and what they eat, this book follows a baby Maiasaurus on its first day out of the nest as it looks for food. Filled with facts and information, it also describes the habits and behavior of the different dinosaurs the baby meets and is perfect for all young dinosaur lovers.

1998 DK Publishing

Jennifer Dussling

Bugs Bugs Bugs!

Bugs Bugs Bugs! is a detailed photographic examination of bugs featuring close-up photography of "the bugs that really bug other bugs," like stag beetles, beetle-hunting wasps, and the praying mantis, to name just a few. This book is filled with fascinating bug facts, and is sure to get either an enthusiastic "COOL!" or "EEEWWW!" from young readers as they pore over both the text and the photos.

1998 DK Publishing

Rita Golden Gelman

Illustrated by Mort Gerberg

More Spaghetti, I Say!

Minnie the monkey loves spaghetti, and she can eat it all day every day, in every possible way. But how much spaghetti is too much? When your friend Freddie feels bad because you won't play with him or when your tummy hurts from too much spaghetti? In this humorous, rhyming tale with an interesting twist at the end, children will not only learn to sound out compound words, they will also learn about the value of friendship, as they laugh all the way through the story.

1977 Cartwheel Books/Scholastic Inc.

Beginning Readers 4–7

Charles Ghinga
Illustrated by Jon Goodell
Mice Are Nice

This sweet story takes place in a pet shop, where a little girl has gone to find the perfect pet. The little mouse is giving her the "big sell" on why mice are better than all the other pets—no dropping feathers, no chewing slippers, no making you sneeze—as the girl examines all the pets in the store. From the simple rhymes and charming illustrations, you can guess who goes home in the little girl's pocket.

1999 Random House Children's Books

David L. Harrison
Illustrated by Hans Wilhelm
Wake Up, Sun!

This beginning reader offers children a clever barnyard tale. A dog is awakened by the bite of a flea in the middle of the night and assumes that it is morning and time for the barnyard to wake up. As he wakes each animal, not realizing that it is the middle of the night, the animals fear that the sun has forgotten to rise. Illustrated with comical and colorful pictures, this book features large print, simple words, and two lines per page, making it easy to read and understand.

1986 Random House Children's Books

Arthur Books

Arthur is a little chimpanzee with a precocious younger sister named Violet, both of whom children will easily be able to relate to as the chimp's experiences so closely parallel their own. There are several books in the Arthur series for young readers who find themselves wanting more of these beautifully illustrated stories of growing up. In *Arthur's Loose Tooth,* Arthur is afraid that when his tooth falls out it's really going to hurt, but he's also afraid to pull it out himself. In *Arthur's Camp-Out*, Arthur is sure he knows everything about camping, but he gets frightened alone in the woods. Arthur thinks having a pen pal is better than anything—even his little sister—in *Arthur's Pen Pal*...until he finds out his pen pal's true identity. In *Arthur's Funny Money,* Arthur learns about earning and saving money to buy a new T-shirt and cap. The books teach reading as well as how to deal with the everyday, sometimes confusing, dilemmas that come along with growing up.

Arthur's Pen Pal *(1976)*
Arthur's Funny Money *(1981)*
Arthur's Loose Tooth *(1985)*
Arthur's Camp-Out *(1993)*
HarperCollins

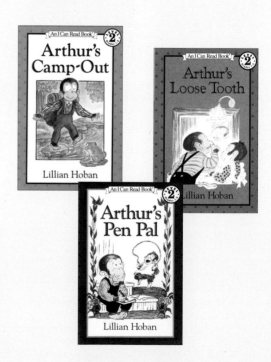

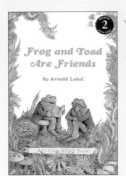

Caldecott
Honor

Frog and Toad Are Friends

Frog and Toad are the very best of friends, and children will learn to love this classically illustrated book with its loving stories of friendship. There are five separate chapters, which will give children a sense of accomplishment as they are able to read each independently. These adventures also make great read-aloud tales for younger children, with simple tales about a swim the friends take together, the search for a lost button, looking forward to spring, and waiting for the mail.

1970 HarperCollins

Frog and Toad All Year

Join everyone's favorite amphibians in another collection of short, chapter-length tales abut their activities throughout the seasons, including a special holiday celebration. Children will love reading about Frog and Toad sledding in the winter, hunting for signs of spring, and all that melting chocolate ice cream in the summer. There are additional Frog and Toad books in the series as well.

1976 HarperCollins

Mouse Soup

In this clever tale of mouse ingenuity, little Mouse finds himself in a predicament: Weasel is getting ready to make soup, and mouse is one of the major ingredients. Mouse has four short chapters to invent a plan to outsmart the weasel and get himself out of hot water—literally. Children will be rooting for our clever little hero, and anxiously reading their way to his eventual victory over the weasel.

1977 HarperCollins

Mouse Tales

Seven little mouse brothers are getting settled in for the night, and they ask their mouse father to tell them a story before sleep. Father does them one better and tells them seven short stories, one for each of the mouse brothers. Perfect for bedtime reading, these stories are short enough so that parents can alternate reading with their children or read the entire book aloud.

1972 HarperCollins

Owl at Home

In another classic book by Arnold Lobel, we meet Owl, who lives by himself in a cozy, warm home. There are four simple stories in this book: In the first, Owl invites Winter into his cozy home on a blustery evening. In the other three stories, he finds strange bumps in his room, makes "tear-water tea," and is followed home by a new friend after an evening's stroll in the woods. As in all of Lobel's books, the two-color illustrations are lovely and offer visual clues for beginning readers.

1975 HarperCollins

Beginning Readers 4–7

Amelia Bedelia Books

In this hilarious series of books, children will meet Amelia Bedelia, the housemaid who does everything she is asked to do—just not exactly as you might expect her to do it. Amelia follows orders literally. If you ask her to draw the curtains, she's likely to get out her sketch pad and draw a picture. If you ask for cereal with your coffee, you are likely to get cereal *in* your coffee, and instructing her to be sure to use the bib when feeding the baby ends up with Amelia wearing the bib. There are many books in this series, each one filled with hysterical literal mix-ups, which always have Amelia on the verge of getting fired—however, her huge heart and amazing cooking and baking always save her job. Somehow, at the last minute, just when you're sure she has to go, out comes her lemon meringue pie or a juicy strawberry tart, and all is well. The books offer great lessons in figures of speech, and children love the wordplay and trying to figure out what Amelia will do every time she is given instructions.

Illustrated by Fritz Siebel

Amelia Bedelia (1963)

Illustrated by Wallace Tripp

Come Back, Amelia Bedelia (1971)

Illustrated by Lynn Sweat

Amelia Bedelia and the Baby (1981)

HarperCollins

Stephen Krensky

Illustrated by Davy Jones

Bones

In this early reader, children will learn all about the bones in their skeleton, including which bones are longest and shortest, and how they protect the organs inside your body. After all, without bones we would just be blobs, or jellyfish, or even worms. This early science reader is perfect for curious children with an interest in science and biology. The illustrations are well executed, not too technical, and easy to understand, as is the text.

1999 Random House Children's Books

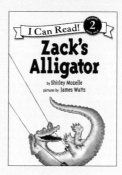

Shirley Mozell

Illustrated by James Watts

Zack's Alligator

There are several books in the *Zack's Alligator* series for interested readers. This volume is the first of the series and is loaded with fun and silliness, both within the text and in the illustrations. When Zack receives Bridget, the alligator he ordered through the mail, she is tiny enough to be used as a key chain. But when Zack soaks her in water, she not only comes to life, she grows and grows. Bridget is also fond of wrestling the garden hose, swinging on the monkey bars, and doing cartwheels. Bridget's zany antics will keep kids reading this book and others in the series.

1989 HarperCollins

Beginning Readers 4–7

Lucille Recht Penner
Illustrated by Jada Rowland

The Statue of Liberty

No other symbol is more representative of America than the *Statue of Liberty* that stands in New York's harbor. This easy-to-read and well-illustrated book brings the history of this great statue to life, from the first drawings to its creation in France as a gift to the United States, its shipment in pieces to New York, and its reconstruction and installation on Liberty Island.

1995 Random House Children's Books

James Skofield
Illustrated by R. W. Alley

Detective Dinosaur

By now you've probably noticed that there are an awful lot of dinosaurs in children's books. This particular book features three short mysteries about a bungling, derby-wearing dino detective that will have young readers giggling while they solve the simple mysteries. The art is filled with visual gags and humor, and the only stumbling block may be the long dinosaur species names—for the parents that is! Kids will pick them up in no time.

1996 HarperCollins

Cynthia Rylant
Illustrated by Suçie Stevenson

Henry and Mudge

Henry has no brothers and sisters, and he doesn't have many friends who live in his neighborhood—but what he does have is Mudge, one hundred and eighty pounds of slobbering bull-mastiff fun. These books chronicle Henry and Mudge's adventures together and their loving, protective friendship. Each book consists of five to seven short chapters that are easy to read and illustrated in full color. Once your children meet Henry and Mudge, they are going to want more—luckily, there are over thirty books in this classic series for beginning readers.

1987 Simon Spotlight

Susan Jeffers on her favorite things: stories and drawing....

I love to draw. I have always loved to draw. I go to school every week, now, to learn how to draw better.

My mother was an artist who taught my sister and me the rules of drawing and how to make light and shadow in our pictures.

I love stories. My father, who performed in *Vaudeville*, a famous variety show in the 1930s, tap danced and recited "Hiawatha's Childhood" as his bedtime good night. My mother read comic books to my sister and me when we were sick. They both read all the fairy tales to us from a series called *My Book House*. Major artists included in these books who have inspired me my whole life were N. C. Wyeth, Aubrey Beardsley, and Jesse Wilcox Smith. I loved how beautifully their illustrations were drawn and the simple powerful emotion that they expressed. I would stare at them again and again...I still do.

After I graduated from Pratt Institute School of Art, just by chance, my first job was at a children's book publishing company. Working in the art department, I looked at the art that I was preparing for new books, and I had a moment of certainty that I could do this, too.

Later, after my first book was published, I figured out that in this field of writing and illustrating for children lay two of my most favorite things, stories and drawing.

Since I know what natural artists and storytellers children are, it is an honor to have them as colleagues, critics, and company.

I have been inspired by my adult colleagues as well in working with Rosemary Wells on the McDuff books, and Steven Kellogg who always makes me laugh out loud. I want to live in his world of adored animals and friends big and small.

See individual listings for books written or illustrated by Susan Jeffers on pages 32, 46, 228, and 230.

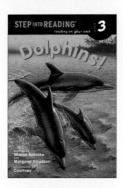

Sharon Bokoske and Margaret Davidson
Illustrated by Richard Courtney

Dolphins!

Children—and quite a few adults—are fascinated by dolphins, and this book is a great read for children interested in the many amazing interactions between dolphins and humans. Children will learn that dolphins are mammals, not fish, even though they live in the ocean and that they seem to have some sort of kindly connection to humans. Facts and stories of unusual dolphin behavior are presented clearly, and the illustrations offer clear visuals to support the text.

1993 Random House Children's Books

Martha Brenner
Illustrated by Donald Cook

Abe Lincoln's Hat

This nonfiction reader features longer and more difficult words as well as longer sentences. Children will learn all about Abe Lincoln's early years as a struggling lawyer who didn't have much money, the story behind that big black stovepipe hat, and details of his early legal cases. These stories are told with a great deal of humor—did you know Lincoln used to store important papers under that hat while he wore it?—as well as bold illustrations to keep children interested.

1984 Random House Children's Books

Illustrated by Marilyn Hafner

The Missing Tooth

Robby and Arlo are the best of friends. They dress alike and do everything together; however, their friendship is tested over a silly bet about which one of them will lose the next tooth. The illustrations are humorous and provide many clues to help move readers through the text, and the story also offers a good lesson on friendship and maintaining relationships for middle graders.

1988 Random House Children's Books

Illustrated by Patricia Wynne

Hungry, Hungry Sharks

There are no more feared or ferocious fish in the ocean than the many varieties of sharks. In this book, children will learn that some sharks are very small, and that they rarely attack humans. Sharks actually predate dinosaurs on Earth, and some are smaller than your hand. Still others have innumerable sharp teeth, and it is true that they never stop swimming or go to sleep. These fun facts and many more are contained in this book, which is perfect for shark-obsessed children.

1986 Random House Children's Books

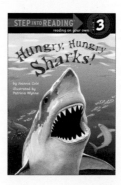

Beginning Readers 4–7

Beginning Readers 4–7

Mark Dubowski

Titanic: The Disaster that Shocked the World!

Most children are familiar with the *Titanic* disaster, but this book offers a unique approach to the story of the "safest" ship ever built and its ultimate fate when it encountered an enormous iceberg. Filled with both archival photographs and realistic illustrations, this book also offers picture/information sidebars and an extensive glossary of the nautical terms used to tell the story.

1998 DK Publishing

Frank Murphy
Illustrated by Richard Walz

George Washington and the General's Dog

Both children and adults are interested in learning about presidents and their pets. This story of a lost dog that then-General Washington found wandering on a battlefield is both touching and historically accurate. Washington was an animal lover, and he rescued the dog himself and made sure that it got back to General Howe, its rightful owner, who had the forethought to inscribe his ownership on the dog's collar.

2002 Random House Children's Books

Justine and Ron Fontes (Level 3)

Abraham Lincoln: Lawyer, Leader, Legend

Featuring maps, archival photographs, a glossary, and an index, this biography of Lincoln's middle years and presidency presents facts and information-from Lincoln's humble beginnings and his love of reading to his path to the presidency—in a ways that is suitable for newly independent readers.

2001 DK Publishing

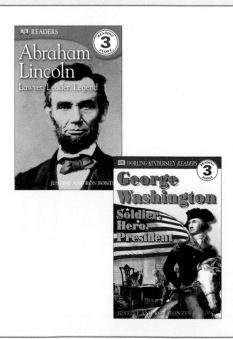

George Washington: Soldier, Hero, President

This biography effectively combines illustrations and archival photographs to give newly independent readers a comprehensive portrait of Washington from his early years to his activities as a farmer, a statesman, a general during the American Revolution, and as president. Maps, an index, and a glossary are included.

2001 DK Publishing

Natalie Standiford
Illustrated by Donald Cook

The Bravest Dog Ever: The True Story of Balto

Based on a true story, this account of Balto the sled dog, who led a team of dogs over fifty-three miles of ice and snow to deliver medicine in northern Alaska during the 1925 diphtheria outbreak, will have children reading and cheering for Balto all the way through the book. The illustrations are realistic and enhance the dramatic story of this truly heroic dog and his role in saving lives during one of the worst disease outbreaks in the history of the United States.

1989 Random House Children's Books

Level 4

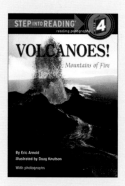

Eric Arnold
Illustrated by Doug Knutson

Volcanoes! Mountains of Fire

Once readers are reading on their own, there is a wide selection of both fiction and nonfiction titles available to them before they move into early-series and first-chapter books. This book focuses on volcanoes, or "the sleeping mountains," and what happens when they "wake up," or erupt. Filled with facts and simple science, this book features realistic illustrations and diagrams, as well as photographs of famous eruptions.

1997 Random House Children's Books

Robert D. Ballard
Illustrated by Ken Marschall

Finding the Titanic

The wreck of the *Titanic* is the subject of many books for children. However *this* book is written by Robert Ballard, the explorer who actually discovered the wreck on the ocean floor, and who personally explored and photographed what he found. Filled with illustrations and photos of the underwater site of the shipwreck, and told from a first-person perspective, this book will fascinate and inspire young explorers.

1993 Cartwheel Books/Scholastic Inc.

Beginning Readers 4–7

Illustrated by Keith Kohler
The Titanic: Lost...and Found

There's a reason that there are so many books on natural disasters and dramatic rescues in this category, and specifically many regarding the sinking of the *Titanic*. The action-filled narrative and drama of the events are perfect for reluctant readers and of especially high interest to boys. This retelling of the *Titanic* story is well illustrated and will prove to be a great addition to any family library, as the thrill and drama of this story will hold the interest of even the most reluctant reader.

1987 Random House Children's Books

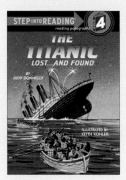

Illustrated by James Watling
Tut's Mummy: Lost...and Found

Ancient Egyptian civilization, pyramids, buried treasure, mummies—it's all here just waiting to be discovered by a new generation of independent readers. With just the right mix of history, facts, and adventure, this account of King Tut, mummification, and Howard Carter's sometimes frustrating five-year search for Tutankhamen's tomb offers drama, excitement, and the thrill of discovery to young readers.

1988 Random House Children's Books

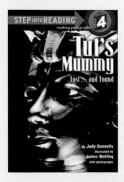

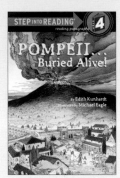

Edith Kunhardt
Illustrated by Michael Eagle
Pompeii...Buried Alive!

There may be no more dramatic tale than the destruction of Pompeii more than two thousand years ago by the eruption of Mount Vesuvius. This book looks at the events of that fateful day from the perspective of the people living there, based on scientific and archaeological discoveries made more than a thousand years later. The illustrations effectively communicate the mounting danger, and the text allows children to imagine what it might have been like to live there.

1987 Random House Children's Books

Alice Low
Illustrated by Jane Manning
The Witch Who Was Afraid of Witches

Just when you thought there was nothing in this category beyond nonfiction, along comes this funny tale of a young witch who is bullied by her sisters into thinking that she really isn't a very good witch. With fun yet moody illustrations, this book portrays Wendy's situation when her sisters go off without her on Halloween and how she discovers her powers and begins using them for good—and for a little revenge on her mean sisters.

1999 HarperCollins

Chapter Book Series
Ages 6-8

Once your child has mastered beginning readers, the next step is early, or first, chapter books. Many of these are available as ongoing series, which help fuel your new chapter-book reader's insatiable appetite. These short novels offer hours of fun with ongoing storylines and favorite characters to follow and feature a wide range of reading levels.

This category is especially important for "reluctant readers"—those children who can read but may not want to or those who are not yet reading proficiently for their grade level. In these cases, the quickest road to reading proficiency is humor, and these books are loaded with it!

The range of choices for readers is vast, from the adventurous to the purely ridiculous. There are mysteries, fantasy stories, animal stories, sports, nonfiction, and even graphic novellas. There are books with and without illustrations and series for boys, for girls, and for both. We've selected a cross-section of the variety of titles and subjects available, balancing interests of gender, reading level, and humor, and books specifically aimed at reluctant readers.

The following section offers reviews of eighteen of the best series available. We have not included reviews for series based on licensed characters, such as those from Disney or Nickelodeon, movie tie-ins, or toy brand extensions. There is nothing wrong with these books, and your child may find it comforting to read about characters he or she feels at home with. However, there are some amazing original characters that were created especially for this category and reading level, and we wanted to introduce them to you. Get ready to enter your child's world through authors and illustrators who have proven staying power, and who exhibit time and again that they know what kids like, what they worry about, and what makes them laugh.

Here are some guidelines to keep in mind when choosing chapter-book series:

- At this age, children like to select their own books, but you can help by leading them to their favorite topics or interests, such as animal stories, science, fairy tales, or sports.

- If you have a reluctant reader on your hands, go for humor—and the more scatological the better. If they keep laughing, they will keep reading.

- Fictionalized versions of historical events are both fun and educational.

- Mystery stories are great for a reader who loves to try to figure things out and solve puzzles.

- When your child discovers favorite characters, or favorite authors and illustrators, look for more books in the same series or by the same author.

- Page counts are also noted in this section for quick reference, as school assignments often require specific page-count minimums on reading assignments.

Tony Abbott
Illustrated by Tim Jessel
Secrets of Droon

This series is all about fantasy and magic, and each volume highlights the adventures of three friends—Eric, Julie, and Neal—in the mysterious land of Droon. It all begins when the three friends are playing in an old storage space in Eric's basement, and something amazing happens. A glittering light and a rainbow-colored staircase appear. As they descend the staircase they enter the land of Droon...and the adventures begin.

1999 *96 pages* **Scholastic Inc.**

Katherine Applegate
Illustrated by Brian Biggs
Roscoe Riley Rules

This very funny early-chapter series stars Roscoe Riley, a rather mischievous, though well-meaning, little guy, who spends a fair amount of time at school in the time-out chair. Featuring short chapters and cartoon-like illustrations, the books are filled with Roscoe's off-the-wall antics and are easy to read, which can be a real confidence booster for young readers. Parents may find some of Roscoe's "super, mega, gonzo" plans a bit much, but there is always a solid lesson to be learned in the end.

2008 *96 pages* **HarperCollins**

Tedd Arnold
Fly Guy

This unlikely and irreverent early chapter-book series is not only hilarious in terms of plot, but also the illustrations are equally laughter-inducing, making this a perfect choice for reluctant readers, especially young boys. Filled with visual puns, slapstick humor, and lots of hyperbole, this series about a fly and the boy who captures him will keep young readers engaged from the very first page to the very last and leave them eager to read the next book in the series.

2005 *30-32 pages* **Cartwheel Books/Scholastic Inc.**

Annie Barrows
Illustrated by Sophie Blackall
Ivy + Bean

Perfect for young girls, this series of books focuses on two very unlikely best friends: Ivy, who wears dresses and sparkly headbands, and the new girl across the street, named Bean, who is a tomboy through-and-through. Sure that they have absolutely nothing in common and could never be friends, they discover that friendship comes from the heart and not appearances. Their slightly supernatural escapades are always entertaining, and the art in these books is charming and serves to point out the girls' differences as well as their similarities.

2006 *120-136 pages* **Chronicle Books**

Jim Benton
Franny K. Stein, Mad Scientist

There is no question that Franny K. Stein doesn't exactly fit in with the other kids in school. The girls all have pretty dolls in frilly dresses, but Franny created her doll, Chompolina, with steel teeth to chomp off the heads of other dolls. Franny's lunch is crab ravioli in pumpkin sauce, theirs is squishy peanut butter and jelly, and when recess comes and they need a bat to play ball, the flying kind she has in her backpack isn't what they are looking for. Franny's mad science skills always manage to make things right in this series, with loads of laughter and funny word-play in the art and the text along the way.

2003 *112 pages*
Simon & Schuster Books for Young Readers

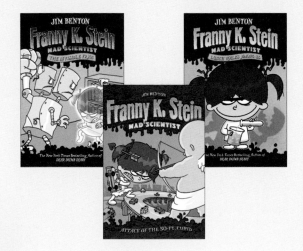

Adam Blade
Illustrated by Ezra Tucker
Beast Quest

In this series, set in a medieval village, young Tom and his friend Elenna are looking for excitement, a quest—and boy do they find it. In each book, the pair is called upon to protect their village or kingdom from some supernatural horror: fire-breathing dragons, ice beasts, sea monsters, and other magical beasts of every possible kind. Using their wits and some wizardry, this clever pair always manages to save the day, and along the way unravel the secrets of Tom's true lineage. Filled with gripping adventure and detailed art, these books are perfect for both boys and girls who want a little more action in their reading.

2007 *80 pages* **Scholastic Inc.**

Nick Bruel
Bad Kitty

This early chapter series is based on the favorite picture book character Bad Kitty, and children who loved the alphabetically inspired mayhem this curmudgeonly kitten created in the picture books will adore her further adventures in these chapter books. Whether she's celebrating her birthday with alphabetical treats or getting the dreaded bath, hanging with Uncle Murray or torturing the poor puppy, there are laughs, brightly colored visuals, and enough mayhem to fill many a chapter, as well as some fun facts from Uncle Murray and a happy resolution after the dust settles.

2008 *144–176 pages* **Roaring Brook Press**

Kate DiCamillo
Illustrated by Chris Van Dusen
Mercy Watson

With its bright, lively, full-color illustrations and clever text, this series about an adorable pig named Mercy, who is adopted into a human family, is a bit of a hybrid between picture books and chapter books and, as such, can be an easy transition to independent reading. Mercy's frolics are generally more fun than dangerous and always involve hot buttered toast—her favorite food—as either the goal or the reward. These books are sweet and simple and can help make the move from read-aloud to reading independently a smooth one.

2005 *80 pages* **Candlewick Press**

Nancy Krulik
Illustrated by John and Wendy
Katie Kazoo, Switcheroo

Her real name is Katie Carew, but the class bully has nicknamed her Katie Kazoo, and is making her life miserable. One day, as Katie wishes she was anybody but herself, a magical wind comes up and —switcheroo— she is turned into other people, even animals! Of course there is always a lesson here, which she learns when she is able to see things from some else's perspective, and a good deed is always accomplished in the end. These well-illustrated books about Katie's "switcheroos" are a lot of fun, and there are additional "fun facts" in each book to help young readers learn more about the subject at hand as well.

2002 *80 pages* **Grosset & Dunlap**

Megan McDonald
Illustrated by Peter H. Reynolds

Judy Moody

Judy, a very precocious third grader, is pretty moody. And it doesn't help that her little brother Stink thinks he knows everything, that she is starting third grade in a new school, and she just isn't in a good mood a lot of the time. This series follows our over-the-top dramatic, but very funny, heroine through her day-to-day life, as she has to deal with learning to handle herself in new situations. The illustrations are cleverly done and enhance the text, and each book has die-cut covers and is the perfect size for tucking into a backpack and taking to school.

2000 *144–160 pages* **Candlewick Press**

Megan McDonald
Illustrated by Peter H. Reynolds

Stink

Readers who loved the Judy Moody series will love this one based on Judy's know-it-all younger brother James, aka "Stink," just as much. The text is filled with verbal puns and funny asides, as well as plenty of solid facts and information. The loving sibling rivalry between Stink and Judy and Stink's very typical school- and family-related antics are relatable for young readers, whether Stink has to do a book report or accidentally kills the class lizard via the garbage disposal when it's his weekend to take him home. With plentiful black-and-white illustrations to help readers move through the stories, these books will provide loads of laughs with every reading.

2005 *112–144 pages* **Candlewick Press**

Mary Pope Osborne
Illustrated by Sal Murdocca

Magic Tree House

Jack and Annie find a tree house in the woods that magically transports them back in time, where they get to experience history and the natural world first-hand. There are over forty books in this bestselling favorite series, and still more to come. Whether they are learning about dinosaurs, mummies, pirates, space exploration, dolphins, polar bears, or the Amazon, with Jack and Annie as their guides this series is a wonderful way for children to learn about historical events in an easy-to-read format.

1992 *64–144 pages* **Random House Children's Books**

Mary Pope Osborne
Illustrated by Troy Howell

Tales from the Odyssey

This six-book series presents Homer's *Odyssey* in language appropriate for middle-grade readers. Each book features a map of Odysseus's journey, an epilogue with information about Homer and the gods and goddesses, and a pronunciation guide. Readers will thrill to adventures and epic battles such as "The Wooden Horse," "The Curse of the Cyclops," and more. These tales are illustrated with pen-and-ink drawings to enhance the reading experience. This series of books takes Homer's epic poem and translates all of its mystery and wonder into a format that is accessible to any reader who loves classic mythology.

2002 *112–128 pages* **Hyperion**

Barbara Park
Illustrated by Denise Brunkus

Junie B. Jones

This series is one of the most popular early chapter series with both boys and girls and features a very feisty main character, whom we follow from her first day of kindergarten through the primary grades. Children relate to Junie B. because her fears and successes mirror their own (it's just that it's funnier when it happens to Junie B.), and because she speaks just as they do (some parents aren't thrilled by this, but the kids love it). She's stubborn and irreverent and prone to the odd tantrum, but she learns from her mistakes, and underneath her not-always-perfect behavior there is a goofy sweetness that both parents and children adore.

1992 *80 pages* **Random House Children's Books**

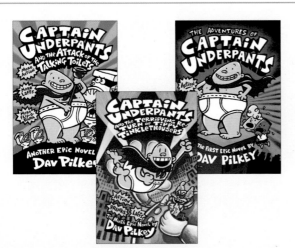

Dav Pilkey
The Adventures of Captain Underpants

If you have a reluctant reader, these books are exactly what you need. They have three things that appeal to all kids, especially boys who don't like to read: they are wickedly funny, brilliantly illustrated, and full of topics like underpants, toilets, poop, and all things gross and disgusting—but in a good way. What is not to love about a superhero who pursues truth, justice, and all things pre-shrunk and cottony—and says "tra-la-la" when he launches into flight? Don't hesitate with this one; it will turn a disinterested child into a reader in no time flat.

1997 *128–144 pages* **Blue Sky Press /Scholastic Inc.**

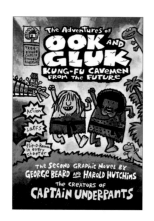

Dav Pilkey

The Adventures of Ook and Gluk: Kung-Fu Cavemen from the Future

From the creator of *Captain Underpants* comes *Ook and Gluk*, a pair of multicultural "kung-fu" cavemen—and if that doesn't pique the interest of your reluctant reader, nothing ever will. Featuring truly wacky storylines with time-traveling cavemen who do their own unique brand of crime fighting with purely hilarious consequences, plus some book-within-a-book flip-comic pages, these books will be read, reread, and shared with friends for a long, long time.

2010 *176 pages* **Blue Sky Press/Scholastic Inc.**

Ron Roy
Illustrated by John Steven Gurney

A to Z Mysteries

You guessed it—there are twenty-six books in this series, one for every letter in the alphabet. This series is a wonderful way to introduce emerging readers to the genre, with mysteries that are not too complicated but suspenseful enough to keep youngsters hooked until they solve each one. These books also teach readers to put together clues and draw conclusions from the facts, as they read through the twists and turns to the always-satisfying conclusion. This series is a winner, from *The Absent Author* all the way through to *The Zombie Zone*, and there are extra "super editions" that augment the series as well.

1997 *72-96 pages* **Random House Children's Books**

Marjorie Weinman Sharmat
Illustrated by Marc Simont

Nate the Great

This young, Sam Spade-style detective can solve any mystery or find any lost object; if you need a case solved, call Nate the Great. In true noir style, Nate likes to work alone; he asks the right questions, gets the facts, narrows down the suspects, and always gets the culprit in the end. With plenty of humor and offbeat cases to solve, along with illustrations by award-winning artist Marc Simont, there is no mystery why young detectives have been reading these books for many years, and will continue to do so well into the future.

1977 *80 pages* **Yearling**

Middle Grade Readers
Ages 8–12

This category of book has exploded in recent years, and the line between middle grade readers and young adult readers can be blurry. We have focused on presenting a wide overview of books for eight- to twelve-year-olds that range from the classics to the most contemporary. These books vary widely in subject matter and reading level, so we encourage you to participate in your child's selection process. At this age, children most often want to select their own books, based on their interests and the recommendations of their friends. However, this is an age that still needs some parental oversight in the areas of mature content or subjects and reading levels. Selecting a book above your child's reading or maturity level can turn a positive reading experience into a discouraging one.

This category is a mix of genres—general fiction, family sagas, mystery, adventure, horror, humor, fantasy, sports, and more—you name it, it's available for readers in this age group. The books in this section range from the classic tales you grew up with to titles with subjects that are trend-driven, such as vampires, wizards, and dystopian fiction. All of these books are equally important if they keep your child curious and reading.

There are award-winning authors galore in this category, and we will note them with each review. But only a very small number of books win the annual coveted literary awards. The most acclaimed titles in children's literature live in this section, from *Little Women* to *Superfudge, James and the Giant Peach* to *Island of the Blue Dolphins, Mrs. Piggle-Wiggle* to *The Chronicles of Narnia.* There is something here for every reader—including parents! These are also the books that populate school reading lists, and many will become treasured additions to your family library, to be read and reread for generations to come.

Here are some guidelines to keep in mind when choosing books for middle grade readers:

- Look for books on subjects that interest your child and subjects or themes that coordinate with their current studies at school.

- Be mindful of reading levels and sensitive subject matter—but also try to select books that will stimulate and challenge your children and encourage discussion.

- Pay attention to your child's school reading lists; often such lists can be found at your local bookstore or from the teacher or school librarian.

- When it comes to the classics, we have chosen to review them in their original formats—but many are also available in abridged formats if your child is intimidated by their length.

- Page counts are also noted in this section for quick reference as school assignments often require specific page-count minimums on reading assignments.

Joan Aiken

The Wolves of Willoughby Chase

The action in this heart-stopping novel never lets up, as readers follow the adventures of cousins Bonnie and Sylvia in 19th-century England. When Bonnie's parents embark on an ocean voyage, the girls are left in the care of a distant fourth cousin, Miss Slighcarp, who has a very evil plan in mind. After being sent to a horrible orphanage by Miss Slighcarp, the girls realize they must rely upon their wits to make their escape and assure that Miss Slighcarp is stopped. Complicating matters is a pack of wild wolves, migrating through the area via a mysterious tunnel from Russia. This classic gothic tale is a thrill ride from start to finish.

1963 *168 pages* **Doubleday**

Louisa May Alcott
Illustrated by Scott McKowen

Little Women

Great storytelling stands the test of time, and readers of all ages will never forget the March sisters: loving Meg, rebellious Jo, sweet Beth, pretty Amy—and their wise and supportive Marmee. The story follows the four sisters from childhood to adulthood and all that comes in between: financial hardship and the privations of war; sibling rivalries and enduring friendships; courtship, love, and marriage; and career aspirations. Though the book was written in 1868, the sacrifices made, tragedies endured, and ultimate success and happiness these young women experience remains both timeless and genuine for today's readers. Readers will rejoice as each of the March sisters finds her own true path in ways she could never have expected.

1868 *536 pages* **Sterling Classics**

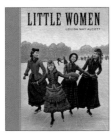

Lloyd Alexander

The Chronicles of Prydain Series

Lloyd Alexander is regarded as a master of fantasy fiction, and the five books that comprise The Chronicles of Prydain—*The Book of Three, The Black Cauldron, The Castle of Llyr, Taran Wanderer,* and *The High King*—have become classic titles in the fantasy genre. This epic series can be compared to mythology in the way that Taran, a young pig-keeper, becomes the hero of the books, growing from a young, inexperienced boy to a man of courage and conviction. Taran yearns for a bigger life, to go into battle and prove himself, and readers will not be disappointed as they follow him on his legendary journey.

The Book of Three *(1964)*

The Black Cauldron *(1965)*

The Castle of Llyr *(1966)*

Taran Wanderer *(1967)*

The High King *(1968)*

190-272 pages **Henry Holt**

Middle Grade Readers 8–12

123

Laurie Halse Anderson

Fever 1793

This historical novel takes a fascinating look at the yellow-fever epidemic that devastated Philadelphia in 1793, eventually wiping out almost 10 percent of the city's population. In the novel, we meet sixteen-year-old Mattie Cook, her widowed mother, and her grandfather, who run a coffee house in the city. As the yellow fever epidemic begins to spread and the fear of contagion casts suspicion everywhere, Mattie's comfortable life is destroyed. When her mother falls victim to yellow fever, Mattie and her grandfather must flee the city to save their lives. Upon their return to Philadelphia after the epidemic has passed, Mattie is a more capable young woman, ready to assume control of the family business.

2000 *256 pages* **Simon & Schuster Books for Young Readers**

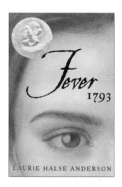

Tom Angleberger

The Strange Case of Origami Yoda

When Dwight brings an origami Yoda finger puppet to school, the sixth-graders can't decide if it's an oracle or just a wad of green paper. The advice the puppet offers isn't very "Dwight-like," and the Yoda doesn't even seem to use his voice. This comic novel is really about boys who are just discovering girls and all the complicated social interactions involved in the "I-like-her-but-does-she-like-me?" sixth-grade world. Told with varying typefaces, what appear to be crumpled handwritten pages, and some cartoon-like illustrations, this novel of sixth-grade manners is funny and just right for any reader, especially young boys who need a little humor to keep them involved in a story.

2010 *160 pages* **Amulet Books**

Richard and Florence Atwater
Illustrated by Robert Lawson

Mr. Popper's Penguins

Mr. Popper is a house painter who dreams of being an arctic explorer. He loves his wife and children but spends all his free time reading and dreaming about exploration. After he writes a fan letter to Admiral Drake, the most amazing thing happens—the Admiral sends him a penguin named Captain Cook. When one penguin turns into twelve, Mr. Popper has to come up with a plan—they can't all sleep in the refrigerator. He creates "Popper's Performing Penguins," a traveling stage show featuring his mischievous penguins. This classic is perfect for confident readers and makes an excellent chapter-a-night read-aloud for younger children.

1938 *139 pages* **Little, Brown and Company**

Newbery Honor

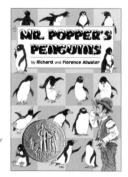

Avi

Newbery Award

Newbery Honor

Newbery Honor

The True Confessions of Charlotte Doyle

This swashbuckling adventure yarn takes place on the high seas in the year 1802, as twelve-year-old Charlotte sails from England to Rhode Island aboard a ship with a crew always on the verge of mutiny and a captain who is both ruthless and crazy. When Charlotte's passage to America is arranged by her father, she is still a proper young girl looking forward to an uneventful journey. Readers will be electrified by her transformation into a brave and determined member of the crew and her survival during such a perilous journey—which results in her being wrongfully accused of murder and sentenced to hang for a crime she did not commit.

1990 *240 pages* **HarperCollins**

Crispin: The Cross of Lead

Historical fiction comes alive in the able hands of award-winning author Avi, and readers will become engrossed in this tale of life in feudal 14th-century England, where the King, the lords of the manors, and the church leaders are equally corrupt. As the book opens, we meet Crispin at the funeral of his mother, accompanied by the parish priest, who may be his only hope of learning his true origins. When the priest is murdered soon after, Crispin is blamed. Penniless and near starvation, Crispin runs off to find a better life and to find out more about his own history. Two follow-ups to this thrilling historical novel complete Crispin's story and his quest for his rightful name.

2002 *272 pages* **Hyperion**

Nothing but the Truth

Subtitled a "documentary novel," *Nothing but the Truth* tells a story of an act of rebellion by a high school student that gets turned into a national act of treason and civil disobedience. Convinced his teacher hates him, Philip Malloy commits a minor infraction that he hopes will get him transferred out of her homeroom: he hums rather than sings the national anthem. Using multiple points of view, as if it were a documentary rather than a work of fiction, this novel is about two things that every middle school student can relate to: the misuse of power and the failure to communicate.

1991 *177 pages* **Orchard Books/Scholastic Inc.**

Illustrated by Brian Floca
The Poppy Stories

The Poppy stories are a series of six books about the woodland animals of Dimwood Forest. In *Poppy*, a group of anthropomorphized animals, including mice, owls, porcupines, and others, live under the despotic rule of Ocax, a hoot owl who promises to protect the mice from other threatening animals. But the owl himself is the biggest threat to the very mice he purports to protect. When the little mouse Poppy's fiancé, Ragweed, is killed by Ocax, Poppy sets out to find another place to live and to prove that Ocax is a villain and not a protector. The other books in the series are *Ragweed* (actually a prequel to the series, but written after *Poppy*), *Poppy & Rye*, *Poppy's Return*, *Poppy and Ereth*, and *Ereth's Birthday*.

1995 *192 pages* **HarperCollins**

Middle Grade Readers 8-12

The Eyes of the Amaryllis

Over thirty years ago, the ship *Amaryllis* was caught in a hurricane, and all aboard perished. The captain's widow, Geneva Reade, has been waiting all those years for a message she is sure her husband will send from beneath the sea. Now her granddaughter Jenny has come to stay, to assist her as she recovers from a broken ankle. But Geneva is not the only one watching the sea for a message; a man named Seward, and now Jenny, wait as well. This haunting mystery poses many questions for young readers as it winds to a surprising conclusion.

1977 *136 pages* **Farrar, Straus & Giroux**

Kneeknock Rise

This story begins when Egon visits the town of Instep for the annual fair and hears the story of something called Megrimum, that lives atop Kneeknock Rise and shrieks and moans on stormy nights. Egon is fascinated and decides to do what no one has ever done before: climb the rise to find the source of the mysterious sounds. When he discovers what is really making those sounds, no one in Instep believes him, preferring to continue to take charms and offerings to the mysterious Megrimum. This book has been described as a sort of fable or allegory for man's desire to have something larger than himself to believe in.

1970 *144 pages* **Farrar, Straus & Giroux**

Newbery Honor

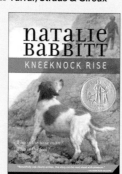

The Search for Delicious

The Prime Minister is writing a new dictionary for his country, and is looking for the perfect word or item to define *delicious*. No one can agree: Is it *apples*, or *pudding*, or something else entirely? So the king sends the Prime Minister's adopted son, Gaylan, to poll the citizens in the countryside. What he discovers is a country on the verge of a civil war, and the queen's evil brothers stirring up the townspeople. Alternately funny and touching, this story will hold the interest of young readers—especially if they are at all curious about what *delicious* really means.

1969 *192 pages* **Farrar, Straus & Giroux**

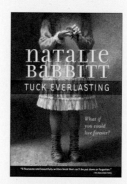

Tuck Everlasting

Imagine that you have come upon a real fountain of youth, and you have to choose whether to live forever at the age you are now or to age normally like the rest of the world. That is the choice faced by Winnie, a ten-year-old runaway, when she stumbles upon the magic spring and discovers the unusual Tuck family secret. At first, she is willing to go along with the Tucks, until Jesse Tuck explains to her what it really means to be eternally seventeen. This novel is beautifully written and offers plenty of suspense but also addresses some very serious questions about death and the natural cycle of life.

1975 *160 pages* **Farrar, Straus & Giroux**

Lynne Reid Banks
The Indian in the Cupboard

This is the first and most popular book in a series about a young boy named Omri and the two magical birthday gifts that change his life: a plastic Indian and an old chest. Omri isn't thrilled with either gift, but the magic begins when he puts the Indian in the cupboard; turn the key once and the Indian comes to life, turn it again, and he reverts to a plastic figurine. The real action starts when he adds a cowboy figurine to the cupboard. Eventually, the two figurines become friends, but until that point, there is a lot of action and just enough magic to keep the story moving. For interested readers, the series continues with four more books: *The Secret of the Indian, The Return of the Indian, The Mystery of the Cupboard,* and *The Key to the Indian.*

1985 *192 pages* **Doubleday**

J. M. Barrie
Illustrated by Scott McKowen
Peter Pan

This enchanting story of the boy who won't grow up can't be beat. Perfect for read-aloud nightly chapters or for those who are reading on their own, this magical story of Peter and his exploits with Wendy and the Darling family defines what it means to be a true classic. Since 1904, children have thrilled to the adventures of Peter, Wendy, Tinkerbell, the Lost Boys, and Captain Hook; met mermaids, Indians, and pirates; and wished for some fairy dust and a Neverland of their own. Combining magic and wonder with heart-stopping adventure, *Peter Pan* is a book that once read is never forgotten.

1904 *160 pages* **Sterling Classics**

John Bellairs Mystery Trilogy

Many young readers may be surprised to know that the subject of witches and magic had been a staple of children's literature for years before there was a young wizard named Harry Potter. The eerie John Bellairs trilogy that begins with *The House With a Clock in Its Walls,* and continues with *The Figure in the Shadows* and *The Letter, the Witch, and the Ring,* offers mystery, witches, and magical happenings galore. The series begins when recently orphaned Lewis Barnavelt comes to live with his Uncle Jonathan. What he soon finds out is that both his Uncle Jonathan and their next-door neighbor, Mrs. Zimmerman, are witches—but more importantly, Lewis himself has magical powers. As the series continues, there are clever mysteries to solve and powers to be learned and properly used, all of which adds up to a bewitching series of mysterious tales that children will love trying to solve as they read.

Illustrated by Edward Gorey
The House With a Clock in Its Walls *(1973)*

Illustrated by Mercer Mayer
The Figure in the Shadows *(1975)*

Illustrated by Richard Eigelski
The Letter, the Witch, and the Ring *(1975)*

155–188 pages

Puffin

Middle Grade Readers 8–12

Judy Blume's list of awards is nearly as long as her bibliography; among the most notable are the National Book Foundation's Medal for Distinguished Contribution to American Letters and the Library of Congress Living Legend Award. With more than twenty-five books for children in print, three for adults, and surely more to come, Judy Blume's books remain favorites with readers from age seven to seventy. She doesn't shy away from the tough issues or the sensitive and controversial ones. Her books have been banned and even burned, but more importantly, they have been read and loved by generations of children who want to read books about kids they can relate to and understand. Blume writes about real children in real-life situations—and like life, some are fun and silly, some, serious. But her characters are always authentic, and they respond to their situations in realistic and surprising ways.

Freckle Juice

Nicky and Andrew are in the same class; Nicky has freckles and Andrew wants freckles, because he thinks that if he had them, his mother wouldn't notice when his face was dirty and make him wash so often. When Sharon, the class trickster, offers Andrew a disgusting recipe for "freckle juice," a drink that will give him freckles, he falls for it. In the end, Andrew realizes that Nicky wants to get rid of the very freckles that Andrew so desperately wants, and this humorous story offers a solid lesson on a difficult subject to understand: that we all need to learn to be happy with who we are.

1978 *48 pages* **Yearling**

Blubber

Perhaps no one is able to interpret what it feels like to be a middle-grader better than Judy Blume. The theme of this novel is peer pressure and bullying; two subjects Blume recognized and addressed long before today's media focus on the subject. Jill is very aware of the social hierarchy in her class, and she knows that Wendy, the class president, is a bully, but she doesn't want to make waves, even when Wendy begins to torture Linda, who is a little overweight, by teasing and calling her *Blubber*. As the book progresses, Jill begins to understand the damage that can be done by "going along" with bad behavior.

1976 *160 pages* **Yearling**

Iggie's House

When Iggie's family moves to Japan, Winnie is devastated and left without her best friend. Then the Garber family moves into Iggie's house, making them the first African American family on very-white Grove Street; Winnie decides to be the neighborhood welcoming committee. As tensions in the neighborhood escalate, bringing the issue of racism out into the open, Winnie takes up the cause and circulates a petition in support of the Garber family. There's just one problem: the Garber children don't want to be a cause—they just want to make new friends.

1975 *128 pages* **Yearling**

The One in the Middle Is the Green Kangaroo

This is the first book published by Judy Blume, and its publication marked the start of an unparalleled career in children's literature. Freddy has an older brother and a younger sister. He's tired of being squashed in the middle like the peanut butter in a sandwich and is looking for a way to stand out. When his school puts on a play, he sees his chance and tries out; after all, no one in his family has ever been in a play before. Freddy gets a small part in the play, but more importantly, he gets to prove to everyone, including himself, how special he is just for being Freddy.

1969 *48 pages* **Yearling**

Superfudge

This book is the second title in the Fudge series, and our hero, Peter, is in for a lot of transitions. His mother is pregnant, his father has decided to write a book, the family is moving, Peter will be going to a new school, his ever-annoying little brother Fudge, who thinks he knows everything, will be in the same school as him, and oh, yeah—there's this girl named Joann McFadden.... Peter learns a lot in one short year, and readers will be laughing and learning those life lessons right along with Peter and his irrepressible brother Fudge.

1980 *176 pages* **Dutton**

Otherwise Known as Sheila the Great

Though this book features some familiar characters from the Fudge series, it is actually a stand-alone novel about Sheila Tubman, one of Peter Warren's classmates. When her family rents a summer vacation home outside New York City, Sheila must learn to face some of her fears, like spiders, ghosts, thunderstorms, the dark, dogs, and water—the kind you have to learn to swim in. Sheila's new friends and family help her work through these issues, and she learns both to face her fears and that pretending to know everything may not be the best strategy after all.

1972 *144 pages* **Dutton**

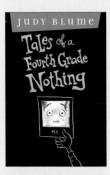

Tales of a Fourth Grade Nothing

This is the first book in the beloved Fudge series by Judy Blume. At the heart of the story is Peter Warren Hatcher, who is constantly annoyed by his younger brother Farley Drexel Hatcher—who hates his name so much he demands to be called "Fudge" instead. Peter can't seem to do anything without Fudge somehow getting in the way or ruining his plans. He's sure that his parents actually like Fudge better and feels that Fudge never receives the punishment he deserves. Any reader with a younger sibling will be able to relate to Peter's frustration with Fudge's antics and also see the love that Fudge has for Peter in this laugh-out-loud funny book.

1972 *128 pages* **Dutton**

L. Frank Baum
Illustrated by Scott McKowen
The Wonderful Wizard of Oz

Many readers are unaware that this book is the first of fifteen books in Baum's "Land of Oz" series and that Dorothy's adventures in Oz continue long after she meets the infamous Wizard of Oz. This now-iconic tale of Dorothy and Toto in Oz is a great jumping-off point for readers who like action, adventure, and a whole lot of magic in the books they read. This introduction to the Land of Oz is also a perfect choice for parents who would like to read aloud a chapter a night rather than a shorter storybook.

1900 *176 pages* **Sterling Classics**

Pseudonymous Bosch
The Name of this Book Is Secret

Not only is the name secret, but so is the author. Readers who love a good mystery, filled with twists, supernatural events, off-beat humor, word games, and anagrams to decipher, will gobble up the quirky tale of Cassandra and Max-Ernst, two eleven-year-olds determined to solve the mysterious death of an old magician. As they search for the magician's missing notebook, they encounter villains who are seeking the same notebook and accumulate some very strange information along the way. This very funny mystery will have readers longing for more, and since this is the first in a series, that particular wish will be granted.

2007 *384 pages* **Little, Brown and Company**

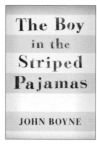

John Boyne
The Boy in the Striped Pajamas

Bruno's father, an officer for "The Fury," as he calls it, is transferred from Berlin to a mysterious place in Poland called "Out-With." From his new bedroom window, Bruno can see a camp where all the inhabitants wear striped pajamas. Bruno's curiosity about this place leads him to befriend a boy named Shmuel. Readers familiar with the Holocaust will be able to determine what is going on before young Bruno does, as his friendship with Shmuel becomes dangerous and leads to a shocking ending. Though it is written appropriately for a middle-grade audience, parents should consider reading this book with their children if they are unfamiliar with the Holocaust.

2006 *240 pages* **David Fickling Books**

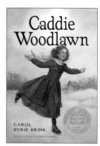

Newbery Award

Carol Ryrie Brink
Caddie Woodlawn

Based on the life of the author's grandmother, whose family moved from Boston to settle in Wisconsin in the 1860s, this story of brave and plucky Caddie Woodlawn is an accurate portrayal of a pioneer girlhood. Caddie is a tomboy and is allowed to run free on the prairie with her two brothers, much to the chagrin of her mother and the snobbish Annabelle, who think that she should learn to act like a proper young lady. This novel teaches readers the meaning of tolerance and understanding, and considering when it was written, deals sensitively with the issues relating to Native Americans—though today's readers may find it dated in that particular respect.

1935 *288 pages*
Simon & Schuster Books for Young Readers

Frances Hodgson Burnett

Little Lord Fauntleroy

Cedric Errol is an American-born boy whose English father dies young, leaving Errol to inherit the title of Lord Fauntleroy. Young Cedric has been called back to England to learn the ways of the aristocracy from his grandfather. Upon his arrival, it is clear that Cedric's affectionate manner and more "common" American upbringing are in direct conflict with his grandfather's cooler demeanor. In the end, this is a story about the obligations of family, the ways in which Cedric's grandfather learns from his young grandson to be more sympathetic and compassionate, and how Cedric learns to use those same traits to become a better sort of nobleman.

1886 *256 pages* **Puffin**

Illustrated by Scott McKowen
A Little Princess

This reversal of the usual rags-to-riches tale offers young readers a valuable lesson in patience and compassion. After living a life of luxury in India with her adoring father, Sara Crewe is placed in an English boarding school for young ladies in order to receive a proper education. Sara finds London very different from India; Miss Minchin, the owner of the school, turns out to be a cruel and uncaring woman. When Sara's father dies penniless in India, she goes from being the "princess" of the school to living in a cold and lonely room in the attic and must join young Becky as a scullery maid to earn her keep.

1904 *208 pages* **Sterling Classics**

Illustrated by Scott McKowen
The Secret Garden

Mary Lennox comes to live with her distant uncle at Misselthwaite Manor in the Yorkshire moors after both of her parents perish in a cholera epidemic. She is an impudent and spoiled little girl, prone to fits and temper tantrums. Mary soon meets her invalid cousin Colin, who lives most of his life locked away in his room, and finds that though he may be sickly, he is as spoiled as she is. When she discovers a secret garden on the estate behind a long-locked door, Mary, her friend Dickon, and Colin learn how to tend and restore the garden, and by so doing they begin to bloom as well.

1911 *248 pages* **Sterling Classics**

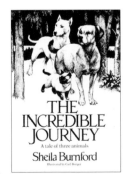

Sheila Bunford
The Incredible Journey

This classic story is about three house-pets, a young labrador retriever, an aging bull terrier, and a clever Siamese cat, and their amazing journey together through the wilds of Ontario, Canada, to be reunited with their owners. The Hunter family must take a trip to England, and leave their pets with a friend who lives 250 miles away. The lonely animals decide to search for their owners. These animals do not converse in English dialogue, but the writing makes their love for each other and the hardships and many obstacles they face together, vividly clear. This is a riveting story that has been enthralling young readers and animal lovers for generations.

1996 *160 pages* **Delacorte Press**
(Originally published in 1961 by Little, Brown and Company)

All that is required to enter Alice's magical world is a patient reader and a suspension of belief in the world as we know it, for once Alice steps down into the rabbit hole, or through the looking-glass, things become "curiouser and curiouser." These books, with their classic illustrations, make perfect first read-aloud chapter-a-night stories for children who have begun to outgrow picture books; each chapter contains a complete adventure or introduces a new character. Children will be entranced as they meet some of the most memorable characters in all of children's literature: the white rabbit, the mad hatter, the Cheshire cat, the mock turtle, Tweedle Dee and Tweedle Dum, the very short-tempered Red Queen, and so many more. Much has been said about the supposed "mathematical codes" in the books or the author's use of opium to fuel the creation of some of their more fantastic elements, but in the end, all you need to know about the two Alice books can be read in the faces of children as they listen to the stories and dive into the illustrations—they are enraptured, transported, and completely involved in the adventures.

Illustrated by Scott McKowen
Alice's Adventures in Wonderland
1865 *136 pages* **Sterling Classics**

Illustrated by John Tenniel
Through the Looking-Glass
1871 *208 pages* **Puffin**

Newbery Award

Betsy Byars
The Summer of the Swans

Like many fourteen-year-old girls, Sara is absorbed in her own life and problems. She hates her hair and her changing body and has spent the summer feeling either jealous of her older sister or sorry for herself. Sara wonders what it would be like to just fly away like the swans on the lake where she takes her mentally disabled younger brother Charlie. One night, Charlie leaves the house to find the swans and becomes lost. What follows is the longest day of Sara's life as her family and the community pull together to find her brother, and Sara learns that caring about others is much more important than worrying about herself.

1970 *144 pages* **Viking**

Newbery Honor

Gennifer Choldenko
Al Capone Does My Shirts

In 1935, twelve-year-old Moose Flanagan's father gets a job as an electrician at the prison on Alcatraz Island, where the most famous mobster of all time, Al Capone, is currently incarcerated. Moose's mother hoped that this move would allow the family to enroll Moose's autistic sister into a special school in San Francisco, but when that doesn't work out, Moose ends up having to care for her when he'd rather be playing on the baseball team. While the setting and themes of this novel seem intense at first glance, it is still a laugh-out-loud funny story about the dilemmas that families face and how they cope with them.

2004 *240 pages* **Putnam**

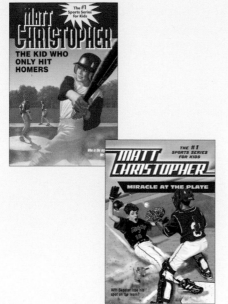

Matt Christopher is America's preeminent writer of sports stories for middle-grade readers. Though he is best known for thse baseball-themed titles, he has written about many other sports as well, including football, soccer, basketball, hockey, lacrosse, extreme sports, and more. Christopher's books are perfect for young boys who are reluctant readers but avid sports fans; they are filled with relatable action on topics of high interest and written in clear and easily understandable text. Each of the titles also contains a mystery element to keep readers involved. In *The Kid Who Only Hit Homers,* readers meet Sylvester, a boy who loves baseball but isn't the best hitter—until he meets the mysterious Mr. Baruth and begins to hit homer after homer. In *Miracle at the Plate,* readers will meet Tommy and Skeeter, who are both competing for a spot on the same team. Skeeter is a great batter but a lousy fielder, and Tommy is just waiting to replace him on the team. The competition that pits them against each other and how they work out their differences is at the heart of this well-loved page turner.

The Kid Who Only Hit Homers *(1972)*

Miracle at the Plate *(1967)*

129–151 pages **Little, Brown and Company**

Andrew Clements
Illustrated by Brian Selznick
Frindle

Nick Allen is ten years old and has a real gift for trying to annoy his teachers. When one of his pranks backfires, he is given an assignment to write an extra paper on how new words get into the dictionary. Doing the research gives Nick a great idea: he is going to invent his own word—*frindle*, which means "pen," the kind you write with. When the whole school starts calling pens *frindles*, things quickly get out of hand. There is after-school punishment, but there is also some national publicity—and in the end *frindle* is actually added to the new dictionary, and a young boy learns that he can accomplish something pretty big.

1996 *112 pages* **Atheneum**

Carlo Collodi
Pinocchio

We all know the story of Pinocchio, the wooden puppet who wanted to be a real boy, and his creator Geppetto—or do we? Here's a clue that what you know may differ greatly from the original: Pinocchio does meet a talking cricket in Collodi's original tale—and then he squashes him dead. In the original story, Pinocchio is a prankster: he's long on gumption, but he's greedy and low on scruples. He is in some ways both a hero and an antihero at the same time. Filled with dark humor and a very theatrical sense of farce, this book offers plenty for competent readers looking for the original story behind the classic.

1882 *288 pages* **Puffin**

Named as a "living legend" by the Library of Congress, author Beverly Cleary is a multiple award-winning author whose books have been translated into more than a dozen languages. For young readers who have been introduced to her many unforgettable characters, such as Beezus and Ramona, Henry and Ribsy, Ralph S. Mouse, Ellen Tebbits, Henry Huggins, Otis Spofford, and so many more, she is more of a national treasure. The better question is not whether children have read her books but how many of her books they have read. Her clever and funny stories deal with family and school issues that all children can understand, and though we are only mentioning a few here, Cleary has written more than 30 books for young readers to choose from.

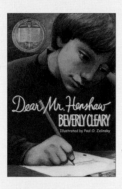

Newbery Award

Illustrated by Paul O. Zelinsky
Dear Mr. Henshaw

Leigh Botts is having a difficult time adjusting to his parent's divorce; he misses his father and he does not like being the new kid in town at all. A second-grade assignment to write a letter to his favorite author, Boyd Henshaw, starts a correspondence that brings Leigh to a place of acceptance and helps him build his self-confidence as well. The story is told primarily through letters between Leigh and Mr. Henshaw and then switches to diary entries as Leigh takes the author's advice to keep a journal.

1983 *144 pages* **HarperCollins**

The Mouse and the Motorcycle

When Ralph the mouse comes out from behind the knothole in the wall of his hotel-room home, he finds a toy motorcycle that one of the guests has left behind. Of course, he just has to take it for a spin, but when the ringing phone startles him, he and the bike end up in the waste basket. Luckily, the little boy who owns the toy comes back for it and finds both the toy and Ralph. He teaches Ralph how to ride the motorcycle, and a great new friendship begins.

1965 *208 pages* **HarperCollins**

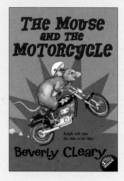

Ralph S. Mouse

There is trouble at the Mountain View Inn, the hotel where Ralph S. Mouse lives. First, Ralph's cousins come for a visit and wreck his motorcycle, and then they get noticed—so now there is talk of an exterminator. Ralph persuades his friend Ryan to take him to school, and at first Ralph is a big hit. But he really doesn't love running around in that maze all day, one of Ryan's classmates has broken his motorcycle, and what if the school hires an exterminator too? Ralph has to use his head to turn this situation into a more positive one.

1982 *192 pages* **HarperCollins**

Ramona and Her Father

Ramona's father has lost his job, and no one in the house on Klickitat Street is in a very good mood. Ramona just wants everybody to be happy, and so she tries to cheer everyone up. Being Ramona, this results in her sister Beezus calling her a pest, her cat not eating his food, her teacher accusing her of not having any manners, and her parents losing patience with her antics. But when her father tells her that no matter what, he wouldn't trade her for a million dollars, Ramona knows that everything will work out somehow.

1975 *192 pages* **HarperCollins**

Newbery Honor

Ramona Quimby, Age 8

Ramona has finally turned eight years old, and she feels like a really grown-up girl. She gets to help Beezus make dinner, she rides the bus all by herself, and she even tries hard to be nice to pesky Willa Jean. After all, she is in the third grade now—so why does everybody, especially her teachers, think that she is such a nuisance? Well, maybe she did accidentally squish a raw egg into her hair, and she did throw up in class, but still...Ramona has far too much pep and attitude to let those things get her down, and she does her best to fix the situation—in typical Ramona style.

1981 *208 pages* **HarperCollins**

Newbery Honor

The Artemis Fowl Series

If you prefer your criminal masterminds to be teenagers, and funnier than they are evil, then this is the series for you. The author describes this series as "*Die Hard* with fairies," but make no mistake—these fairies are not sweet little Tinkerbells. Think impish warlocks, vain sprites, flatulent pixies, and other members of the elite LEP, short for Lower Elements Police, or more tellingly, LEPrecon. Artemis Fowl's primary mission is to rebuild his family's fortune after the disappearance of his father, and there is nothing legal about how he goes about doing it in the eight books of this hilarious series. These books take the action around the world, including Siberia, France, Morocco, Ireland, and the fictional Lower Elements, to name only a few of the exotic locales. Both boys and girls will find much to love and laugh at as they follow Artemis Fowl's sinister and always highly amusing exploits and nefarious plots to acquire more and more money. These books are also available as graphic novels.

288–320 pages **Disney Hyperion**

Middle Grade Readers 8–12

This bestselling series put dystopian fiction on the map for today's young readers when the first book, *The Hunger Games,* was published in 2008. The novels take place in a land once known as North America, now called the nation of Panem, which consists of the Capitol and twelve outlying districts. Every year, all twelve districts are required to send one boy and one girl between the ages of twelve and eighteen to participate in the "Hunger Games," a vicious and frightening battle to the death, televised and watched by all of Panem. To the winner goes a life of safety and plenty for their family, but there can only be one winner, and for the losers death is a certainty. Katniss Everdeen competes for her district and in the process inspires a revolution. The Capitol is angry, and so is President Snow. This powerful series of books will have young readers racing through their reading and rooting for Katniss from the first page of *The Hunger Games* all the way through *Catching Fire* and to the thrilling conclusion in the third and final book, *Mockingjay.*
Note: these books are most appropriate for older or more mature readers.

The Hunger Games *(2008)*

Catching Fire *(2009)*

Mockingjay *(2010)*

384–400 pages **Scholastic Press/Scholastic Inc.**

The Dark Is Rising Sequence

This multiple-award-winning fantasy series incorporates Celtic and Welsh mythology and legends into a five-volume tale of good versus evil. It all begins in the first book, *Over Sea, Under Stone,* when the Drew children, Simon, Jane, and Barney, realize that there is something more to their great uncle than they knew. The mystery begins as they start to unravel the clues in an ancient treasure map they find in the attic. And so begins their quest to aid the forces of Light over the Darkness. As the series continues, the Drew children, Will Stanton, and a boy named Bran are joined together by destiny in a series of battles against the Dark. There are elements of the Arthurian tales here, and each book is filled with mystery and adventure as the children embark on quests, battle with crystal swords, search for golden grails, and meet a dog that can "see" the wind. This series is an excellent starting point for young readers who may not have read much in the fantasy genre, as there is a strong and beautifully written mystery tale behind all of the magic that will keep them coming back for more.

Over Sea, Under Stone *(1966)*

The Dark Is Rising *(1973)*

Greenwitch *(1974)*

The Grey King *(1975)*

Silver on the Tree *(1977)*

Newbery
Honor

Newbery
Award

148–288 pages **Margaret K. McElderry**

Karen Katz on the inspiration a new baby can bring...

When I was twenty, fresh out of art school, I wanted to be a children's book illustrator. I painted and drew and made lots of little storybooks. One book I made was for Maurice Sendak, asking him if I could take his illustration class. I never gave it to him. Then, life took me in many other directions. I went through an assortment of careers as a costume designer, a quilt maker, a fabric artist, and a graphic designer.

Twenty years later, my husband and I adopted a beautiful baby girl from Guatemala. My life suddenly changed and I knew I wanted to live my dream and create children's books. This tiny, little, adorable baby was all I needed to be totally inspired. Everything she did sparked a new idea for me. My first book, *Over The Moon*, was the story of my daughter's adoption. I was fortunate enough to be asked to write and illustrate it. My career was born. As my daughter grew, each new milestone brought me more inspiration. Forty-five books later, my daughter's baby DVDs and photos still inspire me.

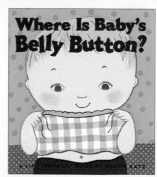

Along the way my inspiration has come from so many other sources...toys, greeting cards, napkins I've scribbled on, babies everywhere, Mexican ceramics, fabrics, Chagall, Matisse, children's art, primitive paintings, and many, many amazing authors and illustrators. To name just a few of my inspirations: Lucy Cousins, Sam Williams, Helen Oxenbury, Harriet Ziefert, Rosemary Wells, Mo Willems, Little Bear, Winnie-the-Pooh, Spot, Biscuit, Corduroy...the list goes on and on.

We never know where our inspiration will come from. I certainly didn't know that when this little baby was put into my arms she would inspire me to create the children's books I dreamt of when I was nineteen.

See individual listings for books by Karen Katz on pages 15, 238, and 247.

Illustrator Karen Katz

Robert Cormier
The Chocolate War

This dark novel deals with the issues of conformity and "mob rule" in a boys' school named Trinity High and is not recommended for those readers who cannot deal with disturbing subjects or who require a neat-and-happy ending. It is a brilliantly written and often searing portrayal of what it means to be an individual who chooses to "disturb the universe." Trinity is ruled by a school gang called the Virgils. When Jerry refuses to play along in a prank involving the school's annual chocolate sale, he suffers the dramatic consequences. *Note: for older or more mature readers.*

1974 *270 pages* **Alfred A. Knopf**

Cressida Cowell
How To Train Your Dragon

This fun series of books with black-and-white, childlike illustrations is just right for newly independent readers who like a heavy dose of silliness and humor with their adventure stories. Hiccup Horrendous Haddock III is not a natural hero, as he explains it—he has to work hard at it. Hiccup and his fellow young warriors-in-training must first pick out baby dragons from the dragon nursery and then begin to train them. Fortunately Hiccup speaks "Dragonese," and after a rather bumpy and quite comical training period, he succeeds in training his very stubborn dragon.

2003 *240 pages* **Little, Brown and Company**

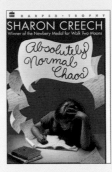

Absolutely Normal Chaos

Thirteen-year-old Mary Lou has to keep a journal as part of her summer English requirement, and she has plenty to write about. She has a boisterous family, and now her annoying seventeen-year-old cousin Carl Ray has come to stay with them. Her best friend has gone boy-crazy, and Alex, a cute classmate of hers, has been hanging around an awful lot. When a car accident leaves Carl Ray (who recently received an anonymous gift of money) in a coma, Mary Lou looks back at the journal she has been keeping and wonders how she was so unaware of what's been going on around her during a pretty eventful summer.

1990 *240 pages* **HarperCollins**

Bloomability

Thirteen-year-old Dinnie has lived in thirteen states in twelve years, moving every time her father sees what he mysteriously calls an "opportunity." Dinnie's father is on the road, her brother is in jail, and her sixteen-year-old sister is going to have a baby, when suddenly Dinnie is kidnapped (not literally, but that's how it feels). Her aunt and uncle take her to a private school in Switzerland where her uncle works. As Dinnie adjusts to her new school and new, international friends, she gains a better understanding of her world, her family, and the gift she has been given—realizing that she has been rescued from a family that was falling apart.

1999 *288 pages* **HarperCollins**

Chasing Redbird

Zinnia is the quiet middle child in a large family in rural Appalachia, who is having a difficult time dealing with the death of her beloved Aunt Jessie. She's also struggling to find and accept her own identity while trying to work out a few family mysteries that she doesn't fully understand. When she discovers an overgrown path at the edge of the family farm, she is determined to clear the path and see where it leads her. This sensitively told coming-of-age novel is perfect for middle-grade girls who are desperate to find their place in their family, their school, and the world at large.

1997 *272 pages* **HarperCollins**

Granny Torrelli Makes Soup

Rosie has always been best friends with Bailey, the boy who lives next door. It has never mattered to either of them that Bailey is blind—they've always managed to work around any difficulties that have come up—but now things have changed. Rosie and Bailey are attending different schools, and they are making new friends and having new experiences separately for the first time. And frankly, they are both feeling a little out of sorts and jealous of the other. Rosie shares her concern with her beloved Granny Torrelli, who proves to be not only a great cook, but also a good listener and advisor.

2003 *160 pages* **HarperCollins**

Multicultural

Newbery Award

Walk Two Moons

Told with a great deal of compassion, this novel about a very sensitive subject explores the effect on a family when the mother leaves. Salamanca Tree Hiddle is thirteen when her mother disappears, and she works through her grieving process during a cross-country trip with her slightly odd grandparents to retrace her mother's steps. As the tale unfolds, told as a story-within-a-story that Sal tells her grandparents on their journey, we begin to see the parallels between Sal's life and the story of her friend Phoebe Winterbottom, who also lost her mother. Along the way, Sal comes to terms with her feelings, is comforted by her Native American background, and finds the ability to move forward.

1994 *288 pages* **HarperCollins**

Newbery Honor

Illustrated by David Diaz

The Wanderer

This thrilling tale of a perilous sea voyage, which is part-mystery, part-adventure novel, and ultimately a coming-of-age story, could be compared to *The Perfect Storm*—if that book had a happier ending and was written for middle-grade readers. Thirteen-year-old Sophie convinces her adoptive parents to allow her to accompany her uncles and male cousins on a voyage from Connecticut to England, in a forty-five-foot sailboat, to visit her grandfather. Along the way, she proves her bravery to the all-male crew under both dangerous and life-threatening circumstances. Through her journal, we learn more about this remarkable, sometimes dreamy, other times stubborn, girl and her complicated family history.

2000 *320 pages* **HarperCollins**

Middle Grade Readers 8–12

Christopher Paul Curtis

Newbery Award

Coretta Scott King Award

Bud, Not Buddy

Bud is an African American teenager during the middle of the Great Depression. Bud is convinced that his father is jazz musician Herman E. Calloway, named in a flyer he finds in his suitcase. That's not all that he carries with him; he also has the book he's writing, called *Bud Caldwell's Rules and Things for Having a Funner Life and Making a Better Liar Out of Yourself*, which interjects a great deal of humor into his story. Along the way, Bud has to learn to fend for himself and deal with racism, the privations of the Depression, his own fear, and near-constant hunger. He also discovers how jazz music may provide both the family and self-respect he is seeking.

1999 *256 pages* **Delacorte Press**

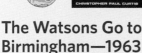

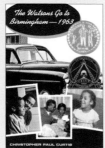

Coretta Scott King Award

Multicultural

Newbery Honor

The Watsons Go to Birmingham—1963

Kenny works hard in school and tries to live up to his parents' expectations, but his sister is pretty eccentric, and his older brother, Byron, is steadily working his way towards juvenile delinquency. Kenny's parents decide that the time has come to bring Byron to Birmingham for the summer. This book deals frankly with racism and the careful planning required for a black family traveling south in 1963, as they most likely will not be able to get food or lodging on the road once they pass into the southern states. What the reader knows—that the family doesn't—is the history-in-the-making they are about to drive into.

1995 *224 pages* **Delacorte Press**

Roald Dahl

Illustrated by Quentin Blake

The BFG

The BFG is a lovable Big Friendly Giant, who, in Dahl's inimitable style, speaks a language all his own that children will have no problem understanding. The other giants are mean and eat children regularly, but the BFG is a vegetarian of sorts; he doesn't eat "human beans," only the rather disgusting "snozzcumbers." The BFG snatches young Sophie from the orphanage she lives in, because she sees him blowing sweet dreams into the ears of children. Sophie and the BFG then come up with an ingenious plan to vanquish the evil child-eating giants. Quentin Blake's illustrations add humor and whimsy to this magical tale.

1982 *208 pages* **Puffin**

Illustrated by Quentin Blake

Charlie and the Chocolate Factory

Charlie Bucket is a poor boy who lives near Willie Wonka's chocolate factory and is lucky enough to win one of five golden tickets that will allow him inside to meet Mr. Wonka and see all the marvels that the factory holds. Children love the fact that, in Dahl's strange and funny fantasies, truly evil people always meet their demise in the most literally appropriate and funny manner, and in this case revenge is actually sweet. Within these pages, children will meet the Oompa Loompas, the spoiled Veruca Salt, and the gluttonous Augustus Gloop. Laugh-out-loud funny from start to finish, this story may require eating some chocolate along the way.

1964 *155 pages* **Puffin**

Illustrated by Lane Smith
James and the Giant Peach

When reading Dahl's stories, embracing the ridiculous is required. When James Henry Trotter's parents are killed in an unfortunate rhinoceros accident, he must live with his vile Aunt Sponge and Aunt Spiker. When James receives a bag of magic crystals that he is told can end his life of misery, things start to look up—until James accidentally spills those crystals on an old peach tree in the yard. When that tree grows one really enormous peach, James climbs inside and rolls away to a life filled with adventure and new and unusual friends. This book begs to be read aloud, or for independent readers, again and again.

1961 *144 pages* **Alfred A. Knopf**

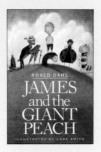

Illustrated by Quentin Blake
Matilda

Matilda may only be four years old, but she is already a genius. Now if only all the adults in her life weren't so stupid. She escapes her unhappy home life by going to the library, where she discovers literature and teaches herself to read and finds a supporter in Miss Honey, a teacher at her new school, who actually understands her. Readers will be rooting for Matilda as she extracts her hilarious revenge on all of the people in her world who have wronged her. In Dahl's books, the evildoers are vanquished, usually in as disgusting a manner as possible—which, rather than frightening young readers, appeals to their sense of justice.

1988 *240 pages* **Viking**

Illustrated by Quentin Blake
The Witches

In this clever tale, the Grand High Witch has a fiendish plan to eliminate all the children in England, and our hero, a young orphan living with his wise grandmother, overhears her plans to turn the children into mice —and then bring out the mousetraps. Fortunately, his grandmother knows all about witches and how to outsmart them, but before he has a chance to speak with her, he is turned into a mouse himself. Will he manage to outsmart the witches before they complete their master plan? Of course he will, and readers will be laughing all the way through this charming and funny story.

1983 *208 pages* **Farrar, Straus & Giroux**

Karen Cushman
Catherine, Called Birdy

Told through the diary entries of a young noblewoman in medieval England, this historical novel accurately portrays the life and times of Birdy, who is fourteen years old in the year 1290. We learn many fascinating facts about medieval life at court, from religious practices to rituals of courtship and marriage. Birdy keeps turning down the suitors her father chooses for her, and as a result nearly ends up wed to a much older nobleman. Readers will be fascinated by the details of her life and how much of her future is not entirely within her control. There is also an extensive afterword about the time period in which the novel is set.

1994 *176 pages* **Clarion Books**

Newbery Honor

Marguerite de Angeli
The Door in the Wall

The term *door in the wall* is a metaphor for trying your best until you find a way to overcome the obstacle that confronts you. This novel, set in England in the Middle Ages, features a boy who hopes to become a knight like his father. However, he becomes ill and loses the use of his legs, and when both of his parents are called away, he is abandoned by the family servants who fear the plague has struck him. He is rescued and cared for by Brother Luke, taught to swim and carve wood and eventually called upon to save the castle by use of his wits.

1949 *128 pages* **Doubleday**

Newbery Award

Antoine de Saint-Exupéry
The Little Prince

This story about love, loneliness, and the meaning of life could be off-putting for middle-grade readers if it were not so beautifully written and illustrated. This book is commonly read in classroom settings because it is also a great tool for teaching the meaning of allegory and metaphor. The Little Prince appears to a man whose aircraft has crashed into the desert, and they begin a long discussion about life on Earth compared to the Little Prince's home planet, called B-612, different ways of seeing and understanding, and knowing the truth in your heart. This is a moving and beautiful story that children understand intuitively.

1943 *96 pages* **Harcourt Children's Books**

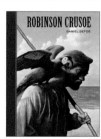

Daniel Defoe
Illustrated by Scott McKowen
Robinson Crusoe

Written in 1719, this classic saga of adventure, kidnapping, pirates, cannibals, and survival has certainly stood the test of time. Robinson Crusoe lived a turbulent life prior to becoming the lone survivor of a shipwreck that lands him on an uninhabited island with only the captain's dog and two cats for company. He struggles to overcome his despair and is forced to use his wits to develop the skills he needs to survive. Before he is rescued, Crusoe saves a man from a tribe of cannibals, and they become friends and companions. This book demonstrates the virtues of patience, hard work, and ingenuity, and the courage it takes to survive under the most difficult circumstances.

1719 *304 pages* **Sterling Classics**

Meindert DeJong
Pictures by Maurice Sendak
The Wheel on the School

When Lina asks her teacher why the storks no longer come to Shora to nest as they used to, the simple query turns into a quest that mobilizes an entire Dutch village to take action. The teacher instructs the children to consider why the storks never come—because if you ask the question, you can discover answers and begin to make changes. The students do exactly that and by so doing inspire the entire community to take action. Sendak's simple black-and-white illustrations elegantly illuminate the easy-to-read story of townspeople who worked together until their dream came true.

1954 *312 pages* **HarperCollins**

Newbery Award

Julia DeVillers and Jennifer Roy
Trading Faces

This first book in a trilogy about twin sisters Emma and Payton Mills follows a predictable plot device that never goes out of style—identical twins who switch places—made even more fun by the fact that the authors themselves are identical twins. The twins are excited to begin seventh grade in a new school. Things are going along nicely for both girls when Payton suffers an embarrassing burrito-related mishap at lunch, and Emma comes to her aid by temporarily (she thinks) switching places with her. Filled with humor and teen drama, this case of mistaken identity is sure to be a hit with middle-grade girls.

2008 *320 pages* **Aladdin**

Illustrated by Tony DiTerlizzi
The Spiderwick Chronicles

Since they are written in the form of "as told to" novels, the authors themselves play a role in this series of books that begins with a letter left at a tiny bookstore for the authors by the Grace children—Mallory and twins Simon and Jared—telling of their move to the Spiderwick Estate and their discovery of a Faerie world they never knew existed. These charming, small-format books are lavishly illustrated with fairies, goblins, trolls, dwarves, and many other creatures the likes of which the Grace children could never have imagined. There are eight books in the series and an additional four books, such as field guides, advice on the care and feeding of sprites, and others, that accompany the main series. This series is perfect for boys and girls—these are not your sweet little fairies, and there is plenty of mystery, action, and adventure to keep readers involved in the stories of Spiderwick Estate.

2003 *128-142 pages*
Simon & Schuster Books for Young Readers

Illustrated by Bagram Ibatoulline

The Miraculous Journey of Edward Tulane

This is a timeless story about love, loss, and learning to love again. Edward Tulane is a china rabbit owned by a little girl named Abilene. He's a vain little guy, used to being pampered, until the day he is accidentally dropped overboard on an ocean voyage. Fate takes Edward from the ocean into a fisherman's net, then to a hobo, and then to a dying child. He is broken and repaired, and finally ends up, a bit battered but with a heart that has grown bigger and softer with every new human he has come in contact with. The sepia tones and full-color illustrations are both detailed and expressive and serve the soft nature of the text well.

2006 *228 pages* **Candlewick Press**

Because of Winn-Dixie

Newbery Honor

Ten-year-old Opal is at the Winn-Dixie grocery store when a big, old, stinky stray dog creates a ruckus in the produce department. Then the dog smiles at her— really smiles—and before she has time to think, she claims the dog is hers, is named Winn-Dixie (she has to think fast), and must have gotten into the store by mistake. With the help of Winn-Dixie, Opal begins to adjust to life in a new town with her preacher father and without her mother, who abandoned the family. As she begins to make new friends and deal with her sadness and loss, she comes to a place of acceptance—all thanks to a dog who really can smile.

2000 *184 pages* **Candlewick Press**

Illustrated by Yoko Tanaka

The Magician's Elephant

When Peter Augustus Duchene is sent to the market to buy fish and bread, he makes a fateful decision—he goes to the fortune teller's booth instead and spends his money to ask if his sister, who he believes to be dead, is still living. The shocking answer he receives, that she still lives and that an elephant will lead him to her, leaves him confused but also jumpstarts a series of miraculous events. That night, a magician appearing in town accidentally conjures an elephant that crashes through the roof of the theater, killing a socialite. So begins DiCamillo's mystery/fable of longing, hope, and compassion, illustrated with Tanaka's softly drawn, magical black-and-white images.

2009 *208 pages* **Candlewick Press**

Illustrated by Timothy Basil Ering

The Tale of Despereaux

Newbery Award

This novel in four parts is reminiscent of the best aspects of fairy tales. We meet four characters who are outcasts, and each strives for something that is beyond what is expected of him or her. Despereaux is a little mouse with big ears who falls madly in love with a princess. Princess Pea appreciates Despereaux, despite her father's hatred of rodents. Chiaroscuro is a rat that craves light and soup. Miggery Sow is a peasant girl who is a bit slow and hard of hearing, who dreams of becoming a princess. DiCamillo ties these four stories together neatly and, combined with Ering's delicate pencil drawings, shares valuable lessons about love, hope, and forgiveness.

2003 *272 pages* **Candlewick Press**

The Tiger Rising

Rob Horton is a sixth grader who has both literally and figuratively locked his feelings away in his suitcase after the death of his mother. Rob and his father have moved to Florida, hoping for a fresh start, but they are both so full of grief that it affects everything around them. Two things begin the healing process for Rob: he meets another new student who also feels like an outcast, and he discovers a caged tiger behind the hotel. The animal represents the opportunity for freedom—literally for the tiger and freedom from grief for Rob—as Rob allows himself to get close to someone again.

2001 *128 pages* **Candlewick Press**

Franklin W. Dixon
The Hardy Boys Series

In 1927 the world was introduced to Frank and Joe Hardy, teenage brothers and amateur detectives who solve mysteries, and the serialized mystery format has been going strong ever since. Over the years, the original twenty-five books have been revised, reissued, and rewritten to keep up with the times, and several more modern iterations have been created in paperback formats as well. For the purists, however, there is nothing like the original mysteries in the "collect them all" hardcover formats. Here's a fun fact for fans of the series: the author's name, Franklin Dixon, is a pseudonym—and since their inception, the books have been ghostwritten by a number of authors. With over a million copies of these books sold every year, Frank and Joe continue to introduce young boys and girls to the world of crime solving.

1927 *192 pages* **Grosset & Dunlap**

Chris d'Lacey
The Fire Within

Contrary to the cover, this book is not all fire-breathing dragons and epic battles—though it does possess a fair amount of dragon lore. College student David Rain rents a room from a woman named Liz and meets her eleven-year-old daughter, Lucy, who creates and sells clay dragons that seem to possess magical powers. When Lucy creates a special dragon for David named Gadzooks, he is hesitant to accept it, but when he does, it inspires him to write a story, which provides the reader with a story-within-a-story plot. David's story doesn't end well and has a potentially disastrous effect on Gadzooks—because Lucy's special dragons die if they are not loved.

2001 *352 pages* **Orchard Books**

William Pene du Bois
The Twenty-One Balloons

This brilliant novel mixes the best elements of fantastical storytelling and adventure in one award-winning package. Professor Sherman is a retired schoolteacher, bored with his life, who sets out on an exciting and solitary mission: to circumnavigate the globe by himself in a hot air balloon. Unfortunately, he is forced to land on the island of Krakatoa, where he meets a very unusual society of people. The descriptions of the inhabitants, their twenty-day months, and their gourmet food-based government will entrance readers, as will their escape with the Professor from the island. In the end, the professor must explain how he is discovered on a raft powered by over twenty balloons when he took off with only one.

1947 *192 pages* **Viking**

Newbery Award

Jeanne DuPrau
The City of Ember

This book is the first novel in the four-book post-apocalyptic "Books of Ember" series, and for readers who love dystopian fiction, this series will keep them turning pages from the first book all the way through the fourth. Ember is an underground city that is slowly running out of both supplies and the power needed to keep it running. The main characters, Lina Mayfleet and her friend Doon Harrow, must decode a message and follow a series of clues left by the original builders of Ember in order to find a way to save Ember and safely exist in the outside world—a world they never knew existed.

2003 *270 pages* **Random House Children's Books**

Illustrated by Quentin Blake and N. M. Bodecker

The Half Magic Series

This well-loved, classic series of seven books has been a middle-grade favorite from the original publication of *Half Magic* in 1954 through the subsequent publications of *Knight's Castle, Magic by the Lake, The Time Garden, Magic or Not?, The Well-Wishers,* and *Seven-Day Magic,* which completed the series in 1962. The new editions feature cover art by Quentin Blake, but the wonderful interior art by the original illustrator, N. M. Bodecker, remains the same. In this series, we follow the adventures of Katherine, Mark, Jane, and Martha, who find a magical coin that grants half-wishes—which causes some very funny consequences until the children learn to double their wishes in order to have them granted in their entirety. The subsequent books follow the original characters and their own children through further magical adventures that include meeting Robin Hood and Ivanhoe, "thyme" travel, and so much more. The books are filled with clever wordplay, hilarious situations, and a whole lot of magic, and today's readers will love them as much as their parents and grandparents did.

1954 *208 pages* **Harcourt Children's Books**

Walter Farley
Illustrated by Keith Ward
The Black Stallion Series

Walter Farley's series about perhaps the most famous fictional horse in children's literature began with the 1941 publication of *The Black Stallion* and was followed by thirty-three additional books about the black stallion, his descendants, and other horses as well. For horse-loving readers, this series is the gold standard. Each book is well written, with its own compelling story, and all lovingly portray both the horses and the humans they come in contact with. Each book stands on its own, and though there are some continuities from book to book, they can be read in order or independently of each other. The series begins with an ill-fated ocean voyage from India to England, where Alec Ramsay meets Black, a wild horse. When the ship eventually founders, leaving Alec and Black on a desert island together, they experience adventures on the island before they are eventually rescued. If the young reader in your family loves horses, this series is guaranteed to become a favorite.

1941 *288 pages* **Random House Children's Books**

Louise Fitzhugh
Harriet the Spy

Harriet wants to become a famous author. In order to do that, she needs to become an astute observer and learn to understand why people do the things they do—and she has to write everything she observes in her notebook. In other words, Harriet has to become a spy. Every day, she follows the same "spy route" and compiles information, bluntly stating the facts as she sees them. When her notebook accidentally ends up in the hands of her classmates, feelings are hurt and Harriet becomes an outcast. Readers will relate to Harriet because she is a very real character; she's flawed, and she makes mistakes, just like they do.

2000 *304 pages* **Delacorte Press**
(Originally published in 1964 by Harper & Row)

Middle Grade Readers 8–12

Illustrated by Louis Slobodkin

The Moffats

Meet the Moffats, four children and their hard-working, widowed mother, who live in a simpler time in the village of Cranbury. The oldest, Sylvie, is very clever but not terribly responsible. Twelve-year-old Joey considers himself the man of the house—sometimes. Janey looks at the world in a rather upside-down way, and the littlest Moffat, Rufus, seems to get into the biggest trouble. Children will love reading about the Moffat children's exploits, like accidentally getting stuck in a bread box at the local delicatessen. These curious mistakes and adventures never result in any harm or danger, though they do provide plenty of laughs and general silliness.

1941 *224 pages* **Harcourt Children's Books**

Illustrated by Louis Slobodkin

The Hundred Dresses

Dealing with bullying is not a new issue for children's books. In this lovingly illustrated and sensitively told story, we meet Wanda Petronski, a recent refugee from Poland, who is poor, shabbily dressed, has a "funny" name, and lives in the "wrong" part of town. Her tormentors in school are Peggy and Maddie, who tease Wanda when she says she has one hundred dresses and sixty pairs of shoes. When Peggy and Maddie want to make amends, they find out that Wanda's family has moved to a place where they will not be shunned for their origins. This book is an excellent tool for teaching the negative power of words spoken without thought.

1944 *88 pages* **Harcourt Children's Books**

Illustrated by Edward Ardizzone

Pinky Pye

Since 1958, this tale of a plucky, stray black kitten who adopts the Pye family has been a regular on school reading lists and a favorite among children. When the Pye family goes on vacation for the summer, they discover a black kitten with one white paw on their doorstep. Though they already have a dog named Ginger and a cat named Gracie, when little Pinky joins the family, everything changes. This kitten isn't afraid of anything, she boxes with Gracie, and she can even type. In this charmingly illustrated book, the children decide to help Pinky type out her story of how she came to live with them and the adventures they have together.

1958 *272 pages* **Harcourt Children's Book**

Sid Fleischman
Illustrated by Peter Sís

The Whipping Boy

The prince and pauper role-reversal is common enough in literature, but in this case it is executed perfectly. In the 1700s, the tradition in royal households was that only the king could whip a prince for an infraction. But since kings were not always available to administer the punishments, each prince had a "whipping boy," who was flogged in his stead for any misdeeds committed. In this case, the royal in question is named Prince Brat (and he is one), and his whipping boy is the clever peasant Jemmy, who plans to run away. Prince Brat beats him to it and takes him along on a swashbuckling adventure in which Jemmy's skills far outdistance Prince Brat's.

1986 *96 pages* **Greenwillow Books**

The Ranger's Apprentice Series

This popular fantasy series from Australian author John Flanagan, which has been published in sixteen countries, includes twelve books. The tale is set in the medieval fantasy world of Araluen and follows the adventures of a young orphan named Will, who must choose between becoming an apprentice Ranger (whose goal is to keep Araluen safe from invaders, traitors, and other threats to the kingdom) or a life working in the fields. Realizing his options are limited, Will chooses to join the Rangers, a sort of unofficial police force. Will is joined in his adventures by his friend, Horace, and his mentor, Halt, as he begins to learn the skills required to become a Ranger—which include camouflage, knife throwing and fighting, weaponry, and the art of seen and unseen movements. The series follows Will's progress as a Ranger's apprentice with new and perilous adventures (with humans and more fantastical creatures as well) in each book.

2005 *272 pages* **Puffin**

Ian Fleming
Illustrated by John Burningham
Chitty Chitty Bang Bang

This was Ian Fleming's only book for children, but if you are going to write only one book for children, this well-loved bestseller will do nicely. The very eccentric Pott family certainly would not buy an ordinary car, and Chitty Chitty Bang Bang is anything but ordinary. The car drives, of course, but it also flies, and floats, and doesn't even need a driver. This enchanting, magical tale of the adventures of the Pott family as they try to nab a notorious gang of robbers—with lots of help from Chitty Chitty Bang Bang—will have readers laughing and cheering all the way through the book.

1964 *160 pages* **Random House Children's Books**

Victoria Forester
The Girl Who Could Fly

Piper McCloud is the daughter of conservative farmers who are concerned with fitting in, and she can fly. They home school her and keep her away from others, so Piper is lonely. One day she meets Dr. Letitia Hellion, who offers Piper a chance to come to her school, a school for children like Piper who have special powers. Soon she realizes that things are not what they appear to be. The evil Dr. Hellion's real mission is to remove the students' special powers by altering their DNA. What happens next will have readers anxiously turning the pages as they race to the ending of this tale about friendship and embracing your authentic self.

2008 *352 pages* **Feiwel & Friends**

Middle Grade Readers 8–12

Hilary Knight on the importance of "three"…

THREE is a great number—in life, literature, and learning, be they little pigs, kittens, or blind mice, in my particular case they would include:

1. My father, CLAYTON KNIGHT, born in Rochester, NY. Studied art in Chicago under the eye of his idol George Bellows, served in World Wars I and II, was famous for his aviation paintings and his comic strip, "Hall of Fame of the Air."

2. My mother, KATHARINE STURGES, born in Chicago, studied art in Japan in 1917 (while my father was flying planes over Germany). She did picture books for Chicago's Volland Publishers, then moved to New York to work in fashion and magazine designs throughout the 1920s and 30s, an era unmatched for style and originality.

3. My teacher, REGINALD MARSH, at Manhattan's Art Students League, who taught me what I had not absorbed from my parents. (What I had absorbed was, for instance, my father's love of hand lettering for his book jackets and cartoon strips; and my mother's Asian influences: in her gold leaf-embellished painting, her exotic and fantastic birds wore earrings!) Reginald Marsh gave me strict but stretchable anatomy lessons that certainly helped me send ELOISE skibble down the Plaza's hallways.

My three favorite illustrators (all from my family's library):

1. Maurice Boulet de Monvel—my visual interpretation for Eloise comes from his many books of mischievous enfants in the late 1800s.

2. Edmund Dulac—his dense, detailed watercolors for fairy tales from China to the Middle East to icy seas of Scandinavia.

3. Ernest Shepard—anything and everything he drew, with a line true, effortless, and hilarious.

See individual listings for books illustrated by Hilary Knight on pages 81 and 229.

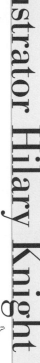

Illustrator Hilary Knight

This magical fantasy begins with the story of twelve-year-old Meggie Dolchart as she discovers that her father Mortimer, a bookbinder, has a magical gift—when he reads aloud, he is able to bring people and items in the books he reads into the real world. Meggie learns that when she was three years old, her father read a book called *Inkheart* aloud to her mother. Suddenly, Meggie's mother and her two cats disappeared into the book, and three villains from the book entered the real world. When those men come back to find Meggie and her father, nothing will ever be the same. There are two sequels to this book, *Inkspell* and *Inkdeath,* which continue and conclude Meggie's magical adventures.

Inkheart *(2003)*

Inkspell *(2005)*

Inkdeath *(2008)*

535-704 pages **Chicken House/Scholastic Inc.**

The Thief Lord

Twelve-year-old Prosper and his brother flee Hamburg after the death of their mother. Their mother often spoke to them of the wonders of Venice, and so they head there. Once there, they fall in with a gang of street urchins and orphans who are cared for by a Robin Hood-like figure who claims to steal from the rich to care for the gang. When the boys' Aunt Esther hires a detective to look for them, the action increases, with mysterious missions and chase scenes throughout Venice. Meanwhile, a soft-hearted detective discovers that the "Thief Lord" is actually a man from a wealthy family. Filled with magic and nonstop action, this mystery will keep readers riveted until the surprising and stunning ending.

2002 *352 pages* **Chicken House/Scholastic Inc.**

Paula Fox
Illustrated by Eros Keith
The Slave Dancer

In this powerful, historically accurate novel, readers will get a first-hand look at the horrors of the slave trade. In 1840, Jessie is thirteen years old and running an errand for his mother when he is kidnapped on the New Orleans docks and taken aboard a slave ship. Jessie hates everything about the ship, even the slaves themselves. One night there is a shipwreck, and the only survivors are Jessie and a young slave named Ras. Parents should be cautioned that this book deals frankly with the realities of the slave trade—the most difficult passages are also the most historically accurate—which may be a tough subject for sensitive readers.

2001 *192 pages* **Atheneum/Richard Jackson Books**

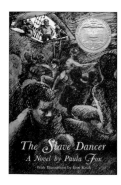

Newbery Award

Neil Gaiman

Illustrated by Dave McKean

Coraline

This complex, modern horror story may be too frightening for younger readers but will prove to be a thrilling read for those old enough to handle the drama, suspense, and sinister characters. Coraline is an intelligent and resourceful girl. The mystery begins when Coraline finds a door that leads to a parallel "Other World." Everything looks like her own home but better: more toys and games, and another mother and father, just like her parents but with buttons instead of eyes. The Other Mother offers Coraline a chance to stay in the Other World forever if Coraline will allow buttons to be sewn into her eyes as well. This book is also available as a graphic novel.

2002 *176 pages* **HarperCollins**

Illustrated by Dave McKean

The Graveyard Book

This award-winning ghost story from the master of middle-grade thrillers has everything you would expect and something you might not—an entire cast of benevolent and even loving ghosts. When a family in England is stabbed to death, the youngest child slips away and ends up in a neighboring graveyard. The ghosts who reside in the graveyard adopt him and name him Nobody Owens (Bod for short). Bod has many adventures, both in and out of the graveyard, with his mentor, Silas, a character who is neither living nor dead. As Bod grows up, he will learn Silas' secret, and confront the fact that his own family's killer is still looking for him.

2008 *320 pages* **HarperCollins**

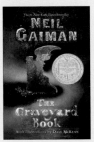

Newbery Award

Ruth Stiles Gannett

Illustrated by Ruth Chrisman Gannett

The three books in this enchanting series are narrated by a boy whose father, Elmer Elevator, rescues a baby dragon and describe the friendship and further adventures that result from Elmer's kindness and bravery. This charming series also features the stylized art of the author's stepmother, which succeeds in offering frequent, detailed black-and-white illustrations to move the plot forward. It all begins when Elmer befriends a stray cat who turns out to have magical powers. The cat asks Elmer to help rescue a baby dragon that fell from a cloud and bruised its wing and is now being held captive on Wild Island. How Elmer accomplishes the rescue, by the use of such everyday items as lollipops, rubber bands, and a comb, will captivate young readers. In the second book, *Elmer and the Dragon*, the reader is treated to more adventures of Elmer and the dragon on various exotic islands. In *The Dragons of Blueland* (which can be read as a stand-alone novel), Elmer is asked by the dragon to help him save his family from dragon hunters. All three of these books are perfect for chapter-a-night read-alouds and can also be easily read by newly independent readers.

My Father's Dragon *(1948)*

Elmer and the Dragon *(1950)*

The Dragons of Blueland *(1951)*

96–112 pages **Random House Children's Books**

Jean Craighead George

Middle Grade Readers 8–12

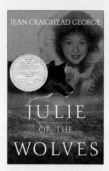

Julie of the Wolves

Newbery Award

This is a riveting tale of a young Inuit girl forced to learn to live on her own, who joins a wolf pack in the arctic tundra. Miyax has learned the ways of her people from her beloved father Kapugen. When she attends school, her name is changed to Julie, and the only thing about school she likes is her pen pal in San Francisco. As life in the village becomes threatening, Julie runs away, hoping to get to San Francisco. Readers will be inspired by Julie's ability to survive in the wild and adapt to life in the wolf pack and the choices she must make when she returns to civilization.

1972 *192 pages* **HarperCollins**

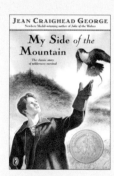

Newbery Honor

My Side of the Mountain

Thirteen-year-old New Yorker Sam Gribley is fed up with the world he lives in and runs off to live on his grandfather's rustic mountain property. He begins his journey with a penknife, a ball of cord, a flint and steel, and about forty dollars. Readers will be amazed by what it really takes to survive in the wild, as Sam makes fire without matches, catches his own food, creates a shelter, befriends animals to ward off loneliness, and trains a peregrine falcon (named Frightful) to hunt. Sam survives blizzards, hunters, his own fear, and all that nature can throw at him, with a great deal of humor mixed into his more exciting exploits.

1959 *172 pages* **Puffin**

Fred Gipson
Old Yeller

Set in a small Texas town just after the Civil War, this now-classic tale of a boy and his dog has compelling characters, a historical setting, a loving family, and a heroic dog. Travis is fourteen years old when the story begins. When a stray yellow dog steals the family's meat, Travis wants to kill him—until the dog rescues his little brother from an angry bear. From that point on, Travis and Old Yeller are best friends. The ending is perhaps one of the most heartbreakingly tragic in children's literature: Old Yeller is bitten by a rabid wolf, and Travis must kill his loyal friend to prevent his suffering.

1956 *192 pages* **HarperCollins**

Newbery Honor

Kenneth Grahame
Illustrated by Michael Hague
The Wind in the Willows

This classic children's book was first published in 1908 and has been one of the best-loved children's stories ever since. This version, with the exquisitely detailed paintings of Michael Hague, has been a family favorite for more than thirty years. Readers meet the main characters, Mole, Rat, Toad, and Badger, and many other animals, in the woods near Mole End, and follow them on their woodland adventures. Each chapter contains a complete adventure, which makes this a perfect chapter-before-bedtime reader. This loving story begs to be read aloud, and the language is also appropriate for newly independent readers.

1908 *216 pages* **Henry Holt**

Roderick Gordon and Brian Williams

This four-book series features an archaeological mystery and an alternate society theme, as readers follow the adventures of fourteen-year-old Will Burrows, his archaeologist father, and his friend Chester. Will's family is dysfunctional; his father is an eccentric obsessed with exploring abandoned tunnels and other local archaeological sites, and Will is a bit of a teen outcast himself, pale with white hair and not many friends. When his father goes missing, it's up to Will to use what he has learned about archaeology to find him, and with Chester at his side he enters a subterranean tunnel that leads to a strange, parallel underground world called The Colony. Will is confronted by people who look like him and claim to be his relatives. Can Will find his father and return to life above ground— and who are these people who claim to be his real family? As Will struggles to survive, issues of identity and sibling rivalry, as well as an ongoing mystery, will keep readers involved, and the cliff-hanger ending will send them off and running for the next book in the series.

Tunnels (2007)

Deeper (2009)

Freefall (2010)

Closer (2011)

496–672 pages **Chicken House/Scholastic Inc.**

René Goscinny

Illustrated by Albert Uderzo

The Asterix Series

Created in France in 1959, this series of thirty-four graphic novels has been translated into more than one hundred languages, including English in 1961. The series focuses on a village of ancient Gauls, who are preoccupied with resisting a Roman invasion. The main characters are Asterix, who is intelligent and shrewd, his cohort Obelix, who, having fallen into cauldron of magic potions as a baby, has superhuman strength, and Dogmatix, Obelix's dog. In the course of the series, they have many adventures, drink magic potions, visit many countries, interact with Cleopatra and Julius Caesar, and much, much more. The books are loaded with dark humor and some not-so-subtle political references and are perfect for readers who like a lot of humor and action in their reading, as well as reluctant readers who may feel less intimidated by the comic-book-style graphic novel format.

1959 *48 pages* **Orion**

Middle Grade Readers 8–12

Tim Green
Rivals

This fast-paced baseball-themed novel has all the suspense and action of a major-league game and a whole lot of intrigue as well. Josh is thrilled when his baseball team makes the playoffs. Not only is this good for Josh, it also means a trip to Cooperstown, home of the Baseball Hall of Fame. But when an injury sidelines him for a game or two, he begins to suspect foul play is involved. Josh and his friend Benji develop a plan to expose the truth—but there's a lot more than a playoff championship at stake.

2010 *272 pages* **Harper**

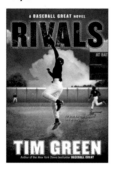

John Grisham
Theodore Boone: Kid Lawyer

Theo Boone is thirteen, and while has hasn't taken the bar yet, he does spend all his free time hanging out at the courthouse, giving his friends legal advice and watching *Perry Mason* reruns. Theo finds himself in a complicated situation when an illegal immigrant who has witnessed a murder comes to him with evidence that the person on trial is guilty. Theo may be only thirteen, but he has to make a very adult decision, and it might not be what readers will expect. This legal thriller will open up a lot of discussion among middle-schoolers about doing the right thing in a tough situation.

2010 *263 pages* **Dutton**

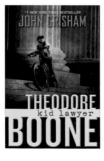

The Homework Machine

Fifth-grader Brenton is a computer whiz; in other words, he's a nerd. The three classmates in his school workgroup don't believe Brenton when he tells them he has invented a machine that can do their homework perfectly, until he demonstrates it to them. At that point, Judy, Kelsey, and Sam form an alliance—each for their own reasons. The story is told in flashbacks, through police interviews with the students, their families, and school officials, though why the police are involved is not revealed until the end. This story raises questions about family, ethics, and integrity in a way that is easily understood by middle-grade readers.

2006 *160 pages*
Simon & Schuster Books for Young Readers

The Talent Show

Cape Bluff, Kansas is demolished by a huge tornado, and the school principal has decided that in order to help raise both morale and money to rebuild, the school should hold a talent show. The description of the tornado is vividly told and will be as thrilling to readers as the show auditions are funny. On the night of the show, yet another tornado hits, taking the electrical power with it. The show must go on and it does, with quite surprising results. This well-told story of a community pulling together for a cause, and the conclusion that sometimes people exceed our expectations, offers valuable lessons to young readers.

2010 *224 pages*
Simon & Schuster Books for Young Readers

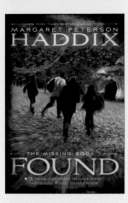

The Missing Series

Thirteen-year-old Jonah and his friend Chip have always known they were adopted, and it's never been a big deal to either of them—until now. Both boys begin receiving some strange and frightening letters with cryptic messages, such as "You are one of the missing." Jonah, his sister, Katherine, and Chip try to untangle the mystery, but things start to get even more ominous when they discover the FBI is involved. This suspense-filled series will keep readers guessing just how Jonah, Katherine, and Chip will survive being pulled in different directions by very powerful forces.

2008 *320 pages*
Simon & Schuster Books for Young Readers

The Shadow Children Series

Imagine a world where families are allowed only two children. Illegal third children, known as "shadow children," must live in hiding. Should they be found, there is only one punishment: death. Luke is such a child—and as a result he has been hidden his whole life. He's never had a birthday party or even a friend. Confined to the attic, his only view of the outside world is through an air vent. One day he sees the face of a girl in another house's window after her family of four has left the house. Is it possible that he is not the only hidden child? This series, including titles *Among the Hidden*, *Among the Impostors*, and *Among the Betrayed*, poses many questions for readers about totalitarian regimes, defying authority, and the value of living freely.

1998 *160 pages*
Simon & Schuster Books for Young Readers

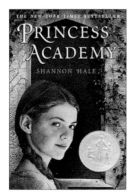

Newbery Honor

Shannon Hale
Princess Academy

Don't let the title fool you—though this book is about a Princess Academy, it's also all about "girl power," and our heroine, Miri, is no shrinking violet. When the king announces that the prince will choose a bride from her village and Miri is forced to attend the Princess Academy to learn how to be a princess, she agrees to go—reluctantly. It is her courage and spunk, plus her ability to speak and understand a mysterious silent language called "quarry speak," that turn Miri into a leader among the girls. As to who the prince chooses... you'll have to read this unusual coming-of-age tale to find out.

2005 *320 pages* **Bloomsbury Children's Books**

The House of Dies Drear

Thirteen-year-old Thomas is fascinated by the old house his father has bought; it has a history as a stop on the Underground Railroad, it's filled with secret passageways, and it may be the site of buried treasure. The fact that two slaves and the abolitionist Dies Drear were murdered there just adds to the mystery—even if it is a little creepy. As strange and sometimes frightening things begin to happen, Thomas starts to piece together the mystery of the house's history. This is a dramatic story of a black family living in a house that played a key role in the abolition of slavery, and it has an astounding and unexpected ending.

1970 *256 pages* **Aladdin**

M.C. Higgins, the Great

When Mayo Cornelius (M.C.) Higgins' grandmother Sarah came to what is now called Sarah's Mountain as a runaway slave, the beautiful, wild mountain became home to the future generations of the Higgins family. But now things have begun to change and not for the better. A strip-mining company is mining on the mountain, and the slag heap of waste piling up above and behind M.C.'s home threatens to collapse and bury it at any moment. M.C. yearns for independence but must also come to terms with his own values, prejudices, and beliefs in order to deal with both an impending ecological disaster and his family's future.

1974 *240 pages*
Simon & Schuster Books for Young Readers

The Planet of Junior Brown

In this book, Hamilton takes on a number of troubling issues within a gritty New York City setting featuring an obese, mentally-disturbed eighth-grader named Junior Brown. Junior is a musical prodigy, yet his controlling mother removes the strings from his piano and overfeeds him to keep him close by. Junior's friend Buddy and the school janitor are Junior's only friends and supporters. They are aware of his mental issues and the dangerous consequences of his home life and come up with a plan to teach him to survive on his own. This brilliantly written novel doesn't shy away from social issues that have no simple answers.

1971 *244 pages* **Aladdin**

Kevin Henkes
Olive's Ocean

This lovely coming-of-age novel deals with the many questions that come with growing up. Martha is twelve years old and is headed to Cape Cod for a summer vacation with her family. Just before she leaves, she receives a journal entry from the mother of her classmate Olive, who was recently killed in a car accident. Like Martha herself, Olive wanted to be a writer. Martha has much to think about this summer: Why did Olive die, and is her grandmother dying too? Will Jimmy Manning be her boyfriend? Will she become a writer? So many questions and no easy answers—middle-grade readers will be sure to relate.

2003 *224 pages* **HarperCollins**

Marguerite Henry

Illustrated by Wesley Dennis

Justin Morgan Had a Horse

Known for her award-winning and well-loved horse stories, author Maguerite Henry based this historical novel on the story of how one specific breed of American horse came into being. The year is 1791, and a Vermont schoolmaster named Justin Morgan has received a two-year-old colt called Little Bub as repayment of a debt. Little Bub is a runt, but Morgan believes in him and asks his student Joel to train him. Joel realizes that the colt is something special; he can outrun the thoroughbreds and pull heavier loads than a pair of oxen. This book tells the true story of the father of a new breed of horse named after his owner—the Morgan.

1954 *176 pages* **Aladdin**

Illustrated by Wesley Dennis

King of the Wind: The Story of the Godolphin Arabian

This wonderful story of the love of a stable boy for a remarkable Arabian stallion is a fictionalized biography of the Godolphin Arabian, whose blood runs through the veins of many of the best thoroughbreds today. Sham has a white spot on one heel, considered a symbol of great speed; he also bears a wheat-shaped mark on his chest, a symbol of great misfortune. The stable hand Agba saves him from being killed for that ominous marking, and he and the colt become friends for life. Eventually Sham and Agba find an owner who appreciates Sham's speed and bloodlines, and Sham goes on to sire generations of champion racehorses.

1948 *176 pages* **Aladdin**

Illustrated by Wesley Dennis

Misty of Chincoteague

Paul and Maureen Beebe live with their grandparents near the island of Chincoteague (off the coast of Maryland and Virginia), home of the wild Chincoteague ponies. Every year there is a round-up of the wild ponies, and this year Paul and Maureen are determined to capture the wildest pony of all, Phantom. Nobody is more shocked than Paul when he succeeds in capturing Phantom along with her foal Misty. This wonderful story of two teenagers who love horses offers a compassionate portrayal of the relationship between horses and humans and addresses the dilemma inherent in domesticating wild animals. Based on actual events in the author's life, its realism adds to the compelling storytelling.

1947 *176 pages* **Aladdin**

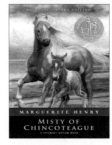

Illustrated by Wesley Dennis

Stormy, Misty's Foal

For those who breathlessly read every word of *Misty of Chincoteague*, the sequel will have readers racing through this eventful novel to the very last page. Misty is about to give birth to her first foal when a hurricane hits. The Beebe family is terrified that Misty and her unborn foal will not survive the storms and flooding. They do, and the foal is named Stormy in honor of the storm she was born in. However, the storm killed more than half of the wild ponies on the islands, and now it is up to the Beebe family to raise enough money to help rebuild the herd that has always lived wild and free.

1963 *224 pages* **Aladdin**

The Adventures of Tintin Series

This series of graphic novellas was created by Belgian artist Georges Remí, who wrote them under the name Hergé, and has been published in more than eighty languages throughout the world. The series is set in the early twentieth-century, and the main character, Tintin, is a young Belgian reporter who is generally accompanied on his many adventures by his faithful fox terrier, Snowy. There are twenty-four books in the series, and they cover a range of topics, but each involves a central mystery that the clever and logical Tintin must solve in order to escape great peril or certain death. Each book is filled with humor and sometimes ridiculous situations, but there is a rather subversive political undertone to these books as well. Parents should be cautioned that these books are not without controversy for their sometimes anti-semitic themes and racial stereotyping, and although some of that has been corrected for more recent printings, there remain some disturbing undertones in a few of the books—though certainly not in all.

1945 *62 pages* **Little, Brown and Company**

The Bunnicula Series

Bunnicula, A Rabbit Tale of Mystery is the first book in this mystical series of not-too-scary mysteries narrated by Harold the dog and Chester the cat, which are perfect for newly independent readers. Bunnicula looks like a normal bunny, but at night that little black spot on his forehead seems to spread around his ears to meet the black markings on his back, and it starts to look more like a cape...and when he curls up his lip—hey, are those fangs where his normal rabbit buck teeth should be? Yes, it's true, Bunnicula is a vampire bunny, but he doesn't drink blood—he's a vegetarian who sucks the color out of vegetables. In the first book, Harold and Chester try to kill Bunnicula by driving a raw steak through his heart, but eventually the three animals become more like friendly adversaries. The crazy antics continue in *The Celery Stalks at Midnight*, *Howliday Inn*, and *Nighty-Nightmare*.

Deborah and James Howe
Illustrated by Alan Daniel
Bunnicula: A Rabbit Tale of Mystery *(1979)*

James Howe
Illustrated by Leslie H. Morrill
The Celery Stalks at Midnight *(1983)*

Illustrated by Lynn Munsinger
Howliday Inn *(1982)*

Illustrated by Leslie H. Morrill
Nighty-Nightmare *(1987)*

112–208 pages **Atheneum**

The Outsiders

This dramatic novel, written in 1967 when the author herself was only sixteen, remains a classic story of the conflicts between social classes in high schools. Ponyboy sees the world he lives in clearly defined by two groups: the "Socs" (socials), who have money and power and can easily get whatever they want and the "Greasers," who live on the outside of the Socs' world. Ponyboy is proud to be a greaser, but he is also confused and sensitive. Ponyboy's world makes sense to him until one fateful night when his best friend kills a Soc, and he realizes that pain feels the same no matter who you are. This is a powerful novel dealing with serious issues.

1967 *192 pages* **Viking**

Rumble Fish

Parents should be aware that this book brings up some troubling and mature themes that are realistically dealt with and do not necessarily result in happily-ever-after endings. Rusty James is the toughest guy in a gang of high school kids; any respect he has gotten has been earned with his fists. He wants to be just like his older brother, Motorcycle Boy, a legendary tough guy who has always been around to bail him out when he gets in trouble. What he doesn't realize is that his older brother is no longer interested in a tough and violent life and has many regrets.
Note: for older or more mature readers.

1975 *144 pages* **Delacorte Press**

That Was Then, This Is Now

All of S. E. Hinton's books deal with mature themes, and in this case, the theme is the limits of friendship. Two young men who have been friends since childhood begin to grow up and realize that they have very different plans for the lives they want to live. Until recently, Mark and Byron did everything together, but things are starting to change. Is Mark jealous of Byron's new girlfriend, or is it that Byron is no longer interested in street fighting? Mark suddenly has a lot of money, and eventually Byron realizes that Mark is selling drugs. Byron now faces a tough decision: does he call the police and betray his best friend or do nothing?

1971 *160 pages* **Viking**

Carl Hiaasen
Hoot

Bestselling adult-fiction author Carl Hiaasen serves up a funny ecological mystery, filled with his usual cast of bumblers, misfits, and generally befuddled-but-lovable characters. This book is especially good for reluctant readers who need humor and a large helping of crazy antics to keep them reading. Roy's introduction to Florida includes getting beaten up by the local bully—which isn't good, but if it hadn't been for that, he'd never have seen the "running boy." On the trail, Roy encounters potty-trained alligators, a fake-fart champion, and eventually the boy himself, an eco-avenger out to protect the habitat of some burrowing owls.

2002 *314 pages* **Alfred A. Knopf**

Newbery Honor

Tove Jansson
The Moomin Series

There are nine books in this series from Sweden that was originally created in 1945. The Moomintrolls are a family of sweet and friendly trolls that live within a forest in Finland. Readers have fallen in love with the charming characters in these books. The Moomins have many adventures together as a family and separately, but each adventure is a gentle one; there are perils, but they are never frightening and are always quickly resolved in a gentle and loving manner. These books are all about a caring family and a warm community of friends, and their gentle ways as they adventure through amusement parks, wildernesses, tree houses, secret caves, flowing rivers, and all the other pleasures of Moominland. For interested readers, there are several bound collections of the Moomin comic strips and also a few Moomin picture books for younger children.

1945 *176–192 pages* **Farrar, Straus & Giroux**

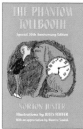

Norton Juster
Illustrated by Jules Feiffer
The Phantom Tollbooth

The continued popularity of this allegorical tale is attributable to several factors: its illustrations are wonderful and illuminate the storytelling, it appeals equally to adults and children, and it's a perfect title to read aloud or independently. Milo is bored with everything—school, the city he lives in, his books, his toys—everything. One day he finds a toll booth in his room with a blue envelope attached that says, "For Milo, who has plenty of time." What happens next is anything but boring. Not since Alice went down the rabbit hole has there been such a riot of adventure in one book.

1961 *256 pages* **Random House Children's Books**

Diana Wynne Jones

Howl's Moving Castle

Diana Wynne Jones is known for her ability to weave humor throughout her books, which are mix of fantasy, fable, and old-fashioned quest novels. Readers will be entranced by the magical events that take place in this book and will also be laughing all the way through the magical love story/fantasy adventure. When the Wicked Witch of the Waste turns Sophie into an old lady, Sophie seeks refuge in the wizard Howl's moving castle. Howl is by reputation an "eater of souls," but in truth he, too, is under the witch's curse until he can find the girl of his dreams and end his contract with the fire demon.

1986 *336 pages* **Greenwillow Books**

House of Many Ways

While this book revisits some of the magical characters readers first encountered in *Howl's Moving Castle,* it can be easily read on its own. Charmain is a young girl who is sent to look after the household of her great uncle. Uncle William's house is filled with magical rooms and ways, and as Charmain reads her great uncle's books, she discovers that she possesses some of his magical gifts as well. This subtly comic fantasy is populated by many wonderful characters. Through her experiences, Charmain is transformed from an unsure young girl into an adventuresome and confident young woman.

2008 *416 pages* **Greenwillow Books**

Marianna Mayer on stories that inspire illustrations…

From early childhood I knew what I wanted to do when I grew up. There was never any doubt. I loved books and wanted to write and illustrate children's books. Looking back, I wonder when that desire first emerged. But from my earliest memory it just seems it was ever present. I was an only child for a decade before my sister was born. My dearest, closest friend was my small dog, Tony, a shaggy black-and-white rescue. I had lots of animals growing up, though. Our place was overrun with all kinds…ducks, geese, rabbits, horses and ponies, chicks, cats and kittens, canaries, parakeets, giant turtles, and all manner of tropical fish. But Tony was my constant companion. If we were not outdoors playing, I was reading books to her, even before I could actually read. I loved picture books and fairy-tale collections. I could not get enough, and like many children I never tired of hearing the same stories over and over again.

Many of those books were without pictures, so I would imagine illustrations for each story. I started making books well before my school years. I majored in art, and at 18 I was writing and illustrating children's books and submitting them to publishers. The children's publishing industry was very different when my first children's book was accepted. Full-color picture books were rarely published. And fairy tales were only found in anthologies with very few black-and-white line illustrations.

I tried for many years to convince my editors to agree to my doing a version of a classic fairy tale or folktale in a full-color, illustrated picture book format. The argument was always the same: why would anyone want to buy a single tale when they could buy many in just one book? But I persevered, and finally my editor, Judith Whipple at Four Winds Press, was persuaded to give me a contract to do my own version of *Beauty and the Beast*. On the strength of that book's success, a genre was launched, enabling me to follow with many other titles.

Charles Dickens, Lewis Carroll, the Brothers Grimm, Hans Christian Andersen, and Beatrix Potter are authors who very much inspired me as a youngster. Their vivid storytelling style encouraged me to try to create stories that will reach readers of any age.

See individual listings for books by Marianna Mayer on page 219.

Author/Illustrator Marianna Mayer

Carolyn Keene
The Nancy Drew Series

The Nancy Drew mystery series, featuring a teenaged girl detective, launched in 1930 and has been going strong ever since. In the following years, the books have been reissued, updated, and revised to keep up with changing times, and more modern versions, such as *The Nancy Drew Files,* have been published as well. The original books have sold over eighty million copies and have been translated into more than twenty-five languages, far outselling the "Hardy Boys" series. Nancy's mysterious adventures (along with her boyfriend, Nick Nickerson) in the original, hardcover, "collect them all" format remain just as popular today. For those who are curious, Carolyn Keene is a pseudonym—since their inception, the books have been ghostwritten by a number of authors over the years.

1930 *192 pages* **Grosset & Dunlap**

Newbery Honor

Jacqueline Kelly
The Evolution of Calpurnia Tate

In this story, set in rural Texas in 1899, twelve-year-old Calpurnia (Callie) Tate is the only girl in an upper-crust family of seven, and she is slowly becoming aware that her family's expectations for her life and her own hopes for what it can be are in direct conflict. Her mother foresees a life of corsets and a formal debut into society; Callie is happiest when exploring the natural world with her grandfather (together they discover a new form of plant life and attempt to have it officially recognized). The focus of the book is on Callie's struggle to achieve her hopes and dreams within the limits of her family's expectations as a new century approaches.

2009 *352 pages* **Henry Holt**

Katy Kelly
Illustrated by Gillian Johnson
Melonhead

This first book in a series for newly independent readers is filled with the humorous escapades of nine-year-old Adam Melon (Melonhead to his friends), whose enthusiasm often exceeds both his abilities and his capacity to predict the hilarious outcomes of his various schemes. For Melonhead, a simple climb up a tree requires the fire department's "Jaws of Life" to get him down, so you can imagine what happens when he tries to come up with a suitable science project. Illustrated with fun black-and-white drawings that help new readers to move through the text, this series is also perfect for young boys who need a lot of humor and silliness in order to keep them reading.

2009 *224 pages* **Delacorte Press**

Liz Kessler
Illustrated by Sarah Gibb
The Emily Windsnap Series

In the first installment in this eight-book series about seventh-grader Emily Windsnap, Emily is a young girl just like everyone else, except that she has never learned how to swim. But readers will soon find out that Emily is nothing like anyone else, for when she begins swimming lessons, her legs turn into a fishtail, and she is soon gliding through the water as a mermaid. Emily has a lot of questions, but her mother's memory is a bit foggy on the facts. Soon she meets another mermaid who takes her to an underwater mermaid school, where Emily discovers more about both the merpeople and her heritage as she searches for her father.

2004 *208-224 pages* **Candlewick Press**

Jeff Kinney

Diary of a Wimpy Kid Series

This six-book (and growing) series can best be described as a hybrid between traditional and graphic novels. The main character is Greg Heffley, a middle-schooler whose story is told through his diary entries, which are accompanied by his cartoon illustrations. Greg is dealing with all the issues that come up for boys in middle school: girls, popularity, his parents and siblings, and his nerdy friends. Greg's humor is pretty subversive and his deadpan diary entries would be funny on their own, but when coupled with the cartoons, they ascend to the hilarious on nearly every page.

2007 *224 pages* **Amulet Books**

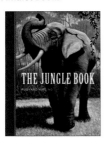

Rudyard Kipling
Illustrated by Scott McKowen

The Jungle Book

Kipling's *Jungle Book* is probably best known for the "Mowgli Stories" of the man-cub raised by wolves. But the original book holds many more stories that will entrance and entertain children as well. Between the covers of this book, readers will also meet Rikki Tikki Tavi, the cobra-fighting mongoose; Toomai, the boy who sees the elephants dance; Quiquern, the heroic Eskimo who saves his tribe from starvation; Kotick the white seal; Shiv and the grasshoppers; and many more. The thrilling stories in this book make wonderful family read-aloud stories and are also perfect for independent readers who are looking for some truly gripping and slightly fantastical stories to read.

1894 *352 pages* **Sterling Classics**

Newbery Award

Newbery Award

From the Mixed-Up Files of Mrs. Basil E. Frankweiler

This classic has engrossed readers for over forty years, and given them a whole new perspective on visiting museums. Young Claudia feels that her family doesn't appreciate her, and she decides the only way they ever will is if she runs away—just long enough so that they can miss her. However, she wants to run to somewhere comfortable, beautiful, and very elegant. That problem is solved by making her destination the Metropolitan Museum of Art in New York City. When Claudia sees a beautiful statue of an angel, she knows she can't go home until she finds out more about it...which leads her to Mrs. Basil E. Frankweiler.

1967 *176 pages* **Atheneum**

The View from Saturday

Sixth-grade teacher Mrs. Olinski must form a team of students to compete in an academic bowl requiring general knowledge, and nobody knows why she chooses Noah, Nadia, Ethan, and Julian over the more obvious honors students in her class. The story unwinds as each of the four students, who meet to prepare and have tea together each Saturday, tell their own stories; and the ways that they come together and interlock is revealed. They win the competition, of course, but more interesting is how their individual experiences with kindness and respect teach them to seek those qualities in others. This beautifully written novel will be one that readers won't want to end.

1996 *128 pages* **Atheneum**

No More Dead Dogs

When Wallace has to write a book report on *Old Shep, My Pal*, he makes it perfectly clear that he hated the book and that he is tired of reading classic books in which the dog always croaks at the end. So Wallace's teacher sends him to detention, to sit in the auditorium where the stubborn English teacher is directing a play of—you guessed it—*Old Shep, My Pal*. Wallace's suggestions to "punch up" the production anger Rachel, the head of the drama club—but in the end, his ideas are incorporated, he and Rachel discover they are meant for each other, and maybe this time the dog might actually survive for a change.

2000 *192 pages* **Hyperion**

Schooled

Thirteen-year-old Capricorn (Cap for short) Anderson has never watched TV, never tasted pizza, and never been to school; he was home schooled by his grandmother on a "hippie commune" farm. When his grandmother falls from a tree and must be hospitalized, Cap is thrust into the home of a social worker and sent to a school where he has no idea how to fit in. How Cap handles his predicament, and the way in which he ends up changing and enriching the lives of the students he meets rather than conforming to their standards, may cause readers to look at the social structures in their own schools with newly opened eyes.

2007 *224 pages* **Hyperion**

Ingrid Law
Savvy

Everybody in the Beaumont family has a single magical power that comes to them when they turn thirteen, but it's different for each person. Mibs is about to celebrate her thirteenth birthday, and she has no idea what her power will be. Just before her big day, her father is seriously injured in a car accident. Mibs is certain that her power will be able to wake him up from his coma. After many mix-ups, she does "reach" her father and discover her power, which is the ability to read the thoughts of anyone who has ink on their body—from tattoos to marks from a ballpoint.

2008 *352 pages* **Dial**

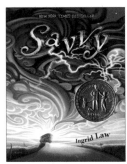

Newbery Honor

Robert Lawson
Rabbit Hill

Though this children's classic was written more than sixty years ago, it has lost none of its charm, and its gentle lesson about how humans and animals are interdependent will resonate with children today just as it did upon its original publication. The animals that live near Rabbit Hill are excited because they have heard that some "Folks" are moving back into the "Big House," which has been empty for some time. The animals are a little nervous, too; they wonder if the new people will be kind and plant the garden or if they will be mean and like to hunt like some of the previous residents.

1944 *128 pages* **Viking**

Newbery Award

Middle Grade Readers 8–12

Madeleine L'Engle

The Time Quintet

For almost fifty years, middle-grade readers and adults have been transported into the marvelous world of the Murry family. In the first book of the quintet, *A Wrinkle in Time*, Meg, her brother Charles Wallace, and her friend Calvin must venture through a tesseract—an actual wrinkle in time—to rescue their father, who is being held captive by an evil presence. In the second book, *A Wind in the Door*, Charles Wallace falls ill, and Meg, Calvin, and their teacher must travel inside him to make him well (and prevent the evil Echthros from carrying out his plans for the universe as well). *A Swiftly Tilting Planet* finds both the Murry and O'Keefe families working together, along with a unicorn, to prevent a potential nuclear war; and in *Many Waters*, Meg's younger siblings embark on some time travel back to the time of Noah, to a desert oasis that is in the midst of a brutal war. The last book in the quintet is *An Acceptable Time*; Meg and Calvin are now married and have a daughter named Polly, who finds herself trapped 3,000 years in the past. These allegorical tales have compelled readers not just because they are beautifully written, but also because their themes reinforce the true power of love and emphasize that all people must make moral choices.

A Wrinkle in Time *(1962)*

A Wind in the Door *(1973)*

A Swiftly Tilting Planet *(1978)*

Many Waters *(1986)*

An Acceptable Time *(1989)*

256–384 pages **Farrar, Straus & Giroux**

Julius Lester
Illustrated by Tom Feelings

Newbery Honor

To Be a Slave

When Julius Lester set out to write this book, he created something for middle-grade readers that had not existed previously; he created a book about what it actually felt like to be a slave—to be bought, sold, and owned like a piece of property. He did this by virtue of extensive research interwoven with actual slave narratives and historical documents, and the result is one of the most remarkable books about the condition of slavery ever written for readers of any age. This book is both a compelling, can't-put-it-down read and a valuable historical document about one of America's least proud eras and those who survived it.

1968 *176 pages* **Puffin**

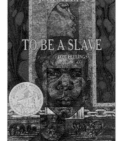

Middle Grade Readers 8–12

Ella Enchanted

Gail Carson Levine's re-imagining of Cinderella is one that girls today can relate to and understand. Ella was cursed (or blessed, depending on how you look at it) at birth with the gift of obedience by the fairy Lucinda. The story follows a familiar path; however, in this version Ella learns that she can rescue herself and her prince by doing the right thing in a difficult situation, which will also break the curse—she has to say no to the one thing she wants to say yes to. Readers will cheer for a heroine who has smarts and guts, and who gets her prince through methods that spring from her humor and bravery.

1997 *240 pages* **HarperCollins**

Ever

This novel is rooted in mythology, bringing the reader into a world where a god in human form falls in love with a mortal woman. As the author explores the meaning of love and immortality, the reader will meet Kezi, the beautiful weaver, who falls in love with Olus, the Akkan god of the winds. The risks of this love are great: if Kezi and Olus succeed in their quest, they will be together and immortal forever; if they fail, it is Kezi who risks death as a human sacrifice. For young girls who love a romantic tale with a lot of action, this might be the best book—ever.

2008 *256 pages* **HarperCollins**

Fairest

There are connections in this tale to the traditional *Sleeping Beauty*, but the awakening of the main character in this novel is more metaphorical than actual. Readers will be able to relate to the world Aza lives in, where beauty, grace, elegance, and the ability to sing are valued. Unfortunately, Aza is awkward, clumsy, and homely, but she can sing beautifully, "throw" her voice, and mimic any voice she hears. Aza is blackmailed into using her abilities to make it appear as if the new queen is singing. Upon discovery of the ruse, Aza must flee for her life, and it is then that she begins to understand her own strength of character.

2006 *336 pages* **HarperCollins**

Newbery Honor

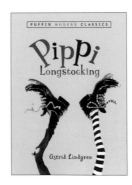

Astrid Lindgren
Pippi Longstocking

Pippi Longstocking and her remarkable adventures have entertained boys and girls alike for more than sixty-five years. Pippi is capable, independent, and strong enough to lift a horse, and her motto is "Don't you worry about me. I'll always come out on top." There are four books in this series about the adventures of the little girl with the too-big shoes, mismatched stockings, and red braids sticking out from her head. Along with her friends Tommy and Annika, Pippi has adventures galore, as she spins wild tales and gets into interesting (but never dangerous) situations. Every child would love a best friend like Pippi, and by reading these books he or she will surely get one.

1945 *160 pages* **Puffin**

Illustrated by Pauline Baynes

The Chronicles of Narnia

It has been said that readers should read The Chronicles of Narnia three times: first in childhood, second in early adulthood, and finally later in life. Whether you read each of the seven books once or thrice, it is certain that you will never forget them. These books are filled with lessons both literal and allegorical and deal with themes of good versus evil and the importance of faith and hope in our world. The timeless nature of the stories and adventures assures that children who discover them today will certainly be sharing them with their own children in the years to come. In *The Lion, the Witch, and the Wardrobe,* four children—Peter, Susan, Edmund, and Lucy Pevensie—enter a wardrobe and are transported to a magical land called Narnia, where they meet the lion Aslan and help him rescue Narnia from the evil White Witch who has held the land in a state of perpetual winter. In *Prince Caspian,* the children are called back to Narnia by Prince Caspian, who is fighting to save the land from his Uncle Miraz, who has usurped the throne that is rightfully Caspian's. *The Voyage of the Dawn Treader* brings the children back to Narnia to embark upon a perilous journey with Prince Caspian to find the seven lords who were banished when Miraz usurped control of Narnia; and in *The Silver Chair* (the first book that does not feature the Pevensie children), Prince Caspian calls Eustace Scrubb and Jill Pole to Narnia to search for his son, Prince Rilian. *The Horse*

and His Boy takes place during the reign of the Pevensie children in Narnia and focuses on Bree, a talking horse, and a boy named Shasta who, after a long captivity, are making their way back to Narnia and freedom. *The Magician's Nephew* travels back in time to tell the story of how Aslan the lion created Narnia and how evil first entered that magical world. The final book in the series, *The Last Battle*, chronicles the end of the land of Narnia. Filled with gripping adventures, fantastical creatures, and valiant battles, these books are guaranteed to capture the hearts and imaginations of any reader who loves epic storytelling.

The Lion, the Witch, and the Wardrobe *(1950)*

Prince Caspian *(1951)*

The Voyage of the Dawn Treader *(1952)*

The Silver Chair *(1953)*

The Horse and His Boy *(1954)*

The Magician's Nephew *(1955)*

The Last Battle *(1956)*

176–256 pages **HarperCollins**

Jack London

The Call of the Wild

Though this classic wilderness adventure title was written for adults, it has long been a staple of middle-grade reading lists for its brilliant writing, and it is considered to be Jack London's masterpiece. Readers will be captivated by the life story of Buck, a domesticated dog who, through a series of difficult and cruel events, has to learn how to survive and work in the Alaskan wilderness, until the day he, too, must answer "the call of the wild." Parents should be aware that there are fairly realistic scenes of cruelty and violence in this book, but the story of this loyal and loving dog with a huge heart remains a story worth sharing.

1903 *134 pages* **Puffin**

White Fang

This story of a half-wolf/half-dog named White Fang has been a classic since its original publication in 1906. Considered to be a companion novel to *Call of the Wild*, in which a domesticated animal eventually returns to his wild roots, this novel takes the opposite course and is told from the viewpoint of a wild animal who learns to trust the kindness of humans. Set in the Yukon Territory during the Klondike Gold Rush, the novel deals with the complicated themes of morality and redemption. Parents should also be aware that there are scenes of cruelty and violence to both animals and humans within the story.

1906 *248 pages* **Viking**

Hugh Lofting
The Story of Doctor Dolittle

There are twelve books in this well-loved series about the doctor who can talk to animals. Dr. Dolittle prefers his animal patients to his human ones, and in the course of the first book, readers will discover that he can talk to the animals in their own languages, which is extremely helpful when you are treating them for illnesses. Children have loved reading about the adventures of the rotund and kindly naturalist and all of his "wild" friends since the first book was published in 1920, and the books have lost none of their charm and humor in the years that followed.

1968 *176 pages* **Yearling**

Maud Hart Lovelace
The Betsy-Tacy Series

The ten books in this delightful series, written between 1940 and 1955, focus on an enduring friendship between Betsy Ray and her best friend, Tacy. One of the unique characteristics of these books is that the characters age as the books progress to the final book. The series begins with *Betsy-Tacy*, when Betsy is five years old and meets her lifelong friend Tacy, and continues with *Betsy-Tacy and Tib, Betsy and Tacy Go Over the Big Hill, Betsy and Tacy Go Downtown, Heaven to Betsy, Betsy in Spite of Herself, Betsy Was a Junior, Betsy and Joe, Betsy and the Great World,* and *Betsy's Wedding.* Though the books are set in a simpler time, they deal with the issues that girls still deal with today: shyness, siblings (Betsy is one of eleven children), friendship, love, death, and the dreams of a young girl who hopes to write stories herself one day.

1940 *144 pages* **HarperCollins**

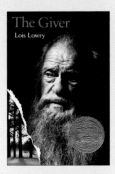

The Giver

This dystopian novel is set in a future society, where poverty and violence have been eradicated at a great cost: everyone looks alike, most cannot see color or hear music, and along with undesirable societal conditions, free will has been eradicated as well. In each generation, one person is selected to carry the history of the society's past and become "The Receiver." In this story, that person is twelve-year-old Jonah. Once Jonah receives the history of his people and he becomes conscious of the restrictions of his community, he and the previous Receiver work together to bring back the ability to feel to the people in their world.

1993 *192 pages* **Houghton Mifflin Books for Children**

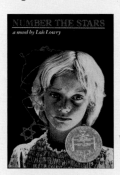

Number the Stars

This story about the evacuation of the Jews from Denmark offers readers a Holocaust story that demonstrates that the bravery and humanity of people can be mobilized to thwart great evil. On September 29, 1943, information was received by the Danish Resistance that the Jews of Denmark were to be rounded up and sent to death camps. Annemarie and her family arrange to smuggle the Rosen family out of the country at great risk to themselves. They succeed in doing so but not without many close calls along the way. Unlike many stories of the Holocaust, this one ends happily, as the Danish government welcomes the Jews back after the war.

1989 *144 pages* **Houghton Mifflin Books for Children**

The Batboy

Mike Lupica, one of the most prominent sports reporters in America, has written thirteen (so far) sports-themed novels for middle-grade readers. This baseball-themed story focuses on fourteen-year-old Brian, who gets his summer dream job: batboy for his hometown's major-league team. To Brian, this is also a way to connect with his absent father, a man who loved baseball so much, he left his family to pursue the sport. Through this job, Brian hopes to reconnect with his father, and he never expects that a more vital connection will be made with Hank Bishop, a former steroid user making a comeback.

2010 *247 pages* **Philomel**

Miracle on 49th Street

This holiday-themed basketball story is sure to wring a few tears out of even the most jaded middle-grade sports fans, even the boys. Josh Cameron is a basketball superstar playing for the Boston Celtics, and he's got it all: the championship ring, the adoring fans, and the clean-cut, good-guy image. What he doesn't have is a family—until the day twelve-year-old Molly Parker approaches him in a parking lot and tells him she's his daughter, the child of the only woman he has ever loved, who recently passed away. Readers will be cheering for spunky Molly all through the book, as she turns Mr. World Champion into dear old dad.

2006 *256 pages* **Philomel**

Safe at Home

Nick Crandall is a twelve-year-old foster kid who feels like he doesn't fit in anywhere. He sure doesn't fit in with his foster parents, who are both professors and who don't know anything about sports, and he doesn't fit in on his school's varsity team either. But Nick has to prove that he can fit in while he has a chance, and he's determined to do it on the team and at home; but most importantly, Nick needs to prove it to himself.

2008 *192 pages* **Philomel**

Middle Grade Readers 8–12

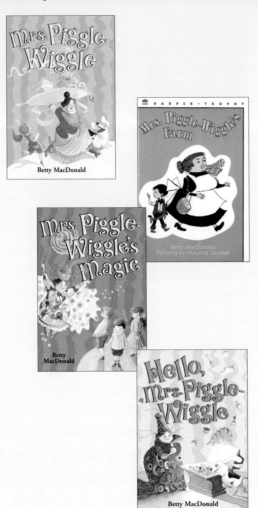

Mrs. Piggle-Wiggle Books

For newly independent readers, both boys and girls, the magical Mrs. Piggle-Wiggle is just the ticket to keep them reading and loving every minute of it. Mrs. Piggle-Wiggle lives in an upside-down house in a neighborhood filled with children—children with good hearts and bad habits. The neighborhood parents come to Mrs. Piggle-Wiggle for help curing those bad habits because she has a treasure-chest filled with crazy magical cures, given to her by her deceased pirate husband. For the child who interrupts too much, there is a powder that when blown on the child renders him temporarily mute; the "Radish Cure" is for children who won't take baths; the "Selfishness Cure" labels everything a child owns with his/her name, causing embarrassment and ridicule; and there are many more, each of them equal parts silly and effective. These books teach children proper behavior through exaggerated negative consequences—but rather than being preachy, all of Mrs. Piggle-Wiggle's "cures" teach the virtues of common sense and good behavior through tricks, games, laughter, and a whole lot of silliness and love.

Illustrated by Alexandra Boiger
Mrs. Piggle-Wiggle (1947)

Illustrated by Alexandra Boiger
Mrs. Piggle-Wiggle's Magic (1949)

Pictures by Maurice Sendak
Mrs. Piggle-Wiggle's Farm (1954)

Illustrated by Alexandra Boiger
Hello, Mrs. Piggle-Wiggle (1957)

136-192 pages **HarperCollins**

Patricia MacLachlan
Sarah, Plain and Tall

This beautifully written book tells the story of a mail-order bride from the Maine coast who answers the ad of a widower with two children who lives on the Midwestern prairie. The story is told from the perspective of the children—Anna and her younger brother Caleb. Sarah and the family communicate by letter initially, and eventually she comes out for a one-month trial. Anna and Caleb are constantly in fear that Sarah will not like them, Papa, or the land-locked life they lead and worry that she will leave them. Since this is the first of five books about the family, readers can be assured that she does not.

1985 *64 pages* **HarperCollins**

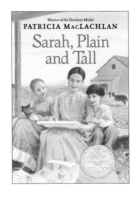

Newbery Award

11 Birthdays

Amanda and Leo have been best friends forever, and since they share the same birthday, they have celebrated their birthdays together for the last 10 years. But this year, they are turning 11, which is a pretty big deal, and Amanda and Leo haven't been on speaking terms for a while. After their eleventh birthdays, something very strange begins to happen: they keep waking up and repeating that same day. This strange event allows them to heal the rift in their friendship and to experiment with ways that different actions or decisions change the outcome of their repetitious birthday.

2009 *272 pages* **Scholastic Press/Scholastic Inc.**

Finally

Most children just can't wait to grow up, to reach that magic age when they can finally do all the things they have been waiting to do for so long. According to the family rules, when Rory turns twelve, she can wear contacts, get her ears pierced, get a pet, own a cell phone, stay home alone—and finally be able to ride in the front seat of a car. With a clever surprise ending, this contemporary novel about growing up is a perfect fit for tween-age girls who are in a hurry to look, act, and feel older than they really are.

2010 *304 pages* **Scholastic Press/Scholastic Inc.**

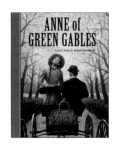

Lucy Maud Montgomery
Illustrated by Scott McKowen

The Anne of Green Gables Series

This classic series is about one of the most unforgettable characters in children's literature: the outspoken, red-headed girl named Anne Shirley, who comes to live at Green Gables as a foster child and whose story begins with an error and ends with love. Marilla and Matthew Cuthbert, the owners of Green Gables, send away for a boy orphan who needs a home to come live with them and help out on the farm. What they get instead is a feisty, talkative, and irrepressible eleven-year-old girl named Anne. While at first they consider sending her back, Anne's winning ways, vivid imagination, and sunny disposition change their minds forever. Anne does manage to get into more than her share of scrapes and trouble along the way, but none of them cause any lasting harm. Through the eight books in the series, we follow Anne from childhood to adulthood as she experiences all the love and losses that come with life: the death of Matthew, giving up a scholarship to stay behind and help Marilla both emotionally and financially, the joy of her years teaching school in Avonlea, and her devoted friendship, which turns into something much deeper, with Gilbert Blythe. Readers who continue on with this series will learn that Gilbert and Anne, sworn enemies in the first book, do eventually marry in the last. The books in this series are so beautifully written, it's no wonder middle-grade girls have been longing to visit Prince Edward Island in Canada since the first young girl cracked the spine of *Anne of Green Gables* in 1908.

1908 *312 pages* **Sterling Classics**

Brandon Mull
Illustrated by Brandon Dorman

Fablehaven

This book is the first in a six-book series about a mystical encampment called Fablehaven, which was established centuries ago to prevent the extinction of magical creatures—the kind we read about in books but aren't sure really exist. They do exist, and Kendra and Seth's grandfather is the caretaker of this mysterious haven for greedy trolls, mischievous satyrs, plotting witches, spiteful imps, and jealous fairies, to name only a few species. Maintaining order among these magical creatures isn't easy, and when Seth's curiosity gets the better of him, all sorts of mayhem may be unleashed upon an unsuspecting world.

2006 *368 pages* **Aladdin**

Lauren Myracle

Eleven

Perfect for preteen girls dealing with all the angst related to approaching the teen years, this novel effectively captures what it feels like to be on the cusp of adolescence. The book begins as Winnie celebrates her eleventh birthday and ends a year later on her twelfth. What a difference a year can make; Winnie's best friend appears to be dropping her for a new friend, and Winnie is becoming closer to Dinah—an awkward girl she used to pity. Throw in some family drama, a surly older sister, and a crush or two, and you've got a relatable stew of tween angst.

2004 *208 pages* **Dutton**

Phyllis Reynolds Naylor

Shiloh

This moving tale of a boy who rescues an abused dog, set in rural Virginia, poses interesting ethical questions for readers. Marty is eleven when he finds Shiloh, a dog that has run away from his owner. Marty knows the owner and fears that Shiloh will be injured or worse if he returns him, but his family is poor, so taking in a dog that needs feeding is not something his parents will allow. Marty does return the dog, but Shiloh returns to Marty again—this time seriously hurt by his owner. The decision Marty makes about keeping the dog means doing some things that readers will not expect and offers topics for discussion.

1991 *144 pages* **Atheneum**

Newbery Award

Garth Nix

The Keys to the Kingdom Series

The seven-book *The Keys to the Kingdom* series begins on a Monday. Arthur Penhaligon is a normal boy who finds himself in an unusual situation that begins in a dream when a mysterious stranger hands him a key shaped like the minute hand of a clock. When he wakes up, he is actually holding that key. As the week goes on, Arthur and his friends, Leaf and Suzy, have to do battle with some strange creatures, and in order to protect themselves and a magical house at the center of the universe, they must use all their powers (magical and practical) to defeat Lord Sunday and the enemies who are closing in from all sides.

2003 *336–368 pages* **Scholastic Press/Scholastic Inc.**

Roxie Munro on creative illustration for nonfiction…

I grew up in a small village on the Chesapeake Bay in Maryland. My parents were great readers—we were probably the only address in our rural county in the '60s that got the "Saturday Review of Books." By age eleven, I had read all the books in our small elementary school's library; the Thursday visit by the county bookmobile was the week's highlight. But my favorite book, with beautiful detailed watercolors, was *Andersen's Fairy Tales*, illustrated by Arthur Szyk.

In college, I studied art, and, after living in Washington, D.C., moved to New York City when *The New Yorker* started buying my art for covers. Looking for freelance work, I showed my portfolio to an adult book editor, who suggested I see Donna Brooks, a great children's book editor. Although I told her "I don't do bunnies and bears; don't do cute," she thought I had something to offer children. I did my first book, *The Inside-Outside Book of New York City* (a *New York Times* Best Illustrated Award winner) with her. She taught me that nonfiction for children can be as original and creative as fiction.

Working on a painting, maybe a maze landscape, I sometimes imagine myself within the scene. Suddenly, I am in the tiny car on the winding road or swinging down the big-city avenue. My family took long "road trip" vacations—as a child, I would have loved *Go! Go! Go!* I travel a lot now and have visited 10 of the 12 biomes in *EcoMazes*. The research for my books can be the most fun part!

See individual listings for books by Roxie Munro on pages 61 and 207.

Author/Illustrator Roxie Munro

Five Children and It

The five children in this story are Robert, Anthea, Cyril, Jane, and Lamb, brothers and sisters whose family has moved from London to the British seaside town of Kent. When digging in the sand one day, they awaken a grumpy creature called a Psammead—or Sand Fairy. The good news is that the Sand Fairy can grant them one wish each day that will last until sunset. The bad news is that the wishes keep going absurdly awry. Readers will enjoy this quaint fantasy romp as they laugh through the children's mishaps and wonder what they would wish for if they had the opportunity to have their own wishes granted.

1902 *272 pages* **Puffin**

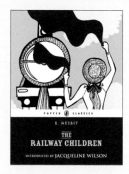

The Railway Children

The Waterbury family must move to a house named Three Chimneys, near the railway in the British countryside, when their father, who worked at the foreign office, is falsely accused and imprisoned for selling secrets to the Russians. The three children become friendly with the station porter, Albert Perks, and one of the regular passengers referred to as "the Old Gentleman," who is helpful in assisting the family to prove that their father is innocent. This lovingly told tale of the truth being brought to light will satisfy readers and also inform them of the social and economic issues of the time in which it was written.

1906 *304 pages* **Puffin**

Mary Norton
Illustrated by Beth and Joe Krush
The Borrowers

The Borrowers are the Clock family—mother, father, and siblings Pod, Homily, and Arrietty—a tiny family of "little people" who live under the floorboards of a quiet country house in England, undetected by the "human beans" that live in the house above them. They survive and furnish their home with little trinkets, morsels, and scraps they "borrow." They've lived unnoticed for years, but when a young boy comes to live at the house, he sees Arrietty and she befriends him, an action that imperils the family. This is the first in a series of five charming books about The Borrowers, and interested readers can follow their continued adventures in *The Borrowers Afield, The Borrowers Afloat, The Borrowers Aloft,* and *The Borrowers Avenged.*

1953 *192 pages* **Harcourt Children's Books**

Robert C. O'Brien
Illustrated by Zena Bernstein
Mrs. Frisby and the Rats of NIMH

In this wonderful fantasy tale, filled with suspense and bravery, we meet Mrs. Frisby, a widowed field mouse with four young children. Mrs. Frisby knows it's time to move her family to their summer living quarters, but Timothy, her youngest, is ill with pneumonia and cannot be moved. With no one else to turn to she seeks the assistance of the strange rats that live nearby. As it turns out, the rats of NIMH are an extremely intelligent breed who assist Mrs. Frisby in a way she could never have imagined. In return, she helps them with an even more dangerous assignment: freeing "laboratory enhanced" rats from captivity in a science lab.

1971 *240 pages* **Atheneum**

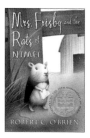

Newbery Award

Island of the Blue Dolphins

Based on a true story, this saga of a young girl's survival after being left alone on a deserted island will inspire readers. Off the coast of California is an island inhabited by an indigenous tribe. When a Russian man comes to the island to prey on the wildlife, the tribe realizes they must flee the island, and Karana is accidentally left behind. As the years pass and she waits for the ship that will surely come to rescue her, Karana learns to build shelter, find food, clothe herself, and defend herself from the feral dogs on the island. The tale of Karana's survival (and eventual rescue) is a story not easily forgotten.

1960 *192 pages*
Houghton Mifflin Books for Children

Sing Down the Moon

Told from the point of view of Bright Morning, a young girl of the tribe, this version of the famous Long Walk of 1863 to 1865, in which the Navaho People were taken by the "Long Knives" (American soldiers) and forcibly marched over 200 miles from Arizona to Fort Sumner, New Mexico, will captivate readers. As Bright Morning and her friend Bright Star are tending to Bright Star's flock, the girls are kidnapped by Spaniards to be sold as slaves. Bright Morning manages to escape and return to her people just before the tribe is taken from their homes, forced on the Long March, then held captive for years. Bright Star and her husband manage to escape and return to their former home.

1970 *144 pages*
Houghton Mifflin Books for Children

The Black Pearl

Ramon Salazar's father is the most famous pearl dealer in Baja, California, and now that Ramon is a partner in his father's company, he dreams of finding a pearl so large that Sevillano, his father's best diver, will treat him with respect. He learns to dive from a superstitious local named Soto Luzon, dives into the lagoon that Luzon claims is ruled by the "manta diablo" (giant manta), and finds a giant pearl—the "Pearl of Heaven." Luzon warns Ramon that the pearl will bring bad luck, and the manta diablo will want it back. Unable to sell such a valuable pearl, Ramon's father donates it to the church, setting off a series of events that will surprise and thrill readers.

1967 *144 pages* **Houghton Mifflin Books for Children**

Mary Pope Osborne
The Mysteries of Spider Kane

This engaging series of short mysteries is perfect for newly independent readers. The plots are suspenseful and the action moves quickly enough to hold their interest as they try to solve the mystery along with Spider Kane. In each book, our intrepid and brilliant multi-legged detective is asked by a fellow insect to solve a simple mystery; he is honor bound to do so by his secret organization, M.O.T.H., which stands for "Mission: Only To Help." As much fun to read alone as they are to read aloud to younger children, these books will quickly have readers stuck fast in their mysterious web.

1992 *240 pages* **Yearling**

The Great Gilly Hopkins

In this riveting story, we meet eleven-year-old Gilly Hopkins, who has been in more foster homes than she can remember. She is brilliant, brash, and out of control most of the time. Gilly is sure that one day her real mother (who writes occasional letters) will come and rescue her, especially now that she has been placed with the weirdest foster family yet, the Trotters. Gilly is a tough kid who is determined to create a plan to get her real mother to rescue her, but when the rescue doesn't work out quite as planned, she is forced to consider that perhaps living with the Trotters may not be quite so bad after all.

1978 *160 pages* **HarperCollins**

Bridge to Terabithia

Jess Aarons and Leslie Burke are unlikely best friends who meet when tomboy Leslie beats Jess in the fifth-grade race he had hoped to win. Together, Jess and Leslie create a secret kingdom in the woods called Terabithia, and the only way to get to their "castle" is via a swinging rope over a river gully. In Terabithia, they share their hopes and dreams and tell stories, and their friendship grows until tragedy strikes. When Leslie goes to Terabithia alone one day, there is an accident as she swings across the gully, and she is killed. Jess must learn to deal with grief and sorrow in this stirring tale of friendship and loss.

1977 *144 pages* **HarperCollins**

Jacob Have I Loved

This novel deals with the issues of sibling rivalry and self-reliance in a manner that preteens and teens can easily relate to. Caroline and Sara Louise are twins, and though Caroline started out small and sickly, she is somehow always getting more attention from everyone in the family than Sara Louise, who is kinder, smarter, prettier, and more talented. Sara Louise must learn to deal with this issue by using her gifts and finding the strength within herself to live life on her own terms and change her future. This moving story of family dysfunction and the courage it takes to rise above it and chart your own course will inspire readers.

1980 *224 pages* **HarperCollins**

Rodman Philbrick
Freak the Mighty

Tearjerker alert: this moving tale of the unlikely friendship between two outcasts will not only teach tolerance and understanding, but also what it means to be a true friend. Max is large, awkward, and learning disabled, and he lives with his grandparents while his father is in prison for murdering his mother. Undersized and physically disabled Kevin is brilliant but needs braces and crutches to get around. Together they become Freak the Mighty: Max puts Kevin on his shoulders to give him mobility, and Kevin's intelligence defends them from the bullies' mocking. Sadly, Kevin's disease progresses and he dies, but Max is left with wonderful memories and a more positive sense of himself and his capabilities.

1993 *176 pages* **Blue Sky Press/Scholastic Inc.**

Newbery Honor

Newbery Honor

Newbery Honor

Hatchet

For those who like their reading filled with action and adventure, Gary Paulsen's books offer an abundance of both. While Brian is flying in a small plane to visit his father, the pilot has a heart attack and dies, forcing Brian to crash-land the plane in the Canadian wilderness. Brian has no idea how long he will be stranded and must figure out how to make a fire, find food, and protect himself with only the hatchet his father had given him. The fifty-four days he spends in the wilderness prior to being reunited with his father also provide him with the time to come to terms with his parents' divorce.

1987 *208 pages* **Atheneum/Richard Jackson Books**

Dogsong

Inuit Russell Suskitt is disillusioned with modern life and interested in the lore and adventures of the "old ways" of his people. The shaman Oogruk, who owns the only team of sled dogs in the village, understands Russell's desire for old traditions and helps him to train himself and the dogs for an adventure that will help Russell find his own way. Russell seeks his own "song" as he travels the unforgiving tundra, ice floes, and mountains with his team of sled dogs and is changed by the people he meets and his unexpected adventures along the way. Parents are advised that there are intense scenes in this book that may not be appropriate for younger readers.

Multicultural

1985 *192 pages*
Simon & Schuster Books for Young Readers

The Winter Room

This quiet coming-of-age tale takes place in a farmhouse in Northern Minnesota. Eldon's great uncle Nels tells stories of the old country, the family, and the possibly mythical "Woodcutter" around the wood stove in the living room, or "winter room," where the family gathers to pass the time on the cold winter nights. Interwoven with Great Uncle Nels' tales is Eldon's own story of life on the farm, the changing seasons, and the powerful and terrible story of the Woodcutter—which may or may not be true—but which changes everything for Eldon and his brothers. Though softer than Paulsen's usual fare, this story is no less powerful in its effect on readers.

1989 *128 pages* **Scholastic Press/Scholastic Inc.**

Eleanor H. Porter
Pollyanna

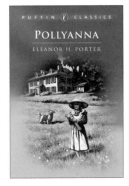

In this sweet and old-fashioned tale, we meet Pollyanna, an unwanted orphan whose optimistic spirit and way of using the "Glad Game" to turn life's lemons into lemonade is still winning hearts almost one hundred years after the book's original publication. When Pollyanna moves in with insensitive Aunt Polly, she still manages to make the best of it and befriends even the most unfriendly people in town. Ultimately even Pollyanna's positive spirit is broken when she is struck by a car and loses the use of her legs. But when the entire town rallies around her, she finds the bright side of her situation—and learns to walk again.

1927 *288 pages* **Puffin**

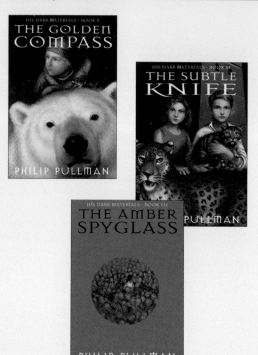

Phillip Pullman

His Dark Materials Trilogy

This epic trilogy introduces a world that is parallel to our own, but much more mysterious, dangerous, and filled with daemons, winged creatures, and armored polar bears that live alongside humans—as well as a substance called "Dust," so powerful that it can either unite the multiple worlds in the series or destroy them. Readers will cheer for Lyra, her daemon Pantalaimon, Will, and other characters, each more fantastical than the last, as they battle the ultimate forces in an effort to assure that good will triumph over evil. In *The Golden Compass,* we meet Lyra and her daemon Pantalaimon as the arrival of her uncle, Lord Asriel, pulls her into a battle in the far north to save the stolen children and help Iorek, the armored bear, save his people. In *The Subtle Knife,* Lyra journeys through the Aurora to a city in another world, where she meets Will, and they join forces to find Will's long-lost father, resulting in Lyra's kidnapping. In the conclusion of the series, *The Amber Spyglass,* Will and Lyra journey to the "Land of the Dead," where they learn the true origin of "Dust" and fight to free all the worlds of the dark substance.

The Golden Compass *(1995)*

The Subtle Knife *(1997)*

The Amber Spyglass *(2000)*

352–518 pages **Alfred A. Knopf**

Ridley Pearson

Illustrated by Tristan Elwell

Kingdom Keepers Series

In this four-book series from award-winning author Ridley Pearson, readers are transported to the "happiest place on earth"—Disney World—where some decidedly unhappy things are happening when the park closes for the night. In this quite fantastical tale, Finn Whitman and four other Orlando teens, who are hired as models for holographic theme-park guides, find themselves pitted against the classic Disney villains in a battle for the theme park and perhaps the world beyond. The Disney Imagineers use a new technology called DHI—Daylight Hologram Imaging—and Finn and his friends are transformed into hologram projections that guide guests through the park. As it turns out, there is a scary side effect that happens at night, as Finn and friends are transported back to the park to battle the villains—or are they dreaming? Over the course of the four books in this series, there are thrills, perils, and battles to be fought and won against Maleficent and a mysterious group called the Overtakers. This series provides more thrills and heart-stopping action than the Haunted Mansion and Space Mountain combined.

Kingdom Keepers: Disney After Dark *(2009)*

Kingdom Keepers II: Disney at Dawn *(2009)*

Kingdom Keepers III: Disney in Shadow *(2010)*

Kingdom Keepers IV: Power Play *(2011)*

336–560 pages **Disney Hyperion**

 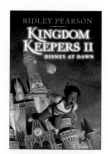

 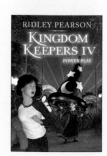

Newbery Award

Ellen Raskin
The Westing Game

Long a staple of school reading lists, this fascinating novel centers on sixteen mysteriously chosen people who must come together in a building on Lake Michigan called Sunset Towers to solve the mystery of who killed Sam Westing. They are read Sam's will, which offers a puzzle that they must solve in teams of two—with each pair getting a different set of clues. Each duo is given $10,000 to play the game—but to the pair that solves the murder goes Sam Westing's 200-million-dollar fortune. Readers will be drawn into the mystery as they try to solve it along with those playing the game.

1978 *192 pages* **Puffin**

Marjorie Kinnan Rawlings
Illustrated by N. C. Wyeth
The Yearling

This classic about a boy and the fawn he loves is certain to require a few tissues from all who read it. Jody lives in the backwoods with his parents and has always wanted a pet—but poverty and the cost of another mouth to feed prevents it. One day, while in the woods, Jody is bitten by a poisonous snake and must kill a deer to use its liver to draw out the toxin. In doing so, he orphans a fawn he names Flag, who becomes his constant companion. But as Flag grows up, Jody must choose between his beloved pet and his family, resulting in a terrible struggle between Jody and his mother.

1938 *528 pages* **Aladdin**

Wilson Rawls
Where the Red Fern Grows

This well-loved tale of a boy named Billy and his two redbone coonhounds, Old Dan and Little Ann, has been on middle-grade reading lists for years, and for good reason. Billy works to save the money to buy the two puppies and trains them to be the best coon hunters around. The story follows Billy and his dogs through their training and coon hunting competitions, as the bond between master and dogs grows ever stronger. But alas, there are perils for hunting animals, and the ending of this compassionate story is certain to bring tears to the eyes of anyone who has ever loved a dog.

1961 *208 pages* **Delacorte Press**

Rachel Renee Russell
Dork Diaries

This three-book series is about fourteen-year-old Rachel Russell, the new girl at a private middle school. In the first book, subtitled *Tales from a Not-So-Fabulous Life,* we learn of Rachel's hilarious attempts to fit in via her diary entries, coupled with her funny illustrations. Rachel has to deal with the resident "mean girl" and her posse, the "CCP" (cute, cool, and popular girls). Her further adventures in the next books, subtitled *Tales from a Not-So-Popular Party Girl* and *Tales from a Not-So-Talented Pop Star,* keep the side-splitting antics and embarrassing moments coming as Rachel continues her not-so-easy voyage of self-discovery.

2009 *288 pages* **Aladdin**

Percy Jackson & the Olympians

This five-book series became an instant sensation when the first book was released. These wonderfully written stories about a group of young demigods—the result of the gods of Greek mythology mating with humans in the present—set up an unusual plot. As if being a teenager isn't hard enough, try being a teenager with god-like powers that you can't control any better than your hormones. And that's where Camp Half-Blood comes in. Percy Jackson has problems at school, and problems at home, and some pretty mysterious and scary people keep trying to kill him. His mother brings him to Camp Half-Blood, where he learns the truth of his parentage: his father is actually Poseidon, god of the sea. All the other campers are also half-human offspring of the gods and, like him, have been brought to the camp to be trained to use and understand their powers. Throughout the five books in the series, Percy and his fellow demigods must do battle with any number of mythological beings that still exist (though artfully disguised) in our world. There are mythical beasts galore, such as satyrs, minotaurs, cyclopes, sirens, muses, and manticores, to name only a few. Plus, our young heroes must also deal with the sometimes angry and often jealous gods themselves—Zeus, Athena, Poseidon, Hades, Titan, and others—along the way. Each of these adventure-packed books is also filled with all the humor you would expect from a group of teenage demigods dealing with their vain and legendary ancestors, along with a few budding romances as well. Both parents and young readers will find much to love about these books—they are filled with thrilling stories of myth and legend and cleverly mixed with the problems that face teenagers and our world today. Middle-grade readers can relate to the characters, who in the end are really just searching for their own identities in the world—even if their world is a bit more epic in scale than the one we mere mortals inhabit.

The Lightning Thief *(2005)*

The Sea of Monsters *(2006)*

The Titan's Curse *(2007)*

The Battle of the Labyrinth *(2008)*

The Last Olympian *(2009)*

288–400 pages **Disney Hyperion**

The Red Pyramid (The Kane Chronicles, Book 1)

From the author of *Percy Jackson & The Olympians* comes a new series steeped in the myth and magic of ancient Egypt. When Sadie and Carter accompany their Egyptologist father to a British museum, they couldn't have imagined what would happen next. Their father blows up the Rosetta stone and looses five ancient Egyptian gods, including Set, who has evil plans. Carter and Sadie discover their heritage and their magical powers, which must now be used to save the world from Set's destructive plans. Filled with laugh-out-loud humor, this book and its sequels will be hits with readers.

2010 *528 pages* **Disney Hyperion**

Harry Potter

Since the publication of the first title in the series, the adventures of adolescent wizard Harry Potter have become the bestselling children's series the world over and a cultural phenomenon, as well loved by adults as they are by the middle-grade readers for whom they were written. The seven books in this series follow Harry and his friends Hermione and Ron, from their first days together at Hogwarts School of Witchcraft and Wizardry through young adulthood. Each book offers memorable characters and magical creatures galore, as well as fantasy and magic, but also larger themes about love, prejudice, emotional growth, coming of age, and death. Each book chronicles a year in Harry's life and wizardly education at Hogwarts. In the first book, *Harry Potter and the Sorcerer's Stone,* we learn Harry's mysterious origins and how he came to Hogwarts; we also meet most of the characters who will recur throughout the series and follow the beginning of Harry's education and understanding of what it means to be a wizard. In *Harry Potter and the Chamber of Secrets,* Harry and his friends investigate a fifty-year-old mystery that might explain some recent sinister events at Hogwarts and learn more about the evil Voldemort and his own time as a student there. In *Harry Potter and the Prisoner of Azkaban,* Harry begins his third year, learns more about the death of his parents, and deals with the knowledge that a possible participant in their deaths, Sirius Black, may be targeting him

for death as well. In *Harry Potter and the Goblet of Fire,* Harry is forced to compete in the Triwizard Tournament against his will and must not only complete a series of dangerous tasks, but also determine who is forcing him to and why. In *Harry Potter and the Order of the Phoenix,* Harry deals with the reappearance of Voldemort and his personal connection to him and secretly teaches his classmates to fight the dark arts. In *Harry Potter and the Half-Blood Prince,* Harry and his friends struggle with adolescence, learn new potions from an old textbook, which may not be reliable, and discover still more about Voldemort's history and powers. In the final book in the series, *Harry Potter and the Deathly Hallows*, Voldemort gains control of the Ministry of Magic, and Harry and his companions must fight him in a final battle at Hogwarts.

Harry Potter and the Sorcerer's Stone (1998)

Harry Potter and the Chamber of Secrets (1999)

Harry Potter and the Prisoner of Azkaban (1999)

Harry Potter and the Goblet of Fire (2000)

Harry Potter and the Order of the Phoenix (2003)

Harry Potter and the Half-Blood Prince (2005)

Harry Potter and the Deathly Hallows (2007)

309–896 pages **Arthur A. Levine Books/Scholastic Inc.**

Louis Sachar

Illustrated by Julie Brinckloe

Sideways Stories from Wayside School Series

The Wayside School is wacky from the first floor to the thirtieth; there is no nineteenth floor, and the architect who built it made a mistake—instead of building 30 classrooms next to each other like a regular school, he built them "sideways"—on top of each other—resulting in a 30-story tower (or it would be if it had a nineteenth floor.) The students and teachers in the school are wacky as well, and each book in this series features 30 funny stories about these eclectic residents of the Wayside School. But, as you might imagine, strange things happen when readers get to chapter 19—in one book it's missing, and in another it's backward. Early readers will love these comical stories with black-and-white illustrations, especially the crazy antics that always seem to occur on the thirteenth floor, of course. There are three books in the original series for newly independent readers: *Sideways Stories from Wayside School, Wayside School is Falling Down,* and *Wayside School Gets a Little Stranger,* and two math-related spin-offs: *Sideways Arithmetic from Wayside School* and *More Sideways Arithmetic from Wayside School.*

1998 *128-160 pages* **HarperCollins**

Holes

As a result of a curse on Stanley Yelnats' great-great-grandfather, Stanley ends up at a juvenile detention facility in the Texas desert. Overweight and lonely, Stanley tries to excel at the camp's one activity—digging holes exactly five feet deep and five feet across. Told in a first-person narrative, a story that drifts between the past lives of Stanley's relatives and the present moment, this odd novel beautifully creates a multilayered puzzle that may actually have those daily holes Stanley is digging become his salvation and change the course of his life forever.

1998 *272 pages* **Farrar, Straus & Giroux**

Newbery Award

Cynthia Rylant
Missing May

Foster child Summer is having a difficult time dealing with the death of her foster mother, May, but of more concern is how her foster father, Ob, is coping—which is not very well at all. Summer fears that her existence doesn't offer Ob enough reason to go on living and is worried when Ob claims he has seen a sign that May is on her way back from the spirit world. Along with her friend Cletus, Summer and Ob begin a journey to see a medium who they hope will explain things to Ob and offer some reassurance to all of them about life, death, and the afterlife—if there is one.

1992 *112 pages* **Orchard Books/Scholastic Inc.**

Newbery Award

Angie Sage
Illustrated by Mark Zug

Septimus Heap Series

In this magical and mysterious fantasy series, Septimus Heap is the seventh son of a seventh son and has wondrous magical powers. For readers who might be a bit too young for the Harry Potter books, this series is just the ticket, with just as much magic, some fun, and a few illustrations. There are five books in the series: *Magyk, Flyte, Physik, Queste,* and *Syren.* Septimus' adventures begin when he is stolen at birth from his family of wizards, pronounced dead, and replaced by a baby girl with violet eyes named Jenna, who has some magic of her own. The books are filled with humor and all the charms, potions, conjurations, and medieval alchemy readers would expect, as well as the forces of the sinister "Darke Magyk."

2005 *576–656 pages* **Katherine Tegen Books**

Newbery Honor

Gary D. Schmidt

The Wednesday Wars

Holling Hoodhood is in seventh grade in the year 1967, and everything around this eleven-year-old is changing. The country is at war in Vietnam, his sister wants to run away and be a flower child, and worst of all, every day in the afternoon all the Catholic kids in his class go to Catechism, the Jewish kids go to Hebrew school, and Holling, as the lone Presbyterian, has to stay and read Shakespeare with Mrs. Baker—who hates him. This sensitively told coming-of-age story is often quite funny while dealing with all the miseries of growing up in a time of change.

2007 *272 pages* **Clarion Books**

Illustrated by Garth Williams

The Cricket in Times Square

With illustrations by Garth Williams, this timeless story of a country cricket named Chester, who ends up in the heart of New York City, has enchanted middle-grade readers for over fifty years. Readers will follow Chester and his new friends—a streetwise city mouse and cat, along with their human friend Mario—on their big-city adventures and witness Chester's noble attempt to assist Mario's family. For interested readers, there are six sequels to enjoy as well: *Tucker's Countryside, Harry Cat's Pet Puppy, Chester Cricket's Pigeon Ride, Chester Cricket's New Home, Harry Kitten and Tucker Mouse,* and *The Old Meadow.*

1960 *144 pages* **Farrar, Straus & Giroux**

Newbery Honor

The Genie of Sutton Place

Tim is a young boy who is staying with his crotchety old Aunt in New York City. He's not happy about being there and fears he may never see his dog again. But things change when he finds one of his father's old archaeological notebooks: by reciting a spell he finds buried in the notebook's pages, he summons Abdullah, a real genie. Life on Sutton Place may never be the same, but for Tim, it's never been better.

1994 *192 pages* **Farrar, Straus & Giroux**

183

Caldecott Award

Brian Selznick

The Invention of Hugo Cabret

It's unusual for a book in this category to win the Caldecott award, but this is a rare book: a 544-page, fully-illustrated novel for middle-grade readers. In the early twentieth century, twelve-year-old Hugo is an orphan who lives in the Paris train station, where he tends the clocks and steals what he needs to live. This is a highly visual mystery filled with intrigue, including a notebook belonging to Hugo's father that contains a hidden message, a stolen key, and a mechanical man called an "automaton" that lurks, unmoving, in a museum. Hugo is determined to solve the mystery of the automaton and make it move once again.

2007 *534 pages* **Scholastic Press/Scholastic Inc.**

Anna Sewell
Illustrated by Scott McKowen

Black Beauty

Often referred to as the "autobiography of a horse," this well-loved horse tale is told in the first person by Black Beauty himself. Black Beauty begins life as a handsome colt with a strong spirit, galloping with his mother, Duchess, in the country meadows of England. Hard times force his owners to sell him, and Black Beauty bravely leaves his happy, comfortable life for one filled with hard labor and cruel masters. Even though he has a series of harsh owners and must work as a lowly cab horse in London, his spirit is never broken. The determination and uncompromising spirit of a beautiful horse has made this story a classic.

1877 *208 pages* **Sterling Classics**

Jeff Smith

Bone Series

This full-color graphic-novel series has been compared to The Lord of the Rings in terms of its epic fantasy scope—only it's a lot funnier and fully illustrated. The series begins when the three Bone cousins, Fone Bone, Phoney Bone, and Smiley Bone are run out of Boneville, jump-starting their adventures. Over the course of the nine books, they survive being separated in a vast desert and an attack of the Rat Creatures, and they confront dragons, mountain lions, erupting volcanos, and the Lord of the Locusts—all in an attempt to save the valley. There is as much thrilling action as there is humor in this series, and it's perfect for reluctant readers or any readers who like a few laughs along with their adventure stories. The series consists of nine books: *Out from Boneville, The Great Cow Race, Eyes of the Storm, The Dragonslayer, Rock Jaw: Master of the Eastern Border, Old Man's Cave, Ghost Circles, Treasure Hunters,* and *Crown of Horns,* plus four spin-off titles as well.

2005 *144–224 pages* **Graphix/Scholastic Inc.**

Jon J Muth on literature as a reminder of the possible...

I first decided to create books for children because I wanted to communicate with my children in every possible way. They were starting their journeys into the wilderness of being human and I'd been part of the way through, so I thought I could help them understand how they might carve their own paths. Many people have their first heart-opening experience in childhood: an awareness of that innate and natural connection between playfulness, joy, and curiosity, and what is sacred and holy and meaningful. It often gets *explained* out of them. Literature has always been a reminder for me of what's possible. Human beings do very little without models, and literature has an intimacy and power that can't be overestimated.

Leo (Lev Nikolaivich) Tolstoy, as a writer, has always been my greatest inspiration.

In my illustration, I find inspiration in many forms: Brancusi's sculptures, Gao Xingjian's paintings, Valentin Serov's paintings and drawings, Daisy Youngblood's clay work. In children's books, Wolf Erlbruch, Ed Young and Lisbeth Zwerger, and Peter Sís are constantly reinvigorating me and making me want to draw and paint better than I can. Lately, watching the movement of light and colors and form as my children play in the yard, nature has become my biggest inspiration.

See individual listings for books written and illustrated by Jon J Muth on pages 62, 86, 89, and 229.

Author/Illustrator Jon J Muth

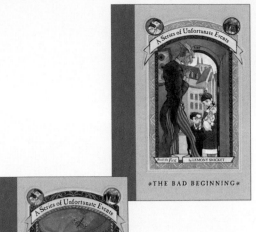

THE BAD BEGINNING

THE WIDE WINDOW

THE REPTILE ROOM

Illustrated by Brett Helquist

A Series of Unfortunate Events Series

This very funny and not-so-scary series of thirteen (of course, the unluckiest number) novellas follows the troubled adventures of the Baudelaire orphans—Violet, Claus, and Sunny—who have been placed with their sinister Uncle Olaf after a house fire of mysterious origin kills their parents. Count Olaf not-so-secretly sets out to abuse and perhaps kill the three in order to embezzle their inheritance. With over sixty million copies in print, and translated into forty-one languages, this series of tragically funny books has been a hit from the first volume, *The Bad Beginning,* to the last—*The End.* The titles of the books alone give readers an indication of the mayhem the three orphans are in for in each of these hilarious, dark mysteries. Every book is thirteen chapters long, and filled with all the evil deeds, madness, and murder that Uncle Olaf and his cohorts can come up with to obliterate the children and get his hands on their inheritance. The gothic, black-and-white illustrations add to the somber feel of the text but are also filled with the same sense of fun and far-out humor as the story. There is no question that readers will speed through each of these books to find out what exactly happens to the poor little Baudelaire orphans, and they will be laughing all the way. The series includes: *The Bad Beginning, The Reptile Room, The Wide Window, The Miserable Mill, The Austere Academy, The Ersatz Elevator, The Vile Village, The Hostile Hospital, The Carnivorous Carnival, The Slippery Slope, The Grim Grotto, The Penultimate Peril, The End,* and many additional spin-off titles and companion books.

1999 *176–224 pages* **HarperCollins**

Robert Kimmel Smith
Chocolate Fever

Henry Green loves chocolate—all kinds of chocolate in all forms. Chocolate cookies, cakes, candy bars, syrup, milk, cereal, you name it. If it's chocolate, he loves it, and if he could, he'd eat it for every meal, every day. Is there such a thing as too much chocolate? Henry doesn't think so—until one day when he breaks out in strange chocolaty-brown spots and is diagnosed with "Chocolate Fever." Henry doesn't want to be poked by doctors or stop eating chocolate, so he runs away, and that's when this hysterical story really takes off. Readers will be laughing, and probably craving chocolate, all the way through this book.

1972 *96 pages* **Putnam**

Zilpha Keatley Snyder

Illustrated by Alton Raible

The Egypt Game

In this classic mystery novel, we meet April Hall and Melanie Ross, two girls fascinated by anything having to do with Egypt. Together they create "The Egypt Game," filled with well-researched rituals, costumes, secret codes, belief systems, and ancient practices; soon they are joined by Melanie's brother, Marshall, and three other kids from the neighborhood—Elizabeth, Toby, and Ken. They play their game in an abandoned lot behind an antique shop, until strange things start to happen—someone is murdering children in the area, and the group fears their Egypt game has gone too far. Readers will be eager to find out the identity of the real culprit.

1967 *224 pages* **Atheneum**

Illustrated by Alton Raible

The Headless Cupid

This intricate story is part mystery, part ghost story, and 100 percent great reading from beginning to end. David and his younger siblings must deal with the fact that their father has remarried, and they now have a new, and somewhat odd, stepsister—Amanda, who aspires to be a witch. She dresses in bizarre costumes, studies black magic, and even has a "familiar"—a crow named Rolor. Amanda promises to instruct David and his siblings in the supernatural, but when the house they live in appears to actually be haunted, things start getting strange. Is there really a ghost, or is Amanda up to something?

1971 *224 pages* **Atheneum**

Jerry Spinelli

Maniac Magee

Maniac Magee is positioned and told as a folktale, which allows its theme of racism to be expressed more freely. "Maniac" Magee lives on his own in a town clearly divided on racial lines. He is a white boy who can run faster and hit balls better than anyone in town and is innocent of any differences between the black and white families. In fact, he has been lovingly taken in by feisty Amanda Beale and her black family. Maniac soon realizes that someone has to intervene to make the townsfolk more tolerant; he confronts their ignorance, and brings the two sides of town together in friendship.

1990 *192 pages* **Little, Brown and Company**

Wringer

This novel confronts the issue of peer pressure among middle-graders in a direct way, with a troubling premise that may be difficult for some readers. Nine-year-old Palmer is nervous about his approaching tenth birthday. In his town, all the ten-year-old boys have to become "wringers"—boys who wring the necks of pigeons at the annual pigeon shoot. The thought of this makes him sick—and what will happen when his buddies discover that he has been hiding a pet pigeon in his room? Readers will sympathize as Palmer must decide whether to give in to peer pressure and become a wringer or follow his heart.

1997 *240 pages* **HarperCollins**

Middle Grade Readers 8–12

187

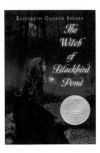

Newbery Award

Elizabeth George Speare
The Witch of Blackbird Pond

Kit Tyler is sixteen years old in 1697, when she leaves her grandfather's home in Barbados to live with her aunt and uncle in a Puritan colony in Connecticut. To say she doesn't fit in with the rigid and intolerant religious community is an understatement; Kit is used to dressing well, swimming, and speaking her mind. She becomes friendly with outcast Hannah Tupper, a Quaker who had been cast out of the Massachusetts colony and accused of being a witch. When a deadly illness strikes the village, initially both Hannah and Kit are accused of being witches. Eventually they are exonerated, but through the process Kit learns not to judge others too harshly.

1958 *256 pages* **Houghton Mifflin Books for Children**

Johanna Spyri
Illustrated by Scott McKowen
Heidi

For over a century, this story of a sweet girl who teaches everyone she comes in contact with how to love has been read by generations of adoring readers. Heidi is brought to live with her cold and hermit-like grandfather in the Alps, where she meets her friend Peter and his blind grandmother. Heidi's sunny disposition thaws even her icy grandfather's heart. When Heidi is then brought to the city as a companion to disabled Klara, she is miserable, though she and Klara do become friends. Eventually Heidi comes back to her beloved Alps and grandfather. Klara joins them as well and learns to walk again with Heidi's help.

1879 *272 pages* **Sterling Classics**

John Steinbeck
The Red Pony

This classic coming-of-age story may be difficult for sensitive readers. Jody is ten years old, and when his father buys him his own red pony, he is thrilled. The pony is too young to be ridden, but Jody loves and cares for him, and begins training him to take the saddle and lead. One day while Jody is at school, the pony is caught in a fierce storm. Though Jody lovingly nurses him, the pony dies, and Jody is devastated. Some time later, Jody assists his father with a mare's difficult birthing—and when the mare dies, Jody must raise the newborn colt himself, bringing the story full circle.

1933 *128 pages* **Penguin Classics**

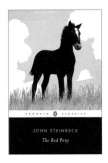

Noel Streatfeild
Illustrated by Diane Goode
Ballet Shoes

Three adopted sisters, Pauline, Petrova, and Posy, live with their adoptive Nana in England as they await the return of their great uncle Matthew, who has been on an extended paleontology expedition. Matthew has been gone so long that the girls must go to work to help support the family; since they have all been taking ballet lessons, they take to the stage. Each of the girls has a different dream: Pauline wants to be a famous actress, Posy a prima ballerina, and Petrova an airplane pilot. In the course of the story, they each learn that they can pursue separate dreams and still remain a family.

1993 *256 pages* **Yearling**

Robert Louis Stevenson

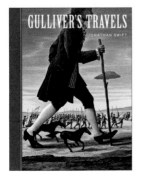

Kidnapped

This gripping adventure has been a classic for over a century and, in that time, has lost none of its original force. David Balfour leaves his simple life in the Scottish lowlands after his father's death to find his only living relative, his uncle Ebeneezer. David is unaware of the "bad blood" between his father and uncle; and when they meet he finds that Ebeneezer has no intention of granting him his rightful inheritance and instead has David kidnapped to be sold into slavery in North Carolina. David survives a shipwreck and many other swashbuckling adventures before his eventual escape and return to Scotland to claim his inheritance.

1886 *304 pages* **Penguin Classics**

Illustrated by Scott McKowen

The Strange Case of Dr. Jekyll and Mr. Hyde

This classic tale of good and evil residing within the same person is a masterful combination of horror, fantasy, and science fiction, written as only a master like Stevenson could. A good doctor's hunger for knowledge leads him to perform extreme scientific experiments—on himself. The results are astounding: good and thoughtful Doctor Jekyll develops an alter-ego, the horribly evil Mr. Hyde. This book about the dual nature of man, both good and evil, is an eerie thrill ride and will not be forgotten by anyone brave enough to read it all the way through.

1886 *96 pages* **Sterling Classics**

Illustrated by Scott McKowen

Treasure Island

When it comes to swashbuckling pirate stories, there are none that compare with *Treasure Island*. This novel has it all: a one-legged old salt with a parrot on his shoulder, a treasure map where *X* marks the spot, the line "Yo-ho-ho, and a bottle of rum!" and the most infamous, charming, and deadly villain of all pirate stories, Long John Silver. Add raging seas, mutiny, bravery, buried treasure, and a cast of unforgettable characters, and you have arguably the best pirate adventure story ever written. Though it was first published in 1881, it has lost none of the force or power of a tale well told.

1881 *232 pages* **Sterling Classics**

Jonathan Swift
Illustrated by Scott McKowen

Gulliver's Travels

Readers will love following the adventures of the kindly surgeon Lemuel Gulliver as he travels from one wondrous and strange land to another, and all will be entertained by the ironic and satirical humor in the text as well as the humanitarian lessons about tolerance and acceptance that are presented along the way. Gulliver visits four lands: Lilliput, where he is a giant among tiny people; Brobdingnag, where he is a tiny person among giants; the magical ruins of Laputa; and the land of the Houyhnhnms, gentle horses ruthlessly ruled by ugly, apelike humans.

1726 *320 pages* **Sterling Classics**

Illustrated by Carson Ellis

The Mysterious Benedict Society Series

This series will keep readers who love a great mystery hooked on reading through all three books. Reynie Muldoon is an eleven-year-old orphan who responds to a mysterious ad seeking "a gifted child looking for special opportunities," and the next thing he knows he and his three friends—Kate, Constance, and Sticky—are in training to become "The Mysterious Benedict Society." Readers will be captivated by their around-the-world adventures, as they are taken to an isolated location to be trained by the mysterious Mr. Curtain, a criminal mastermind who is scheming to take over the world. The four friends realize that the only way to foil his plans is to work together, and the reader will join them, working with the Mysterious Benedict Society members to figure out the clues in order to expose Mr. Curtain's evil plans for world domination. The next two books in the series are *The Mysterious Benedict Society and the Perilous Journey* and *The Mysterious Benedict Society and the Prisoner's Dilemma*.

2007 *400–512 pages* **Megan Tingley Books**

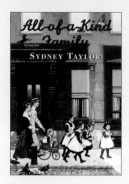

All-of-a-Kind Family Series

This special series illuminates what life was like for a Jewish immigrant family living in New York City just prior to World War I. Readers will experience life through the eyes of the five girls in the family—Ella, Charlotte, Henny, Sarah, and Gertie—and their little brother Charlie. For fans of historical fiction like the "Little House" series, these books and their urban setting offer another view of American life. In many ways, life is simple for this family. There are plenty of activities and adventures for the girls: going to the library, swimming at Coney Island, and shopping trips to the Rivington Street Market. The girls also create their own fun by playing hide-and-seek with buttons Mama has hidden in the living room, telling stories, and playing make-believe, but they do get into a fair amount of mischief as well. Integrated throughout the books are the traditions of Jewish life, and readers unfamiliar with the holidays and celebrations of Judaism will learn about them as the family celebrates the Sabbath and major holidays throughout the year. Judaism forms the tie that binds this family together, but many of the immigrant cultural experiences are relevant to any immigrant group; for example, the parents speak Yiddish but learn English from the girls, who answer queries in Yiddish with responses in English. The series follows the girls as they mature and marry, through the war years, and beyond; as each follows her own dreams and creates her own "all-of-a-kind" family.

All-of-a-Kind Family *(1951)*
189 pages **Yearling**

More All-of-a-Kind Family *(1954)*

All-of-a-Kind Family Uptown *(1957)*

All-of-a-Kind Family Downtown *(1972)*

Ella of All-of-a-Kind Family *(1978)*

J.R.R. Tolkien

The Lord of the Rings Trilogy

This trilogy is required reading for fans of fantasy fiction. Epic in scope and infused with moral lessons about good and evil, these books are often considered the standard by which other fantasy series are measured. With unforgettable characters, like the menacing Dark Lord Sauron, the hobbits Bilbo, Frodo, Merry, Pippin, and Sam, Gimli the Dwarf, Legolas the Elf, Boromir of Gondor, and the tall, mysterious stranger called Strider as their guides, this series draws readers into a nonstop adventure. The tales focus on the Dark Lord Sauron's efforts to regain control of the third of the three Rings of Power so that he can rule all of Middle-earth. That ring, called the Ruling Ring, is, oddly enough, in the possession of the hobbit Bilbo Baggins, who bequeaths it to his cousin Frodo along with a most dangerous quest: Frodo must journey across Middle-earth and deep into Mordor, the land ruled by Sauron, cast the ring into the Cracks of Doom, and destroy it. The story of that quest, undertaken by Frodo and the other members of the Fellowship of the Ring, comprises "The Lord of the Rings" trilogy.

The Fellowship of the Ring *(1954)*

The Two Towers *(1954)*

The Return of the King *(1955)*

352–448 pages
Houghton Mifflin Harcourt

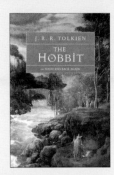

The Hobbit

For readers of fantasy fiction, there may be no more beloved character than the hobbit Bilbo Baggins. In this story, we meet Bilbo and follow him on an epic adventure with Gandalf the Grey to retrieve a stolen fortune from the dragon Smaug. Along the way, they meet giant spiders, hungry wolves, elves, dwarves, and a terrifying subterranean creature named Gollum—from whom Bilbo wins a golden ring. This book serves as an introduction to the Lord of the Rings trilogy, which readers will be eager to begin when they finish this book.

1937 *256 pages* **Houghton Mifflin Books for Children**

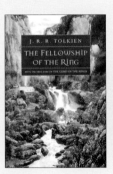
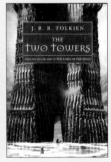
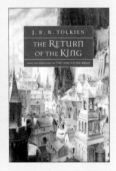

James Thurber
Illustrated by Marc Simont

The 13 Clocks

James Thurber did not write many books for children, but he did contribute this classic story. Though Thurber usually illustrated his own books, he was losing his sight as he wrote this novel, and Simont's illustrations illuminate the text beautifully. This tale features a wicked duke, who is always cold and thinks he has killed time; his lovely niece, who is always warm; and of course, the required handsome and valiant Prince, who eventually rescues both time and the princess. Filled with broad humor and evil deeds, this book has all the elements of a great fairy tale, and then some.

1950 *124 pages* **New York Review Books**

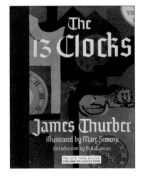

Mary Pope Osborne on linking the past to the present...

Why did I choose to write children's books? Actually I don't feel I ever actually chose to write children's books. I wanted to be a poet and a journalist. But one day I was "seized" by the voice of a young girl, so I went up to the roof of our old tenement building in New York City and began writing her story. I wrote and wrote, and every day I wrote more. When I'd finished, I showed the story to a friend who showed it to a literary agent who showed it to an editor who wanted to publish my story as a book for young adults.

Now, thirty years later, I've published over 100 children's books. I can honestly say I've never gotten bored with my work. Writing for children presents countless opportunities for self-expression and for learning about new subjects. I've written historical novels, picture books, biographies, mysteries, and the Magic Tree House Series. I've also retold many ancient stories of the Bible, as well as Greek, Norse, and Celtic mythology. I love linking the past to the present. That's probably why I'm particularly affected by the work of children's writers of the past, such as J.R.R. Tolkien, C. S. Lewis, Laura Ingalls Wilder, Beatrix Potter, William Steig, Arnold Lobel, Margaret Wise Brown, and James Marshall.

The writer Jean Rhys once said that all literature from all times was like a great lake; and the job of the writer is to keep filling the lake. I don't believe that children's literature is a little "kiddie pool" off to the side of the great lake. I like to imagine we're all contributing to the same mighty source, drop by drop.

See individual listings for books by Mary Pope Osborne on pages 118, 119, 175, and 220.

Mildred D. Taylor
Roll of Thunder, Hear My Cry

This novel deals frankly with the issues of racism and discrimination during the 1930s in rural Mississippi. Cassie Logan's family owns the land they work and live on, but that does not give them immunity from the terrifying "night riders," brutal attacks, lynchings, illness, and financial woes that come along with being an African American family during the Great Depression. The book follows Cassie over a turbulent twelve-month period, and for interested readers, the Logan family saga continues with *Let the Circle be Unbroken*, *The Road to Memphis*, and a prequel, *The Land*.

1976 *296 pages* **Dial**

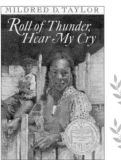

Newbery Award

Coretta Scott King Honor

Theodore Taylor
The Cay

Young Phillip is aware that his mother is prejudiced toward black people, and though he doesn't agree with her views, he has nothing else to compare them to. When World War II breaks out, Phillip and his mother set sail from their Caribbean island home for Virginia. Their ship is sunk by the Germans, and Phillip and his mother are separated on different rafts. A blow to the head renders Phillip blind, and he must rely on his raft-mate, an older black man named Timothy, for survival when they land on an unpopulated island. Timothy teaches Phillip how to survive on the island and also that the color of a man's skin is irrelevant.

1969 *144 pages* **Delacorte Press**

Mary Poppins Series

Readers will be happy to know that there are eight books about Mary Poppins, a most magical nanny. When Mary Poppins comes to Number Seventeen Cherry Tree Lane to be the nanny for twins Jane and Michael Banks, their world is forever changed. What other nanny can slide up a banister, pull an armchair out of her bottomless carpetbag, and make medicine taste like a lime cordial? But that is only the beginning; throughout the books Mary Poppins' magic allows Jane and Michael to enjoy the most fabulous adventures. They meet the King of the Castle and the Dirty Rascal, visit the upside-down house of Mr. Turvy and Miss Topsy, dangle above the park clutching a bunch of balloons, talk with cats on a distant planet, learn to dance with their own shadows, and so much more. The books are *Mary Poppins, Mary Poppins Comes Back, Mary Poppins Opens the Door, Mary Poppins in the Park, Mary Poppins from A–Z, Mary Poppins in the Kitchen, Mary Poppins in Cherry Tree Lane*, and *Mary Poppins and the House Next Door*.

1934 *224–336 pages* **Harcourt Children's Books**

Middle Grade Readers 8–12

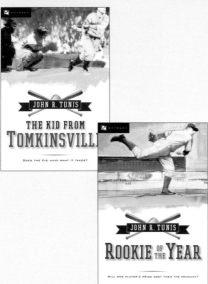

The Kid from Tomkinsville

This baseball story is so well written that readers can feel the crack of the bat as it hits the ball. Roy Tucker is an innocent country boy when he is called up from a small-town team to help the Dodgers out of a slump, he is overwhelmed by the grand lifestyle available in the world of professional baseball. His talent and career are nurtured by Dodgers veteran Dave Leonard, who teaches him that he must work hard if he is to succeed. When a freak accident threatens his pitching career, Roy is sure his dream has ended, until he realizes the value of perserverance, and goes on to play as an outfielder.

1940 *304 pages* **Sandpiper**

Rookie of the Year

In this riveting baseball story, Tunis focuses on the importance of teamwork in the midst of a championship race. Spike Russell hopes that he can still motivate his team, the Dodgers, to the pennant race, even though they are ten games behind the Cardinals. But in order to do that, he needs to bring his brilliant but irresponsible rookie pitcher in line, because his actions are threatening the team's chances and Spike Russell's job as well. The book demonstrates how star players alone can't win a game and what it takes to be a team.

1944 *240 pages* **Sandpiper**

Illustrated by Scott McKowen
The Adventures of Huckleberry Finn

In this classic American story, readers meet young Huck Finn, a boy who has no mother and whose father is a brutal drunk. To escape from life with his father, Huck fakes his own death and runs away. When Huck takes off on his adventures around Mississippi (some on foot, and some by river raft), he meets many memorable characters and has many unique and formative experiences. Most notable is Huck's friendship and travels with former slave Jim, which allow Huck and the reader to examine the complicated issue of racism and slavery.

1884 *320 pages* **Sterling Classics**

Illustrated by Scott McKowen
The Adventures of Tom Sawyer

The character of Tom Sawyer has come to represent American boyhood in a more innocent time. Filled with adventures, mishaps, tricks, and pranks, this book about a boy growing up in a nineteenth-century Mississippi River town is certainly a classic. Readers will laugh as Tom pulls pranks to try to get others to do his chores, like whitewashing a fence, and thrill to his adventures, such as robbing a grave with Huck Finn or getting lost at night in a frightening cave with Becky.

1876 *224 pages* **Sterling Classics**

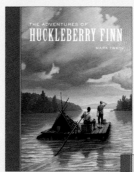

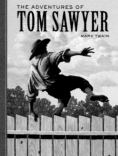

Jules Verne
Illustrated by Scott McKowen

20,000 Leagues Under the Sea

Sometimes literature can actually inspire reality rather than imitate it, and that is the case with this thrilling undersea adventure by Jules Verne. When he wrote this book of science fiction about Professor Aronnax and his dangerous journey under the sea to see what creatures lived there, Verne imagined a vessel that would take him deep into the ocean—the submarine *Nautilus*, which had yet to be invented. Readers will thrill to the adventures of Captain Nemo and his crew and the amazing, fearsome creatures they found far below the ocean.

1869 *336 pages* **Sterling Classics**

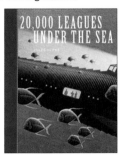

T. H. White

The Sword in the Stone

This stand-alone book is the first of four parts of White's larger work retelling the well-loved Arthurian legends. In this book, young Arthur, called Wart by the Wizard Merlin (who lives life backward), is taught what he needs to know to be a good king. Merlin transforms Wart into a fish, a hawk, an ant, a goose, and a badger, and each transformation teaches him a lesson that will serve him later in life. Merlin also teaches that might does not equal right, and that the only reason to go to war is to prevent war itself. Motivated readers can read Arthur's full story in White's *The Once and Future King*.

1938 *156 pages* **Philomel**

Newbery Honor

A Solitary Blue

Jeff Greene's mother, Melody, left him and his father when he was seven; he has been living with his formal and reserved father, the Professor, ever since. Jeff is overjoyed when, as a teenager, his mother reenters his life with an invitation to visit her for the summer in Charleston. He and his mother reconnect; he loves her warmth and free spirit and looks forward to visiting again the following summer. When he does, everything has changed: Melody has a boyfriend and no time for Jeff, and he returns to his father devastated. The way in which Jeff and his father both heal from that miserable summer offers a satisfying conclusion to this thought-provoking novel.

1983 *256 pages* **Atheneum**

Newbery Award

Dicey's Song

When Dicey's Momma abandoned her family, Dicey was left to take care of her two brothers and sister by herself. Eventually, her mother is traced to an asylum, where she lays near death. Dicey and her siblings make the long, difficult journey to live with an eccentric grandmother they have never known. Dicey hopes that the move will make her burden lighter. But Dicey has a hard time letting go, and she's also growing up and missing her Momma. It takes a serious crisis to bring Dicey and her family together again.

1982 *204 pages* **Atheneum**

The Boxcar Children Series

The original series about the Boxcar Children consisted of nineteen books, though there are over one hundred available today. These classic stories about four plucky orphans—Henry, Jessie, Violet, and Benny Alden—have been well-loved by middle-grade readers for more than eighty years. The four Alden children had been staying at a bakery until the night they heard the baker's wife say that she would take them in—except for Benny (the youngest), who would be sent back to the orphanage. Afraid of being split up, the children run away and make a home for themselves in an abandoned boxcar in the woods. They know this isn't a good solution, but they fear that their legal guardian, their grandfather James Alden, will be cruel to them. After many adventures, the orphans finally meet their long-lost grandfather, who is not at all cruel; he is both kind and wealthy and has been searching for them all along. Their grandfather moves the four children to his home, and has the boxcar brought as well to be used as a playhouse in the backyard. The subsequent books feature the children's adventures at home, at school, and on vacations.

1924 *150 pages* **Albert Whitman**

Kate Douglas Wiggin
Rebecca of Sunnybrook Farm

High-spirited Rebecca is sad to leave her beloved Sunnybrook Farm at age eleven to live with her wealthy but elderly aunts; in return for her help, they will see to Rebecca's education. Neither the aunts nor Rebecca are prepared for each other; Aunt Jane is kind and patient, while Aunt Miranda is strict and quick-tempered, and Rebecca is boisterous and spirited, not at all the young lady she should be. There are many amusing escapades as the three women learn to appreciate and love each other, and Rebecca learns that she can be a young lady and still have a grand, indomitable spirit.

1903 *241 pages* **Penguin Classics**

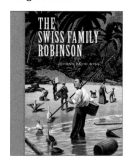

Johann David Wyss
Illustrated by Scott McKowen
The Swiss Family Robinson

This wonderful tale of survival on a deserted tropical island is perfect for middle-grade readers with a hankering for adventure. A storm and shipwreck at sea strands a Swiss pastor and his wife and four sons—Fritz, Ernest, Jack, and Franz—on a tropical island, where their optimistic spirit and cleverness allow them to not only survive, but also to thrive. Luckily for them, the island is abundant with all the fruits, plants, and animals they need, and with the materials they are able to scavenge from the wreck of the ship, they soon build the shelter they need. Add one pet monkey, and you have all you need for a perfect survival story.

1812 *352 pages* **Sterling Classics**

E.B. White

Illustrated by Garth Williams
Charlotte's Web

Charlotte the spider and Wilbur the pig are two of the best-loved characters in children's literature. This story of how they became friends and how Charlotte's clever message woven in her web saves Wilbur from the fate that awaits most farm pigs—the butcher shop—is a true classic. Parents who have not read this lovely book should be aware that Charlotte does die after weaving her miraculous web, which may be difficult for more sensitive readers, but it is handled gently and does not take anything away from the lesson about the true meaning of friendship.

1952 *192 pages* **HarperCollins**

Illustrated by Garth Williams
Stuart Little

Anything can happen in children's books—so it isn't all that strange when the second child in the Little family turns out to be a mouse named Stuart. The Littles lovingly accept Stuart into their family and accommodate his unusual size by making him a bed from a matchbox and sewing him tiny clothing. Snowball the cat isn't too thrilled with Stuart and poses some ongoing-but-very-funny challenges for him. Eventually, Stuart leaves home and strikes out on his own unique and humorous adventures, from racing toy sailboats to substitute teaching, and ultimately finds his place in the larger world.

1945 *144 pages* **HarperCollins**

Illustrated by Fred Marcellino
The Trumpet of the Swan

This is the story of a trumpeter swan named Louis, who is unable to trumpet like the rest of the swans. He can't make any sound at all. If he cannot trumpet his love like a normal swan, how will he ever get the love of his life, Serena, to pay attention to him? Louis goes to school to learn to read and write, but that doesn't help him trumpet. And then one day, his father brings him an actual brass trumpet—and when he plays it, he finally wins Serena's heart.

1970 *272 pages* **HarperCollins**

Jane Yolen
The Devil's Arithmetic

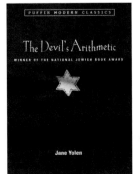

It's Passover, and Hannah is bored to death with hearing her grandparents' stories of the Holocaust and their talk of "remembrance." How can she remember something that happened before she was born? When the Seder progresses to the point when the door is opened for Elijah, Hannah opens the door—and is magically transported back in time, as the orphaned Chana at Auschwitz. What she experiences there will change her view of "remembrance" forever. At a critical moment for Chana, Hanna is returned to her home and family. Parents should be aware that this book deals frankly with the Holocaust and is not appropriate for sensitive readers.

1988 *170 pages* **Puffin**

Middle Grade Readers 8-12

Laura Ingalls Wilder

Illustrated by Garth Williams

The Little House Series

When Laura Ingalls Wilder began the process of writing stories about her life growing up on the unsettled prairies of the Midwest in the 1800s, she couldn't have had any idea that her life and words would still be in print and read around the world more than seventy-five years later. Each book in this series can be read on its own, but when taken together, they offer a first-person account of one family's experience as settlers in what was then an unsettled part of the United States. The books begin when Laura is just five years old and conclude with her marriage to Almanzo and the birth of their daughter, Rose. What happens in the years between makes up the bulk of the series, and above all, these books are a testament to a courageous and loving family who became part of American history. There are nine books in the series: *Little House in the Big Woods, Farmer Boy, Little House on the Prairie, On the Banks of Plum Creek, By the Shores of Silver Lake, The Long Winter, Little Town on the Prairie, These Happy Golden Years,* and *The First Four Years.*

1935 *160–384 pages* **HarperCollins**

Various Authors

The 39 Clues Series

This ambitious series is unique in many ways; it combines reading, online gaming, and card collecting, and though the first book and main story arc was written by Rick Riordan, the rest of the series was written by eight of today's bestselling children's authors in addition to Riordan: Gordon Korman, Peter Lerangis, Jude Watson, Patrick Carman, Linda Sue Park, and Margaret Peterson Haddix. If those talented authors weren't enough, the premise of the series is brilliant, and the online aspect, coupled with the fact that only a few clues are revealed per book, allows readers to play along. Fortunately for new readers of this series, all the books are now available, so they will not have to wait longer than a trip to the bookstore to keep the action moving. Here's what you need to know up front: the wealthy matriarch of the Cahill family has scattered thirty-nine mysterious clues to finding a powerful secret all around the world. Orphaned Amy and Dan Cahill have decided to take on the family, find all thirty-nine clues needed to solve the puzzle, and win the prize. Doing so will involve trips around the globe, plenty of peril and suspense, and having to deal with a seriously not-so-honorable clan of fellow Cahills who want the money for themselves. All that, and these books are also hysterically funny.

2008 *160–240 pages* **Scholastic Inc.**

Innovative Formats

One of the wonderful things about the world of children's books is that as paper and print technology have become more sophisticated, so too has the format of the book itself. There are many different ways that books have been enhanced and innovated; on the bookstore shelves you'll find books with pages that pop up, make sounds, spin, and have textures to touch and parts to move and books with flaps that you can lift and look under to discover clues or just for fun. The engineering behind these books is amazing and offers entertainment and interaction over and over again.

Innovative formats cover many interest areas and ages. You'll discover plenty of reliable information in these books about history, animals, and how things work, as well as classic stories—but many of them are just wild and wacky fun for every age. These are books that teach and offer valuable play and interactive surprises as well.

Here are some guidelines to keep in mind when choosing innovative formats:

- Age matters. For the youngest children, lift-and-look, touch-and-feel, and seek-and-find books with easy text, sturdy flaps, and simple engineering are best.

- Let your child's interests guide your choices; from monsters and dinosaurs to classic stories brought to life, there are many choices that add fun and interactivity to the basic story.

- The more sophisticated interactive books with added value aspects, like letters to open and read, are more suitable for older readers who know to treat a book more gently than a younger child. However, some care is needed when reading these books with all children; they will need to be coached not to rip and tear and to learn to handle them with care.

- These books may be designed for your child's fun and learning, but parents will love them too—so enjoy them together!

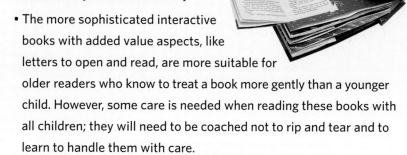

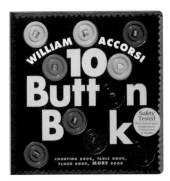

William Accorsi
10 Button Book

Learning to count is made simple with this oversized, double-thick board book. With safety-tested ribbons holding big, colorful buttons sewn into the binding and art created with lively collages of colorful felt, this book allows children to place the buttons into the illustrations on the die-cut pages as they learn to count from one to ten.

1999 Workman Publishing

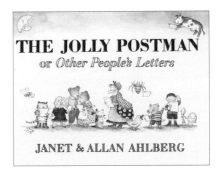

Janet and Allen Ahlberg
The Jolly Postman

For children fascinated by the mail and mail carriers, this book will deliver first-class entertainment. In this delightful book, told in rhyme, the Jolly Postman rides his bike through the fairy-tale kingdom, delivering the mail to the familiar characters that populate children's stories. Every other page features a pocket/envelope with an actual letter inside for children to open up and read. There's a letter from Goldilocks to the Three Bears, a catalog of scary delights sent to the Witch from Hansel and Gretel, and much more.

1986 LB Kids

Marion Bataille
ABC3D

Starting with the lenticular lens on the cover, which shows letters morphing into new letters as you move the book and moving to the dramatic three-dimensional paper engineering inside, both children and adults will be amazed at how Marion Bataille has reimagined both the alphabet and the pop-up book. The book uses only three colors—black, white, and red—each letter pops up and out into a three dimensional representation—and then, as you turn the pages, a clever flip or slide built into the book turns one letter into another. In this case, A is for *Astounding* and Z is for the *Zenith* of paper engineering.

2008 Roaring Brook Press

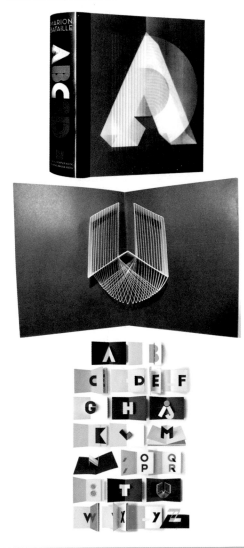

Alpha Bugs

Forget everything you know about bugs, the alphabet, and even pop-up books for that matter. This book not only has cleverly engineered pop-ups, but also lift-the-flaps, scratch-and-sniffs, textures, pull tabs, a wheel that turns, and more. The adorable bugs appear alphabetically in the strangest places, and Carter uses alliteration to introduce them to children; for example, "two terribly timid Tomato Bugs." This interactive book is sure to entertain children with every reading.

1994 Little Simon

How Many Bugs in a Box?

This counting book provides children with an eye-popping, bug-infested tour of numbers one through ten. With each page turn, children will lift the flaps to reveal the insects that pop up and out in numerical order. The pop-ups are fun and engineered to be sturdy enough for younger readers just learning their numbers.

1988 Little Simon

One Red Dot

If the premise of this book is uncomplicated—find the one red dot in each paper sculpture—the execution of that premise is anything but. Each double-page spread features one fantastical, three dimensional, boldly colored paper construction—some with tabs, slides, and actual clicking sounds. This visual game of hide-and-seek, combined with sophisticated paper engineering, will fascinate parents and children alike. Due to the more complex concept and somewhat delicate design, this book is not appropriate for young children.

2005 Little Simon

Yellow Square

David Carter once again takes the idea of paper engineering far beyond the traditional pop-up and into the realm of three-dimensional visual art in this astounding book. As with *One Red Dot,* this book is too conceptual and delicate for the littlest children, but parents and older children will find the search for the yellow square in these paper sculptures fascinating. Other materials are used in addition to paper: plastic netting, yarn, and wax paper effectively enhance the dimensionality of the unique paper constructions.

2008 Little Simon

Rod Campbell
Dear Zoo

This classic first lift-the-flap book has been a hit with toddlers for more than twenty-five years. The story involves a little boy who writes to a zoo, asking for a pet. Each time he receives a crate from the zoo, children can open the flaps to see which animal he has been sent. This simple storyline leads to laughter, as the zoo sends one inappropriate animal after another—which the young boy sends back—until the last crate arrives and brings with it a surprise ending.

1982 Little Simon

Anne Carter
Illustrated by Jan Pieńkowski
Dinnertime

This pop-up is a sly tribute to the circle of life in the animal world. Brightly colored, nonthreatening animals populate the pages, each with a wide-open, three-dimensional mouth ready to eat the creature on the previous page. First frog eats fly, then vulture eats frog, gorilla eats vulture, and so it goes with each successively larger animal. Young children will happily eat up every gory detail of this survival-of-the-fittest pop-up book.

1981 Candlewick Press

Jen Green
Tutankhamen's Tomb

Opening this book allows young explorers to take a three-dimensional tour of both Tutankhamen's tomb and ancient Egyptian history. Using illustration and actual photographs of ancient sites, this book offers mummies, hieroglyphics to decipher, jars to open, pages to peer through, timelines, maps, pop-ups, pull tabs, cross-sections, and flaps—everything needed for a fully interactive reading experience.

2006 Barron's Educational Series, Inc.

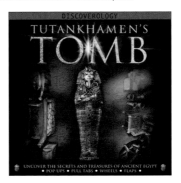

Chuck Murphy
Color Surprises

Each page or spread of this book features a primary-colored square that children can lift, push, slide, or open to reveal a sliding, slithering, or bouncing pop-up animal that embodies each color. It might be a blue parrot or a green snake, until the final spread, which features an entire aquarium's worth of brightly colored fish swimming across the pages. This book is designed for young children, but some parental supervision is required to assure that the pop-ups are not damaged by enthusiastic toddlers.

1997 Little Simon

The Ology Series

Though the books in this series cover diverse and thrilling subjects for adventurous readers (there are more titles in the series than are represented here), it is what they have in common that sets this series apart. Each book features an extraordinary number of interactive components, including (but absolutely not limited to) booklets, flaps, fold-outs, pull-outs, pop-ups, personal notes, letters, drawings, maps, textures, spells, potions, pendants, and so much more. Since they are written as journals or field guides, the reader is included in the adventures and can use all the added components to solve various mysteries, crack the cases, or make discoveries right along with the "as told by" fictionalized author/expert. These books offer hours of fun—but the facts, history, and information presented also offer a learning experience that is interactive and un-put-down-able. There is something in this series for every young explorer, investigator, or budding scientist.

Dr. Earnest Drake, Edited by Dugald A. Steer
Dragonology:
The Complete Book of Dragons
2003 Candlewick Press

Emily Sands, Edited by Dugald A. Steer
Egyptology:
Search for the Tomb of Osiris
2004 Candlewick Press

Dr. Earnest Drake, Edited by Dugald A. Steer
Monsterology: The Complete
Book of Monstrous Beasts
2008 Candlewick Press

Lady Hestia Evans, Edited by Dugald A. Steer
Mythology: Greek Gods,
Heroes, & Monsters
2007 Candlewick Press

Captain William Luber, Edited by Dugald A. Steer
Pirateology:
The Pirate Hunter's Companion
2006 Candlewick Press

Spencer Blake, Edited by Dugald A. Steer
Spyology:
The Complete Book of Spycraft
2008 Candlewick Press

Archer Brookes, Edited by Nick Holt
Vampireology:
The True History of the Fallen
2010 Candlewick Press

Master Merlin, Edited by Dugald A. Steer
Wizardology: The Book of
the Secrets of Merlin
2005 Candlewick Press

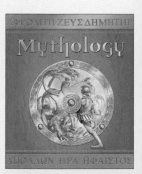
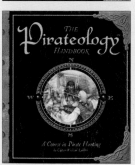

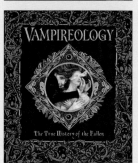

P. H. Hanson
My Granny's Purse

This wonderful book is overflowing with things you would expect to find in a real purse and many surprises as well. There is a comb, a mirror, keys, and sunglasses, of course, but also a wrench, a compass, a passport, jewelry, chocolates, and family photos. Filled with removable objects which provide maximum play value for curious children, the text of the book and the contents of the purse tell the story of an adventurous grandmother who offers plenty of advice along the way. Two similar titles, *My Grandpa's Briefcase* and *My Mommy's Tote*, are also available.

2003 Workman Publishing

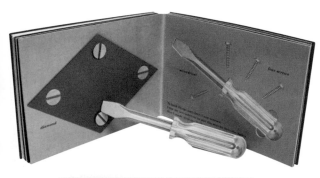

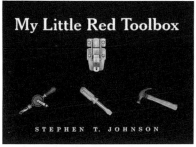

Stephen T. Johnson
My Little Red Toolbox

This sturdy book for boys is a bit of a hybrid; it is a book that teaches counting, colors, and shapes, and it is also a toy with seven sturdy removable tools that really work. Children will love playing with a saw that makes noise when it cuts wood (corrugated cardboard in the book), a drill with moveable parts, a screwdriver with screws that turn, a wrench with bolts that tighten, a hammer made for pounding nails, and a pencil, ruler, and erasable slate perfect for for drawing up plans.

2000 HMH Books (Franchise)

Matthew Reinhart and Robert Sabuda

Robert Sabuda and Matthew Reinhart, working both as a team and individually, have elevated the concept of pop-up books and paper engineering to previously unforeseen heights. Each of the books in this series is fully interactive: pages pop up and out, images transform from one thing to another, objects spin and slide, there are gatefolds at the corners and tabs to pull and push, and every turn of the page offers young readers a startling and unexpected surprise. Whether the subject is fairies, dinosaurs, mythology, or sharks, these books are suitable for either boys or girls and will captivate parents as well. The special effects these two master paper engineers accomplish in their books are always astonishing—young readers will continuously ask "how did they do that?" as they marvel at the seemingly magical (and always breathtaking) possibilities of stunning illustrations on cleverly folded paper.

**Encyclopedia Mythologica:
Fairies and Magical Creatures** (2008)

**Encyclopedia Mythologica:
Gods and Heroes** (2010)

**Encyclopedia Prehistorica:
Mega-Beasts** (2007)

**Encyclopedia Prehistorica:
Dinosaurs** (2005)

**Encyclopedia Prehistorica:
Sharks and Other Sea Monsters** (2006)

Candlewick Press

Maurice Sendak and Arthur Yorinks
Illustrated by Matthew Reinhart
Mommy?

The text of this monster-filled pop-up book consists of two words. One is a question: "Mommy?" The other, the answer: "Baby!" Even with a limited number of words, there is a story here, and it is told visually through the brilliant collaboration of an award-winning trio of children's authors and illustrators: Arthur Yorinks, Maurice Sendak, and Matthew Reinhart. In this not-too-scary tale, perfectly suited for children who like a more thrillingly interactive read, a little boy wanders into a haunted house in search of his mommy. The boys asks each mad scientist and monster the same question, "Mommy?" The pop-ups and special effects are as amazing as the way he disarms the monsters. He gives a pacifier to Dracula, removes Frankenstein's bolts, and (with an impressive spinning element) unwraps the Mummy. The final spread features one monster of a conclusion with all the characters literally flying up and out of the book, as our hero finds his Mommy—the Bride of Frankenstein.

2006 Michael di Capua Books/Scholastic Inc.

Innovative Formats

Roxie Munro
Go! Go! Go!

This sturdy, oversized interactive book is sure to keep toddlers and preschoolers entertained for hours. With two big, full-page fold-outs and many lift-and-look flaps and moving parts, this book featuring things that go and will keep busy fingers and imaginations going through multiple readings. Firemen put on their gear and head off to fight a fire, horses are saddled and gallop off on a steeplechase track, a submarine voyages to the bottom of the sea, and race cars race for the checkered flags. Munro has managed to combine two childhood favorites—things that go and interactivity— in one great book.

2009 Sterling

David Pelham
Sam's Sandwich

This clever and very funny lift-and-look book actually resembles a sandwich, with a cover designed to look like bread and layers of ingredients that Sam adds to the sandwich he makes for his sister Samantha. However, it's what children see as they lift and look under the expected ingredients, such as tomatoes, lettuce, cheese, pastrami, and hard-boiled eggs, that will have them squealing. Devious Sam has added a few ingredients of his own—some truly icky bugs. Each reveal of a fly, a worm, a slug, a caterpillar, or a group of ants nestled into the more traditional sandwich fare will have children howling with laughter.

1991 Dutton

Old MacDonald: A Hand-Puppet Board Book

There are plenty of board books that integrate finger puppets into the book, some of which we have reviewed elsewhere in this guide. What makes this book (and the other books from Scholastic in this series for infants and toddlers) so much fun is the creative format—a five-fingered glove with an animal puppet for each finger, and an embroidered, plush cloth sing-a-long book are built into the palm of the glove. It's both simple and genius, and allows children and adults to sing, *oink, moo, meow*, quack, bark, and act out the song from beginning to end.

2007 Cartwheel Books/Scholastic Inc.

Robert Sabuda

Innovative Formats

Lewis Carroll
Alice's Adventures in Wonderland

In this pop-up version of *Alice's Adventures in Wonderland,* Robert Sabuda manages two impressive feats: he abridges Lewis Carroll's original text without losing the essence of the story, and he also takes the original John Tenniel illustrations and turns them into dramatic, three-dimensional works of art that appear to actually fly up and out of the pages. Sabuda's explosive paper engineering, including a masterpiece depicting Alice surrounded by a deck of flying cards, enhance this classic tale for a new generation of readers.

2003 Little Simon

J. M. Barrie
Peter Pan

In Sabuda's hands, the classic story of Neverland, with its pirate ships and familiar characters of Peter, Tinkerbell, Wendy, and Captain Hook, is transformed into a three-dimensional marvel. The story is abridged and presented in small booklets that open on each page, perfect for young readers. The pop-ups that accompany the text are amazing in their ingenuity and ability to surprise the reader and enhance the story. This timeless tale is brought to life in an entirely fresh and exciting style, featuring pull tabs, moveable art, and even a final spread featuring Captain Hook actually sliding down a tree.

2008 Little Simon

L. Frank Baum
The Wonderful Wizard of Oz

For this book, published to commemorate the one hundredth anniversary of the publication of L. Frank Baum's *The Wonderful Wizard of Oz*, Robert Sabuda pulled out all the stops, creating this masterful paper-engineered pop-up retelling of the story, using as inspiration the original art created by W. W. Denslow. The special effects include a hurricane that actually spins, removable green-lensed glasses for children to wear as they view the Emerald City (and which also reveal a secret message on every page), and a hot air balloon that appears to inflate three-dimensionally before the reader's eyes, to name only a few. This dazzling retelling of a treasured family classic will become a book that children reach for again and again.

2000 Little Simon

The Movable Mother Goose

Reinterpreting the traditional Mother Goose rhymes for children with animals in the place of the human characters offers a new twist on the classic rhymes. Add Sabuda's brilliant paper engineering, pop-ups, pull tabs, foil, and all manner of three-dimensional effects to the mix, and these familiar rhymes reach a new level. This book offers plenty of action, but is still sturdy enough for careful youngsters who will thrill at four-and-twenty whimsical, sunglass-wearing blackbirds bursting from a pie.

1999 Little Simon

Rufus Butler Seder

Scanimation Books

All you need to know about scanimation is that the technology built into the book makes turning the pages create the illusion that the images on the page are moving in a fluid, realistic manner. Unlike lenticular lenses, which cause an image to appear to move when physically adjusted to a different angle (which parents may be more familiar with), scanimation allows the visual perception of movement with a turn of the page and without moving the book or changing the reader's point of view. The result is both realistic and magical at the same time. All three of these books use this technology, along with simple rhyming text, to tell a story that involves movement. In *Gallop!*, children will watch as black-and-white horses run, eagles soar, and chimpanzees swing from the branches. In *Swing!*, sports of all sorts are explored in moving black-and-white images. Baseballs seem to fly directly at the reader, bicycle wheels spin, skaters twirl, and much more. *Waddle!* features full-color images of animals that slither, slide, flap, and prance across the pages. These books are sturdy, well constructed, and will mesmerize young children for hours, while older children try to figure out just exactly how the process works.

Gallop! *(2007)*

Swing! *(2008)*

Waddle! *(2009)*

Star Wars *(2010)*

Wizard of Oz *(2011)*

Workman Publishing

Innovative Formats

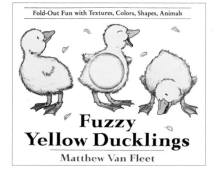

Matthew Van Fleet
Fuzzy Yellow Ducklings

Perfect for infants and toddlers, this long, fold-out book is filled with shapes, colors, and textures, making it an excellent first touch-and-feel book. Each spread features a shape—a circle, a rectangle, a crescent—and within each shape, a texture—fuzzy, wooly, bumpy. Lift the right-hand flap, and you will find the corresponding animal—a duckling, a sheep, or maybe a frog. With text limited to three descriptive words per page, this straightforward book teaches three early concepts (shapes, colors, and textures) under one cover.

1995 Dial

Peter Yarrow

Paul O. Zelinsky

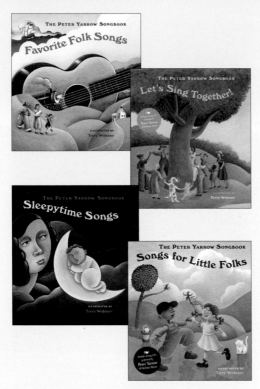

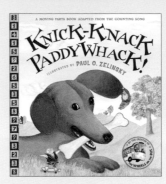

Knick-Knack Paddywhack!

Through some very clever paper engineering, Paul Zelinsky takes the traditional children's song "This Old Man" and adds pull-tabs, pop-ups, and lift-the-flaps to create a "moving-parts" book that gives a fresh spin to the classic counting song. Pull the tab and the dog gets a bone, the old man's bicycle wheels spin as he goes rolling home, and that's not all—there's a whole lot of knick-knack-paddywhacking going on all through the book in unexpected ways. This sing-along story is filled with interactivity from the first page to the last, where several old men go rolling—down a hillside—home.

2002 Dutton

Illustrated by Terry Widener
Peter Yarrow Songbooks

Peter Yarrow, member of the iconic '60s folk trio Peter, Paul & Mary and a musical legend in his own right, turns his focus toward music for children with this four-book series of four songbooks—each featuring a sing-along CD with twelve fully-produced songs. Whether it's a calming song for bedtime like "All Through the Night," or "Hush Little Baby," or songs that beg to be sung together, like "Blue Tail Fly" and "Home on the Range," these songs are the ones we all grew up singing and the ones we want to sing with our children as well. Each song is illustrated by Terry Widener, and each book also features the music, chords, and lyrics in the back for those who might want to pick up a guitar and strum along. Perfect for long car rides and family sing-alongs, these books will offer hours of singing and dancing for every family and at least one, if not all, should be part of every family's musical library.

Favorite Folk Songs *(2008)*
Let's Sing Together *(2009)*
Sleepytime Songs *(2008)*
Songs for Little Folks *(2010)*
Sterling

The Wheels on the Bus

This moving-parts book brings a favorite song to life for young children. It is filled with easy-to-manipulate flaps, tabs, and other interactive parts: the wheels on the bus actually do "go round and round" and the wipers really go "swish, swish, swish," as the bus picks up passengers all over town. There are many funny visual gags in the art, and children will love the ending: the bus pulls up to the library, where a folk singer is performing. What do you think he's singing?

1990 Dutton

Innovative Formats

Fairy Tales,
Folktales & Anthologies

For many of us, the love of reading began with the fairy tales and folktales read to us as bedtime stories. We learned simple moral tales via Aesop's fables, our first superheroes were the gods and goddesses of Greek and Norse myths, we learned about American folk heroes like Johnny Appleseed and Paul Bunyan, and we first learned about magic and good versus evil from the fairy tales by the Brothers Grimm, Hans Christian Andersen, and Charles Perrault.

These tales have survived all these years not just because they are brilliantly written, but because they all still have something to teach us about how we live today. They exist in many forms, including anthologies and collections of the original tales, beautifully illustrated versions of a specific tale, or themed collections. The books we have chosen are some of the best available in a wide variety of categories and reading levels. Some are picture books to read aloud to younger children, some are graphic novels, and others are more appropriate for a middle-grade reader. No family library should be without a few well-selected choices from this section.

Here are some guidelines to keep in mind when choosing fairy tales, folktales, and anthologies:

- Age and reading level come first; start with picture-book formats for the youngest children, and move on to some of the more comprehensive collections to read aloud or for independent readers.

- There is excitement, fun, humor, and magic in these tales to appeal to all, from the very youngest child to the more sophisticated reader.

- One cautionary note: the original versions of many fairy tales do not have happy endings (unlike the TV or movie versions your child may be familiar with), so when using an anthology of original stories, you should read them first to determine whether or not they are appropriate for your child.

- Myths and legends and stories about pirates and dragons are thrilling adventure stories but may also have some violence or content that is not suitable for younger children; parents should preread these stories to determine whether or not they will upset their child.

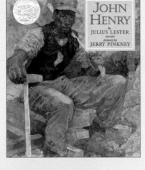

Illustrated by Jerry Pinkney

Aesop's Fables

These traditional fables are brought to life by award-winning illustrator Pinkney's lush and detailed watercolors, in full-page art and smaller illustrations as well. Many of the classics are here, such as "The Tortoise and the Hare" and "The Lion and the Mouse," but there are also some lesser-known stories included. Through these gloriously illustrated fables children will learn classic lessons, such as "don't count your chickens before they hatch" and many more.

2000 Chronicle Books

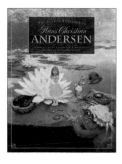

Retold by Margaret Clark
Illustrated by Christian Birmingham

The Classic Treasury of Hans Christian Andersen

This treasury of Andersen's fairy tales is not all inclusive, but it does offer a selection of eight of his best-loved tales, including "The Ugly Duckling," "Thumbelina," "The Steadfast Tin Soldier," "The Emperor's New Clothes," "The Little Match Girl," "The Little Mermaid," "The Nightingale," and "The Princess and the Pea." The illustrations set this book apart from other collections of its kind; Birmingham's beautiful paintings, while realistically rendered in great detail, are also filled with magic and wonder that will capture children's full attention as they read or listen to these classic tales.

2002 Running Press

D'Aulaires' Book of Greek Myths

This version has been the "go to" standard for Greek myths since its publication in 1962. Written in language that can be easily undersood by children of read-aloud age and also easy enough for those reading on their own, the myths in this book have stood the test of time. The illustrations are magnificent, and considering the subject matter, not too scary for young children. No family library should be without this definitive collection of all the thrilling exploits of Zeus, Athena, Hera, Pandora, the Titans, Poseidon, and the all the rest of the fascinating Greek gods and goddesses.

1962 Doubleday

D'Aulaires' Book of Norse Myths

This companion to *D'Aulaires Book of Greek Myths*, originally published in 1967, was out of print for many years until its reissue in 2005. Children can once again thrill to the adventures of Odin, Thor, and Loki, as well as bizarre monsters, elves, sprites, gnomes, and more than a few giants with ancient grudges to settle. This volume is lavishly illustrated and broken into short, focused chapters, perfect for reading one story at a time or as many as you want to read in a single sitting. There is adventure, magic, and fantasy galore; these myths are perfect for children who want a little more action and adventure in their stories.

1967 New York Review Books

Fairy Tales, Folktales & Anthologies

Armand Eisen
Various Illustrators
A Treasury of Children's Literature

This single-volume anthology offers a solid overview of children's literature and includes excerpts of longer works like *Pinocchio, Alice in Wonderland, The Wind in the Willows,* and others, and also an abundance of nursery rhymes, poems, fables, folktales, and fairy tales as well. Featuring the illustrations of sixteen different artists, this book covers a lot of ground, whether you are looking for the story of Paul Bunyan or Cinderella or Aesop's fables. One of the advantages of anthologies is that you can get a sense of what interests your child and follow up with more specific single-title stories or author-themed collections.

1992 Houghton Mifflin Books for Children

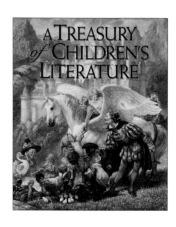

Amy Ehrlich
Illustrated by Diane Goode
The Random House Book of Fairy Tales

As the author of this book says in her introduction, fairy tales serve a dual purpose; yes, they are meant to enchant and entertain, but they also reinforce the messages that goodness, using your wits, and inner beauty can conquer all, that children should always take the righteous path and avoid bad and evil deeds, and that perpetrators of evil will be punished. While these messages may not always hold true in real life, it is comforting to young children. The illustrations in this collection are lighthearted and whimsical, and each story features both full-color and black-and-white illustrations.

1985 Random House Children's Books

Howard R. Garis
Uncle Wiggily's Story Book

These classic tales of everybody's favorite gentleman rabbit have been entertaining children for decades and will no doubt continue to do so for decades to come. Uncle Wiggily is a very kind and compassionate rabbit, and his stories always focus on either a human or an animal who needs advice, kindness, or understanding in a difficult or frightening situation. Whether he is helping a little boy who is afraid to go the dentist, dealing with chicken pox, or rectifying bad behavior, he always does so quietly and by example, rather than with a lecture. These innocent stories deal with a myriad of common situations that children are familiar with and can offer helpful advice and coping skills.

1921 Grosset & Dunlap

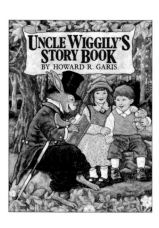

Michael Hague

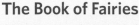

The Book of Dragons

This gloriously illustrated book features seventeen short dragon-related tales from many familiar authors such as Kenneth Grahame, J.R.R. Tolkien, E. Nesbit, Elizabeth Coatsworth, C. S. Lewis, and more and includes folk tales from China, Italy, and Germany. Hague's classical illustrations take care with every detail of these dragons in richly hued watercolors and tightly controlled black-and-white sketches. With art so vivid children can count every scale on the dragons' backs and lush backgrounds filled with detailed images of nature and animals, there is as much to thrill the reader in the art as in the stories themselves.

1995 HarperCollins

The Book of Fairies

While there is no doubt that little girls are enthralled by all things fairy related, from sparkly wings to magical powers, there is plenty in this book for little boys too. Not all these fairies are sweet and delicate in nature; some are quite crotchety and mischievous. The book includes short excerpts from *Thumbelina, Peter Pan, The Flower Babies,* and six other tales as well as extensive notes on the stories at the back. Hague does here what he does best: invests the color and pen-and-ink drawings with magnificent details and as much magic and mystery as any fairyland could hold.

2000 HarperCollins

The Book of Pirates

Children have always been fascinated by the lives of pirates, from Captain Kidd and Long John Silver to Captain Hook, and that is exactly what is to be found in this collection of eleven classic pirate yarns from authors such as Robert Louis Stevenson, Arthur Conan Doyle, J. M. Barrie, Washington Irving, John Masefield, and others. The artwork is filled with all the details of pirate life, including incredibly detailed renderings of their ships and their clothing, in both color and pen-and-ink drawings. This classically illustrated anthology with its dark-and-moody scenes of the ocean at night and detailed natural settings will have children poring over the illustrations as they engage with the stories of the dirty deeds and exploits of the scallywags onboard.

2001 HarperCollins

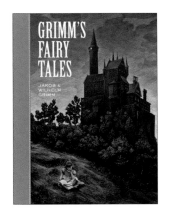

Grimm's Fairy Tales

This collection presents 120 of the Grimm's tales in their original form. All of your favorites are here, including "Cinderella," "Snow White," "Hansel and Grethel," "Rapunzel," "Rumpelstiltskin," "The Golden Goose," "The Frog Prince," and many more. A caution to parents is in order: these are the original versions of the tales, not the prettified versions you've seen in movies or on television—the villains are frightening, the consequences of bad behavior and evils that happen to those who are good can be gruesome, and the endings are not always happily ever after— so we encourage pre-reading these tales to determine whether or not they are appropriate for your children. That said, these classic once-upon-a-time tales are also filled with magic, action, adventure, and thrills galore, which might be just right for older children, and certainly for adults.

2009 Sterling Classics

Fairy Tales, Folktales & Anthologies

Dav Pilkey on freedom from perfection...

I owe so much to the influence of James Marshall (*George and Martha*) and Arnold Lobel (*Frog and Toad*). I fell in love with their books as an adult, in particular their gentle humor and compassion. When I was a kid, I loved to draw and make up stories. I didn't worry about drawing things perfectly or spelling things correctly. I just wanted to get my ideas and stories on paper. I loved the freedom that came with creating stories just for fun. Once I got published, I spent years traveling to different schools and talking with kids about my books. I was surprised to learn that most of the kids I met didn't consider themselves to be artists or writers. Many thought they had to be able to draw perfectly to be an artist. They had also convinced themselves they needed to spell perfectly in order to be writers. Everywhere I went, I met kids who were stifled creatively because of their fears of imperfection.

Ever since then, my goal has been to encourage kids to be creative without worrying about being perfect. That's how *Captain Underpants* came along. I designed each book to contain two or three "mini-comics" created by the stories' protagonists, George Beard and Harold Hutchins. George and Harold's simple, silly, and wildly imperfect mini-comics turned out to be one of the most popular parts of each book—and that inspired me to give "the boys" a chance to create their own full-length novels, *The Adventures of Super Diaper Baby* and *The Adventures of Ook and Gluk, Kung-Fu Cavemen from the Future*.

My hope is that George and Harold's examples will give kids permission to invent their own stories without concern for perfectionism, and so far, it seems to have worked. Every year, I get hundreds of original comics and stories from kids. These stories were all made for one reason—for fun! And isn't that what creativity is all about?

See individual listings for books by Dav Pilkey on pages 119 and 120.

Virginia Hamilton

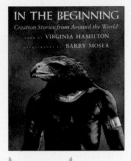

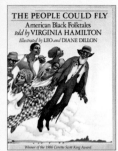

Newbery Honor

Illustrated by Barry Moser
In the Beginning: Creation Stories from Around the World

Here are twenty-five creation myths from around the world, drawn from myths and legends as well as the Bible and other religious books. Hamilton stays as true to the legends as possible without trivializing or making any judgments about the various ways in which people of the world, from ancient times to the present, view the ultimate mystery of creation. With celebrated artist Barry Moser's brilliant illustrations at the beginning of each story and detailed historical notes in the back, this book will provide fascinating reading for many families. The stories are best read aloud to little ones, but once children are reading independently, they will have no trouble reading the text on their own.

1988 Harcourt Children's Books

Illustrated by Leo and Diane Dillon

Coretta Scott King Award

The People Could Fly: American Black Folktales

The twenty-four stories presented here, by an award-winning master storyteller and the multiple award-winning artists Diane and Leo Dillon, run the gamut from fanciful and funny to magical and mysterious, and everything in between, as they address the common theme of a human's need for freedom. There is beauty in the text, in language sometimes colloquial and other times not, but always moving and perfectly matched with the Dillons' peerless illustrations, alternately heartbreaking and joyous. This is one of those books that should be on every family's bookshelf regardless of ethnicity, because although these folktales may have their beginnings in African tradition, the stories are very much about American freedoms.

1985 Alfred A. Knopf

Margaret Hodges
Illustrated by Trina Schart Hyman
Saint George and the Dragon

This award-winning and faithful adaptation of a story segment from Edward Spencer's "The Faerie Queen" tells the story of the Lady Una and the Red Cross Knight she engages to slay the dragon that threatens her kingdom. Brilliantly re-told by Hodges, this tale of a chivalrous knight and his brave deeds is brought to glorious life by the classic artistry of Trina Schart Hyman. Each painting is filled with plants, flowers, and other wonders of nature, as well as knights in armor, dragons, and faeries, and each includes loads of period details in the clothing, castles, and the magical world in which the tale is set. Not only an engaging story of heroic deeds, this book is also an artistic masterpiece to be enjoyed for years to come.

1984 Little, Brown and Company

Caldecott Award

Charles and Mary Lamb
Illustrated by Joëlle Jolivet
Tales From Shakespeare

This collectible, abridged edition of the 1880s classic features a die-cut slip case and new illustrations, which lend it a more contemporary feel. When these tales were originally written, the idea was to take classic Shakespeare plays and put them into a more approachable prose format for those who find the original language and structure intimidating. Coupled with Jolivet's more contemporary art style, plays including *Much Ado About Nothing*, *Macbeth*, and others come alive in clear, easily understood language.

2007 Abrams Image

Fairy Tales, Folktales & Anthologies

Julius Lester

Caldecott Honor

Johnny Appleseed

The story of Johnny Appleseed is based on a real man, John Chapman, born in Massachusetts in 1774. Through the years, the details of his life as a fruit grower have been embellished, and we are left with the folktale about the man who planted apple-tree seeds wherever he went. Regardless of the facts, this wonderful folktale is an American classic, and Kellogg's version brings it to the page with charming illustrations and careful attention to all the plants and animals that Appleseed was likely to have encountered.

1988 HarperCollins

Illustrated by Jerry Pinkney
John Henry

This retelling of the African American legend of John Henry, written by master storyteller Julius Lester with illustrations by multiple award-winning artist Jerry Pinkney, brings to life the tall tale of America's fabled "strongman." Beginning with his birth, witnessed by animals who appear throughout the story, this is a tale of man versus machine, as John Henry uses his mighty arms like sledgehammers to blast through the Allegheny Mountains, competing against the mechanized steam drill to make the tunnel needed for the railroad. He wins, of course, but parents should be warned that he dies shortly after. However, this is not a depressing story but a story of a life lived well and with a great deal of heart.

1994 Dial

Paul Bunyan

When it comes to American tall tales there is certainly none so tall as the story of Paul Bunyan and Babe, his blue ox. According to legend, Bunyan single-handedly created the Great Lakes, The St. Lawrence River, the Great Plains, and the Grand Canyon. These fanciful tales of the world's strongest man and biggest lumberjack have been entertaining children for years, and this book will continue the trend for years to come. Children will laugh at the whimsical art, such as pictures of baby Paul lifting a cow over his head, and hang on every word.

1984 HarperCollins

Illustrated by Jerry Pinkney
Uncle Remus: The Complete Tales

This collection brings together all of the Uncle Remus folktales, originally transcribed from the oral tradition by Joel Chandler Harris over one hundred years ago. They were originally told in dialect, with many clear references to life under slavery; this retelling brings them to a more contemporary audience but retains all the magic of the original Brer Rabbit, Brer Fox, Brer Wolf, and other characters in language easily understood by today's children. Coupled with Pinkney's loving, detailed illustrations in both color and black-and-white, these classic tales are as sure to find an avid audience today as they have for the last century.

1999 Dial

Fairy Tales, Folktales & Anthologies

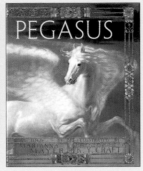

Illustrated by Kinuko Y. Craft

Pegasus

Children have always been fascinated by Pegasus, the horse that can fly. Mayer's thoughtful retelling of the original Greek myth turns the story of Pegasus and the young hero Bellerophon into a perfect read-aloud. The only way that Bellerophon can defeat the horrible Chimera is to enlist the help of Pegasus, the winged horse, but first he must gain the horse's trust. Craft's oil paintings are framed with beautiful borders, and offer sweeping and opulent scenes of the action in this classic tale.

1998 HarperCollins

Illustrated by Kinuko Y. Craft

Baba Yaga and Vasilisa the Brave

In Mayer's capable hands, this Russian folktale—which combines elements readers may recognize from "Cinderella" and "Hansel and Gretel"—becomes a vivid tale of good triumphing over evil, with the requisite happy ending. Vasilisa, whose prize possession is the magical doll her mother made for her, is mistreated by her stepmother and stepsisters after the death of her father. When she is sent to the evil Baba Yaga on an errand, she is held captive and required to complete difficult tasks to secure her freedom. Craft's stunning artwork brings the beautiful Vasilisa annd ugly Baba Yaga to life and enriches this tale of a brave and steadfast young girl.

1994 HarperCollins

Illustrated by Mercer Mayer

Beauty and the Beast

This classic French fairy tale is retold here by a master of the folk- and fairy-tale genre. Unlike what you may be familiar with from television and the big screen, this version is true to the original story of a girl named Beauty who falls in love with a beast/man. The illustrations by Mercer Mayer, filled with magic and wonder, bring this love story vividly to life for a new generation of readers.

1978 Chronicle Books

Illustrated by Kinuko Y. Craft

The Twelve Dancing Princesses

One of the most popular of all the Grimm's fairy tales is retold here with all the drama and romance required to have little girls everywhere strapping on their dancing shoes. When paired with Craft's lush oil paintings, this story of the king's twelve daughters, who arise every morning exhausted, with their new dancing shoes in tatters, and the young boy who solves the mystery will keep little listeners entranced with each reading.

1998 HarperCollins

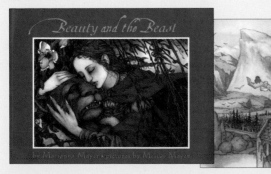

Fairy Tales, Folktales & Anthologies

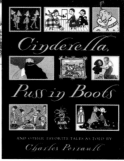

The Olympians

There will eventually be twelve books in this serialized graphic-novel retelling of the Greek myths, and based on the four already published at the time of this writing, it is a series not to be missed. Written and illustrated in comic book-style panels, these tales of love, war, and magical gods and goddesses are perfect for young readers, especially reluctant readers. After all, the Greek gods were really the world's first superheroes, which makes the comic-book style an ideal way to tell their stories. The format is easy to follow, and all the information as well as the art is based on O'Connor's careful research into the myths and legends. The art is filled with action and suspense and will offer many hours of enjoyment. Additionally, each book's endpapers display the Olympian family tree, and the back matter offers notations of Greek words, discussion questions, and further recommended reading.

Athena: Grey-Eyed Goddess *(2010)*

Zeus: King of the Gods *(2010)*

Hera: The Goddess and Her Glory *(2011)*

Hades: Lord of the Dead *(2012)*

First Second Books

Mary Pope Osborne
Illustrated by Michael McCurdy
American Tall Tales

Children have been fascinated by the heroes of traditional American tall tales for centuries, and while there have been separate books about many of them, this compilation brings all of their fabulous figures to life in one volume. Children will learn about the heroic adventures of Paul Bunyan, Pecos Bill, Johnny Appleseed, Davy Crockett, and others. With an introduction and historical notes that explain the origins of these tales and detailed woodcut art by Mike McCurdy, these stories will come alive for a new generation of readers.

1991 Alfred A. Knopf

Charles Perrault
Various Illustrators
Cinderella, Puss in Boots and Other Favorite Tales

These new translations of Perrault's original stories may be a surprise to parents: these classic once-upon-a-time tales do not always end happily ever after. Including "Cinderella," "Puss in Boots," "Little Red Riding Hood," "The Fairies," "Ricky of the Tuft," "Sleeping Beauty," and "Little Tom Thumb," this definitive collection is for older readers who can handle the fact that the wicked wolf does in fact eat Little Red Riding Hood, and Cinderella forgives her evil stepsisters and marries them off to men of noble birth. Each tale is illustrated by a different French illustrator, and historical notes are included for context.

2000 Harry N Abrams

Robert Sabuda on discovering his first pop-up book…

When I was a young boy, I knew I would grow up to be an artist. It seems like I always had a pencil, paintbrush or bottle of glue in my hand! I was also a voracious reader, devouring book after book. For me art and books seemed to go hand in hand, like peanut butter and jelly.

I discovered my first pop-up book when I was about eight years old during a visit to the new dentist in my small, midwest hometown. There was a large, wicker basket in the corner of the waiting room, which clearly had books in it. When I opened one of the books, I was amazed to discover that the pictures stood up! Later that day I made my very first pop-up book, *The Wonderful Wizard of Oz*.

Even when I left home to go to art school in New York City, my love for children's books never faded. During my junior year, I did an internship at a children's book publishing house, and my fate was sealed. Being an intern wasn't glamorous, but I did get to open all the crates and packages in the mailroom that contained original art by the illustrators. Enormous, dramatic scenes by Thomas Locker, delicate, subtle worlds by Barbara Cooney, hilarious characters by James Marshall came to color my impressionable world as a young artist.

I feel honored and humbled to say that I share the same craft as those giants!

See individual listings for books by Robert Sabuda on page 206 and 208.

Fairy Tales, Folktales & Anthologies

Illustrated by Adrienne Segur

The Golden Book of Fairy Tales

This book has been a family favorite since its original publication in 1958. It features twenty-eight favorite tales, including "Sleeping Beauty," "The Frog Prince," "Puss in Boots," "Thumbelina," "Cinderella," "Little Red Riding Hood," "Beauty and the Beast," and many more from the French, German, Russian, Danish, and Japanese storytelling traditions. This collection, which features both full-color and black-and-white illustrations, is one that children have loved for years, and is a welcome addition to any family bookshelf.

1958 Golden Books

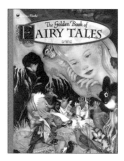

Janet Schulman
Various Illustrators

The 20th Century Children's Book Treasury

Many of the books included in this treasury are included elsewhere in this guide as single volumes— but if you are looking for a great, one-volume overview of classic children's books, this may be just the book for you. There are forty-four titles represented here, from authors ranging from Margaret Wise Brown to William Steig, and just about everyone in between— a convenient overview of the classics. This book is perfect for a long car trip or vacation or any time when you can't carry all your favorite books—with this single volume, you can bring along at least forty-four of them.

1998 Alfred A. Knopf

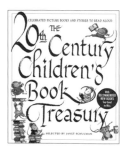

Paul O. Zelinsky

Rapunzel

This is a stunningly illustrated version of a fairy tale often attributed to the Brothers Grimm, but which actually has its origins in French and Italian folktales, as we learn from the author's extensive notes and research. But wherever it originated, this award-winning version, filled with gorgeous, Italian Renaissance-inspired oil paintings, will enchant and captivate young readers and listeners. Rapunzel's famous hair is filled with waves and braids, and manages to look both beautiful and climb-able, the witch is scary and forbidding, and the prince is handsome and kind. This story and its stunning paintings will captivate children from the first page to the last.

1997 Dutton

Rumpelstiltskin

Once again, Zelinsky has created an inspired and award-winning interpretation of a classic Grimms' fairy tale that has been a childhood favorite since it's publication—not incidentally because of how much fun it is to say "Rumplestilskin," and how difficult children know it will be for the miller's daughter to guess the mischievous little troll's name. The paintings here are simply magnificent in their detail, and their golden hues mirror the story, as the poor miller's daughter tries to spin straw into gold. Children will cheer for her success at foiling the plans of the devious troll, who is presented in a way that is more humorous than menacing and should not frighten young children.

1986 Dutton

Poetry

Whether you realize it or not, you have been reading poetry to your children since they were born, and perhaps even before. It starts with simple rhymes and word play, moves to classic nursery rhymes and songs like "Ring Around the Rosie," and progresses to stories and songs with rhythmic language. Children respond to poetry automatically; they don't need to be taught to appreciate it. The reason almost every child loves books by Dr. Seuss is because of the rhythm of the text. This rhythm is also one of the reasons that many parents have a hard time reading Dr. Seuss aloud, since it is often a result of "gibberish" or tongue-twisters. But not all poetry is difficult to read, and the books in this section will make reading poetry with your children a pleasure.

You'll find a little of everything in this section: Mother Goose, the fabulously funny and slightly subversive poems of Shel Silverstein and Jack Prelutsky, classics from Dickinson, Frost, and Longfellow, plus a few anthologies that offer a little bit of everything. You will find books for all ages, from babies and toddlers to teens. It  is advisable to review the books individually to select the right one for your particular child; however, no family library should be without a good poetry anthology that children can grow into over time. Poetry teaches children the beauty of language, how carefully chosen words can take an ordinary thought and turn it into something beautiful. Reading poetry to your children may also turn out to be one of *your* favorite activities and can open up a myriad of discussions and thoughtful exchanges.

Here are some guidelines to keep in mind when choosing poetry books:

- Look for books the whole family can enjoy for years to come; anthologies are especially timeless.

- Increase your children's appreciation of poetry by finding books that appeal to their sense of humor.

- Look for lavishly illustrated books when you're choosing poetry for younger children.

- For older children, reading poetry can help encourage discussion and interpretation of metaphors and similes.

- Look for books that feature stand-alone illustrated poems that appeal to your child's interests, such as nature, animals, romance, holidays, or silliness.

Selected by Jack Prelutsky
Illustrated by Arnold Lobel

The Random House Book of Poetry for Children

The poems collected here are grouped loosely by subject—nature, the four seasons, animals (especially dogs and cats) and other living things, city life, children, home, food, characters, nonsense verse, wordplay, and ghosts and other strange creatures—although there are some that are just unclassifiable. From Emily Dickinson to William Shakespeare, from Lewis Carroll to Ogden Nash, from classic poets to contemporary children's writers such as Jack Prelutsky, Ruth Krauss, Nikki Giovanni, and Dr. Seuss—they're all here in one beautifully illustrated volume of child-friendly poetry.

1983 Random House Children's Books

Paul Fleischman
Illustrated by Eric Beddows

Newbery Award

Joyful Noise: Poems for Two Voices

These poems that celebrate the creatures and sounds of the insect world are written to be read by two voices—sometimes alternating, sometimes together, sometimes softly, and sometimes loudly, but always with a joyful rhythm. These are poems meant to be shared and read together; the lines of each poem are laid out either on the left or the right side of the page to clearly delineate who should be reading, and they are filled with the sound patterns of the insects themselves, from droning bees to buzzing cicadas. The illustrations that accompany the poems are detailed and fascinating, showing the various insects in mid-flight, resting, feeding, or playing.

1988 HarperCollins

Douglas Florian
Poetrees

The poems in this collection all celebrate trees, from familiar ones, like birches and oaks, to some fantastically named (but very real) varieties, like the dragon tree, monkey puzzle tree, and baobab tree. The collages that illustrate this book were created on paper bags with an amalgam of media, including oils, pastels, chalk, and even rubber stamps, in a way that effectively mimics the wide variety of trees depicted in the poems. The book features a "Glossatree" at the end with facts about the trees featured in the poems, as well as a brief bibliography for teachers, students, and parents interested in more information about trees.

2010 Beach Lane Books

Poetry

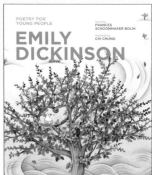

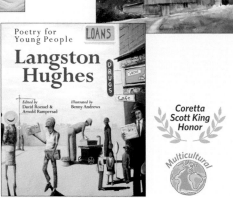

Each book in this series for middle-grade readers contains a brief biographical sketch of the poet with information about the times in which he or she was writing and features full-color illustrations as well as definitions of words that young readers may not be familiar with. There are additional books available in this series that will be of interest to poetry lovers.

Poetry

Edited by Edwin Graves Wilson, Ph.D.
Illustrated by Jerome Lagarrigue
Maya Angelou

This collection of twenty-five poems from Dr. Maya Angelou form a tapestry of her life and work in support of the historic struggles of the African American people, and they are filled with the sense of hope and spiritual strength for which Maya Angelou is known throughout the world. Included in this collection are "Harlem Hopscotch," "Me and My Work," "Still I Rise," and many more.

1994 Sterling

Edited by Frances Shoonmaker Bolin
Illustrated by Chi Chung
Emily Dickinson

Though Emily Dickinson is perhaps known best for her somewhat odd and reclusive lifestyle, this volume brings forth thirty-five poems from the incredibly productive poet, as well as information about her other artistic pursuits, such as painting with watercolors. The poems include "I'm nobody! Who are you?" and "I started early—Took my Dog."

1994 Sterling

Edited by Gary D. Schmidt
Illustrated by Henri Sorensen
Robert Frost

Robert Frost is best known for his poetry celebrating the natural world that he so loved. This collection, featuring twenty-five of his best-known poems, including "Mending Wall," "Birches," and "The Road Not Taken," is arranged by seasons of the year.

1994 Sterling

Edited by David Roessel and Arnold Rampersad
Illustrated by Benny Andrews
Langston Hughes

Langston Hughes is best known for being part of the Harlem Renaissance of black culture in the 1920s and 1930s. His poetry captured the hearts of his people, and addressed their concerns about what it meant to be black in America. His poems about social justice still resonate today. Included in this collection are "The Negro Speaks of Rivers," "Aunt Sue's Stories," "Danse Africaine," "Mother to Son," and "Words Like Freedom."

2006 Sterling

Gyo Fujikawa

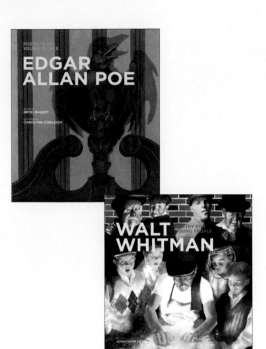

A Child's Book of Poems

There are two hundred poems, proverbs, nursery rhymes, and folk songs presented in this charming collection for young children. Some will be familiar and some new, but each and every one of them is beautifully illustrated by Gyo Fujikawa. From Lewis Carroll's "The Melancholy Pig" to Eugene Fields' "Wynken, Blynken, and Nod," there is a wide variety of both classic and contemporary poems here, and the illustrations feature a truly multicultural mix of children and quite a menagerie of animals, as well as loving depictions of nature.

1969 Sterling

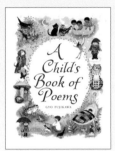

Mother Goose

Mother Goose rhymes are most children's first exposure to poetry, and there are many volumes for parents to choose from. But this version, illustrated by Gyo Fujikawa, is among the most complete available, and also one of the most beautifully illustrated. Parents will be familiar with many of the rhymes here, like "Simple Simon," "To Market," and "Little Boy Blue," but many will be new to them, and will soon become family favorites. The children in the book are a multicultural group of adorable tots, the animals are sweetly presented, and all the illustrations are filled with genuine emotion and joy. No family should be without a comprehensive Mother Goose collection, and this one is sure to be read and enjoyed by generations to come.

1968 Sterling

Edited by Brod Bagert
Illustrated by Carolynn Cobleigh
Edgar Allan Poe

Of the thirteen poems in this collection, some will be familiar to young readers, like the oft-quoted and thrilling "The Raven." Others might be less well known, but are equally interesting. Poe's life was famously filled with tragedy and addiction, and his stories and poems are known to incorporate some of those influences. Also included here are "The Bells," "Eldorado," and "Annabel Lee."

1995 Sterling

Edited by Jonathan Levin
Illustrated by Jim Burke
Walt Whitman

There are twenty-six poems or excerpts from longer poems in this collection from one of America's greatest poets. In addition to some of Whitman's lesser-known poems, this collection features many well-loved favorites, including "I Hear America Singing," "When Lilacs Last in the Dooryard Bloom'd," and the classic mournful poem, "O Captain! My Captain!"

1997 Sterling

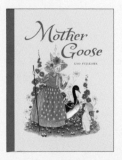

Poetry

Multicultural

Robert Frost
Illustrated by Susan Jeffers

Stopping by Woods on a Snowy Evening

"Whose woods these are I think I know. His house is in the village though; He will not see me stopping here/To watch his woods fill up with snow." So begins one of the best-loved poems of both adults and children throughout the world. In this edition, Susan Jeffers' miraculous snowy illustrations depict a lovely winter scene filled with all the animals one might expect to find in a New England wood, as the old man in the story stops to greet and feed them before he continues his travels. No one will forget the familiar ending: "The woods are lovely, dark, and deep. But I have promises to keep, And miles to go before I sleep, And miles to go before I sleep."

1978 Dutton

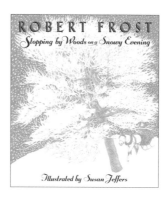

Edited by Elise Paschen
Various Illustrators

Poetry Speaks to Children

This unique collection of ninety-seven poems comes with an audio CD that features about half of the poems read by their original authors. While some of these poems are traditionally for children, others are by renowned adult poets. Children will enjoy hearing the actual poets, such as Robert Frost reading "Stopping by Woods on a Snowy Evening," Langston Hughes reading "The Negro Speaks of Rivers," and Roald Dahl reading "The Dentist and the Crocodile." The illustrations are done by a variety of illustrators and, therefore, are very well suited to the individual poems.

2005 Sourcebooks

Edited by Nikki Giovanni
Various Illustrators

Hip Hop Speaks to Children

This anthology of fifty-one pieces takes poetry to a new level by acknowledging the rhythm and vernacular of hip-hop, rap, and the language of the street as a form of poetry based in the African American community. Like *Poetry Speaks To Children*, this book also comes with an audio CD of performances by the authors, ranging from James Weldon Johnson and Martin Luther King Jr. to Lauryn Hill, Queen Latifah, and Kanye West. The CD makes full use of the rhythms of hip-hop, including influences of jazz, blues, and gospel, while a team of five illustrators lend their unique art styles to the illustrations in the book.

2005 Sourcebooks

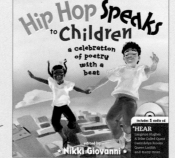

Andy Griffiths

Illustrated by Terry Denton

The Cat on the Mat is Flat

Imagine you wanted to write nine poems for beginning readers. Now consider that it's important that they be as tongue-twister-ish as Dr. Seuss, as irreverent as *Captain Underpants*, and as funny as possible; they must use short words and repetition, and they have to rhyme. Then this is the book that you would write—and your children will laugh so hard they'll forget it's poetry. It's not every day that you find a poem about a dog on a cog who gets chased by a frog around a bog.... These poems are funny and easy to read and perfect for emerging readers with a sense of humor.

2007 Feiwel & Friends

Selected by Caroline Kennedy

Illustrated by Jon J Muth

A Family of Poems

Caroline Kennedy curates and introduces the poetry in this collection and also stresses the importance of including poetry in children's lives as well as encouraging children to try to write poetry. The poems featured lean toward classic poems that parents will be familiar with, but there are also contemporary poets represented here. The illustrations, by award-winning artist Jon J Muth, bring the poems vividly to life with humor, heart, and a sense of wonder and manage to offer visual representations of the words that enhance the force and beauty of the language.

2005 Hyperion

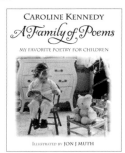

Selected by Lee Bennett Hopkins

Illustrated by David Diaz

Sharing the Seasons: A Book of Poems

This collection of poetry features forty-eight poems organized seasonally, with twelve poems for each season of the year. While some of the poems come from familiar voices, like Carl Sandburg and Karla Kuskin, others will be new to readers. The selection of poems is lovely, but the highlight of this book is award-winning illustrator David Diaz's beautiful and vibrantly colored artwork, which serves to bring both the poems and the seasons to life.

2010 Margaret K. McElderry

Collected by Lee Bennett Hopkins

Illustrated by Hilary Knight

Side by Side: Poems to Read Together

The poems in this collection were selected because they naturally lend themselves to a shared reading experience; they are perfect for reading aloud alone but much more fun to read together. There are many familiar poems in this collection, as well as the work of contemporary poets. The illustrations by the well-loved Hilary Knight are perfectly suited to the poems; they are nostalgic and charming without being old fashioned, and he has also created images of children and animals reading together that appear throughout the book to reinforce the side-by-side reading message.

1991 Simon & Schuster Books for Young Readers

Henry Wadsworth Longfellow
Illustrated by Susan Jeffers
Hiawatha

"By the shores of Gitchee Gumee, By the shining Big-Sea-Water." So begins one of the most memorized and recited poems by grade schoolers everywhere—a true American classic, Longfellow's "The Song of Hiawatha." This illustrated abridgement brings to life the essence of the poem, Hiawatha's journey to manhood so that he can become the leader of his people. The art is breathtaking on every page, filled with the wonders of nature, animals, and even magical spirit guides and will entrance young readers every bit as much as the beauty and elegance of the language, which does in fact, as Longfellow says, "Call to us to pause and listen, Speak in tones so plain and childlike…"

1983 Dial

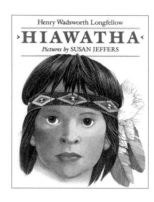

Edited by Bill Martin Jr with Michael Sampson
Various Illustrators
The Bill Martin Jr Big Book of Poetry

This collection is organized by theme: animals, nature, feelings, family, nonsense, and more. Favorites are well represented here, as well as poems that may be less familiar. Unlike other anthologies, this book doesn't feature the work of one illustrator but art from many of today's celebrated picture book artists, including Ashley Bryan, Lois Ehlert, the Dillons, Chris Raschka, Steven Kellogg, and Dan Yaccarino. This approach allows each poem to be paired with an artist whose style is best suited to the poetry and offers much more variety and interest.

2008 Simon & Schuster Books for Young Readers

Jeff Moss
Illustrated by Chris Demarest
The Butterfly Jar

The author of this collection of original poems for young children was the head writer and composer for "Sesame Street," which explains his ability to write short and funny poems that children can easily relate to on such subjects as butterflies, jelly beans, finding a penny, or the bravery required to sleep without a night-light. The simple pen-and-ink line drawings that accompany these poems—some just a line or two long, others running through two pages—serve up just the right amount of humor and visual clues to the poems themselves.

1989 Bantam Books

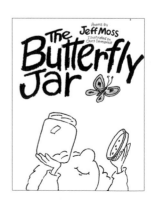

Poetry

Jack Prelutsky

Jack Prelutsky was named the first Children's Poet Laureate by the Poetry Foundation in 2006, and one only has to look at his books to understand why. Prelutsky has an uncanny gift that allows him to write funny, wacky, sweet, and nonsensical poems that children immediately understand and relate to; his poems can be as short as a couple of lines of well-chosen words or much longer poems that keep children laughing and learning—and, in many cases, totally unaware that what they are enjoying is actually poetry: "When the turkey gobble gobbles, It is plump and proud and perky. When our family gobble gobbles, We are gobbling down the turkey." The rhymes may be simple, but the thought behind them is pure genius. These poems are intended to make children laugh and teach them to enjoy wordplay and language. All of these books are just plain fun, with words that leap off the page and practically beg to be sung and danced to. Several of Prelutsky's books have been illustrated with great verve and humor by James Stevenson.

Illustrated by Marjorie Priceman
For Laughing Out Loud
1991 Alfred A. Knopf

Illustrated by Jackie Urbanovic
I've Lost My Hippopotamus
2012 Greenwillow Books

Illustrated by James Stevenson
It's Raining Pigs and Noodles
2000 Greenwillow Books

My Dog May Be a Genius
2008 Greenwillow Books

The New Kid on the Block
1984 Greenwillow Books

A Pizza the Size of the Sun
1996 Greenwillow Books

Something Big Has Been Here
1990 Greenwillow Books

Selected by Jack Prelutsky
Illustrated by Meilo So
The 20th Century Children's Poetry Treasury

The 20th Century Children's Poetry Treasury brings together Prelutsy's own work and the work of many of the poets and writers who came before him, influenced him, and made poetry written specifically for children possible.

1999 Alfred A. Knopf

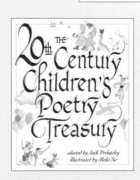

If anyone can be said to truly "own" the category of poetry for children, it would have to be Shel Silverstein. His books of crazy, funny, ridiculous, impossible, magical, and un-put-down-able poetry, coupled with his signature black line illustrations, have changed forever the way that children respond to poetry—and respond they most certainly do, with uncontrollable laughter. Anything can happen in these poems; you might get eaten by a boa constrictor or find a polar bear in the Frigidaire, have somebody steal your knees, see a piglet get a people-back-ride, or even write a poem from inside a lion. There are no boundaries here, just plenty of fun, and some pretty gross and slightly subversive humor as well. All in all, these poems are a lot like your kids: silly, sweet, funny, naughty, and adorable—all at the same time.

Where the Sidewalk Ends (1974)

A Light in the Attic (1981)

Falling Up (1996)

HarperCollins

Selected by Michael Rosen
Illustrated by Bob Graham

Poems for the Very Young

This charming collection of short poems for the very youngest children will bring many new poems to parents in the United States. While there are some classics here that may be familiar, the majority of these short poems and nursery rhymes come from "the other side of the pond." But don't let that stop you—these simple rhymes are often funny and perfect for toddlers. For example; "I can put my socks on. I can find my vest. I can put my pants on—I can't do the rest" (Tony Bradman). Some pages feature a single longer poem, and other pages may have two or three short ones, but each poem is paired with its own illustration. Graham's pastel palette, adorable multiracial children, and softly drawn animals will entrance even the youngest little listeners for hours.

1994 Kingfisher Books

Robert Louis Stevenson
Illustrated by Tasha Tudor

A Child's Garden of Verses

This classic title beautifully marries the timeless poems of Stevenson with the soft, tender, and loving art of award-winner Tasha Tudor. Once you have experienced both, you will realize that, though they were born centuries apart, the pairing of Stevenson's poems and Tudor's art make this the definitive edition of this well-loved title. The poems are by turns sweet and melancholy, and the children in the book's illustrations are charming, slightly old-fashioned, and surrounded by small animals and the blooming, beautiful world of nature. This book of poems is a must-have for every family library.

1961 Simon & Schuster Books for Young Readers

Poetry

Lane Smith on the beauty of simplicity…

I guess I suffer from a bit of arrested development. My tastes and interests never traveled far beyond childhood. The music I listen to is simple. Like the kiddie records I grew up with, whether it's rock, folk, or classical, I don't like too many instruments. I am attracted to fine artists like Paul Klee and Alexander Calder, guys who did a lot with very little. I like Buster Keaton movies: not too many characters, silent, simple, and surreal. This is also what I like about children's books. Good ones are like poetry. You don't have many pages to work with, so everything has to be perfect.

My favorite authors are deceptively simple. Ruth Krauss comes to mind. *The Carrot Seed*, illustrated by her husband, Crockett Johnson, is about as perfect a children's book as you will find. The same goes for Maurice Sendak's *Where the Wild Things Are*. In *It's a Book*, I kept the shapes simple and bold and used mostly primary colors. The designer, Molly Leach, gave the tech-savvy jackass a digital-looking font for his dialog, and gave the book-loving ape a more traditional typeface. Like Crockett Johnson or Charles Schulz, I kept all of the action on a flat plane. No fancy high or low angles to distract the reader. I also showed the full body whenever possible. It's funnier that way. Just one of many tricks I've learned over the years from the greats who have come before me: Remy Charlip, Edward Gorey, Florence Parry Heide, Maurice Sendak, William Steig, Barbara Cooney, Judith Viorst, Leonard Weisgard, and the Provensens, among others.

See individual listings for books written and illustrated by Lane Smith on pages 72, 77, and 141.

Author/Illustrator Lane Smith

Judith Viorst
Illustrated by Cherry Lynne

If I Were in Charge of the World and Other Worries

These poems deal with the real world of childhood: the frustrations and joys, the small celebrations and the big disappointments, apologies, broken hearts, pets, good-byes, secrets, and every feeling they encompass. Children can relate to the subject matter of these poems because they are about the realities of childhood today. There is at least one poem in this book and probably many more that perfectly addresses the way your children feel on any given day. The picture isn't always rosy, but there is an awful lot to laugh about. For example; "If I were in charge of the world I'd cancel oatmeal, Monday mornings, Allergy shots, and also Sara Steinberg." Even though we never know who Sara Steinberg is, can't we all relate to the thought behind the wish? The poems are paired with Lynne Cherry's expressive and elegantly detailed pen-and-ink illustrations.

1981 Atheneum

Selected by Josette Frank
Illustrated by Eloise Wilkin

Eloise Wilkin's Poems to Read to the Very Young

This collection of thirty classic poems for very young children features many poems you would expect from Robert Louis Stevenson, Kate Greenaway, Langston Hughes, and others, but what sets this book apart is beloved illustrator Eloise Wilkin's art. These poems are presented with brightly colored yet softly drawn infants and toddlers at home, at play, in the nursery, in a field of flowers—everywhere you'd be likely to find happy children interacting with their world. The art is comforting and classic, as are the poems in this collection.

2001 Random House Children's Books

Blanche Fisher Wright
The Real Mother Goose

Ask yourself this question: is it possible to raise a child without Mother Goose? I think we all know the answer, and this edition, with its distinctive checkerboard border and bright colorful art, while certainly not the most extensive collection of Mother Goose rhymes, is more than likely the one you, your parents, and perhaps even your grandparents grew up reading. There are hundreds of Mother Goose collections available, but this nostalgic edition has been and continues to be perfect for every generation since its original publication in 1916.

1916 Cartwheel Books/Scholastic Inc.

Dan Yaccarino's Mother Goose

There is something about a Little Golden Book, with its classic golden spine and place for children to write their name inside the cover, that epitomizes children's books. For this book, Yaccarino selected Mother Goose rhymes both familiar and more obscure and then put an entirely new spin on them with his illustrations. The first thing you'll notice is the setting—they are all set in a more urban environment, and they vary in style from 1950s retro chic to the beatnik 1960s and more contemporary times as well. The people and animals romp through the pages in brightly colored, bold art with lots of visual detail in the backgrounds, proving once again that no matter what the setting, these rhymes are timeless.

2003 Golden Books

Growing Up

Growing up really is hard to do. It's filled with new experiences and new transitions, many of which can be confusing to children and can pose some challenging questions for parents as well. The books here focus on key transitions and assist families in dealing with the "big" questions that children will have as they try to understand their relationships and the world around them.

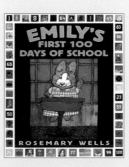

Good manners are important, and so is understanding your feelings. Potty training is a must, and getting ready to go to school can be a challenge. These books can help make those life lessons easier for both parents and children. We have broken down this section into ten sub-sections that deal with the most common issues:

- Potty training
- New siblings
- Starting school
- Family issues
- Feelings

- Special needs
- Moving
- Adoption
- Manners
- The facts of life and puberty

Here are some guidelines to keep in mind when choosing books about growing up:

- Parents should pre-read books on difficult issues such as death and the facts of life/puberty to assure that they align with their own family and/or religious values.

- These books can be very funny and also very frank; the information is accurate, but may be more than a young child can process. The books here vary drastically by age level, and parents should take care to select age-appropriate content.

- These books have been selected to help families feel comfortable discussing difficult issues, as well as to reinforce positive behaviors.

- Sensitive issues such as adoption, divorce, moving, special needs, or death can be difficult to explain to young children. A well-selected book, combined with loving discussion, can ease the process for parents and children alike.

- Relatable stories can ease difficult transitions, and offer children a way to understand their feelings and cope with change.

Potty Training

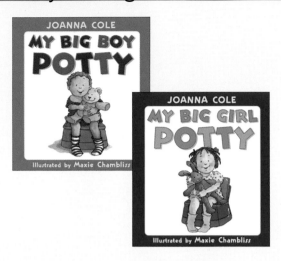

Joanna Cole
Illustrated by Maxie Chambliss
My Big Boy Potty/
My Big Girl Potty

Potty training should be all about success, not failure, and this very upbeat and positive offering—one version for boys, and one for girls—has illustrations that show a supporting cast of parents, toddlers, and even smiling stuffed animals. There is no scariness, yelling, or recrimination here, and there is acknowledgment that accidents do happen and success takes time. There is also a page in the back of the book with tips for successful potty teaching for parents.

2000 HarperCollins

Alona Frankel
Once Upon a Potty Boy/Girl

There are two versions of this bestselling potty-training book (over four million copies sold since its publication)—one for boys and one for girls. It is small in size to perfectly fit little hands, with charming illustrations that take children through the basics (showing a chamber pot rather than a toilet), with the characters of Joshua for the boys and Prudence for the girls. The focus is on building confidence and pride in the child's accomplishment of this daunting achievement, so that, as the author explains it, "he sat on the potty as a little child and got up feeling ten-feet tall."

1980 Firefly Books Ltd.

Growing Up

Karen Katz
A Potty for Me!

When you think about it, the idea of combining a potty-training book with a lift-the-flap book is sort of brilliant. For parents who loved Karen Katz's adorable early-concept board books, her potty-training book is a natural follow-up. The little child in the story gets a potty as a gift, but getting her to use it isn't easy— a challenge many parents can relate to. The text is upbeat and encouraging, with simple exclamations like "That's okay!" and "Yeah! I really did it!," while the art is bright and simple. This book is best used with children on the younger end of the potty-training process or even before potty training begins in earnest.

2005 Little Simon

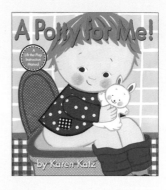

Mo Willems
Time to Pee!

Of all the books on the subject of potty training, this one stands out for several reasons: the dust jacket reverses to become a success chart, it comes with stickers, and it's actually fun. A gang of very encouraging and understanding mice are on hand to guide children through the process, and the stickers reflect every situation in a positive manner, with celebratory mice exclaiming everything from "Nice Try!" and "Oops!" to "You did it!" and "Do it again!" This is the perfect potty-training book for children who need a little more tangible reinforcement and a whole lot of celebration when they succeed.

2003 Hyperion

Taro Gomi
Everyone Poops

There are parents who love this book and those who don't, but it's rare to find a toddler who doesn't find it fascinating and funny. The concept is pretty basic: everyone who eats—be it human, animal, or fish— poops. The text is simple: "An elephant makes a big poop. A mouse makes a tiny poop." The illustrations of the animals' back ends and their poops, along with short commentary on size, shape, and smell, may make some parents queasy, but they generally make children howl with laughter. Hopefully, that laughter comes as they read it while sitting on the potty.

2003 Kane Miller

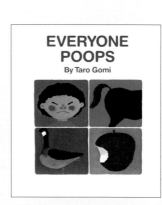

Stan and Jan Berenstain

The Berenstain Bears' New Baby

In this charming book, Mama and Papa Bear help Little Bear adjust to the big and small changes in life when a new baby comes. The familiar Berenstain Bears have helped children adapt to new experiences in more than fifty books, and this one is no exception. Very loving and positive in tone and featuring familiar characters that children relate to, it has a definite "look on the bright side" approach that will work well with toddlers and preschoolers.

1974 Random House Children's Books

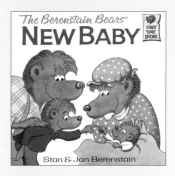

John Burningham

Illustrated by Helen Oxenbury

There's Going to Be a Baby

This picture book about a new baby is just right for young children. It's approach, that of an ongoing conversation between a mother and toddler about the new baby that takes place over an extended period of time—represented by the changing seasons—cleverly addresses the time it takes to actually have a baby. The combination of Burningham's simple text—the toddler's ask questions such as "When is the baby going to come?" "What will we call the baby?" and "What will the baby do?"—and Oxenbury's bright, boldly drawn illustrations of what he imagines might happen will bring a smile to parents and toddlers alike.

2010 Candlewick Press

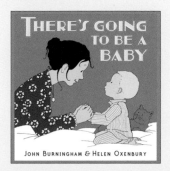

Joanna Cole

Photography by Margaret Miller

The New Baby at Your House

This wonderful book uses large photographs and a mix of multi-ethnic toddlers, families, and siblings to not just discuss, but also actually demonstrate all the feelings that a toddler or preschooler might have about a new baby. Parents can point to the pictures and ask their children to identify and name the feelings on the faces of the children as they read; they are easily understood visually by even very young children. There is also an introductory note for parents at the beginning of the book with advice on preparing older children before the new baby comes home as well as helping them adjust to their new sibling.

1999 HarperCollins

Mercer Mayer

The New Baby

For toddlers familiar with Mayer's "Little Critter" books, and even those who are not, this book offers an easy-to-understand, child's-eye view of how frustrating a new baby can be to an eager older sibling. Babies don't pay attention when you read to them, they cry when you make silly faces, and they do not understand jokes at all. Eventually Little Critter figures out what you can do with a baby and how to be (in this case) a big brother. This book is perfect for toddlers excited about a new baby, who might not understand that babies don't really do all that much—at first.

2001 Random House Children's Books

Growing Up

Heidi Murkoff

Illustrated by Laura Rader

What to Expect When the New Baby Comes Home

The "What to Expect Kids" series by the creators of the bestselling *What to Expect When You're Expecting* books addresses the issue of new siblings in an easy-to-understand way for preschool children. Using a question-and-answer format featuring "Angus the Answer Dog," typical questions such as "Why do babies cry so much?" and "Why do babies get so many presents?" are frankly and simply explained. The illustrations and the device of the Answer Dog cleverly allow children to prepare themselves emotionally and come to terms with what life with a new baby brother or sister will be like.

2001 HarperFestival

Starting School

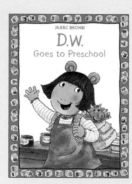

Marc Brown

D.W. Goes to Preschool

Many children are familiar with the adventures of Arthur the aardvark and his little sister D.W. This book for new preschoolers by D.W. is full of calming, reassuring advice for toddlers who may be nervous about beginning preschool. D.W.'s advice to preschoolers is upbeat and matter-of-fact as she acknowledges that some kids are sad when they say good-bye to their parents but also reassures them that parents come back at day's end so "it's no big deal." Children will learn what to expect from preschool, all the things they'll learn, and the fun they'll have. This book will be helpful in calming fears and creating realistic expectations for young children who have the jitters about that first day of preschool.

2003 Little, Brown and Company

Katie Davis

Kindergarten Rocks!

Dexter is fine with starting kindergarten, really he is. His stuffed dog Rufus might be just a teensy bit scared, but not Dex, nope, not at all. Big sister Jessie sees what's going on, and reassures her brother by telling him that "kindergarten rocks!" This story of one young boy's apprehensions and his big sister's reassurances is funny and told though Dexter's first-person thoughts and concerns; Katie's answers are in clever cartoon-like speech bubbles, and even Rufus the stuffed dog becomes part of the action. The text and illustrations cleverly address many of the possible outcomes of the first day of school—good and bad—including having so much fun you just can't wait to go back the next day.

2005 Harcourt Children's Books

Laura Numeroff and Felicia Bond
If You Take a Mouse to School

By the time children get to preschool or kindergarten, most of them will be familiar with at least one of the "If You Give A..." books, and this one, focusing on starting school, doesn't disappoint. First the mouse wants your lunch box, then a sandwich, and maybe a snack; he'll want to play soccer, then build a house, then make some furniture...you get the idea. Our friend mouse is up to his usual cause-and-effect tricks. Somehow this formula never gets old and just keeps working for generation after generation of young children. Using a familiar character to address the ins and outs of the school day can make this transition more comfortable for anxious children.

2002 HarperCollins

Joseph Slate
Illustrated by Ashley Wolff
Miss Bindergarten Gets Ready For Kindergarten

This book is populated by an entire alphabet of animals, including the title character, a border collie with a trusty cockatiel as her assistant. As Miss Bindergarten gets dressed and prepares her classroom with mobiles, posters, a goldfish, a vase of autumn leaves, and more, her students are alphabetically getting ready for the new school year as well: "Adam Krupp wakes up. Brenda Heath brushes her teeth. Christopher Beaker finds his sneaker." With a glossary in back that identifies each animal—for example, Adam is an Alligator—this book gives children many reasons to get excited about the first day of kindergarten.

1996 Dutton

Rosemary Wells
Emily's First 100 Days Of School

In recent years, schools across the country have begun to celebrate the one-hundredth day of school with parties and other exciting activities. In this book, Rosemary Wells uses her signature animal characters to represent the teachers and students who are using those one hundred days to learn about numbers. Emily's school bus is number three, her mother knows fifty-six ways to answer "How Do I Love Thee?" and so it goes, until they get to the big milestone one-hundredth day party. This book offers a creative way for little students to mark the milestones of the school year and to keep the learning going the entire time.

2000 Hyperion

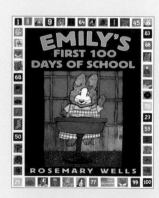

Growing Up

Marc Brown and Laurene Krasny Brown

Dinosaurs Divorce:
A Guide for Changing Families

There may be no family issue more difficult to explain to young children than divorce. There are so many feelings involved, so many new words to understand, and big changes to family life as well. This book uses cartoon dinosaurs and frank text to explain these changes to young children and includes chapters on having two homes, stepparents and siblings, celebrating holidays, and more, and features a glossary of divorce terms and what they mean. Nothing can make this family transition pleasant and worry-free, but this book should prove to be very helpful by addressing childrens' concerns in language they can understand.

1986 Little, Brown and Company

Todd Parr

The Family Book

Known for his use of bold, bright colors and simply executed black line drawings, author Todd Parr explores the varieties of what family can mean in language young children can easily understand. Whether a family is big or little, looks alike or different, is clean or messy, has one parent or two, or has two mommies or two daddies doesn't matter—what matters is the way that all families are the same: they all love to hug, celebrate special days, be together, and love and help each other.

2003 Megan Tingley Books

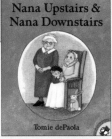

Tomie dePaola

Now One Foot, Now the Other

In this book, Bobby's grandfather has had a stroke (though that word is never used), and Bobby is frightened because his parents have explained that his grandfather might not recognize them right away. Grandfather Bob, who Bobby is named after, helped teach Bobby to walk, built towers out of blocks with him, and told him stories. Now, when grandfather comes home from the hospital and is getting better, it's Bobby's turn to teach those things to grandfather. Bobby knows that his grandfather remembers as he holds his hands and says, "Now one foot, now the other." This story deals with a serious issue with a great deal of love and compassion—parents should be forewarned that it will likely bring tears to their eyes, and their children will see it as a story of hope and love.

1981 Putnam

Tomie dePaola

Nana Upstairs & Nana Downstairs

Many young children have to deal with the death of a grandparent or great-grandparent, in some cases at an age where the concept of death is both frightening and confusing. This sweet autobiographical story is about four-year-old Tommy, who loves to visit his grandmother and great-grandmother every Sunday. Tommy's grandmother is always busy downstairs, but his great-grandmother is always upstairs in bed because she is ninety-four years old. When Nana upstairs dies, young Tommy is upset, and his mother comforts him by reminding him that she will always live in his memories whenever he thinks of her. Death is a complicated subject to address with young children, but this book does so in a gentle, loving manner.

1973 Putnam

Marlo Thomas and Friends
Free To Be...You and Me

This freshly illustrated version of the classic book for families, originally published in 1973, carries on the legacy of the classic. Whether families are opening this book together for the first time or parents remember it from their own childhoods and are now sharing it with their children or grandchildren, it remains as fresh and filled with love as it always has. The new illustrations by award-winning artist Peter H. Reynolds enhance the original content while at the same time paying homage to how unique it was. It is packed with poems, stories and songs, and messages to children and families that are positive: empowerment, diversity, the virtues of equality, kindness, and self-determination. This edition of the book also includes a CD of the songs and music.

2008 Running Press

Judith Viorst
Illustrated by Erik Blegvad
The Tenth Good Thing About Barney

The loss of a pet can be very difficult for a young child, whether it's a fish, a hamster, or in this case, a young boy's beloved cat, Barney. The family decides to have a funeral for Barney, and the boy's mother asks him to think of ten good things to say about Barney—but he can only think of nine. Later, when working in the garden with his father, he discovers the tenth—Barney's body can help flowers grow—and decides that's "a pretty nice job for a cat." This book does mention heaven, so families with a different belief system may choose to make an appropriate substitution when reading.

1971 Atheneum

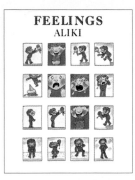

Aliki
Feelings

For children, learning how to identify and understand their feelings is not quite as easy as you might think. This book uses simple text and art to demonstrate and name different feelings and explain in a very basic sense what causes us to feel the way we do. In any given day a child can experience many feelings—happy, excited, sad, nervous, proud—and this book will help each child understand all of his or her emotions.

1984 Greenwillow Books

Nancy Carlson
I Like Me!

This elegy to self-esteem is told by a very enthusiastic piglet who knows that she is her own best friend. She likes everything about herself and knows the best way to take care of herself as well: she eats good food, keeps herself clean, exercises, reads good books, and even draws lovely pictures. This confident piglet knows that she may make mistakes, but she always cheerfully tries again, teaching children that a positive self image is vital to a happy life.

1988 Viking

Growing Up

Growing Up

Todd Parr
It's Okay to Be Different

This book for very young children teaches about diversity and acceptance in very simple language. These concepts can be challenging to explain to toddlers, and this book is helpful for dealing with social situations that require explanations, such as adoption, disabilities, family structures, ethnic diversity, and more—and it does so with a sense of fun, straightforward language, and brightly colored, minimalist illustrations.

2001 Megan Tingley Books

Multicultural

Todd Parr
The Feelings Book

Featuring Todd Parr's signature bold colors and simple visuals, this book is perfect for toddlers and very young children who are just beginning to understand what feelings are and how to express them. Some of the illustrations and descriptions of emotions are very direct, and little ones will have no problem identifying happy smiles or tears of sadness; others, such as depictions of "lonely," "scared," or "silly," though thoughtfully presented, might require a little more parental explanation, depending on the child.

2000 Megan Tingley Books

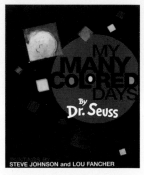

Dr. Seuss
Illustrated by Steve Johnson and Lou Fancher
My Many Colored Days

The concept of equating moods with colors is not a new one, but this book communicates it in a way that is easily understood by children. The simple poetry of this book differs from more familiar Seuss titles, featuring concise, short couplets rather than his usual rollicking style, but thanks to the vivid paintings by Johnson and Fancher, this inspired method of interpreting moods as colors comes luminously to life on every page.

1996 Alfred A. Knopf

Charlotte Zolotow
Illustrated by Arnold Lobel
The Quarreling Book

Some days just start out badly; it can begin with a little thing, and before you know it a bad mood is passed from person to person. Mr. James forgets to kiss Mrs. James before he goes to work. Mrs. James is cross about this and snaps at Jonathan. Distracted, Jonathan forgets his galoshes and umbrella and gets soaked in the rain. Suddenly everybody is having a bad day—until a sweet little dog comes along and helps them spread happiness instead of negativity. This book teaches children that bad moods do occur but that they also have the ability to change the direction of a bad day with positive actions.

1963 HarperCollins

Mo Willems on starting his career at the age of seven...

The best thing about being an author/illustrator is that you can begin your career at age seven. I sure did! That's about the time I created "Lazer Brain," an inept space hero who lost his brain in a laser accident. Creating the adventures of "Lazer Brain" wasn't pretend, it was a *real* comic, *really* written and *really* drawn for the same *real* audience I write for now, *real* kids.

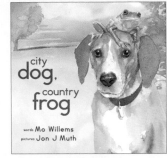

My classmates who wanted to be doctors or lawyers could only pretend to practice their professions, it would be many years before they actually set a fractured bone or litigated. But, as a young author/illustrator, I was doing the actual, professional work of creating and disseminating stories.

The thrill of figuring out a character or coming up with a funny line or hearing from my audience what they liked about a story was palpable then, exactly as it is now. I'm continually thankful that, unlike the other seven-year-olds in my class, I forgot to stop drawing and making up stories.

See individual listings for books by Mo Willems on pages 86, 97, and 238.

Author/Illustrator Mo Willems

Nancy Carlson
Arnie and the New Kid

Addressing the issue of children with disabilities without lecturing can be a challenge, but this picture book handles it with grace and humor. Phillip is the new kid in school, and he is different from the other kids because he uses a wheelchair; since the children don't know how to include him, they tend to ignore him. When Arnie falls down the stairs and ends up on crutches, he and Phillip become friends, and he realizes that they have a lot in common. Because of that lesson, their friendship continues long after Arnie's cast comes off.

1990 Puffin

Jennifer Moore-Mallinos
Illustrated by Marta Febrega
My Friend Has Down Syndrome

As more children with Down syndrome are "mainstreamed" into traditional school and camp programs, children who are unfamiliar with the condition will have questions that need to be answered. This book tells the story of two little girls at summer camp, one who has Down syndrome and one who does not. They become fast friends and help each other in different and unexpected ways. A short section at the back of the book offers additional tips and advice for parents on discussing Down syndrome with their children.

2008 Barron's Educational Series, Inc.

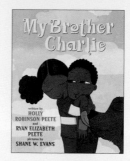

Holly Robinson Peete and Ryan Elizabeth Peete
Illustrated by Shane W. Evans
My Brother Charlie

In this loving story told by young Callie, we learn that Callie and Charlie are twins; they have always been together, and they love many of the same things. We also learn that Charlie has autism, which can occasionally make things difficult—there are times he might ruin a play date or just not want to talk. These situations and more are dealt with in a caring and supportive manner, with illustrations that enhance the text and help to explain the issues that can accompany autism. Based on Holly Robinson Peete's true family story, the book also contains an afterword that explains more about the condition.

2010 Scholastic Press

Jeanne Whitehouse Petersen
Illustrated by Deborah Kogan Ray
I Have a Sister—My Sister Is Deaf

In this lovingly told story, a young girl talks about her sister, who is deaf. She explains that her sister does all the same things that other children do; she loves to run and jump and play just like all children. She can feel the cat purring in her lap and even play the piano—but she cannot hear. As readers follow the story of the two children through their day, they will learn that being deaf means differences in communication and some limitations, but they are outweighed by the interests that all children have in common.

1977 HarperCollins

Pat Thomas
Illustrated by Leslie Harker

Don't Call Me Special: A First Look at Disability

Written by a psychotherapist and counselor, this book helps preschoolers understand physical disabilities and offers a very direct and positive look at the full and happy lives lived by the disabled. It explains the various types of equipment that may be required to assist disabled children with their needs, and encourages young children to ask questions and confront the social issues and situations that come up when dealing with a disability.

2002 Barron's Educational Series, Inc.

Adoption

Jamie Lee Curtis
Illustrated by Laura Cornell

Tell Me Again About the Night I Was Born

Actress Jamie Lee Curtis is the mother of two adopted children. Her engaging and often amusing explanation of how an adopted child joins a family is just right for preschoolers who love to hear reassuring stories about their birth. The illustrations are charming and filled with fun bits of visual humor, and the facts about adoption, birth mothers, and family adjustments are dealt with honestly but sparingly, in a manner easily understood by young children.

1996 HarperCollins

Karen Katz
Over the Moon: An Adoption Tale

Perfect for parents who have traveled a great distance to adopt a child and parents who have adopted children with a different ethnic background than their own, this tale of adoption starts with "Once upon a time..." and ends with "forever and always"—the promise of adoption. Katz's colorful, pattern-filled illustrations of smiling babies and parents and the accompanying text keeps the mood light and reassuring as the parents tell the story of making a long journey to bring home the baby that was meant to become part of their family.

1997 Henry Holt

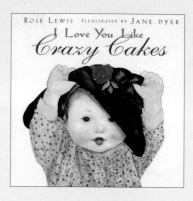

Growing Up

Rose Lewis
Illustrated by Jane Dyer

I Love You Like Crazy Cakes

This lovingly written and illustrated book describes the story of a Chinese girl adopted by an American family. It begins with a woman writing to China, asking to adopt from the big room of babies who are missing mothers, because she is a mother missing something too—a baby. The process of the adoption is explained in just enough detail that you can use it as a way to tell your own story, but what is clear all the way through in the text and illustrations is the instantaneous love and ongoing connection between the mother and daughter.

2000 Little, Brown and Company

Todd Parr

We Belong Together: A Book About Adoption and Families

Every family with an adopted child decides when the time is right to discuss adoption. For those who do so in the toddler years, this book can be a great help. With Parr's signature bright rainbow of simply drawn graphics, this book discusses home, love, and family (all easily understood by very young children), and never actually mentions the word *adoption*. The focus here is on all the ways that people can become a family and what it means to share your heart and your home with those you love.

2007 Megan Tingley Books

John McCutcheon
Illustrated by Julie Paschkis

Happy Adoption Day!

For many families with adopted children—especially those with children adopted from China—Chinese adoption day, often referred to as "Gotcha Day," is cause for great celebration. The text of this book is song lyrics (the musical score is included at the back) written to celebrate this special day—after all, there is a special birthday song, why not a song just for adoption day? The illustrations have a bright folk art feel, the child at the center of the celebration is clearly Chinese, and the family and friends are represented as multiethnic as well.

1996 Little, Brown and Company

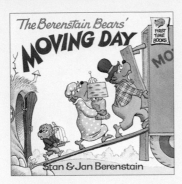

Stan and Jan Berenstain
The Berenstain Bears' Moving Day

The Berenstain Bears' "First Time Books" were created to help young children understand and cope with new experiences and changes in their lives. In this case, Brother Bear is just a cub who loves his home in the mountains and isn't at all sure how he feels about moving to the big tree house in Bear Country. Youngsters will be able to relate to his concerns: Will he have friends? Will he like living there? Children will be reassured when the transition goes smoothly, and life for Brother Bear is even better in the new tree house.

1981 Random House Children's Books

Teresa and Whitney Martin
Big Ernie's New Home: A Story for Children Who Are Moving

This book about moving doesn't shy away from the many complicated feelings that children have about moving to a new house or neighborhood. It gently acknowledges that at first they may feel sad or mad, lonely, and perhaps even anxious. Big Ernie, the main character, feels all of those things, but gradually he realizes that his home still has all the familiar comforts he's used to, and with some parental support, he ventures out to meet new friends and have exciting adventures in his new neighborhood.

2006 Magination Press

Constance W. McGeorge
Illustrated by Mary Whyte
Boomer's Big Day

Rather than focusing on a child's confusion about moving, this story is told from the perspective of Boomer, a Golden Retriever. Boomer wakes up one morning to chaos: there are strangers with boxes, he can't find his toys, and what happened to his morning walk? After being stuck in a cramped car, he is released into an empty house, and when the furniture comes in, nothing is where it should be. The art is filled with humor, and Boomer's moods and body language are expressively communicated.

1996 Chronicle Books

Judith Viorst
Illustrated by Robin Preiss Glasser
Alexander, Who's Not (Do you hear me? I mean it!) Going to Move

Those who loved *Alexander and the Terrible, Horrible, No Good, Very Bad Day* will remember that when Alexander gets frustrated, he threatens to move to Australia. But when Alexander's family needs to relocate a thousand miles from home, this defiant middle-grader puts his foot down. After some parental reassurances (he can call his friends long-distance now and then and maybe even get a dog), Alexander begins to pack and say good-bye to his "special" people and places. Filled with humor and illustrations that communicate Alexander's every mood, this book will go a long way toward reassuring children about a family move.

1995 Atheneum

Growing Up

Aliki
Manners

In this book, all the "dos" and "don'ts" of common social interactions are presented in a cartoon-style series of vignettes with speech bubbles, a manner that young children can easily process. Witty commentary and asides are provided by two small birds and several other animals in the margins, who watch the interactions on each page and keep the lessons from becoming too pedantic while keeping children engaged.

1990 Greenwillow Books

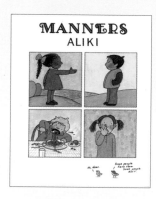

Whoopi Goldberg
Illustrated by Olo
Whoopi's Big Book of Manners

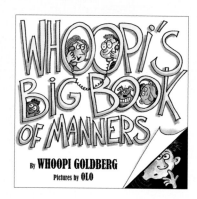

Populated by an integrated mix of animals and humans, this very animated and sometimes quite silly illustrated guide to manners will have both children and parents laughing as they learn the ins and outs of good manners. The lessons are solid, and the art will captivate and surprise children with random animals (like a big lizard casually riding a bus with people) and with the expressions on the faces of the characters as they react to both polite behavior and major faux pas with visible glee or shock. There is advice for parents here as well, to model appropriate behavior for their children and set good examples for them to emulate.

2006 Hyperion

Laurie Keller
Do Unto Otters

Populated by a couple of crazy otters, a bunny, and a wise old owl, not to mention various and sundry acerbic insects, this tribute to The Golden Rule is a hilarious homage to doing the right thing. By using recognizable situations and characters with a fairly broad sense of humor, this book will teach children to treat others the way they would like to be treated. Keller's art is filled with funny asides and visual gags, and there are verbal acrobatics in the text that will have children learning how to behave and giggling the entire time.

2007 Henry Holt

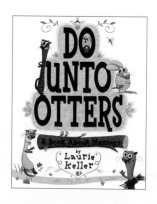

Growing Up

Munro Leaf
Manners Can Be Fun

This classic title, originally published in 1936, has been reissued for a new generation of readers. Many parents and grandparents learned their first etiquette lessons from Leaf's simple stick figures and characters cleverly named the "Mefirsts," the "Pigs," the "Whineys," and others, which even very young children can easily understand and relate to. Children will learn what to do and say when they meet new people, table manners, controlling their voices, and other basic manners. There are also blank pages at the back for children to draw and write what they have learned.

1936 Universe (Rizzoli International Publishers)

Munro Leaf
How to Behave and Why

Written in 1946 as a follow-up to *Manners Can Be Fun*, this book quickly became even more popular than the original title. While it does emphasize good manners, this book is focused on getting along with other people, and making and keeping friends by behaving properly. Leaf once again uses simple stick figures and clear concise text to explain how to get along with others: "You have to be HONEST, you have to be FAIR, you have to be STRONG, and you have to be WISE." According to the author, once you have learned those four things, you have learned how to behave and why.

1946 Universe (Rizzoli International Publishers)

Peter Mayle
Illustrated by Arthur Robbins
Where Did I Come From?

The question broached by this title can come at any time, and parents are rarely prepared to answer it when it does. This book offers a frank and factual answer to that question, suitable for children between four and eight, in a format chock-full of humor and cartoon-like illustrations that can make the discussion a whole lot easier on Mom and Dad. Having said that, parents are advised to review this book before reading it with their children, as it discusses anatomy, sex, orgasm, and other related subjects in a very funny but also direct manner that may not be suitable for some families.

1977 Lyle Stuart

Peter Mayle
Illustrated by Arthur Robbins
What's Happening to Me?

There is no question that the arrival of puberty brings an entire new set of questions and concerns for both parents and children. Because puberty can begin anytime—sometimes starting as early as eight or nine—parents are advised to have a book on the subject available when needed. This particular book is geared toward children aged eight and up, and like its predecessor, *Where Did I Come From?*, it offers all the facts of puberty in a hilariously illustrated but also frank and factual format. While children are more likely to read this book on their own, parents are still advised to review this book due to the frank content and illustrations.

1975 Lyle Stuart

Growing Up

Lynda Madaras with Area Madaras
Illustrated by Simon Sullivan
The "What's Happening to My Body?" Book for Girls/Book for Boys

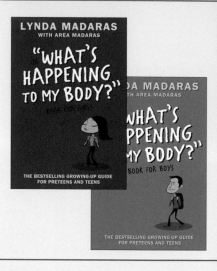

Talking about puberty with tweens and teens isn't easy; finding a resource with one edition for boys and one for girls helps. Both books present the facts in a straightforward manner, include illustrations that explain bodily functions, and deal effectively with emotional and social issues—from dating and romantic feelings to peer pressure and boundaries and also more serious subjects like STDs and eating disorders. Each book has a section dealing with the bodily changes in the opposite sex, making sure readers get enough information on how puberty affects both boys and girls. These books are appropriate for children nine and up to read independently, but parents are advised to review them first to be sure they are comfortable with the content.

2007 Newmarket Press

Lynda Madaras and Area Madaras
Illustrated by Simon Sullivan, et.al.
My Body, My Self: For Girls/For Boys

These two books by the authors of the *What's Happening to My Body?* books skew toward the younger end of the nine-to-twelve age group, and focus exclusively on puberty for either boys or girls—not both. Using a more humorous and colloquial tone, with chapter headings such as "B.O. & Zits: Is Puberty the Pits?" they still present solid factual information but do not go into more graphic sexual detail. The most unique aspect of these books is that they are designed for tweens and teens to use interactively—by filling out forms, taking quizzes, and doing exercises and worksheets that can assist them in developing a positive body image and enhancing self-esteem. These books are an excellent starting point for children who have not yet begun or are just beginning to enter puberty—they offer solid support and facts without overwhelming them with information they may not be mature enough to handle.

2007 Newmarket Press

JoAnn Loulan and Bonnie Worthen
Illustrated by Marcia Quackenbush and Chris Wold Dyrud
Period. A Girl's Guide

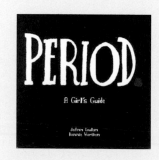

Most parents know that the time to talk to their daughters about menstruation is before it occurs—but since you can't predict exactly when it might begin, it's a good idea to be prepared in advance. This book is a very reliable source of information for girls from age eight or nine and up and has the added benefit of an excellent parent's guide at the back to advise parents how and when to talk to their daughters about this rite of passage and the other changes in their bodies. This book communicates a positive message about self-esteem and body image, diversity, and the differences between reality and images of women in the media, and provides a few handy charts for girls to fill in so that they can begin to identify the early signs and learn to keep track of their menstrual cycles.

2001 The Book Peddlers

Nonfiction & Reference

Selecting nonfiction and reference books is a lot like trying to find a limit to the universe: the depth and breadth of available options is immense.

Though a wealth of material is available on the Internet, finding reliable information online can sometimes be more difficult than a quick trip to the library or searching for facts in a dictionary or encyclopedia. How many of us remember poring over those clear pages showing the circulatory system of the human body? That research experience is still available in books and in formats that offer even more exciting interaction and information. In this chapter, we will focus on the five largest and most important categories: United States and world history, general reference (including dictionaries), single-volume encyclopedias and thesauri, how things work, science and nature (including dinosaurs), and cookbooks.

Within these categories you'll find books for all ages. In the bookstore's nonfiction section you'll also find many titles that fall outside of these groups—for example, books that have a more specific focus on a historical event or a single animal species—so we encourage you to spend time in this area to go beyond our recommendations.

Here are some guidelines to keep in mind when choosing nonfiction and reference books:

- Let your child's interests guide your choices and encourage discussion, questions, and further investigation and research—which, depending on the age, may also include online research.

- When looking at dictionaries and thesauri, age matters. A dictionary for a younger child will feature more illustrations, large, bold type, and simpler definitions than one for a middle grader.

- Science and nature books also vary widely by age. For a younger child, look for photographs, illustrations, or a blend of both; most importantly, look for an exciting visual orientation. For an older child, more sophisticated topics and facts provide valuable information, while additional online links may also be helpful.

- When it comes to cookbooks, books that encourage family involvement and supervision are strongly recommended, and nutritional information should be addressed and easy to understand.

- Books on the subject of "how things work" vary greatly in detail and level of sophistication. Parents are advised to select these books with their children to ensure age, interest, and reading-level appropriateness.

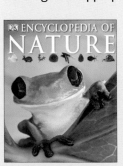

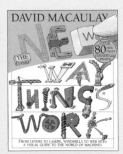

Jennifer Armstrong
Illustrated by Roger Roth

The American Story: 100 True Tales from American History

American history is filled with great stories—some familiar, others lesser known—and many of them are recounted within this wide-ranging, single-volume history book. Organized by time period, beginning with "Settlement and Colonies (1565–1778)" and ending with "Brave New World (1946–2000)," this illustrated compendium offers cultural and political information about the events that shaped our nation, as well as the unusual personalities, such as Carrie Nation, Typhoid Mary, Babe Ruth, and many others who made America the country we know today.

2006 Alfred A. Knopf

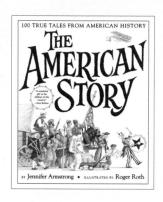

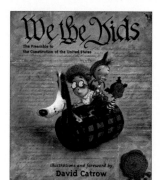

David Catrow

We the Kids: The Preamble to the Constitution of the United States

For anyone who's ever had to memorize this important bit of American history and wondered (as the author explains in his foreword) "Why couldn't the guys who wrote this just use regular English?", this picture book is for you and your kids. The text is the verbatim preamble, but Catrow uses the conceit of three children and a dog on a camping trip to explain via quirky and humorous illustrations each of the concepts in ways children can easily understand. This book comes complete with a glossary and introduction, titled "Big Words, Big Ideas," so that children may finally understand what "domestic tranquility" or "blessings of liberty" mean, and get a good laugh while they learn.

2002 Dial

Kenneth C. Davis
Illustrated by Matt Faulkner

Don't Know Much About American History

This author brings his successful formula for adult books into the world of children's books by using his trademark question-and-answer format. Fully illustrated and loaded with fun facts, sidebars, quotes, and timelines, this book introduces readers to the original settlers on the east coast through their movement west, the indigenous peoples of the Americas, the formation of government, wars, slavery, and everything in between in clear, easy-to-understand language. It is suitable for readers eight and up, but even parents will learn a few things about American history from this nontraditional history book.

2003 HarperCollins

Nonfiction and Reference

Nonfiction and Reference

Author Jean Fritz has managed to do what many might think impossible—focus on significant moments and key figures in American history and write about them in a way that makes them interesting, understandable, and just plain fun for middle-grade and younger readers. There is plenty of great material here, and lots of action and important information is presented in each book, but perhaps the most notable aspect of these books is that they are hilarious. We all remember learning about Ben Franklin's kite and key and Paul Revere's famous ride, and some of us may even remember that Sam Adams was a Patriot before he was a brand of beer, but if we had learned about our forefathers from these books we might also remember that the individual states never wanted to be "united," and even printed their own money. In each book, readers will learn some of the back story, including where famous Americans grew up and their jobs before they became part of our history. There are also fun facts galore: Did you know that Paul Revere had sixteen children? Or the reason John Hancock's signature is so big on the Declaration of Independence is because he was mad at King George? How about the fact that King George was pigeon-toed, and blushed a lot? Readers will learn all this and more with this wonderful series of picture books that teaches history in a way that makes it easy to learn and remember.

Jean Fritz

Illustrated by Margot Tomes
And then what happened, Paul Revere? *(1973)*

Illustrated by Trina Schart Hyman
Why don't you get a horse, Sam Adams? *(1974*

Illustrated by Margot Tomes
Where was Patrick Henry on the 29th of May? *(1975)*

Illustrated by J. B. Handelsman
Who's that stepping on Plymouth Rock? *(1975)*

Illustrated by Margot Tomes
What's the big idea, Ben Franklin? *(1976)*

Illustrated by Trina Schart Hyman
Will you sign here, John Hancock? *(1976)*

Illustrated by Margot Tomes
Can't you make them behave, King George? *(1977)*

Illustrated by Tomie dePaola
Shh! We're writing the Constitution *(1987)*

Putnam

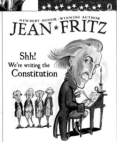

Ruby Bridges
Ruby Bridges Goes to School: My True Story

This level-two reader offers newly independent readers a chance to learn the story of school integration from the first-person narrative of Ruby Bridges, who in 1960, at six years of age, bravely walked past an angry mob in New Orleans to become the first African American child to attend an all white school—and by so doing changed American history. The courage and bravery required to take those first steps toward ending racial segregation are well communicated through both text and archival photographs. For older readers there is a book titled *Through My Eyes,* also by Ruby Bridges, with more detail and information.

2009 Cartwheel Books

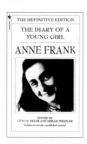

Anne Frank
The Diary of a Young Girl

In terms of first-person accounts of the terrors of the Holocaust, no book compares with this one. A longtime staple of middle-grade reading lists as well as adult Holocaust scholarship, Anne's story of her family's forced hiding from the Nazis in an attic in Amsterdam, and the brave people who assisted them, has touched the hearts of all who have read it. In a story that is in turns touching, poignant, and brave, readers learn from Anne herself what it was like to be hidden—and can read in the afterword of her eventual capture and death. Parents should be aware that this book deals frankly with the Holocaust and may not be appropriate for sensitive readers.

1993 Bantam Books

Russell Freedman
Lincoln: A Photobiography

The author's research for this book was extensive, and readers will reap the benefits as he examines the early life and legends surrounding one of America's most fascinating presidents. The first half of the book focuses on Lincoln's early years, self-education, and work, and the latter on his presidency and assassination, via extensive use of drawings, archival photographs, and documents. There is a wealth of information here that does not shy away from the controversies of his presidency. The book also includes a listing of historical sites to visit and excerpts from Lincoln's writings.

1987 Clarion Books

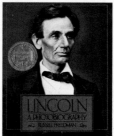

Newbery Award

David C. King
Various Illustrators
Smithsonian Children's Encyclopedia of American History

Maybe you were the kind of kid who loved to read encyclopedias; if you weren't, you will be now— and so will your kids. This single-volume history of America begins in the year 1000 and covers every major event until the year 2002. Illustrated with paintings, drawings, timelines, documents, photographs, artifacts, cultural touchstones, and images both iconic and new, this book offers not just the facts, but also a comprehensive and visual history. Appendixes include lists of the presidents, state facts, the full Declaration of Independence, the Gettysburg Address, the Constitution, and more.

2003 DK Publishing

Betsy Maestro
Illustrated by Giulio Maestro

A More Perfect Union: The Story of Our Constitution

This accessible history of the writing of the Constitution is just right for young scholars who need to understand how our government was formed. With a focus on the decisions that created the organization of the government and led to the "Great Compromise," this book shows what a group of people can do when they work together for a common cause. The book also has great information at the back, including a timeline of events, dates of ratification, information on the attendees of the Constitutional Convention, and simple summaries of the articles of the Constitution.

1987 HarperCollins

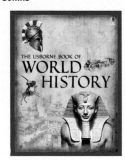

Anne Millard and Patricia Vanags
Illustrated by Joseph McEwan

The Usborne Book of World History

Undertaking world history in a single volume is a daunting task, and yet this book offers a huge amount of information in a visual and easy-to-understand format. Readers will be able to examine historical events from early civilizations to the twentieth century with a focus on different peoples and cultures and the help of a geographical time chart and an extensive index with recommendations for further reading.

2009 Usborne

Mary Ling
Various Illustrators

DK First Encyclopedia

Perfect for four- to eight-year-olds, this visual encyclopedia offers a wealth of information across a broad spectrum of topics, including science and nature, world regions, people and societies, the human body, technology, the universe, and more. Using photographs and incorporating simple quizzes, games, and color-coded links to related information, this book will boost learning, encourage imagination, and keep children interested. This book offers an easy-to-understand format that will also support school curriculum.

2002 DK Publishing

Scholastic Reference Editors

Scholastic Children's Encyclopedia

This encyclopedia is geared toward middle-graders aged nine to twelve, with over 600 entries and more than 2,000 illustrations offering timelines, maps, "Did You Know" boxes, and highlighted "Amazing Facts." An extensive reference section, which includes maps, a countries table with names, flags, capitals, populations, a table of states, presidents, plant- and animal-classification charts, weights and measures conversions, and so much more. This book is a great general family reference title, featuring extensive information across a wide spectrum of topics.

2004 Scholastic Reference/Scholastic Inc.

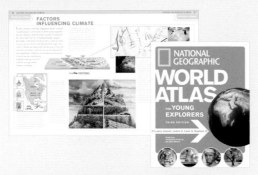

National Geographic World Atlas for Young Explorers

This world atlas offers more than just maps—it also explains the different type of maps, from topographical and physical to political, and teaches children how to read them. Each map section features photographs and icons representing crops, industries, flags, capitols, languages, and more. Filled with interesting facts and figures, plus thirty-two separate maps that show up to twenty different political and physical features, this book will prove to be very useful for supporting school reports and projects with accurate and easy-to-understand information about the continents, countries, and states of the world.

2007 National Geographic

Editors of Time for Kids Magazine
Time for Kids United States Atlas

While this atlas offers all the maps and information you would expect about the fifty states of the union, it also offers information that you might not expect: state superlatives, such as the longest, highest, and lowest states; major attractions (manmade and natural); state-specific information; and loads of supporting photographs. In the back of the book, readers will find explanations of longitude and latitude, extensive graphs, and charts comparing the United States to other nations—and, just for fun, a "Where in the U.S." scavenger-hunt game that uses clues, compass directions, landmarks, scales of miles, and more.

2010 Time for Kids

Various Illustrators
The American Heritage Children's Dictionary

Language is always evolving, and this dictionary for middle-graders has added more than 2,000 new words, such as *burqa, akido, hip-hop, sustainable,* and more. It also features 25,000 entries with easily understood definitions, more than 16,000 sample sentences, a phonics-and-spelling guide to assist in building writing skills, and more than 1,500 full-color photographs. This book will assist students with their schoolwork and is a valuable addition to your family library.

2009 HMH Dictionary

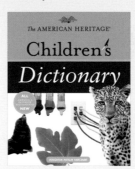

Macmillan Dictionary for Children

Recently revised to be appropriate for 21st century nine- to fourteen-year-olds, this dictionary has long been a favorite for middle-grade students. With 35,000 definitions in clear but not oversimplified language—including common homonyms; newer words, like *velcro, karaoke,* and *Internet*; 1,100 color photographs; drawings; and a reference section that includes maps and a thesaurus—this dictionary should prove to be a valuable resource and fun to browse as well.

2007 Simon & Schuster Books for Young Readers

Nonfiction and Reference

Nonfiction and Reference

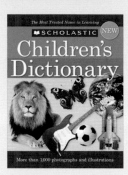

Scholastic Children's Dictionary

New words become part of our language every year, and this dictionary for nine- to twelve-year-olds now includes examples like *rap, DVD,* and *browser,* along with 200 other new entries. This perennially popular student dictionary has everything you might expect, plus Braille and ASL alphabets, maps, flags of the world, facts about the fifty states, and a list of American presidents. With synonym boxes, illustrations, color photographs, and language notes, this popular dictionary offers solid educational support for schoolwork and is definitely browser-friendly.

2010 Scholastic Reference/Scholastic Inc.

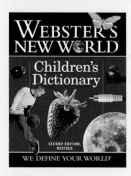

Edited by Michael E. Agnes
Various Illustrators
Webster's New World Children's Dictionary

This dictionary is designed as a transitional dictionary for middle graders seven to twelve years old, who still need a fair amount of illustration but also need solid definitions as well. It includes a miniature pronunciation guide on every page, as well as maps, history, and geography pages, and an introductory thesaurus. A ten-page guide to dictionary usage covers synonyms and homonyms and addresses the issue of how to look up a word you don't even know how to spell.

2006 Wiley

Paul Hellweg
Various Illustrators
The American Heritage Children's Thesaurus

With over 4,000 entries and 36,000 synonyms, the inclusion of each word in a sentence to clarify meaning, and the addition of color photographs to break up the text, this thesaurus is an excellent choice for your family reference library. A four-page explanation of how to use the book appears at the beginning, and an index of antonyms and word groups is featured at the end.

2009 HMH Dictionary

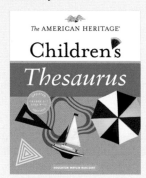

John Bollard
Illustrated by Mike Reed
Scholastic Children's Thesaurus

Is it time for your kids to stop using the word *weird*? This thesaurus offers some other options, like *strange* or *unusual*, and also includes succinct definitions and sentence examples to assist children with written and spoken communication. Playfully illustrated, this book contains more than 500 main "headwords" and 2,500 synonyms—and if readers can't find the word they seek, they can just flip to the index in the back, where they'll find a word listing that sends them to the alternatives they need.

2006 Scholastic Reference/Scholastic Inc.

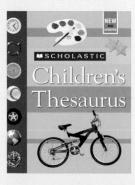

Peter Yarrow on bringing songs to life as books…

Six years ago, after a music career lasting more than four decades, I discovered a new, and in some ways more meaningful, way to share the folk songs that had shaped my life. When I realized that combining a CD with a book that illustrates a song's words could open children's hearts as it shared and taught them what was always most important for me to communicate as a musical artist, I was not only delighted; I became hooked. That's how and why I became (sort of) an author. I don't actually write books (yet). I just record some of my favorite songs with my daughter, Bethany, write some commentary and historical notes, and the editor and illustrator do the rest. I was delighted to find that a song acquires an entirely new life when presented in conjunction with a book. For instance, I have sung "Puff, the Magic Dragon" thousands of times over the years, but reading my "Puff" book to my granddaughter, Valentina, 4, is a totally new experience, revealing how powerful an impression a book can make on a child. Watching the remarkable range of expressions and emotions that pass across Valentina's face as the pages turn, with the music playing in the background, I see that she is actually *living* the Puff story more deeply, and in many ways more meaningfully, than when she simply listened to the song. Now happy, now sad, Puff's arching neck is bent in sorrow. Jackie Paper is leaving him! Valentina's finger touches the sad faces painted in the trees and the rocks, and I see her live the emotions that she thinks Puff is feeling. Yes, after all these years, I am hooked on, and honored to be, a co-creator of books. What a wonderful surprise!

See individual listings for books by Peter Yarrow on pages 91 and 210.

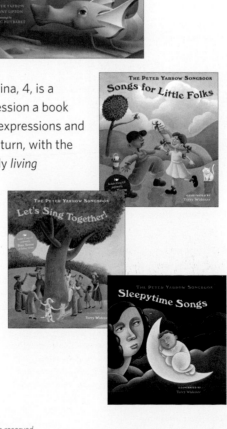

Songwriter/Author Peter Yarrow

Marshall Brain
More How Stuff Works

Based on the website by the same name, this book is perfect for everyone who's ever had a question about the way the things we deal with every day work. It is filled with full-color illustrations to help readers finally understand the workings of a CD, a toilet, a submarine, a cell phone, and an airplane, to name a few of the 135 topics covered in this guide. The book also features fun and interesting sidebars for each entry that present "Did you know?" information and "Cool facts" about the topics explained. This book offers fun and learning for readers young and old alike.

2001 Wiley

John Langone
The New How Things Work

For young readers who are curious about the emerging technologies that have changed the way we live and work, this fun-to-browse book offers some easy-to-understand answers to some fairly complicated questions. In chapters that focus on new technologies in power and energy, transportation, entertainment, manufacturing, tools of medicine, and more, inquiring young minds will finally get the information they have been seeking. Concepts and technologies are explained in clear language and supported by photographs, charts, and diagrams in this comprehensive volume.

2004 National Geographic

Chris Woodford and Jon Woodcock
Cool Stuff 2.0 and How It Works

Ever wonder how night-vision goggles work or what's inside your video game console or what HDTV is? This book takes a detailed look at today's ever-changing technologies and those that may be just around the corner and offers easy-to-understand information. Technology is rapidly changing, and all those e-readers, hand-held devices, and high-tech thing-a-ma-jigs are great—but how exactly do they work? Through full-color graphs, charts, cross-sections, photographs, and concise text, readers will get a handle on lots of new technologies—at least until the next edition comes out.

2007 DK Publishing

Fiona Chandler
Illustrated by David Hancock and John Woodcock

First Encyclopedia of the Human Body

Geared toward children four to eight years old, this introduction to the workings of the human body offers just the right amount of information, with illustrations and photographs to visually support the text. From explanations of what happens to your food after it's swallowed to the number of bones in your body, this book can assist parents in teaching their children how their bodies work and how to keep them heathy. What really sets this book apart is the fact that each section features safe and secure Internet links for children and parents to visit for additional information or text-supporting games and activities.

2004 Usborne

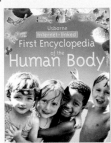

Luann Columbo
Illustrated by Jennifer Fairman and Craig Zukerman

Uncover the Human Body

By utilizing a plastic model of the human body built into this book, readers can explore how the body functions system by system with a simple page turn. Similar to the see-through acrylic pages once used in encyclopedias, this format demystifies the organs, systems, and functions of the human body visually in tandem with the text. Each page examines a specific body system, and closing the book shows them all working together.

2003 Silver Dolphin Books

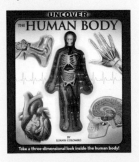

David Macaulay with Neil Ardley
Illustrated by David Macaulay

The New Way Things Work

The author of this fascinating book is a former architect and junior high school teacher who fully comprehends the questions we all have about how stuff works—and more importantly, he can explain it in a visual format that is understandable to children and their parents. The illustrations go a long way toward demonstrating they way things work—and still manage to express humor. This new and updated version of this bestseller from 1988 features an additional eighty pages that deal with all the mind-boggling changes that have been brought by the digital age, from computers to cameras, and every bit and byte of information in between.

1998 Houghton Mifflin Books for Children

David Macaulay

The Way We Work

Readers who learned how things work in Macauley's classic, *The New Way Things Work,* will welcome this book, which takes a detailed and visual look at the mysterious workings of the human body. The author's extensive research shows in his diagrams and cross-sections, and his more humorous takes on and illustrations of bodily functions may be funny, but they are also factual. Everything you ever wondered about your body's composition and functions is here—information on DNA, individual cells, metabolism, respiration, circulation, digestion, elimination, the nervous and endocrine systems, reproduction, and more—in a fully illustrated, easy-to-understand format.

2008 Houghton Mifflin Books for Children

Bill Bryson

A Really Short History of Nearly Everything

In his interesting and accessible hybrid of an encyclopedia, an almanac, and a science book, Bryson takes on the entire universe of science and nature in a kid-friendly, hilariously illustrated and humorously written format. Science can be intimidating for middle-schoolers, but the author takes care to use relatable analogies that bring the loftiest scientific concepts down to earth. This book offers just enough information about a vast number of topics, including chemistry, the cosmos, cells, atoms, earthquakes, asteroids, global warming, recycling, and much more. Every family library should have at least one book of general science information to help parents answer those tricky questions about—nearly everything.

2009 Delacorte Press

Time For Kids Super Science Book

Not only will readers learn about earth, physical, and life sciences, but this book is also designed to dovetail with school curriculum, offering activities and experiments that are easy to do with readily available materials and fully illustrated, step-by-step directions. There is also a bonus section for parents and kids with suggestions and ideas for school science fairs, and information about the proper way to write up your experiments and findings in the same way real scientists do in their labs.

2009 Time for Kids

Charles Taylor, et.al.

The Kingfisher Science Encyclopedia

Updated to cover new technologies and advances in computers, this nearly 500-page volume is chock-full of information about all aspects of science, offering color photographs, charts, diagrams, and more for budding scientists. In chapters ranging from "The Planet Earth" to "Space and Time," readers will find plenty of useful information for science reports, and the browser-friendly format also works well for those who are just curious as well. A reference section in the back offers units of measurement, conversion tables, geometric shapes, and more.

2006 Kingfisher Books

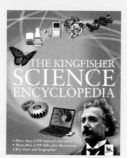

The Usborne Science Encyclopedia

This book is overflowing with science and is beautifully illustrated with both illustrations and photographs that offer readers all the visuals they need to comprehend the text. In chapters focusing on Earth and space, plants, animals, light, sound and electricity, and more, readers will find a ton of information packed into this over-400-page book. For added value, the book also features links to more than 1,000 websites for children and parents to visit for additional information or text-supporting games and activities.

2009 Usborne

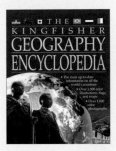

Clive Gifford

The Kingfisher Geography Encyclopedia, 2nd Edition

Suitable for readers in grades four through eight, this almost-500-page book offers information about each country, continent by continent. The highly visual format is accessible, and the information is clearly communicated. This book also offers a broad overview of topics like continental drift, earthquakes, volcanoes, population growth, the Greenhouse Effect, and more. In the reference section of the book, there are facts and charts galore, including ones for life expectancies, literacy, and extinction. The format is easy to browse and offers solid information for curious readers.

2003 Kingfisher Books

Space: A Visual Encyclopedia

While there may not be enough information in each chapter to fill an entire science report, there is plenty of information to get young researchers started, and for those fascinated by all things space-related, this book is sure to please for its use of stunning color photography alone. Chapters cover observing the universe, the solar system, Earth, the moon, the sun, humans and animals in space, and more. Young readers who long to be astronauts are sure to be interested in the sections on space travel and astronaut food.

2010 DK Publishing

Animals: A Visual Encyclopedia

Covering just about everything from anteaters to zebras, this book will offer hours of mesmerizing reading about mammals, birds, fish, reptiles, amphibians, and invertebrates. From the strongest and fastest to the smallest and strangest, this book offers a visual feast of animals, with dazzling and abundant color photographs, graphics, and information, including the relative sizes of the animals compared to humans, natural habitats, family groups, life spans, migration patterns, hunting habits, and conservation status.

2008 DK Publishing

Everything on Earth

Dorling Kindersley is known for its ability to make any subject understandable by use of clear text and eye-catching visuals, and this book brings together the best of the various DK publications in one volume that offers a limited amount of information on a wide variety of subjects. While hardly all-encompassing, there is just enough detail about plants, wildlife, weather, and geography, among other Earth-related topics, to get children interested enough to investigate further on their own.

2010 DK Publishing

Encyclopedia of Nature

This vividly illustrated book offers children a close-up view of the natural world via the use of full-color photographs and clear text. Subjects covered include the natural world, ecology, animals, plants, and the classification of living organisms. This book offers information across a broad array of subjects and, for more computer-savvy readers, is also available as a CD-ROM with additional information and interactive games and activities.

2007 DK Publishing

Roger Priddy
My Big Dinosaur Book

Children are fascinated by dinosaurs, and there are plenty of books on the subject—but not as many targeted to the infant and preschool age group. This book solves that problem nicely and offers a visual guide to the intriguing world of prehistoric creatures. After seeing the bright, simple graphics presented in an oversized and sturdy board-book format, you might just find that your toddler has no problem pronouncing *stegosaurus*.

2004 Priddy Books

Caroline Bingham
First Dinosaur Encyclopedia

For dino-crazy six- to nine-year-olds, this book offers clear color photos and simple text about both the dinosaurs and the periods in which they lived. Wondering how the publisher managed to get photos of long-extinct animals? They use photographs of detailed models, as well as artifacts, to bring these amazing creatures vibrantly to the page for curious readers. In addition to general information about specific dinosaurs, the chapters are arranged chronologically to cover the Triassic, Jurassic, and Cretaceous periods, with selected species featured along the way.

2007 DK Publishing

Touch and Feel Dinosaur

Perfect for toddlers and preschoolers, this durable board-book format not only allows little dino-lovers to identify their favorite prehistoric beasts, but also to touch and feel them, offering a full sensory experience for the youngest readers. With everything from scales and claws to leathery hides, these books are fully interactive and especially good for use with children who might be visually impaired or require a more tactile learning experience.

2002 DK Publishing

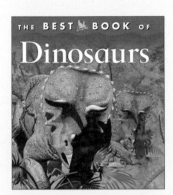

Christopher Maynard
The Best Book of Dinosaurs

Beginning with dinosaur babies hatching from their eggs and including information on what they eat, how they grow, and how they live, this fully illustrated book offers a great introduction to dinosaurs for children in the early primary grades. Chapters discuss plant-eaters, meat-eaters, how dinosaurs hunt for food, extinction, fossil remains and how they are formed, and more. This book also includes an index and provides a glossary, complete with pronunciation guide, for all those long and hard-to-pronounce species names.

1998 Kingfisher Books

Don Lessem
Illustrated by Franco Tempesta
The Ultimate Dinopedia

The dinosaur obsession in children usually peaks between seven and ten years old, and this book is perfectly suited to that age group. Organized by the time periods—Triassic, Jurassic, and Cretaceous—in which the dinosaurs lived, this fully-illustrated book offers a plethora of fun facts and all the details required to satisfy the curiosity of the most avid dino-scholar. It includes chapters covering "How We Know What They Looked Like," "Baby Dinosaurs," and "Great Dinosaur Goofs," as well as topics like habitat, scientific names, and where dinosaurs were discovered.

2010 National Geographic

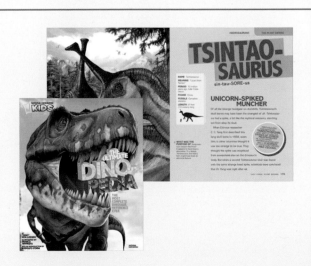

Paul O. Zelinsky on drawing inspiration from the masters...

I'm sure I'm like most people in children's publishing: my interest in making children's books comes from the delight I always felt in reading them. As a child, I was a library addict, but there was also a wonderful bookstore in the shopping center near my home, where I'd go browse during my mother's shopping trips. She would head to a department store, and I'd stay in the bookstore's children's section, looking at the new picture books. (That's how I remember it, anyway.) As I grew older, and shopped on my own, this didn't change. In high school I was still looking at those picture books and enjoying them as art.

I decided to become an artist and thought about painting, not making books. But when I began to consider what, as an artist, I could do in addition to making paintings (a career that supports almost nobody), I thought that picture books would be a great fit.

One of my favorite author/illustrators was William Pène du Bois: his ingenuity captured me totally. The way he drew was admirable, but the things he thought of were spectacular, from the multicultural pizzazz of the picture book *Bear Party* to the technological marvels in *The Twenty-One Balloons*. That novel has something to do with the inventiveness I tried to exercise in my moveable book *Knick-Knack Paddywhack!*

It's probably because of my education, which was in art, not illustration, that I don't usually turn to illustrators when I am figuring out an approach to a book. The artists I've tried to emulate include anonymous embroidery craftswomen, medieval manuscript illuminators, master painters of both the Italian and Northern Renaissance, German Expressionists and even one or two Abstract Expressionists. Plus my great-grandmother: her painting of Hansel and Gretel inspired my own book.

See individual listings for books written and illustrated by Paul O. Zelinsky on pages 134, 210 and 222.

Illustrated by Dave W. Titus

Better Homes and Gardens New Junior Cookbook

You may have had your own copy of this book as a child, but this fully updated, redesigned, and freshly illustrated version is not just bigger and better—it's also healthier, and features more than sixty new recipes. Created to be used by children and parents together, each recipe features short ingredient lists and step-by-step instructions and is accompanied by illustrations and photographs. There is also a chapter focusing on cooking basics, such as kitchen safety, menu-planning, basic nutrition information, and how to read food labels. The book also includes recipes for special celebrations and diabetic substitutions.

2004 Wiley

Illustrated by Dave W. Titus

Better Homes and Gardens Snack Attack!

What could be better than a kid's cookbook filled with forty yummy, easy-to-prepare snacks? The recipes range from quick after-school snack options to others that are hearty enough to be a meal. Each recipe has a short list of ingredients, step-by-step instructions with illustrations and photographs, and nutritional facts. From *"Outrageously Sloppy Joes"* to *"Slam Dunk Veggies,"* there is something here to satisfy every appetite.

2006 Wiley

Rachael Ray
Illustrated by Chris Kalb

Cooking Rocks! Rachael Ray 30-Minute Meals for Kids

Rachael Ray is not just a hit with adults; she also has a strong following among kids, and these recipes may have parents borrowing their kids' cookbook for new ideas. The recipes are nutritious, easy, and designed to take no more than thirty minutes to prepare. Tempting recipes like "Smashed Potatoes with Cream Cheese," "Potato and Apple Home Fries," and "Cherry Tricky Lime Ricky" should get kids' digestive juices flowing, and sections on ethnic cooking and kitchen basics offer a full variety of healthy and satisfying meals.

2004 Lake Isle Press, Inc.

Sandra K. Nissenberg

The Everything Kids' Cookbook

This book offers ninety kid-friendly recipes, but that's not all—it also has tidbits of trivia, and thirty food-related puzzles. Each recipe clearly states the level of difficulty, and features simple ingredient lists and easy-to-follow directions. This book presents information about cooking basics and kitchen safety, with recipe choices like *"Tasty Tacos," "Quick Eating Smores," "Cheese Crusted Fish Fillets,"* and *"Chicken Salad Puffs."* In other words, there is something here for even the pickiest eaters.

2008 Adams Media

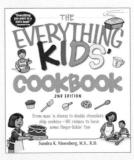

Illustrated by Stephen Gilpin
Betty Crocker Kids Cook!

When it comes to recipes and foods we grew up with, Betty Crocker—if you'll pardon the pun—takes the cake. This book gives kids the lowdown on cooking terms, basic techniques, good nutrition, and kitchen safety, and it also offers sixty easy, tasty, and fun recipes for all three meals, plus healthy snacks as well. Each recipe features illustrations and photographs, ingredient lists, and the required how-to. There is an extensive glossary and important nutritional information as well. The variety of recipes is surprisingly broad, from *"Ooh La La Omelets"* and *"Easy Mac & Cheese"* to *"Purple Cow Shakes"*—all nutritionally balanced and yummy as well.

2007 Wiley

Pillsbury Kids Cookbook: Food Fun for Boys and Girls

If any of these recipes sound like something your kids would eat—*"Bunny Rabbit Pancakes," "Hot Diggity Dog Pizza Boats"* or *"Jiggly Fruit Salad"*—then this is the cookbook for you. Each recipe includes a "Tools You Need" list, clear how-to instructions, a color photo, "Adult Helper" icons, safety information, and easy-to-follow instructions. A complete glossary of cooking terms used in the book and nutritional information is included, and there are recipes for every meal, as well as snacks, desserts, and themed food for holiday parties.

2005 Wiley

Angela Wilkes
Children's Quick and Easy Cookbook

This book offers color, step-by-step photographs that demonstrate each of sixty quick-and-easy recipes visually, in comprehensive chapters that cover "Before You Start" and "Kitchen Rules." Whether your child is in the mood for *"Pita Snacks," "Perfect Pasta," "Lemony Fish Sticks,"* or even *"Baked Alaska,"* the recipes are low on the "cutesy" title factor but high on nutrition and ease. The photos will have kids drooling before they pick up a mixing spoon.

1997 DK Publishing

Stephanie Rosenbaum
Williams-Sonoma Kids in the Kitchen: Fun Food

The twenty-five recipes featured in this book, from *"Rosemary Roasted Chicken"* and *"Stuffed Baked Potatoes"* to *"Parmesan Chicken"* and *"Cheese Quesadillas,"* are sure to please everyone. The book also has chapters that explain getting started, preparing ingredients, preparing your workspace, and knife skills, in addition to nutritional information and an extensive glossary. This is not "kid food," but real recipes for families that are created for kids to cook themselves.

2006 Free Press

Caldecott Medal Books

The bronze Caldecott Medal, which is named after the nineteenth-century English illustrator Randolph J. Caldecott, is awarded annually by the American Library Association to the artist who has created the most distinguished picture book published the previous year. The Caldecott Award has been bestowed on one book each year since 1938. The seal awarded to other notable books of the year, the silver Caldecott Honor, may be bestowed on any number of worthy titles in a given year.

2012 Medal Winner
A Ball for Daisy, by Chris Raschka

2011 Medal Winner
A Sick Day for Amos McGee, illustrated by Erin E. Stead, written by Philip C. Stead

2010 Medal Winner
The Lion & the Mouse, by Jerry Pinkney (page 67)

2009 Medal Winner
The House in the Night, illustrated by Beth Krommes, written by Susan Marie Swanson (page 81)

2008 Medal Winner
The Invention of Hugo Cabret, by Brian Selznick (page 184)

2007 Medal Winner
Flotsam, by David Wiesner (page 85)

2006 Medal Winner
The Hello, Goodbye Window, illustrated by Chris Raschka, written by Norton Juster

2005 Medal Winner
Kitten's First Full Moon, by Kevin Henkes (page 45)

2004 Medal Winner
The Man Who Walked Between the Towers, by Mordicai Gerstein

2003 Medal Winner
My Friend Rabbit, by Eric Rohmann

2002 Medal Winner
The Three Pigs, by David Wiesner

2001 Medal Winner
So You Want to Be President? illustrated by David Small, written by Judith St. George (page 78)

2000 Medal Winner
Joseph Had a Little Overcoat, by Simms Taback (page 82)

1999 Medal Winner
Snowflake Bentley, **illustrated by Mary Azarian, written by Jacqueline Briggs Martin**

1998 Medal Winner
Rapunzel, by Paul O. Zelinsky (page 222)

1997 Medal Winner
Golem, by David Wisniewski

1996 Medal Winner
Officer Buckle and Gloria, by Peggy Rathmann (page 69)

1995 Medal Winner
Smoky Night, illustrated by David Diaz, written by Eve Bunting

1994 Medal Winner
Grandfather's Journey, by Allen Say, (page 70)

1993 Medal Winner
Mirette on the High Wire, by Emily Arnold McCully

1992 Medal Winner
Tuesday, by David Wiesner (page 85)

1991 Medal Winner
Black and White, by David Macaulay

1990 Medal Winner
Lon Po Po: A Red-Riding Hood Story from China, by Ed Young

1989 Medal Winner
Song and Dance Man, illustrated by Stephen Gammell, written by Karen Ackerman

1988 Medal Winner
Owl Moon, illustrated by John Schoenherr, written by Jane Yolen (page 92)

1987 Medal Winner
Hey, Al, illustrated by Richard Egielski, written by Arthur Yorinks (page 89)

Titles in red are featured on the pages indicated. For a complete list of Caldecott Honor Books, visit www.ala.org.

271

1986 Medal Winner
The Polar Express, by Chris Van Allsburg *(page 83)*

1985 Medal Winner
Saint George and the Dragon, illustrated by Trina Schart Hyman, retold by Margaret Hodges (page 217)

1984 Medal Winner
The Glorious Flight: Across the Channel with Louis Bleriot, by Alice and Martin Provensen

1983 Medal Winner
Shadow, translated and illustrated by Marcia Brown, original text in French by Blaise Cendrars (page 28)

1982 Medal Winner
Jumanji, by Chris Van Allsburg (page 83)

1981 Medal Winner
Fables, by Arnold Lobel

1980 Medal Winner
Ox-Cart Man, illustrated by Barbara Cooney, written by Donald Hall

1979 Medal Winner
The Girl Who Loved Wild Horses, by Paul Goble (page 41)

1978 Medal Winner
Noah's Ark, by Peter Spier

1977 Medal Winner
Ashanti to Zulu: African Traditions, illustrated by Leo and Diane Dillon, written by Margaret Musgrove (page 63)

1976 Medal Winner
Why Mosquitoes Buzz in People's Ears, illustrated by Leo and Diane Dillon, retold by Verna Aardema (page 25)

1975 Medal Winner
Arrow to the Sun, by Gerald McDermott

1974 Medal Winner
Duffy and the Devil, illustrated by Margot Zemach, retold by Harve Zemach

1973 Medal Winner
The Funny Little Woman, illustrated by Blair Lent, retold by Arlene Mosel

1972 Medal Winner
One Fine Day, retold and illustrated by Nonny Hogrogian

1971 Medal Winner
A Story A Story, retold and illustrated by Gail E. Haley

1970 Medal Winner
Sylvester and the Magic Pebble, by William Steig (page 80)

1969 Medal Winner
The Fool of the World and the Flying Ship, illustrated by Uri Shulevitz, retold by Arthur Ransome

1968 Medal Winner
Drummer Hoff, illustrated by Ed Emberley, adapted by Barbara Emberley

1967 Medal Winner
Sam, Bangs & Moonshine, by Evaline Ness

1966 Medal Winner
Always Room for One More, illustrated by Nonny Hogrogian, written by Sorche Nic Leodhas, pseud. (Leclair Alger)

1965 Medal Winner
May I Bring a Friend? illustrated by Beni Montresor, written by Beatrice Schenk de Regniers (page 37)

1964 Medal Winner
Where the Wild Things Are, by Maurice Sendak (page 73)

1963 Medal Winner
The Snowy Day, by Ezra Jack Keats (page 49)

1962 Medal Winner
Once a Mouse, retold and illustrated by Marcia Brown

1961 Medal Winner
Baboushka and the Three Kings, illustrated by Nicolas Sidjakov, written by Ruth Robbins

1960 Medal Winner
Nine Days to Christmas, illustrated by Marie Hall Ets, written by Marie Hall Ets and Aurora Labastida

1959 Medal Winner
Chanticleer and the Fox, illustrated by Barbara Cooney, adapted by Barbara Cooney from Chaucer's Canterbury Tales

1958 Medal Winner
Time of Wonder, by Robert McCloskey (page 58)

1957 Medal Winner
A Tree is Nice, illustrated by Marc Simont, written by Janice Udry (page 82)

1956 Medal Winner
Frog Went A-Courtin', illustrated by Feodor Rojankovsky, retold by John Langstaff

1955 Medal Winner
Cinderella, or the Little Glass Slipper, translated and illustrated by Marcia Brown, original text in French by Charles Perrault

1954 Medal Winner
Madeline's Rescue, by Ludwig Bemelmans (page 26)

1953 Medal Winner
The Biggest Bear, by Lynd Ward

1952 Medal Winner
Finders Keepers, illustrated by Nicolas, pseud. (Nicholas Mordvinoff), written by Will, pseud. (William Lipkind)

1951 Medal Winner
The Egg Tree, by Katherine Milhous

1950 Medal Winner
Song of the Swallows, by Leo Politi

1949 Medal Winner
The Big Snow, by Berta and Elmer Hader

1948 Medal Winner
White Snow, Bright Snow, illustrated by Roger Duvoisin, written by Alvin Tresselt

1947 Medal Winner
The Little Island, illustrated by Leonard Weisgard, written by Golden MacDonald, pseud. (Margaret Wise Brown)

1946 Medal Winner
The Rooster Crows, by Maud and Miska Petersham

1945 Medal Winner
Prayer for a Child, illustrated by Elizabeth Orton Jones, written by Rachel Field

1944 Medal Winner
Many Moons, illustrated by Louis Slobodkin, written by James Thurber

1943 Medal Winner
The Little House, by Virginia Lee Burton (page 30)

1942 Medal Winner
Make Way for Ducklings, by Robert McCloskey (page 58)

1941 Medal Winner
They Were Strong and Good, by Robert Lawson

1940 Medal Winner
Abraham Lincoln, by Ingri and Edgar Parin d'Aulaire

1939 Medal Winne
Mei Li, by Thomas Handforth

1938 Medal Winner
Animals of the Bible, illustrated by Dorothy P. Lathrop, selected by Helen Dean Fish

Caldecott Medal Books

Titles in red are featured on the pages indicated. For a complete list of Caldecott Honor Books, visit www.ala.org.

273

Newbery Medal Books

The bronze Newbery Medal, which is named for the eighteenth-century English bookseller John Newbery, is awarded annually by the American Library Association to the most distinguished American children's book published the previous year. The Newbery Award has been bestowed on one book each year since 1922. The seal awarded to other notable books of the year, the silver Newbery Honor, may be bestowed on any number of worthy titles in a given year.

2012 Medal Winner
Dead End in Norvelt, by Jack Gantos

2011 Medal Winner
Moon over Manifest, by Clare Vanderpool

2010 Medal Winner
When You Reach Me, by Rebecca Stead

2009 Medal Winner
The Graveyard Book, by Neil Gaiman, illustrated by Dave McKean (page 151)

2008 Medal Winner
Good Masters! Sweet Ladies! Voices from a Medieval Village, by Laura Amy Schlitz

2007 Medal Winner
The Higher Power of Lucky, by Susan Patron, illustrated by Matt Phelan

2006 Medal Winner
Criss Cross, by Lynne Rae Perkins

2005 Medal Winner
Kira-Kira, by Cynthia Kadohata

2004 Medal Winner
The Tale of Despereaux, by Kate DiCamillo, illustrated by Timothy Basil Ering (page 144)

2003 Medal Winner
Crispin: The Cross of Lead, by Avi (page 125)

2002 Medal Winner
Single Shard, by Linda Sue Park

2001 Medal Winner
A Year Down Yonder, by Richard Peck

2000 Medal Winner
Bud, Not Buddy, by Christopher Paul Curtis (page 140)

1999 Medal Winner
Holes, by Louis Sachar (page 182)

1998 Medal Winner
Out of the Dust, by Karen Hesse

1997 Medal Winner
The View from Saturday, by E. L. Konigsburg (page 163)

1996 Medal Winner
The Midwife's Apprentice, by Karen Cushman

1995 Medal Winner
Walk Two Moons, by Sharon Creech (page 139)

1994 Medal Winner
The Giver, by Lois Lowry (page 169)

1993 Medal Winner
Missing May, by Cynthia Rylant (page 182)

1992 Medal Winner
Shiloh, by Phyllis Reynolds Naylor (page 172)

1991 Medal Winner
Maniac Magee, by Jerry Spinelli (page 187)

1990 Medal Winner
Number the Stars, by Lois Lowry (page 169)

1989 Medal Winner
Joyful Noise: Poems for Two Voices, by Paul Fleischman (page 225)

1988 Medal Winner
Lincoln: A Photobiography, by Russell Freedman (page 257)

1987 Medal Winner
The Whipping Boy, by Sid Fleischman (page 147)

1986 Medal Winner
Sarah, Plain and Tall, by Patricia MacLachlan (page 170)

1985 Medal Winner
The Hero and the Crown, by Robin McKinley

Titles in red are featured on the pages indicated. For a complete list of Newbery Honor Books, visit www.ala.org.

1984 Medal Winner
Dear Mr. Henshaw, by Beverly Cleary (page 134)

1983 Medal Winner
Dicey's Song, by Cynthia Voigt (page 195)

1982 Medal Winner
A Visit to William Blake's Inn: Poems for Innocent and Experienced Travelers, by Nancy Willard

1981 Medal Winner
Jacob Have I Loved, by Katherine Paterson (page 176)

1980 Medal Winner
A Gathering of Days: A New England Girl's Journal, 1830–1832, by Joan W. Blos

1979 Medal Winner
The Westing Game, by Ellen Raskin (page 179)

1978 Medal Winner
Bridge to Terabithia, by Katherine Paterson (page 176)

1977 Medal Winner
Roll of Thunder, Hear My Cry, by Mildred D. Taylor (page 193)

1976 Medal Winner
The Grey King, by Susan Cooper (page 136)

1975 Medal Winner
M.C. Higgins, the Great, by Virginia Hamilton (page 156)

1974 Medal Winner
The Slave Dancer, by Paula Fox (page 150)

1973 Medal Winner
Julie of the Wolves, by Jean Craighead George (page 152)

1972 Medal Winner
Mrs. Frisby and the Rats of NIMH, by Robert C. O'Brien (page 174)

1971 Medal Winner
Summer of the Swans, by Betsy Byars (page 132)

1970 Medal Winner
Sounder, by William H. Armstrong

1969 Medal Winner
The High King, by Lloyd Alexander (page 123)

1968 Medal Winner
From the Mixed-Up Files of Mrs. Basil E. Frankweiler, by E. L. Konigsburg (page 163)

1967 Medal Winner
Up a Road Slowly, by Irene Hunt

1966 Medal Winner
I, Juan de Pareja, by Elizabeth Borton de Trevino

1965 Medal Winner
Shadow of a Bull, by Maia Wojciechowska

1964 Medal Winner
It's Like This, Cat, by Emily Neville

1963 Medal Winner
A Wrinkle in Time, by Madeleine L'Engle (page 165)

1962 Medal Winner
The Bronze Bow, by Elizabeth George Speare

1961 Medal Winner
Island of the Blue Dolphins, by Scott O'Dell (page 175)

1960 Medal Winner
Onion John, by Joseph Krumgold

1959 Medal Winner
The Witch of Blackbird Pond, by Elizabeth George Speare (page 188)

1958 Medal Winner
Rifles for Watie, by Harold Keith

1957 Medal Winner
Miracles on Maple Hill, by Virginia Sorensen

1956 Medal Winner
Carry On, Mr. Bowditch, by Jean Lee Latham

1955 Medal Winner
The Wheel on the School, by Meindert DeJong (page 143)

1954 Medal Winner
...And Now Miguel, by Joseph Krumgold

1953 Medal Winner
Secret of the Andes, by Ann Nolan Clark

1952 Medal Winner
Ginger Pye, by Eleanor Estes

1951 Medal Winner
Amos Fortune, Free Man, by Elizabeth Yates

1950 Medal Winner
The Door in the Wall, by Marguerite de Angeli (page 142)

Newbery Medal Books

Titles in red are featured on the pages indicated. For a complete list of Caldecott Honor Books, visit www.ala.org.

275

1949 Medal Winner
King of the Wind: The Story of the Godolphin Arabian, by Marguerite Henry (page 157)

1948 Medal Winner
The Twenty-One Balloons, by William Pène du Bois (page 145)

1947 Medal Winner
Miss Hickory, by Carolyn Sherwin Bailey

1946 Medal Winner
Strawberry Girl, by Lois Lenski

1945 Medal Winner
Rabbit Hill, by Robert Lawson (page 164)

1944 Medal Winner
Johnny Tremain, by Esther Forbes

1943 Medal Winner
Adam of the Road, by Elizabeth Janet Gray

1942 Medal Winner
The Matchlock Gun, by Walter Edmonds

1941 Medal Winner
Call It Courage, by Armstrong Sperry

1940 Medal Winner
Daniel Boone, by James Daugherty

1939 Medal Winner
Thimble Summer, by Elizabeth Enright

1938 Medal Winner
The White Stag, by Kate Seredy

1937 Medal Winner
Roller Skates, by Ruth Sawyer

1936 Medal Winner
Caddie Woodlawn, by Carol Ryrie Brink (page 130)

1935 Medal Winner
Dobry, by Monica Shannon

1934 Medal Winner
Invincible Louisa: The Story of the Author of Little Women, by Cornelia Meigs

1933 Medal Winner
Young Fu of the Upper Yangtze, by Elizabeth Lewis

1932 Medal Winner
Waterless Mountain, by Laura Adams Armer

1931 Medal Winner
The Cat Who Went to Heaven, by Elizabeth Coatsworth

1930 Medal Winner
Hitty, Her First Hundred Years, by Rachel Field

1929 Medal Winner
The Trumpeter of Krakow, by Eric P. Kelly

1928 Medal Winner
Gay Neck, the Story of a Pigeon, by Dhan Gopal Mukerji

1927 Medal Winner
Smoky, the Cowhorse, by Will James

1926 Medal Winner
Shen of the Sea, by Arthur Bowie Chrisman

1925 Medal Winner
Tales from Silver Lands, by Charles Finger

1924 Medal Winner
The Dark Frigate, by Charles Hawes

1923 Medal Winner
The Voyages of Doctor Dolittle, by Hugh Lofting

1922 Medal Winner
The Story of Mankind, by Hendrik Willem van Loon

Titles in red are featured on the pages indicated. For a complete list of Newbery Honor Books, visit www.ala.org.

Coretta Scott King Award Books

Coretta Scott King Book Awards are given to African American authors and illustrators for outstanding inspirational and educational contributions. The award-winning titles promote understanding and appreciation of the culture of all peoples and their contribution to the realization of the American dream of a pluralistic society. The award was designed to commemorate the life and works of Dr. Martin Luther King Jr. and to honor Mrs. Coretta Scott King for her courage and determination to continue the work for peace and world brotherhood.

2012 Awards
Author: *Heart and Soul: The Story of America and African Americans,* by Kadir Nelson
Illustrator: *Heart and Soul: The Story of America and African Americans,* by Kadir Nelson

2011 Awards
Author: *One Crazy Summer,* by Rita Williams-Garcia
Illustrator: *Underground: Finding the Light to Freedom,* by Shane W. Evans

2010 Awards
Author: *Bad News for Outlaws: The Remarkable Life of Bass Reeves, Deputy U.S. Marshal,* by Vaunda Micheaux Nelson, illustrated by R. Gregory Christie
Illustrator: *My People,* illustrated by Charles R. Smith Jr., written by Langston Hughes

2009 Awards
Author: *We Are the Ship: The Story of Negro League Baseball,* written and illustrated by Kadir Nelson
Illustrator: *The Blacker the Berry,* illustrated by Floyd Cooper, written by Joyce Carol Thomas

2008 Awards
Author: *Elijah of Buxton,* by Christopher Paul Curtis
Illustrator: *Let it Shine,* by Ashley Bryan (page 31)

2007 Awards
Author: *Copper Sun,* by Sharon Draper
Illustrator: *Moses: When Harriet Tubman Led Her People to Freedom,* illustrated by Kadir Nelson, written by Carole Boston Weatherford

2006 Awards
Author: *Day of Tears: A Novel in Dialogue,* by Julius Lester
Illustrator: *Rosa,* illustrated by Bryan Collier, written by Nikki Giovanni (page 41)

2005 Awards
Author: *Remember: The Journey to School Integration,* by Toni Morrison
Illustrator: *Ellington Was Not a Street,* illustrated by Kadir A. Nelson, written by Ntozake Shange

2004 Awards
Author: *The First Part Last,* by Angela Johnson
Illustrator: *Beautiful Blackbird,* by Ashley Bryan

2003 Awards
Author: *Bronx Masquerade,* by Nikki Grimes
Illustrator: *Talkin' About Bessie: The Story of Aviator Elizabeth Coleman,* illustrated by E. B. Lewis, written by Nikki Grimes

2002 Awards
Author: *The Land,* by Mildred Taylor
Illustrator: *Goin' Someplace Special,* illustrated by Jerry Pinkney, written by Patricia McKissack

2001 Awards
Author: *Miracle's Boys,* by Jacqueline Woodson
Illustrator: *Uptown,* by Bryan Collier

2000 Awards
Author: *Bud, Not Buddy,* by Christopher Paul Curtis (page 140)
Illustrator: *In the Time of the Drums,* illustrated by Brian Pinkney, written by Kim L. Siegelson

1999 Awards
Author: *Heaven,* by Angela Johnson
Illustrator: *I see the rhythm,* illustrated by Michele Wood, written by Toyomi Igus

1998 Awards
Author: *Forged by Fire,* by Sharon M. Draper
Illustrator: *In Daddy's Arms I am Tall: African Americans Celebrating Fathers,* illustrated by Javaka Steptoe, written by Alan Schroeder

1997 Awards
Author: *Slam,* by Walter Dean Myers
Illustrator: *Minty: A Story of Young Harriet Tubman,* illustrated by Jerry Pinkney, written by Alan Schroeder

1996 Awards
Author: *The Watsons Go to Birmingham—1963,* by Christopher Paul Curtis (page 140)
Illustrator: *The Middle Passage: White Ships Black Cargo,* by Tom Feelings

Titles in red are featured on the pages indicated. For a complete list of Coretta Scoot King Award Books, visit www.ala.org.

277

1995 Awards
Author: *Christmas in the Big House, Christmas in the Quarters,* by Patricia C. & Frederick L. McKissack
Illustrator: *The Creation,* illustrated by James Ransome, text by James Weldon Johnson

1994 Awards
Author: *Toning the Sweep,* by Angela Johnson
Illustrator: *Soul Looks Back in Wonder,* illustrated by Tom Feelings, edited by Phyllis Fogelman

1993 Awards
Author: *Dark Thirty: Southern Tales of the Supernatural,* by Patricia A. McKissack
Illustrator: *The Origin of Life on Earth: An African Creation Myth,* illustrated by Kathleen Atkins Wilson, retold by David A. Anderson

1992 Awards
Author: *Now is Your Time: The African American Struggle for Freedom,* by Walter Dean Myers
Illustrator: *Tar Beach,* by Faith Ringgold (page 68)

1991 Awards
Author: *The Road to Memphis,* by Mildred D. Taylor
Illustrator: *Aida,* illustrated by Leo and Diane Dillon, written by Leontyne Price

1990 Awards
Author: *A Long Hard Journey: The Story of the Pullman Porter,* by Patricia C. and Frederick L. McKissack
Illustrator: *Nathaniel Talking,* illustrated by Jan Spivey Gilchrist, written by Eloise Greenfield

1989 Awards
Author: *Fallen Angels,* by Walter Dean Myers
Illustrator: *Mirandy and Brother Wind,* illustrated by Jerry Pinkney, written by Patricia McKissack (page 59)

1988 Awards
Author: *The Friendship,* by Mildred L. Taylor
Illustrator: *Mufaro's Beautiful Daughters: An African Tale,* by John Steptoe (page 78)

1987 Awards
Author: *Justin and the Best Biscuits in the World,* by Mildred Pitts Walter
Illustrator: *Half a Moon and One Whole Star,* illustrated by Jerry Pinkney, written by Crescent Dragonwagon

1986 Awards
Author: *The People Could Fly: American Black Folktales,* by Virginia Hamilton, illustrated by Leo and Diane Dillon (page 217)
Illustrator: *The Patchwork Quilt,* illustrated by Jerry Pinkney, written by Valerie Flournoy

1985 Awards (no illustrator award)
Author: *Motown and Didi,* by Walter Dean Myers

1984 Awards
Author: *Everett Anderson's Good-bye,* by Lucille Clifton
Illustrator: *My Mama Needs Me,* illustrated by Pat Cummings, text by Mildred Pitts

1983 Awards
Author: *Sweet Whispers, Brother Rush,* by Virginia Hamilton
Illustrator: *Black Child,* by Peter Mugabane

1982 Awards
Author: *Let the Circle Be Unbroken,* by Mildred D. Taylor
Illustrator: *Mother Crocodile: An Uncle Amadou Tale from Sengal,* illustrated by John Steptoe, written by Rosa Guy

1981 Awards
Author: *This Life,* by Sidney Poitier
Illustrator: *Beat the Story Drum, Pum-Pum,* by Ashley Bryan

1980 Awards
Author: *The Young Landlords,* by Walter Dean Myers
Illustrator: *Cornrows,* illustrated by Carole Byard, written by Camille Yarborough

1979 Awards
Author: *Escape to Freedom,* by Ossie Davis
Illustrator: *Something on My Mind,* illustrated by Tom Feelings, written by Nikki Grimes

1978 Awards
Author and Illustrator: *Africa Dream,* by Eloise Greenfield, illustrated by Carole Bayard

1977 Awards
Author: *The Story of Stevie Wonder,* by James Haskins

1976 Awards
Author: *Duey's Tale,* by Pearl Bailey

1975 Awards
Author: *The Legend of Africana,* by Dorothy Robinson

1974 Awards
Ray Charles, by Sharon Bell Mathis, illustrated by George Ford

1973 Awards
I Never Had It Made: The Autobiography of Jackie Robinson, as told to Alfred Duckett

1972 Awards
17 Black Artists, by Elton C. Fax

1971 Awards
Black Troubador: Langston Hughes, by Charlemae Rollins

1970 Awards
Martin Luther King, Jr.: Man of Peace, by Lillie Patterson

A

Index

Book titles appear in bold. Author and illustrator names appear in italics. Subjects appear in capitals.

Book titles appear in bold. Author and illustrator names appear in italics. Subjects appear in capitals.

Book titles appear in bold. Author and illustrator names appear in italics. Subjects appear in capitals.

281

Index

Index

Book titles appear in bold. Author and illustrator names appear in italics. Subjects appear in capitals.

Book titles appear in bold. Author and illustrator names appear in italics. Subjects appear in capitals.

Index

283

Book titles appear in bold. Author and illustrator names appear in italics. Subjects appear in capitals.

Book titles appear in bold. Author and illustrator names appear in italics. Subjects appear in capitals.

Index

Book titles appear in bold. Author and illustrator names appear in italics. Subjects appear in capitals.

289

Index

Book titles appear in bold. Author and illustrator names appear in italics. Subjects appear in capitals.

Book titles appear in bold. Author and illustrator names appear in italics. Subjects appear in capitals.

Index

Book titles appear in bold. Author and illustrator names appear in italics. Subjects appear in capitals.

Index

Book titles appear in bold. Author and illustrator names appear in italics. Subjects appear in capitals.

293

Book titles appear in bold. Author and illustrator names appear in italics. Subjects appear in CAPITALS.

Index

Index

Book titles appear in bold. Author and illustrator names appear in italics. Subjects appear in capitals.

Book titles appear in bold. Author and illustrator names appear in italics. Subjects appear in capitals.

Index

Index

Book titles appear in bold. Author and illustrator names appear in italics. Subjects appear in capitals.

297

Index

Book titles appear in bold. Author and illustrator names appear in italics. Subjects appear in capitals.

Index

Book titles appear in bold. Author and illustrator names appear in italics. Subjects appear in capitals.

Index

Book titles appear in bold. Author and illustrator names appear in italics. Subjects appear in capitals.

Image Credits

Image Credits

reserved. *The Dragons of Blueland* cover copyright © 1951 by Random House Children's Books, from THE DRAGONS OF BLUELAND by Ruth Stiles Gannett, illustrated by Ruth Chrisman Gannett. Used by permission of Random House Children's Books, a division of Random House, Inc. All rights reserved.

Page 152: *My Side of the Mountain* reproduced by permission of Penguin Books Ltd. *The Wind in the Willows* cover art © 1980 by Michael Hague from the book *The Wind in the Willows* by Kenneth Grahame. Reprinted by permission of Henry Holt Books for Young Readers, an imprint of the Macmillan Children's Publishing Group.

Page 153: *Tunnels* cover art © 2008 by David Wyatt. *Deeper* cover art © 2009 by David Wyatt. *Freefall* cover art © 2010 by David Wyatt. *Closer* cover art © 2011 by David Wyatt. *Asterix and the Golden Sickle* © 1962 Goscinny/Uderzo. Asterix and the Goths © 1963 Goscinny/Uderzo. Asterix the Gaul © 1961 Goscinny/Uderzo.

Page 154: *Theodore Boone: Kid Lawyer* reproduced by permission of Penguin Books Ltd. *The Homework Machine* © cover by Dan Santat. *The Talent Show* © cover by Iacopo Bruon.

Page 155: *Found (The Missing: Book 1)* cover photograph (people) © Getty Images.com/Doug Menuez. Cover photograph (cave) © iStockphoto.com/fotoVoyager.com. Cover photograph (night sky) © iStockphoto.com/Maciej Laska. Cover photograph (clock) © iStockphoto.com/Michal Rozanski.

Page 156: *The House of Dies Drear* © cover by Leo and Diane Dillon. *M.C. Higgins, the Great* © cover by Leo and Diane Dillon.

Page 157: *Justin Morgan Had a Horse* © cover by John Rowe. *King of the Wind: The Story of the Godolphin Arabian* © cover by John Rowe. *Misty of Chincoteague* © cover by John Rowe. *Stormy, Misty's Foal* © cover by John Rowe.

Page 158: *The Adventures of Tintin* © 1979 Hachette Book Group, Inc. *The Adventures of Tintin: Cigars of the Pharaoh* © 1975 Hachette Book Group, Inc. *The Adventures of Tintin: Tintin and the Picaros* © 1978 Hachette Book Group, Inc. *Bunnicula: A Rabbit Tale of Mystery* © cover by C.F. Payne. *The Celery Stalks at Midnight* © cover by C.F. Payne. *Howliday Inn* © cover by C.F. Payne. *Nighty-Nightmare* © cover by C.F. Payne.

Page 159: *The Outsiders* reproduced by permission of Penguin Books Ltd. *Rumble Fish* cover copyright © 1975 by Delacorte Press, from RUMBLE FISH by S.E. Hinton. Used by permission of Delacorte Press, an imprint of Random House Children's Books, a division of Random House, Inc. All rights reserved. *That Was Then, This Is Now* reproduced by permission of Penguin Books Ltd. *Hoot* cover copyright © 2002 by Alfred A. Knopf, from HOOT by Carl Hiaasen. Used by permission of Alfred A. Knopf, an imprint of Random House Children's Books, a division of Random House, Inc. All rights reserved.

Page 160: *Comet in Moominland* cover art © 1946 by Tove Jansson from the book *Comet in Moominland* by Tove Jansson. Reprinted by permission of Farrar, Straus & Giroux Books for Young Readers, an imprint of the Macmillan Children's Publishing Group. *Finn Family Moomintroll* cover art © 1948 by Tove Jansson from the book *Finn Family Moomintroll* by Tove Jansson. Reprinted by permission of Farrar, Straus & Giroux Books for Young Readers, an imprint of the Macmillan Children's Publishing Group. *The Phantom Tollbooth* cover copyright © 1961 by Random House Children's Books, from THE PHANTOM TOLLBOOTH by Norton Juster, illustrated by Jules Feiffer. Used by permission of Random House Children's Books, a division of Random House, Inc. All rights reserved.

Page 161: Images from *Beauty and the Beast* © 1978 by Marianna Mayer, illustrated by Mercer Mayer. Used with permission of Chronicle Books, San Francisco. www.chroniclekids.com.

Page 162: *Nancy Drew* reproduced by permission of Penguin Books Ltd. *The Evolution of Calpurnia Tate* cover art © 2009 by Beth White from the book *The Evolution of Calpurnia Tate* by Jacqueline Kelly. Reprinted by permission of Henry Holt Books for Young Readers, an imprint of the Macmillan Children's Publishing Group. *Melonhead* cover copyright © 2009 by Delacorte Press, from MELONHEAD by Katy Kelly, illustrated by Gillian Johnson. Used by permission of Delacorte Press, an imprint of Random House Children's Books, a division of Random House, Inc. All rights reserved. *Emily Windsnap and the Castle in the Mist* text copyright © 2007 Liz Kessler. Illustrations copyright 2007 Natacha Ledwidge. Reproduced

by permission of Candlewick press, Somerville, MA. *The Tail of Emily Windsnap* text copyright © 2003 by Liz Kessler. Illustrations copyright © Sarah Gibb. Reproduced by permission of Candlewick Press, Somerville, MA. *Emily Windsnap and the Monster from the Deep* text copyright © 2004 Liz Kessler. Illustrations copyright © 2004 Sarah Gibb. Reproduced by permission of Candlewick Press, Somerville, MA.

Page 163: *Diary of a Wimpy Kid, Diary of a Wimpy Kid: Rodrick Rules* and *Diary of a Wimpy Kid: The Last Straw,* DIARY OF A WIMPY KID®, WIMPY KID™, and the Gret Heffley design™ are trademarks of Wimpy Kid, Inc. All rights reserved. Images from *The Jungle Book* © 2007, Illustrated by Scott McKowen. Used with permission from Sterling Publishing Co., Inc. All Rights Reserved. Images from *From the Mixed-up Files of Mrs. Basil E. Frankweiler* © cover by Barry David Marcus. *The View from Saturday* © cover by E.L. Konigsburg.

Page 164: Images from *Gordon Korman No More Dead Dogs* © 2000, by Rick Riordan. Reprinted with Permission granted by Disney•Hyperion, an imprint of Disney Book Group LLC. All Rights Reserved. Images from *Gordon Korman Schooled* © 2007, by Gordon Korman. Reprinted with Permission granted by Disney•Hyperion, an imprint of Disney Book Group LLC. All Rights Reserved. *Savvy* reproduced by permission of Penguin Books Ltd. *Rabbit Hill* reproduced by permission of Penguin Books Ltd.

Page 165: *A Wrinkle in Time* cover art © 2007 by Taeeun Yoo from the book *A Wrinkle in Time* by Madeleine L'Engle. Reprinted by permission of Farrar, Straus & Giroux Books for Young Readers, an imprint of the Macmillan Children's Publishing Group. *A Wind in the Door* cover art © 2007 by Taeeun Yoo from the book *A Wind in the Door* by Madeleine L'Engle. Reprinted by permission of Farrar, Straus & Giroux Books for Young Readers, an imprint of the Macmillan Children's Publishing Group. *A Swiftly Tilting Planet* cover art © 2007 by Taeeun Yoo from the book *A Swiftly Tilting Planet* by Madeleine L'Engle. Reprinted by permission of Farrar, Straus & Giroux Books for Young Readers, an imprint of the Macmillan Children's Publishing Group. *Many Waters* cover art © 2007 by Taeeun Yoo from the book *Many Waters* by Madeleine L'Engle. Reprinted by permission of Farrar, Straus & Giroux Books for Young Readers, an imprint of the Macmillan Children's Publishing Group. *An Acceptable Time* cover art © 2007 by Taeeun Yoo from the book *An Acceptable Time* by Madeleine L'Engle. Reprinted by permission of Farrar, Straus & Giroux Books for Young Readers, an imprint of the Macmillan Children's Publishing Group. *To Be a Slave* reproduced by permission of Penguin Books Ltd.

Page 166: *Pippi Longstocking* reproduced by permission of Penguin Books Ltd.

Page 168: *The Call of the Wild* reproduced by permission of Penguin Books Ltd. *White Fang* reproduced by permission of Penguin Books Ltd. *The Story of Doctor Dolittle* cover copyright © 1968 by Yearling, from THE STORY OF DOCTOR DOLITTLE by Hugh Lofting. Used by permission of Yearling, an imprint of Random House Children's Books, a division of Random House, Inc. All rights reserved.

Page 169: *The Batboy* reproduced by permission of Penguin Books Ltd. *Miracle on 49th Street* reproduced by permission of Penguin Books Ltd. *Safe at Home* reproduced by permission of Penguin Books Ltd.

Page 171: *11 Birthdays* cover art © Digital Vision (RF) Getty Images. *Finally* cover art by Michael Frost. Image from *Anne of Green Gables* © 2004, Illustrated by Scott McKowen. Used with permission from Sterling Publishing Co., Inc. All Rights Reserved.

Page 172: *Eleven* reproduced by permission of Penguin Books Ltd. *The Keys to the Kingdom: Mister Monday, Lord Sunday, Grim Tuesday* cover art by John Blackford.

Page 173: Images from *Go! Go! Go!* © 2009, Illustrated by Roxie Munro. Used with permission from Sterling Publishing Co., Inc. All Rights Reserved. Images from *Mazeways: A to Z* © 2007, Illustrated by Roxie Munro. Used with permission from Sterling Publishing Co., Inc. All Rights Reserved. Images from *Ecomazes: 12 Earth Adventures* © 2010, Illustrated by Roxie Munro. Used with permission from Sterling Publishing Co., Inc. All Rights Reserved.

Page 174: *Five Children and It* reproduced by permission of Penguin Books Ltd. *The Railway Children* reproduced by permission of Penguin Books Ltd.

Page 175: *The Mysteries of Spider Kane* cover copyright © 2006 by Yearling, from *THE MYSTERIES OF SPIDER CANE* by Mary Pope Osborne. Used by permission of Alfred A. Knopf, an imprint of Random House Children's Books, a division of Random House, Inc. All rights reserved.

Page 176: *Freak the Mighty* cover art © 1993 by David Shannon.

Page 177: *Dogsong* © cover by Sammy Yuen Jr. *Hatchet* © cover by Neil Waldman. *The Winter Room* cover art by Larry Rostant. *Pollyanna* reproduced by permission of Penguin Books Ltd.

Page 178: *The Golden Compass* cover copyright © 1995 by Alfred A. Knopf, from *THE GOLDEN COMPASS* by Philip Pullman. Used by permission of Alfred A. Knopf, an imprint of Random House Children's Books, a division of Random House, Inc. All rights reserved. *The Subtle Knife* cover copyright © 1997 by Alfred A. Knopf, from *THE SUBTLE KNIFE* by Philip Pullman. Used by permission of Alfred A. Knopf, an imprint of Random House Children's Books, a division of Random House, Inc. All rights reserved. *The Amber Spyglass* cover copyright © 2000 by Alfred A. Knopf, from *THE AMBER SPYGLASS* by Philip Pullman. Used by permission of Alfred A. Knopf, an imprint of Random House Children's Books, a division of Random House, Inc. All rights reserved. Images from *Ridley Pearson Kingdom Keepers: Disney After Dark* © 2009, illustrated by Tristan Elwell by Ridley Pearson. Reprinted with Permission granted by Disney*Hyperion, an imprint of Disney Book Group LLC. All Rights Reserved. Images from *Ridley Pearson Kingdom Keepers II: Disney at Dawn* © 2009, illustrated by Tristan Elwell by Ridley Pearson. Reprinted with Permission granted by Disney*Hyperion, an imprint of Disney Book Group LLC. All Rights Reserved. Images from *Ridley Pearson Kingdom Keepers III: Disney in Shadow* © 2010, illustrated by Tristan Elwell by Ridley Pearson. Reprinted with Permission granted by Disney*Hyperion, an imprint of Disney Book Group LLC. All Rights Reserved. Images from *Ridley Pearson Kingdom Keepers IV: Power Play* © 2011, illustrated by Tristan Elwell by Ridley Pearson. Reprinted with Permission granted by Disney*Hyperion, an imprint of Disney Book Group LLC. All Rights Reserved.

Page 179: *The Westing Game* reproduced by permission of Penguin Books Ltd. *Where the Red Fern Grows* cover copyright © 1961 by Delacorte Press, from *WHERE THE RED FERN GROWS* by Wilson Rawls. Used by permission of Delacorte Press, an imprint of Random House Children's Books, a division of Random House, Inc. All rights reserved.

Page 180: Images from *Percy Jackson & the Olympians: The Lightning Thief* © 2005, by Rick Riordan. Reprinted with Permission granted by Disney*Hyperion, an imprint of Disney Book Group LLC. All Rights Reserved. Images from *Percy Jackson & the Olympians: The Sea of Monsters* © 2006, by Rick Riordan. Reprinted with Permission granted by Disney*Hyperion, an imprint of Disney Book Group LLC. All Rights Reserved. Images from *Percy Jackson & the Olympians: The Titan's Curse* © 2007, by Rick Riordan. Reprinted with Permission granted by Disney*Hyperion, an imprint of Disney Book Group LLC. All Rights Reserved. Images from *Percy Jackson & the Olympians: The Battle of the Labyrinth* © 2008, by Rick Riordan. Reprinted with Permission granted by Disney*Hyperion, an imprint of Disney Book Group LLC. All Rights Reserved. Images from *Percy Jackson & the Olympians: The Last Olympian* © 2009, by Rick Riordan. Reprinted with Permission granted by Disney*Hyperion, an imprint of Disney Book Group LLC. All Rights Reserved. Images from *The Red Pyramid (The Kane Chronicles, Book 1)* © 2010, by Rick Riordan. Reprinted with Permission granted by Disney*Hyperion, an imprint of Disney Book Group LLC. All Rights Reserved.

Page 181: *Harry Potter and the Sorcerer's Stone* cover art by Mary GrandPré © 1998 Warner Bros. *Harry Potter and the Chamber of Secrets* cover art by Mary GrandPré © 1999 Warner Bros. *Harry Potter and the Prisoner of Azkaban* cover art by Mary GrandPré © 1999 Warner Bros. *Harry Potter and the Goblet of Fire* cover art by Mary GrandPré © 2000 Warner Bros. *Harry Potter and the Order of the Phoenix* cover art by Mary GrandPré © 2003 Warner Bros. *Harry Potter and the Half-Blood Prince* cover art by Mary GrandPré © 2005 Warner Bros. *Harry Potter and the Deathly Hallows* cover art by Mary GrandPré © 2007 Warner Bros.

Page 182: *Holes* jacket art and design © 2008 Vladimir Radunsky from the book *Holes* by Louis Sachar. Reprinted by permission of Farrar, Straus & Giroux Books for Young Readers, an imprint of the Macmillan Children's Publishing Group. *Missing May* cover art by Suzanne Duranceau.

Page 183: *The Cricket in Times Square* cover art © 1960 by Garth Williams from the book *The Cricket in Times Square* by George Selden. Reprinted by permission of Farrar, Straus & Giroux Books for Young Readers, an imprint of the Macmillan Children's Publishing Group. *The Genie of Sutton Place* cover art © 1994 by Ellen Eagle from the book *The Genie of Sutton Place* by George Selden. Reprinted by permission of Farrar, Straus & Giroux Books for Young Readers, an imprint of the Macmillan Children's Publishing Group.

Page 184: *The Invention of Hugo Cabret* cover art by Brian Selznick. Images from *Black Beauty* © 1877, Illustrated by Scott McKowen. Used with permission from Sterling Publishing Co., Inc. All Rights Reserved. *Bone: Crown of Horns* cover art © 2009 by Jeff Smith. *Bone: The Great Cow Race* cover art © 2005 by Jeff Smith. *Bone: Out from Boneville* cover art © 2005 by Jeff Smith.

Page 185: *Zen Ghosts* cover art © 2010 by Jon J Muth. *Zen Shorts* cover art © 2005 by Jon J Muth. *Zen Ties* cover art © 2008 by Jon J Muth.

Page 186: *Chocolate Fever* reproduced by permission of Penguin Books Ltd.

Page 187: *The Egypt Game* © cover by David Frankland. *Maniac Magee* © 1999 Hachette Book Group, Inc.

Page 188: Images from *Heidi* © 2006, Illustrated by Scott McKowen. Used with permission from Sterling Publishing Co., Inc. All Rights Reserved. *The Red Pony* reproduced by permission of Penguin Books Ltd. *Ballet Shoes* cover copyright © 1993 by Yearling, from *BALLET SHOES* by Noel Streatfeild, illustrated by Diane Goode. Used by permission of Yearling, an imprint of Random House Children's Books, a division of Random House, Inc. All rights reserved.

Page 189: *Kidnapped* reproduced by permission of Penguin Books Ltd. Images from *Dr. Jekyll & Mr. Hyde* © 2011, Illustrated by Scott McKowen. Used with permission from Sterling Publishing Co., Inc. All Rights Reserved. Images from *Treasure Island* © 2004, Illustrated by Scott McKowen. Used with permission from Sterling Publishing Co., Inc. All Rights Reserved. Images from *Gulliver's Travels* © 2007, Illustrated by Scott McKowen. Used with permission from Sterling Publishing Co., Inc. All Rights Reserved.

Page 190: *The Mysterious Benedict Society* © 2007 Hachette Book Group, Inc. *All-of-a-Kind-Family* covers copyright © 1984 by Yearling, from *ALL-OF-A-KIND-FAMILY* by Sydney Taylor. Used by permission of Yearling, an imprint of Random House Children's Books, a division of Random House, Inc. All rights reserved.

Page 191: *The 13 Clocks* copyright © Marc Simont.

Page 192: *The Mysteries of Spider Kane* cover copyright © 2006 by Yearling, from *THE MYSTERIES OF SPIDER CANE* by Mary Pope Osborne. Used by permission of Alfred A. Knopf, an imprint of Random House Children's Books, a division of Random House, Inc. All rights reserved. *Magic Tree House* covers copyright © 1992 by Random House Children's Books, from *DINGOES AT DINNERTIME (MAGIC TREE HOUSE #20)* and *CIVIL WAR ON SUNDAY (MAGIC TREE HOUSE #21)* by Mary Pope Osborne, illustrated by Sal Murdocca. Used by permission of Random House Children's Books, a division of Random House, Inc. All rights reserved. *Tales from the Odyssey* images from Mary Pope Osborne *The Final Battle* © 2004 and *The One-Eyed Giant* © 2002, illustrated by Troy Howell by Mary Pope Osborne. Reprinted with Permission granted by Disney*Hyperion, an imprint of Disney Book Group LLC. All Rights Reserved.

Page 193: *Roll of Thunder, Hear My Cry* reproduced by permission of Penguin Books Ltd. *The Cay* cover copyright © 1969 by Delacorte Press, from *THE CAY* by Theodore Taylor. Used by permission of Delacorte Press, an imprint of Random House Children's Books, a division of Random House, Inc. All rights reserved.

Page 194: Images from *The Adventures of Huckleberry Finn* © 2006, Illustrated by Scott McKowen. Used with permission from Sterling Publishing Co., Inc. All Rights Reserved. Images from *The Adventures of Tom Sawyer* © 2004, Illustrated by Scott McKowen. Used with permission from Sterling Publishing Co., Inc. All Rights Reserved.

Page 195: Images from *20,000 Leagues Under the Sea* © 2006, Illustrated by Scott McKowen. Used with permission from Sterling Publishing Co., Inc. All Rights Reserved. *The Sword in the Stone* reproduced by permission of Penguin Books Ltd.

Image Credits

Image Credits

Image Credits